THE FANTASY BOND
Structure of
Psychological Defenses

Robert W. Firestone, Ph.D.

In collaboration with
Joyce Catlett, M.A.

10 9 8 7 6 5 4

Published by The Glendon Association
5383 Hollister Ave., Ste. 230, Santa Barbara, CA 93111

Library of Congress Cataloging in Publication Data

Firestone, Robert W.
  The fantasy bond.

  Includes index.
  1. Psychology, Pathological. 2. Defense mechanisms (Psychology) 3. Resistance (Psychoanalysis) I. Catlett, Joyce. II. Title.
RC454.4.F57   1985   616.89   84-20229
ISBN 0-9676684-0-9 (paperback)

DEDICATION

To my patients, friends, and associates who contributed their honesty and openness by sharing their experience and personal struggle and actively participating in my explorations and conclusions.

CONTENTS

7

ACKNOWLEDGMENTS

The author would like to express his appreciation to Joyce Catlett, M.A., associate and collaborator, for her major contribution to the organization and writing of this book. I am also grateful to Tamsen Firestone and Barry Langberg for their continuing critique and evaluation of the manuscript; to Cecilia Hunt for her initial editing and suggestions; and to Anne Baker and Eileen Tobe for their help in completing the final draft.

I would like to extend my special thanks to Dr. Stuart Boyd for his commentary on the psychotherapeutic community and the concepts that evolved from that setting, and to Dr. Richard Seiden for his interest and criticism of the manuscript. I would also like to express my admiration and appreciation to R. D. Laing for his moral courage in exposing the essential destructiveness in the conventional family unit and perceiving the validity of human suffering and resulting psychopathology emanating from that source.

The names, places, and other identifying facts contained herein have been fictionalized and no similarity to any persons, living or dead, is intended.

FOREWORD

I am honoured to have been invited to write the foreword to Bob Firestone's book, *The Fantasy Bond.*

Dr. Firestone offers vivid and accurate description of a sort of bondage shared by millions of men and women throughout the western world. After living together and being in love for awhile, they begin to feel tied to each other, bound to each other, connected to each other. They are not, except in fantasy. Moreover, they may even go on to feel that they are not separate individual human beings, each with their own centers, points of view, destiny, each with their own deaths awaiting each, separately, but they, we, two, have become one. Who could ask for anything more? Alas, this also is fantasy. However intimately at one we are, *we* could not feel *at* one, *as* one, unless we are not one. Only two or more can be at one. This "at-one-ment" is the very opposite of the fantasy bond as described and depicted by Firestone. The fantasy bond is an illusion, a fantasy; even more, it is virtually and literally, a *mirage.*

There are oases. They are to be found, sometimes, by some of us. But we shall *never* find an oasis in the spell of the mirage.

The descriptive accounts in Firestone's book remind me so much of similar ones from my own professional practice, let alone from my own personal life.

They both said they loved each other but were extremely nasty to each other. Each admitted they were nasty and each accused the other of being nasty. Both were right. Neither could stop it. That's why they came to see me.

They had been married for three years. No children by mutual agreement.

They had begun as appreciative, satisfied, loving lovers. They were almost one, but this ended almost as soon as they married.

Sex quickly turned into a nightmare for both of them. "It's as though," she explained, "we are playing a game of football. He's taking a penalty goal and I'm the goalkeeper." "Yes," he added, "and she never told me the score for three years."

They both agreed thoroughly with the simile metaphor analogy, and both took equal responsibility for embracing it. Among other things, I invited them to imagine a mutual nice image of love making, onto their act of love, but they could not or would not and did not try it out, however deliberately.

They left after three months, in much the same interlock. As Firestone says, they tell themselves they want out of it, but, in fact, they do not dis-interlock.

Why? They are both engulfed by their own miserable mirage of intimacy. They are desperately estranged from each other yet they are terrified to realize that they are simply separate. They could not come together because they could not bear to be apart. They had both become a part of the other. She had become his frustrating mother, who always kept him out, and he had become her impinging, penetrating, raping parents, always trying to get in.

Both felt completely at home. Both loved their home, the typical beautiful home for a miserable mirage between two beautiful people who are ugly to each other.

Firestone's explanation for this state of affairs is that those of us who enslave ourselves in the bondage of the mirage of love are parched for lack of love, and so fearful of giving and getting the love we lack, so terrified of the real thing, that we create our own hell and whine and complain that it keeps on not being the heaven we say we want and want to believe we are in.

For those who are beset by this romantic fantasy illusion mirage, the prime generating factor behind this, Firestone proposes, is that our parents—mothers more primitively than fathers, but fathers as well—did not love us, but pretended to themselves and to us that they did. They generally mistake emotional hunger for love.

In effect, they hate us in practice and love us in theory and induce us to believe them when they define their hate as love. The consequent mystification, confusion and conflict continue to devastate marriages, families, and each generation of children.

Firestone goes on to offer various therapeutic methods in response to this situation. In particular voice therapy, a method whereby people get the incorporated hating parent out of their system by dramatizing their parents' hateful hating attacks on them; attacks which hurt at the time, but went further, the hurt did not mend; the wound did not heal; these hateful hating attacks did permanent *damage*. They did injury to our hearts and souls, the spirit was broken. Procedures were developed to externalize the patient's self-attacks, clearly demonstrating their relationship to parental attitudes.

Firestone's therapy is based on love—genuine love in action, compassionate, forebearing, non-intrusive, skillful in the nitty gritty of psychotherapeutic professional practice.

My own personal experiences of developing a fantasy bond are among the most dreary, boring, agonizing, debilitating and physically dangerous times I've ever lived through. I am out of it now, I hope. Apart from infancy, this kind of bonding happened to me three times. Once in my twenties for about three years. Once in my thirties for about three months. And once in my forties.

Out of my own experience and those of the many sufferers from the varieties of its miserable consequences, I offer this *Knot*, or set of traps. I hope it is both didactic and entertaining.

1. Do you love me?
2. Then believe me.

3. Believe me
4. You don't love me.

5. You don't love anyone
6. You are incapable of love.

7. No one loves you
8. No one could love you

9. Except me.

10. I am the only one who loves you
    You don't love me
    You don't love anyone
    No one loves you
    No one can love you

11. But don't believe me
    Because I say so
    or because I love you

Although
believe me
it's only because I love you
    that I say so

Search yourself
Look into the mirror and see for yourself
You will see that every word I've said is true

Look into your heart
Look into your heart of hearts.

You don't love me
Don't believe me

You know.

R.D. Laing, M.D.

PREFACE

The Fantasy Bond sets forth a new concept of resistance, demonstrating the relationship between the structure and organization of psychological defenses and the fear of change, individuation, and personal power. This work has broadened the concept of resistance in psychotherapy to include an understanding of a core resistance to a "better life."

The problem, according to Dr. Robert Firestone, is that people behave in a way that is motivationally dishonest, reacting perversely to movement in the direction of their stated goals. In other words, they don't really want what they say they want. At this point in post-Freudian time, we all understand that there is an irrational basis to much human behavior; we have gained personal or professional awareness that change, *even positive change,* can have disruptive consequences for people. Success in personal endeavors is dangerous because these changes are symbolic of independence, adulthood, and separateness, and this means relinquishing the Fantasy Bond which has sustained and nourished us over the years.

The concept of a Fantasy Bond is a powerful theoretical construct which unifies neopsychoanalytic and existential frames of reference. The Fantasy Bond originates as an illusion of connection with the mother that is used by the infant to relieve anxiety and emotional pain.

21

Later, it is extended to other individuals, mates, authority figures and other parental substitutes, and destructive bonds are formed which impair the individual's functioning.

The concept of fusion with an idealized mother can be understood in analytic terms as a self-nourishing mechanism to compensate for maternal rejection, neglect, or the deprivation of "love-food" and mature parenting. But at its roots it is also a defense against the indefinable terror and angst of total annihilation which we rather euphemistically call "death anxiety." Maintaining the Fantasy Bond, like other restrictive defense mechanisms, is counterproductive, for it predisposes withdrawal, inwardness, rigidity and other maladaptive sequelae. The process of forming bonds first injures the couple, later the nuclear family, and eventually extends to conventional mores in society at large, which in turn act back on and reinforce the defensive process in the individual.

The book develops the concept of emotional hunger and distinguishes it from parental love with which it is frequently confused. The author analyzes the organization of psychological defenses around the important core defense of the Fantasy Bond and relates this structural process to the basic resistance in psychotherapy. He describes the dimensions of the Fantasy Bond and the secondary defenses that protect this core defense: The idealization of parents and family; the development of a negative or critical view of self; the displacement of negative parental traits onto other objects and the development of a victimized, paranoid orientation to life; the withdrawal into an inward state with accompanying loss of feeling for self; the withholding of affectional responses and capabilities in general; and the involvement with self-nourishing habits and painkillers.

The unique contribution of the concept of the Fantasy Bond underlying resistance to change is crossvalidated by my own two decades of research in the field of self-destructive behaviors. Suicide, the most extreme and dramatic behavior in the continuum of self-destructiveness, is most frequent among the most favored. For example, professionals have higher suicide rates than blue-collar workers. Officers kill themselves more often than do enlisted men; whites have rates much higher than minorities.

Thus we are led to the bittersweet realization that when things get better they may very well get worse. The reason that things "get worse" for us is that we fear giving up the Fantasy Bond of internal gratification although it no longer has any adaptive value. While it is easier to deal with the devil you know, the price of avoiding primal separation and death anxiety is a partial suicide resolution in which one gives up on life. Peace is purchased at the cost of avoiding spontaneous feelings and encouraging a process of emotional anaesthesia—a trade-off in which primal anxieties are ameliorated by sacrificing the zest for life.

Having been acquainted with the development of Dr. Firestone's work for a period of 28 years, I have been able to observe the emergence of his ideas, initially formulated when working with regressed schizophrenic patients. I have seen the evolution of a powerful therapeutic tool and clinical approach. Dr. Firestone extended the work of John N. Rosen in "Direct Analysis" and developed his own systematic theory of schizophrenia. Later he generalized this theory and applied it to a wide range of pathology. He investigated cathartic methods and a powerful Feeling Release Therapy akin to primal therapy and applied his concepts to a new therapeutic methodology that he has termed "Voice Therapy."

Dr. Firestone describes the techniques of Voice Therapy that help the patient become more aware of specific self-critical thoughts and negative attitudes toward others that lead to self-destructive behavior and maladaptive responses. By verbalizing these thoughts in the second person, the patient learns to separate them from his own point of view and make changes in his behavior that are opposed to the dictates of this "voice," which Dr. Firestone conceptualizes as the "language of the defensive process." I see the emergence of Voice Therapy as a new and highly significant addition to the repertoire of psychotherapy.

Dr. Firestone stresses the therapeutic value of friendship in contrast to the destructiveness of bonds or ties of dependency. He believes that the conflict within the patient is one of internal, subjective gratification vs. external interpersonal gratification and that it must be resolved in a social matrix. In our mobile, technological society, however, close, sustained friendships are far from commonplace. Occasionally, circumstances of stress, such as tragedy or war, lead to an enhanced sense of community, a galvanized togetherness which breaks down the usual barriers between people and stimulates communication and a sense of shared experience. Dr. Firestone suggests that the defensive suppression of our primal existential anxieties keeps us from experiencing our true humanity; only in giving up the Fantasy Bond of inward gratification can we relate sincerely to all living beings and interact with others on the basis of genuine friendship and democratic equality.

While you may not agree with all of the ideas expressed in this work, you will appreciate that these findings are not simply theoretical abstractions but are derived from corroboratory clinicial experiences in a variety of settings. The core concepts of this book have been drawn from three diverse populations: the deeply disturbed behavior of regressed schizophrenics; the typical neurotic conflicts of psychotherapy clients; and the everyday behavior of normal, successful people living in a unique pyschological community. The fact that similar behavior can be found in such outwardly different populations underscores both the essential similarity of all human beings and the reliability of the data.

This is not an easy book; it will force you to think. It abounds with paradoxes and seeming contradictions. It challenges deeply held convictions about the world around us. Our beliefs and values about such fundamental subjects as the family, male and female sexuality, child-rearing, and religion are frequently challenged and the reader will surely feel called upon to re-examine his or her own thinking in these most basic areas of belief. This can be a painful process although essentially a liberating one. On the other hand, living as we do in a world dominated by pop psychology pabulum, it is gratifying to discover a fresh outlook and a comprehensive theoretical contribution that can engage us in a process of self-inquiry and intellectual challenge.

Richard Seiden, Ph.D., M.P.H.

INTRODUCTION
Emotional Deadness

Years ago I began searching for answers to a mystery, a seemingly perverse phenomenon about people, that had me deeply puzzled: that is, why most people *choose* an emotionally deadened, self-limiting mode of life. I first focused on this problem when a small group of select patients decided to meet in a rural setting to explore their deepest feelings.

To accomplish this, we came together in the summer of 1971 for a weekend in the wooded mountains near Lake Arrowhead. Our surroundings were peaceful, the atmosphere invigorating. We started talking around 8:00 p.m. Friday. As the hours passed, we began to feel the stress of being continuously with other people. Challenging each other's defenses and remaining in an emotional situation for a long time period were part of this stress.

The exposure of defenses was vigorous and intense. At one point, a young woman, Jane, talked about her rage toward her friend, Mike, who was withdrawn and unresponsive. She confronted him in strong language because she was infuriated at his refusal to reciprocate her feeling for him. Other individuals with similar emotions also attacked Mike's indifference. Mike, a man who could not remember ever crying in his life, finally broke into sobs. In this unfamiliar emotional state he felt terribly disoriented. At first, he did not even know that it was he who was sobbing. He thought the sounds were coming from someone else. But before the night was over, Mike, who had denied his feelings all his life, felt a depth of feeling and a tenderness toward himself and others that he had never experienced.

During subsequent meetings, as I became more skilled in breaking down defenses and creating an accepting atmosphere where people could be themselves, people revealed more and more of their inner pain. Many relived feelings that had been pent up for a lifetime. Occasionally they sobbed or moaned or vented explosive anger. These primitive emotional reactions were followed by dramatic relief and clear insights. The participants were very excited by the encounters and the results, and they expressed appreciation for what they felt had been a remarkable experience. They said they felt closer to themselves and to other people and perceived their lives with unusual clarity.

Those times together were very meaningful to me. I have always been deeply touched by people expressing personal honesty and being loving and accepting toward one another in a truly democratic way. These moments brought me close to myself and made me feel calm and strong. I gave a good deal of thought to the weekend experiences, and I knew that the people's lives during those days together had great value and significance. Their faces changed and their bodies relaxed. They seemed more multidimensional. They felt invigorated and excited, yet when they returned to the city, they lost, sometimes slowly and sometimes very quickly, this edge of feeling and communion with themselves. They resumed their defensive posture and closed off their emotional reactions and sensitivity toward others.

Many of the men and women who traveled to the mountains for those weekends came without their spouses. They came as independent, separate persons, not as one-half of a couple. They were recognized as such, and they flourished for a few days for they were treated as individuals and their sexual identity and attractiveness were confirmed verbally. As a result, they felt better about themselves and had a more positive image of their bodies and sexuality. However, when they returned home, they gave up this good feeling and went back to being half of a couple once more. In returning to their families, they were in fact going back to the "security," the "togetherness," that was more familiar to them than the aliveness and genuine closeness they had experienced in the unfamiliar atmosphere of the mountains.

> Mike stayed feelingful and alive for several days upon returning home. Often he would find tears coming to his eyes as he talked with his wife and son. However, it became more and more

difficult at the end of a long, tedious day for him to get back in touch with his feelings because these emotions were so new and fragile to him. He looked forward to evenings at home, hoping that there he would regain that relaxed, alive state. But his wife, Ann, was threatened by the changes in her husband, by his burst of energy and his tears. She unconsciously wanted him to return to his typical defended state. She was inadvertently helping him cut off his feelings. In the months that followed, it was painful to see Mike become more hardened and more exclusively involved with Ann in a desperate, possessive manner. Mike preferred to cling to an illusion of safety and security with his wife. Mike and Ann were not really hanging on to *each other*; they were clinging to an imaginary link between two people—a fantasized connection, which we call the *fantasy bond*. They were not running the risk of losing something real; they were only protecting a fantasy of love.

There was a great deal of disappointment, because, in spite of these powerful experiences, people soon lost much of the therapeutic value of what they had gained. There was pain in the fact that these feeling people of the weekend, who felt so good and so real, had reverted to so-called normal life in such a short time. I was saddened that all they had left was their memory of having had a profound and meaningful experience and a few important insights, which eventually paled as well.

One thing was clear to me: these people of the weekend were, for the time being, a different breed. They had been emotionally alive whereas in their everyday lives they masked themselves in role-playing, hardness and toughness, paranoia, and other cut-off, nonfeeling states. These people were not in touch with themselves or their real existence most of their waking lives. On the weekend, however, they had pierced the shell of their defenses, and under their facades were deep unresolved feelings of richness and pain. This was not a group of abnormal individuals or patients; it was obvious that these people in their deadened and cut-off states were typical of the mass of humanity.

The fact that people were willing to give up so much of themselves in order to avoid feelings of sadness perplexed me, especially since they obviously felt so good after they expressed the sadness. In a sense, they had committed emotional suicide in order to protect themselves from the painful truth of their experiences. Why did they close off again after opening up and feeling such exhilaration? This was much more than an academic question to me because I, too, wanted to retain this level of interaction.

There was a deep desire on my part to live and experience life in an honest social context on an everyday basis. I wanted to be alive and close to my feelings and to learn more about these mysteries of human behavior. I knew that I had but one life and I valued it. I wanted to live it to the fullest, whether painful or joyous. The closeness and camaraderie of those shared weekends were a vital part of what I desired.

The alive faces and the warmth of those people could not be forgotten. One could not help contrasting their expressions with those of people in the larger society. The defensive posture of most people is etched into their faces and bodies. They live their lives as though they will live forever and can afford to throw away their most precious experiences. Their hardness and insulation make them capable of truly immoral and disrespectful conduct toward one another. Yet these people were essentially the same as the people of the weekend, only under normal environmental conditions. What characteristics of the weekend made possible such an important difference in people's capacity for feeling? How could these elements be incorporated as a style of living?

Since those weekends, I have spent a major part of my life and energy tracing the answers to this puzzle. This book tells the story of my search for understanding the all-encompassing problem of emotional deadness, which characterizes the way the majority of people give up their lives and vital experiences.

Without realizing it, most people become deadened to their emotions. Early in their lives they turn their backs on themselves, their real desires and wants, and substitute self-nourishing habits and fantasies that only serve to deaden them. They have ceased to want what they say they want because real gratifications and accomplishments threaten the process of self-nourishment through fantasy. Because they have been depending since childhood upon these fantasies to give them a sense of accomplishment, they cling to these fantasies rather than relinquish them for anything real. They shy away from success, both interpersonal and vocational, and limit themselves in countless ways. They act as their own jailers, and when they project this attitude, they become paranoid that others are depriving or victimizing them. They are the victims of their own self-denial and withholding. In a sense, people are at the mercy of the defense system that they originally constructed to protect themselves when they were little.

Most individuals are damaged in their psychological development during the earliest years of childhood. In the process of being mishandled and misunderstood, they suffered pain and fear that caused them to spend the rest of their lives in a defensive posture. Because people cannot defend themselves selectively against "bad" feelings, they also lose their ability to feel good. All of us have been hurt to some degree, and to the extent that we insulated ourselves from our feelings of pain and sadness, we have shut ourselves off as feeling people.

When cut off from their feelings in this manner, people cannot tolerate, or become unwilling to feel, their own aliveness, personal wants, and desires. Often they cannot accept simple, straightforward expressions of warmth and respect from another person. Most people are largely unconscious of the fact that they are restricted in this manner. Surprisingly, a good life with loving treatment from either friends or family members would fill them with sadness and anxiety.

> Mike, who had very little feeling for himself, would often find himself close to tears while watching a movie in which the ending turned out unexpectedly well for the characters involved. He especially enjoyed movies in which the villain turned into a "nice guy" or showed some tenderness. He would be particularly touched by this "niceness" if the villain were a parental figure. Mike would try to imagine how it would be if his father or mother or his wife suddenly showed such tenderness toward him. He would feel very sad picturing this, but he would leave the theater to return to his real life of not-so-nice treatment from the people closest to him. Mike firmly believed that he wanted positive recognition and good treatment from these people, when in fact he wanted it only in fantasy and could only tolerate it vicariously in books, plays or movies.

Most people are afraid of leading separate, independent lives and therefore cling to family ties and fantasies of love, which offer the illusion and false promise of connection. People prefer the imagined security of religion and immortality and choose destructive bonds which deny their aloneness. They give up a free existence and the intimacy and closeness that is part of a genuinely loving relationship in a desperate attempt to find fusion with another person.

People cannot deaden themselves emotionally and become defensive without affecting the people closest to them. Therefore, parents who wall themselves off against feeling must inevitably suppress feeling in their young in those areas where they, the parents, feel the most threatened. Live feeling and expressions of vitality cause anxiety to those who are well defended, and this waking-up experience can be very painful. To ward off intrusion on their defenses, parents unwittingly sacrifice their children and damage their self-esteem.

This behavior has far-reaching consequences. The avoidance of pain and feeling drastically distorts people's lives; it makes them resistant to any change in themselves or in their way of life; it shapes rules and roles in society as a fortress against feeling. Recognizing the extent of this destructive process added strong motivation to my search for an alternative way of living.

Over the past 12 years, I searched for and found ways to bring an alive alternative into everyday existence. In an effort to maintain an enriched way of being, my friends and colleagues began to change their habitual mode of living. They abandoned some of their favorite personal escapes and painkillers. They discovered that if they discarded the routines they used to give themselves a false sense of security and stability, this disruption served to add zest to their lives. For the most part, they stopped categorizing or thinking of themselves in static terms and were alive to the possibility of change.

As people revealed themselves openly and became more spontaneous, they began to look more alive, and their appearance changed, sometimes radically. Those who had appeared lifeless and plain-looking before began to have a new sense of vitality, and with the release of repressive energy they became better looking. As they became more responsive to their feelings they were increasingly sensitive to others. It became apparent that those individuals who can tolerate angry feelings in themselves without becoming punishing or judgmental learn to function in a manner that is far less hostile. There is a sharp reduction in toxic, dishonest, and role-playing responses that so often characterize conventional life.

Motivated by their experiences in group interaction, these people gradually evolved into a psychotherapeutic community composed of approximately 95 persons. They succeeded in creating an environment that brought the warmth and aliveness of those weekends into their everyday lives. They are deeply involved in a way of life that minimizes behavior that causes psychological pain to themselves and others.

Research and observation of this unique reference population for a period of more than 12 years has been fruitful and has furnished valuable insights. This unusual laboratory, combined with clinical material from a wide variety of patients, has provided the bulk of data from which our theory is derived.

Many of the questions the author raised years ago have been answered. It is possible for an individual who is willing to face the truth of his or her aloneness to recover feelings of joy and exuberance. However, it would be very difficult, in fact almost impossible, to live this kind of life without the companionship of other people who are emotionally alive. The therapeutic value of friendship must be emphasized, for it is virtually a necessity to share one's struggle with others who support one's individuality and personal freedom. Intimacy without bondage, and closeness without illusions of security enable a person to feel the truth of his or her separateness in a way not possible in a more conventional relationship.

Neurosis originates through a social process and can potentially be altered in a social milieu. The people from the groups and others who joined them, who together created a new social environment, are devoted to ameliorating the destructive repetitive process within themselves and to preventing, as far as is possible, its being passed on to their children. A fundamental understanding of the developmental aspects and dynamics of neurotic defenses has been essential to them in this endeavor.

PART I

THE CORE DEFENSE

Chapter 1

THE FANTASY BOND
A Developmental Overview

Psychological defenses that protected people from suffering emotional pain and anxiety when they were children later play destructive limiting roles in their adult lives. An individual's defense system acts to keep him or her insulated, mechanical, and removed from the deepest personal experiences.

Our defenses can malfunction in a manner that is analogous to the body's physical reaction in the case of pneumonia. In this disease, the body's defensive reaction is more destructive than the original assault. The presence of organisms in the lungs evokes cellular and humoral responses that meet the invasion, yet the magnitude of the defensive reaction leads to congestion that is potentially dangerous to the organism.

In a like manner, defenses that were erected by the vulnerable child to protect him or herself against a toxic environment may become more detrimental than the original trauma. In this sense, one's psychological defenses become the core of one's neurosis.

Our defensive solution acts as a general resistance to change or progress, cuts off our feeling for ourselves, and presents the fundamental problem in any psychotherapy. In our investigation of resistance, we have been confounded by what for us is the single most remarkable fact of human behavior: the perversity with which most people avoid or minimize experiences that are warm or constructive. Most of us reject or manipulate our environments to avoid any emotional interaction that would contradict our early conception of reality, and this fact of human nature may be the single most delimiting factor for all psychotherapies.

The author conceives of neurosis as an inward, protective style of living that leads the individual to seek satisfaction more in fantasy than in the real world. It is the result of the frustration of infantile urges and the primal hunger caused by emotional deprivation in one's childhood. It is the process of reliving rather than living, choosing bondage over freedom, the old over the new, the past over the now. It is the attempt to recreate a parent or parents in other persons or institutions, or even, if all else fails, in oneself. It is the abrogation of real power in exchange for childish manipulations. It is the avoidance of genuine friendship, free choice, and love in favor of familiarity and false safety. In other words, one clings to the emotional deadness of the family and to illusions of safety and security by repeating early patterns with new objects.

In one sense, neurosis is a response to a realistic fear—the terror and anxiety that surround our awareness of death. As a child matures and becomes conscious of his or her own end, the young person uses defenses to protect the self. However, it is a maladaptive procedure because it involves a progessive giving up of our real lives in an attempt to alleviate death anxiety. Indeed, most people prefer to exist in a non-feeling, defended state because to feel for themselves or for another person would make them more aware of their vulnerability and limitation in time.

The basic tenet of my theoretical approach is the concept of a *fantasy bond* (Firestone, 1984). The "primary fantasy bond" is an *illusion* of connection, originally an imaginary fusion or joining with the mother's body, most particularly the breast. It is a *core defense* and is protected by other patterns of thoughts and behaviors (secondary fantasies). The term "fantasy bond" describes both the original imaginary connection formed during childhood and the transference of this internal image of oneness to significant figures in the adult's intimate associations. The process of forming a fantasy bond leads to a subsequent deterioration in the adult's personal relationships. The function of resistance is to protect the individual from the anxiety that arises whenever this fantasy bond is threatened.

It is important to differentiate this specific use of the word "bond" from its other uses in psychological and popular literature. It is not "bond" as in "bonding" (maternal-infant attachment) in a positive sense nor does it refer to a relationship that includes loyalty, devotion, and genuine love. Our concept of the fantasy bond uses *bond* rather in the sense of bondage or limitation of freedom.

For the infant, this fantasized connection alleviates pain and anxiety by providing partial gratification of its emotional or physical hunger. In other words, the fantasy bond is a substitute for the love and care that may be missing in the infant's environment. The more deprivation in the infant's immediate surroundings, the more dependency the infant will have on this fantasy of fusion. The fantasy bond is created to deal with the intolerable pain and anxiety that arise when the infant is faced with excessive frustration. This type of anxiety can be far more devastating to the infant than the frustration itself. Winnicott (1958) has described this reaction:

> Maternal failures produce phases of reaction to impinge- ment and these reactions interrupt the 'going on being' of the infant. An excess of this reacting produces not frustration but a *threat of annihilation*. This . . . is a very real primitive anxiety. (p. 303)

THE CONCEPT OF "LOVE-FOOD"

At the preverbal stage, the state of anxiety is intolerable to the infant and creates a dread not only of separation and starvation, but perhaps even of death. Observing these phenomena in early research, the author concluded that the mother needs adequate emotional resources and an ability to express affection if she is to provide her infant with proper emotional sustenance. She must be able to feed and care for her infant without arousing severe anxiety in the child, and she should be sensitive to the child's needs. In this way, she will enable it to develop into a social being. I have called the product of this ability on the part of the mother "love-food," which implies both the capability *and* the desire to provide for the need-gratification of the infant. In terms of this theory, love-food is necessary for survival in both the physical and psychological sense (Firestone, 1957).

When deprived of love-food, an infant experiences considerable anxiety and pain and attempts to compensate by sucking its thumb and by providing self-nourishment in various ways. At this point in its devel- opment, a baby is able to create the illusion of the breast. An infant who feels empty and starved emotionally relies increasingly on this fantasy for gratification. And, indeed, this process provides partial relief. In working with regressed schizophrenic patients, my colleagues and I observed that some had visions and dreams of white hazes, snow, and the like, sometimes representing the wish for milk and nourishment. One patient described to me a white breast that he saw, and when I asked what came out of it, he said, "Pictures." Thus, fantasy may eventually become "more real" to the seriously disturbed person than does experience in the "real" environment.

In explaining the survival function of schizophrenia, Rosen (1953) has written:

> When a wish for something is so important that it involves a matter of life and death, then, and only then, does the unconscious part of the psychic apparatus spring into action and provide the necessary gratification with an *imagination*. (p. 107–108)

Rosen goes on to report the story of a soldier, lost in the African desert, who imagined that the sand was water and scooped up handfuls of it, which he said "were wet and cool to his touch and refreshing to taste." Such is the power of imagination when one is faced with a situation perceived to be one of life-threatening deprivation.

DETERMINANTS OF THE FANTASY BOND

In the early stages of an infant's development, intolerable feelings of dread, anxiety, and isolation are at times conveyed through the physical interaction between the mother and child. It is impossible for an anxious mother to hide her fears and anxieties from her infant. Her true emotional state is transmitted on a deep level to the child.

In observing rejected infants, the author has noted an important characteristic in their mothers that appeared to damage them. This was the mother's (unconscious) refusal to let herself be affected or moved by the emotional experience of feeding or caring for the child. Other observers have noted that this type of mother seems to avoid her baby's loving looks at the point when the baby first begins to recognize her. This avoidance is usually detrimental to the baby's subsequent emotional development.

The symptoms in such an infant are a general dissatisfaction, often consisting of whining, an inability to relax against the mother's body (or, on the other hand, a desperate clinging to the mother), excessive crying, and a "spaced-out" or pitiful, pinched look on the face. Later, the child appears to avoid love and affection and may have a tendency toward behavior that provokes anger or hostility in others. Sensitive adults may even sense within themselves hostility and feelings of loathing toward an unloved child.

CHARACTERISTICS OF THE INADEQUATE MOTHER AS CONTRASTED WITH THOSE OF THE "GOOD MOTHER"

A particularly destructive type of mother is one whose physical contact with her infant is expressed in an automatic, unfeeling manner or touch. The more contact there is with a well-defended, emotionally cut-off mother, the more damage will be done to the infant. Though inadequate mothers vary in their characteristics, certain qualities stand out as detrimental. Some mothers give their children exaggerated praise and flattery for their physical appearance and abilities. Other mothers tend to talk a great deal *about* their love for their children, but their actions often contradict their words. They may be overly solicitous in one situation, and cold and distant in another. Also fairly common is over-identification with the child, with its accompanying stylized language and use of the pronoun "we"—"now we're going to have our bath."

The "good" or adequate mother, in contrast, has the capacity to tolerate *real closeness followed by separation,* to a greater degree than the mother described above. She has the ability to give sensitive care to her child and to relieve its anxiety without being overprotective.

The "good" mother does not regularly try to put her infant to sleep after a feeding, but is interested in maintaining the contact through play and communication. As the child grows older, the mother offers appropriately varied responses, alternating spontaneous contact with letting-go of her offspring. This mother also copes with acting-out behaviors—whining, excessive crying, tantrums—before these negative patterns become integrated into the child's personality. A "good" mother has little need to reassure her child of a connection because she is better able to tolerate her own separateness as a person. Typically, she also enjoys a close, intimate, and sexually satisfying relationship with her husband.

In terms of the mother-child interaction, it is my hypothesis that the most damaging factor is the presence of habitual physical contact in the absence of genuine emotionality; that is, the mother has withdrawn her affect and her desire for contact with the child, but still offers adequate, or even excessive, automatic physical care or affection.

Other researchers have noticed this particular form of withdrawal in psychotic patients:

> Bateson and Jackson assume that the schizophrenogenic
> mother is a mother who becomes anxious and withdraws if the
> child responds to her as a loving mother; that is, her anxiety and
> hostility are aroused when she is in danger of intimate contact
> with the child. (Grotjahn, 1960, p. 82)

The mother-child dynamics formulated here are the variables that
the author believes to be conducive to the formation of the primary
fantasy bond, with varying degrees of subsequent damage, ranging from
mildly neurotic behavior to, in some cases, schizophrenic regression.

PSEUDO-INDEPENDENCE AND THE PROCESS OF INCORPORATION

The primary fantasy of connection leads to a posture of pseudo-
independence in the developing child—"I don't need anyone, I can take
care of myself"—yet the irony is that the more the person relies on
fantasy, the more helpless he or she becomes in the real world and the
more he or she demands to be taken care of.

Many children feel this false sense of self-sufficiency—or omnipotence—because they have introjected the image of the "good and powerful mother" into themselves. Unfortunately, they generally incorporate her covert rejecting attitudes as well. The more pain and suffering a
child experiences, the more that child will need to incorporate the
mother or the self-mothering process. Erikson (1963), describing the
process of introjection, states that: "In introjection we feel and act as if
an outer goodness had become an inner certainty" (p. 248–249). He
emphasizes that the early defenses of introjection and projection are the
strongest (and most persistent) of all the defenses the child may later
develop.

The incorporated parental attitudes form the basis of the self-
concept. Through introjection, the child has the feeling of being a combination of the good, strong parent and the bad, weak child. The child
now feels that he or she needs nothing from the outside world, but is a
complete, self-sufficient system. The more pseudo-independent the
developing young person feels, the more dependent such an individual
becomes. This is best exemplified in psychotic patients who, at the same
time, have omnipotent delusions and are barely able to take care of
themselves, requiring full-time care from others.

The primary fantasy bond can relieve fear and allay the anxiety of
feeling separate and alone. It can stave off painful feelings of emotional
starvation and emptiness. It creates numerous distortions, however. For

example, in this process the child has a tendency to idealize the parent at the child's own expense. The child must conceptualize him or herself as bad or unlovable in order to defend against the realization that the parents are inadequate. Recognition of real faults in the parent would destroy the bond, or the imagined connection, and the feeling of imagined self-sufficiency.

THE FANTASY BOND IN THE ADULT

The child, and later the adult, defend against the awareness of separateness. For the adult, the primary fantasy also protects one from the terror that accompanies a realization of one's inevitable personal death. Many imaginary connections are used to give this illusion of immortality: the fantasy bond between husband and wife, the bond with one's children, a bond with one's original family, religion, country, or a geographical place.

Bettelheim (1943/1980) observed that a strong fantasized connection formed among the inmates of a compound in a German concentration camp. Facing almost certain death, the prisoners imagined that they would somehow survive as a group, if not individually. On one occasion, the group was forced to stand all night in subfreezing temperatures because two prisoners had tried to escape. More than 80 perished; but the survivors reported that during the event they felt "free from fear and . . . actually happier than at most other times during their camp experiences" (p. 65). When, after the ordeal was over, they were returned to their barracks, they felt relieved but no longer happy or free from fear. "Each prisoner as an individual was now comparatively safer [in reality], but he had lost the [imagined] safety orginating in being a member of a unified group" (p. 66).

Kaiser (1955) has described a "delusion of fusion" that the child develops when threatened by feelings of isolation and separateness. This concept is directly analogous to the concept of a fantasy bond. Kaiser reported that this delusion not only is common in childhood but occurs in many adult situations. He believes that transference in the therapy setting is another attempt on the part of the patient to fuse with a parental figure in order to avoid being a separate individual. To escape from an interaction where he would be an equal (an adult) with the therapist, the patient often retreats to a childish, dependent, submissive posture in a desperate effort to make this primitive connection with another person. The author agrees with Kaiser's perception that the patient wants to form a fantasy bond with the therapist, and the role of therapist often supports the patient's desire. Resistance in therapy derives from this bond, that is, the patient struggles against the therapist as a parental figure whom he or she imagines wants the patient to change.

In summary, the primary fantasy originates in early childhood or infancy to fill a gap where there is environmental deprivation; it "nourishes" the self; and it becomes the motivating force behind self-destructive, neurotic behavior. It is a maladaptive solution that occurs not only in the seriously ill psychotic but also, to a lesser degree, in the neurotic person. No child has an ideal environment, thus all people depend to varying degrees on internal gratification from the primary fantasy.

Defenses Against Threats to the Primary Fantasy Bond

The fantasy process can become functionally autonomous; that is, it can persist for long periods after the deprivation has ceased, and it predisposes behavioral responses. Concomitant to the process of substituting fantasy for real gratification, there is a powerful resistance to accepting anything from the real world. Once the primary fantasy is formed, people often choose to protect it at all costs. Their principal goal then is to maintain the safety and security of this imagined connection. They come to prefer fantasy gratification to real satisfaction and love from others. They tend to develop a cynical view of life and blame others for their failure to achieve their desired goals.

Anything that arouses an individual's awareness of separateness or nonbonded existence provokes anxiety and often leads to hostility, even toward the very people and circumstances that would give the individual the greatest satisfaction. Viewed as attempts to defend the primary fantasy, many irrational, self-limiting, neurotic responses begin to make sense.

Paradoxically, a satisfying sexual experience can be a major disruption to the bond or the fantasy of being connected. The sex act is a real, but temporary, physical connection followed by a sharp separation. Similarly, physical intimacy is a close, affectionate contact with a subsequent separation, and real communication is a sharing of thoughts and feelings followed by a distinct awareness of boundaries. Resentment may be inherent in these separations, which inevitably follow real closeness, though the anger and hostility can be unconscious.

In a bond, these situations are avoided. Moving in and out of closeness is intolerable to those people who have become dependent upon repetitive, habitual contact without much feeling. For example, a woman will often withhold her full sexual response—real satisfaction—to avoid this rejoining and subsequent separation. People avoid real communication because expressing their views implies that they are a discrete entity, that they count, that "they have a vote." This stimulates the fear of separateness and aloneness.

It is the author's conclusion that most people avoid real sexuality, physical intimacy, and honest communication because they don't want to face the fact that each of these transactions has an ending and necessitates a letting go. Each small ending can remind them that everything eventually ends—in death. Genuine love and intimacy challenge the primary fantasy of connection and arouse an acute awareness of mortality. Separateness is intolerable because it fosters an awareness of death. Establishing an imaginary connection with another person can become a major defense against this unbearable anxiety.

Anxious parents attempt to reassure their children *and themselves* that there are no endings. Most parents attempt to maintain an imagined link to safety, security, and immortality for two reasons: first, to relieve and avoid their own anxiety about separation; and secondly, because on a deep level they feel guilty for bringing another human being into a world where the ultimate end is death.

REACTIONS TO POSITIVE EXPERIENCES

Threats to the primary fantasy also create anxiety because they rearouse the painful feelings that were operating at the time the original defense was formed. Most adults don't want to be vulnerable again. Because they fear positive experiences that make them feel deeply about their lives, they avoid them and tend to remain passive, somewhat childish, and may even provoke rejection or bring about disappointment. Because their actions seem to them so perverse and unacceptable, they often speak with duplicity and mixed messages and are generally misleading in their communications. To the degree that they are defended, people no longer really want or pursue what they say they want.

As adults, many people keep intact an idealized image of their parents in the hope that some day their parents will love them or at least approve of them. As a result, their behavior is more conforming, compromising, and conventional, rather than self-directed or independent. Self-hatred and a lack of self-esteeem stem from an idealization of the parents and the introjection of their covertly rejecting attitudes.

JOANNE

Several years ago, a patient of mine, Joanne, recognized that she had reached a point in her therapy where the idealization of her family and her subsequent self-hatred were beginning to be challenged. Writing a letter to friends in her therapy group, she spoke of avoiding contact with them and not wanting to admit the reasons. This highly intelligent woman was extremely sensitive to her defenses and had an unusual understanding of her resistance to abandoning them and taking another chance on people. In her letter, Joanne wrote:

> Not until recently did I let myself see my avoidance as a rejection of real people, as rejecting you. When I've consciously made the choice not to linger and talk after the group, to not talk about myself during the group . . . I never let myself see it as a rejection of people I care about . . . I feel like nothing, no person, no experience is worth giving up my defenses for. I hate seeing that, I hate even more for you to know it, to put it in writing, but it's true. That's how I act, that's how I live my life.
>
> It's really just one basic defense—self-hatred. It was the first "made-up," pretend emotion I created. It seems hard to believe, but I know I was an infant when I seized on hating myself as a way to keep on living. . . . It's a cold, numb feeling where self-loathing was so intense, everything and everyone else is blocked out. Without that feeling, I know I really would have died . . . the only other alternative to self-hatred would be to directly experience rejection, real rejection.
>
> In some twisted way, I structured my whole personality, my behavior, my feeling of "validity" as a person on that made-up emotion. And self-loathing has become so firmly entrenched in my being, it feels like the very core of me—in some crazy way, self-hatred feels like my "life-force."
>
> In all the months and years of therapy, I never saw it so clearly. I eventually saw that feeding my face was a substitute to feeding my vagina, that keeping myself asexual and isolated was keeping a pact with my parents . . . but I never really saw until now how all of that—the fat, the asexual isolation—was keeping my "life-force," my self-hatred intact.
>
> I can't hang on to self-hatred around you any more—even with briefest contact of groups and weekly sessions. No matter how I "insure" the feeling by acts of self-destructiveness during the week—the eating, picking at myself, calling up my mother's voice to ridicule and denounce myself—you just have to see me, I mean really see and address the person that's real in me, to strip

away the self-hate, even for just a second or two. It's like the world falls in on me, I feel like screaming down the hall and doing *anything*—banging my head against the wall—to get back my "life-force" of self-hatred.

When I make jokes at the end of a session, it feels like a desperate attempt to get that self-hatred in force again; it feels like falling off a building and grabbing for ledges to save myself.

In my case, self-hatred was formed very early, to protect myself from the certain total insanity that rejection would have led me into. From there, keeping a layer of fat surrounding me, twisting my face into ugly expressions, kept that basic or primal defense alive in me. (I just remembered that I began being fat at the age of five when a friend of the family began showing an interest in me. It was also a time during which I first acted out self-destructiveness, inflicting a concussion on myself, sitting on a live battery and burning my legs. He was the first to threaten that primary defense . . . by being nice to me.)

Later on, I dealt with the threat of people being nice to me by surrounding myself with not-nice, phony people. And, even then, if they began to respond to anything outside my primary defense, I threw up a barrage of cruel jokes about myself and, worse, about them. I added other superficial defenses, as well, to send up a "smoke screen" to mask the more basic defense. I became an "intellectual," using phony words; I became tough and aggressive to keep people confused and self-protective around me . . . all still in defense of their threatening to strip away my self-hatred.

The "realer" I became (through therapy) and the "realer" all of you have become, the more threatened my "life-force" defense has become. . . . I guess what I'm doing now is exposing the primary defense. I guess I'm ready to risk living for longer and longer periods without that core of self-hatred.

This letter was written over 8 years ago, as some of my later concepts were being developed. This patient, who described herself so honestly, showed a remarkable understanding of herself that was partially ahead of my knowledge at that time. For example, she writes of "calling up her mother's voice" to criticize her during the week. She was referring to the concept of an "inner voice" (Chapter 4), remnants of the incorporated rejecting parental attitudes. Joanne's insight was remarkably perceptive, as I was to discover when I began to experiment more with formulating the self-destructive thought processes of this "inner voice." This was accomplished by having patients verbalize negative thoughts about themselves thereby externalizing their inner dialogue in a dramatic and feelingful release.

The tragedy is that this woman, who was so viciously intolerant of nice treatment as a child that she deliberately burned her legs when someone took an interest in her, could not bring herself to give up her basic defense and eventually left therapy and her friends. Today she is living the isolated life of which she so poignantly wrote.

Joanne's conception of a strong self-hatred being her primary defense was only partly correct theoretically. More precisely, it was the fantasy bond or imagined connection with her family that sustained in her the belief that she could survive alone and take care of herself without ever risking taking anything from the outside world. Her self-hatred was formed as a result of her idealization of her mother, probably before conscious memory. It functioned to maintain her primary fantasy of connection. However, in one sense, Joanne's self-hatred *was* a major defense. By hating herself, she never had to risk rejection or hatred from others; she rejected herself and them first. It was, in fact, a force in her life that ultimately protected her from the dreaded possibility of being hurt again.

CONCLUSION

Human beings desire freedom and individuality, but paradoxically they fight stubbornly against change and progress. Ernest Becker (1964), in writing about the problem of resistance, attempts an explanation:

> It is barely imaginable that one should struggle so hard, except against the relinquishment of real basic inner drives, of irrevocable natural urges [instincts]. . . . But this is to fail to understand human action: the patient is not struggling against himself, against forces deep within his animal nature. He is struggling rather against the loss of his world, of the whole range of action and objects that he so laboriously and painfully fashioned during his early training. (p. 170)

I believe that the concept of the fantasy bond—the illusion of connection to the mother—and all the subsequent actions and thought processes, are a dynamic formulation of the primitive defensive inner world that Becker writes about.

Anxiety arises whenever this inner world is intruded upon, and especially when the fantasy bond, the imaginary connection, and one's pseudo-independence is threatened. Anxiety is aroused, too, whenever there is an awareness of one's separateness and mortality. The author sees resistance as the holding on to an imaginary connection to others, due to the dread of re-experiencing one's sense of aloneness and helplessness. Ultimately, resistance functions in order to protect the individual from experiencing anxiety states that arise from the threats to the neurotic resolution of the basic conflict—the conflict between dependency on inner fantasy for gratification versus a desire for real gratification in the interpersonal environment.

As humans, we are torn between pursuing an assertive goal-directed life, and depending on passive-dependent machinations that assure us of a fantasy bond. How we resolve this basic conflict determines whether we have a free-flowing, changing existence or a static, rigid, defensive posture. The primary fantasy bond is the core defense underlying our resistance to change. It is the major barrier to a full, rich existence.

Chapter 2

HUNGER VERSUS LOVE

Emotional hunger is *not* love, though people often confuse the two. Hunger is a strong need caused by emotional deprivation in childhood. It is a primitive condition of pain and longing which people often act out in a vain and desperate attempt to fill a void or emptiness. This emptiness is related to the pain of aloneness and separateness and can never realistically be satisfied in an adult relationship. Yet many people refuse to bear their pain and are unwilling to accept the futility of attempting to gratify their primitive dependency needs.

When acted upon, hunger is a powerful emotion that is both exploitive and destructive to others. People mistakenly identify this desperate feeling with love and think of this primal longing as genuine affection. They confuse actions that are based on need with true regard for another person.

Feelings of emotional hunger are experienced as deep internal sensations that range in intensity from a dull ache to a sharp painful feeling. Often a person may touch others or express physical affection with ostensibly loving gestures in an attempt to kill off this aching sensation. Many parents offer affection and love when they feel the need for it themselves. This type of physical affection drains the emotional resources of children rather than nourishing them. It is a form of taking, not giving. Many people vehemently claim that they are loving and caring, when in fact they are actually feeling their emotional hunger and dependency.

It is wise to be suspicious of the use of the words "love" or "I love you." If parents examined their motives truthfully, they would discover that they say these words most often not when they feel for their children, but rather when they feel the need for reassurance *from* them. The word "love" is often used in this way, and as a result, children become suspicious and distrustful of real sharing and caring, even when it is sincere. Early in their lives they learned to distrust positive verbal expressions and even physical affection, because more often than not these feelings covertly expressed their parents' need and desperation.

Experiencing the feeling of hunger that comes from unfulfilled emotional needs is bearable, albeit painful, for adults. Unfortunately, most individuals choose to deny or avoid this pain as they did when they were young. They seek every means to kill off their feeling of being rejected or alone. They resort to a fantasy bond, a powerful and effective painkiller, to relieve their fear of aloneness and lessen the ache of hunger.

THE FANTASY BOND AND THE TRADITIONAL FAMILY

Most couples start off feeling real friendship, caring, tenderness, and genuine affection. Their relationship is characterized by mutual respect and separateness. They enjoy sharing and are intensely interested in each other. These characteristics are observable in couples who are not yet in a bond. However, as the partners attempt to achieve permanent security by making emotional commitments and guarantees to each other and themselves, they cease to relate as individuals. They no longer know the other in the true sense. They no longer see each other objectively, having converted the other into a significant figure from the past. Their emotional responses are no longer appropriate to real situations and events but contain elements and distortions based on the frustrations and pains of their childhood. Each individual now merely implements the other's neurosis.

A bond can become a "death" pact in which the relationship has a narcotic effect on the individuals, killing off their pain and feelings of hunger. Often the bond serves as a license to act out destructive behavior because the individuals "belong" to each other and have implicitly agreed that their relationship will last forever.

The myth of love in the traditional couple and the fantasy of parental love are logical extensions of this type of bond. This myth of the family's unconditional love for its members can develop into a shared conspiracy to deny truth and cover up aloneness and pain. As such, it is a concerted effort to avoid the facts of life, death and separateness.

CAROL

Carol was a young woman who was deeply disturbed as a result of growing up in a family where the bond between the parents was extremely destructive. In her family she was lied to about the realities of life and death, extremely overprotected, and intruded upon by an intensely hungry mother. The first time I saw Carol as a patient I thought she was only fourteen or fifteen years old. In actuality, she was in her early twenties. She was barely 5 feet tall and very overweight. Her hair was cut short in an unbecoming style; her eyes were dark and defiant. The awkward, tentative way that she walked and her posture all contributed to a picture of strangeness, of backwardness.

Carol didn't talk—except to tell me her name and a few sketchy details. She looked as if she wanted to speak but she couldn't or wouldn't. She asked a couple of questions near the end of the session and then left, saying that she would see me the following week. This same scene repeated itself over and over for almost a year. Here was a girl who had been stunted in her emotional development and possibly even in her physical growth by events in her formative years, but she was even more damaged by the lies told her about these events. The double messages of the patient's mother, pulling on her, yet claiming love and devotion, drained Carol's vital resources and led to her progressive retreat into fantasy.

Carol's mother, a domineering woman with strong dependency needs of her own, was, in fact, very involved with her daughter. However, her involvement was extremely intrusive. The mother showed little respect for the boundaries between Carol and herself. For example, from the time Carol entered grammar school, her mother constantly questioned her concerning her activities, her thoughts, and her feelings. Later, when Carol was in high school, her mother routinely searched her bedroom, looking for notes or letters from boyfriends. Carol sensed very early that her mother was desperate for information about her personal life and that she longed to know what her daughter was thinking. To protect herself, Carol had begun to withhold her thoughts from her mother. She communicated nothing about herself to her parents and became secretive and inward. Her tendency to hold back personal responses was evidenced by her reserve and shyness in social situations and at school. As she matured, she withdrew more and more into herself and made very few friends during her adolescent years.

After several months of relative silence in her sessions, Carol began to talk sporadically. She mentioned some things she noticed about me—a suit I was wearing, the way my hands looked to her. At the same time, she began to open up and reveal information about herself. She told me of her freshman year at college, when she had locked herself in her dormitory room for 2 weeks, alone, nourished only by the occasional food brought in to her by a concerned roommate. Thoughts of suicide were common during this period in her life. She utilized the thought of suicide to comfort herself, thinking, "If I ever feel too awful, so bad that I can't stand it, then I can always kill myself." The thought of suicide was an important escape for her and acted as a painkiller. Her feelings were quite ambivalent. Frequently, she would offer information and then be overwhelmed with embarrassment and anger.

In spite of the turbulence in the therapeutic relationship, Carol lost 20 pounds during that first year of sessions, a fact mostly attributable to positive transference. I remember thinking then that, if nothing else, the sessions were helpful to her with her weight problem.

After that first year, Carol began to show dramatic progress. First, her appearance changed drastically. Her childish pout was replaced with a soft smile. She seemed to blossom into womanhood during the next few months. She had joined one of the therapy groups, and her fellow group members witnessed a remarkable transformation in her. In the group, she began to talk openly and this openness was now evident in her individual sessions. She started to care deeply for the people in the group and expressed her feelings in a straightforward way. Everyone was affected positively by Carol's warmth and concern. Her perceptions and insights were clear and valuable, and she spoke with compassion concerning each member's struggle. The people in the group developed more tolerance and compassion for themselves as a result of Carol's responses.

Carol's major defense had been one of self-denial and withholding. Her withholding had been a powerful response to her mother's desperate need for love *from* Carol. Holding back her communications from her mother, that is, refusing to share her thoughts and feelings with her, had been the only weapon available to Carol in her struggle to combat the intense emotional hunger and intrusiveness that were directed toward her. After she verbalized her secret suicidal thoughts, however, she chose to relinquish this basic defense on a deep level. She acknowledged, for the first time in her life, the seriousness of her state and was determined to live rather than to act out her retreat from life. Beneath her character armor she had preserved a sense of integrity and honest feelings. Once she stopped withholding her thoughts and feelings, she was free to express her natural interest in life and in other people and became a significant contributor to the group.

HUNGER AND THE MYTH OF FAMILY LOVE

It is a major thesis of this book that the fantasy bond in the traditional family causes a tremendous amount of innocent, unnecessary suffering. Denying primitive hunger and pain and pretending connections that, in fact, do not exist, lead to fundamental distortions of each person's sense of reality. It is a great burden on everyone to play this game of "let's pretend."

In many families the members constantly complain and make accusations such as, "You don't really love me;" yet on another level they refuse really to believe their own complaints. When these accusations are made, a person generally responds with immediate guilt reactions. There are angry protestations that they *do* in fact love the other, but that the others don't love them. And so it goes, back and forth, with melodramatic scenes and manipulations. "If you really love me, then why is it necessary to go out with the boys?" "Why can't you show a little consideration for your family and give up that girl?" "If you really loved me, how could you forget our anniversary?—my birthday?" "How could you leave me and go out when you know how I worry?" There are hundreds of variations of these manipulations and games that people act out with each other while professing eternal love. On some level, everyone knows they are lying, which is why they are so defensive and dishonest.

It is virtually impossible to convince "loving parents" that they in fact don't love their children and family. They feel the sensation of their deep hunger and need in the pit of their stomachs—the *feeling* of hunger really does exist.

> During one of my psychotherapy groups, one mother cried out to her daughter, "If I don't love you, what is this burning feeling inside me?" She had been continually abusive and disrespectful to her daughter, yet she insisted that she loved her. She *did* have a burning feeling, but it wasn't love. It was a restless, powerful hunger to be nurtured and to feed off this young person. This woman did not love her daughter or her son, who was also in the group. As a result of the manipulations and distortions

designed to protect the fantasy of her love, both children had been severely damaged in their capacity to feel or even think.

This mother's hunger and oversolicitousness were still being manifested in the present and were characteristic of her destructive child-rearing. She spoke of the horror she felt when her daughter had attempted suicide, but even in this she demonstrated a lack of real feeling, for she was concerned primarily with the grief that she herself experienced at the time, not with her daughter's suffering.

Her burning emotion was not love or anything resembling it because it had fractured her children's ability to live and experience their lives. It had restricted them and led them to close off their feelings. It undermined their confidence and sense of personal worth.

Many parents are handicapped like this mother and cannot offer genuine love or affection to their children on an operational or observable level. In my study of families, I have seen countless examples of well-meaning parents carrying on behavior that is destructive and injurious to their children, while claiming to love their children and have their best interests at heart. These parents are telling the truth, albeit defensively, when they state that they did the best they could for their children. It is true that they did the best that they were capable of, but they simply weren't capable of meeting their children's needs. Parents have often been too psychologically damaged themselves to provide a healthy climate.

The fact that parents are supposed to love their children creates a sense of pressure and obligation on immature parents, which only compounds the problem. Many have grown up with a feeling of resentment and hostility about duties and obligations. These feelings of anger and hatred are then acted out consciously on their children. *If the concept or illusion of unconditional parental love were withdrawn from the child-rearing scene, it would be better for all concerned.*

An honest, unloving father or mother will do far less damage to his or her child than a role-playing, "loving" parent. A rejecting and unloving parent will cause a child pain, but a dishonestly rejecting parent causes the child pain and makes him or her feel "crazy." This type of parent causes the child to become unsure of the ability to think and perceive correctly and ultimately causes the son or daughter to develop symptoms of psychological illness. When parents cannot bear to know that they are rejecting their children, they systematically cut off the children's opportunity to express themselves. Hiding the truth forces the children to bury their pain, which interferes with the possibility of healing.

Many children do not feel love for their parents either. After they have been damaged in their early years, they tend to have a self-centered, exploitive interest but no real feeling for their parents as people. Because their original affectionate feeling toward their parents was rejected, they become withholding and inward. Like their parents, children feel strong sensations of dependence and need that they mistakenly refer to as love. Both parents and children sense, on some level, the underlying truth about the myth of love in the family but neither is courageous enough to cope with it forthrightly and place it in true perspective.

THE OPERATIONS OF LOVE

In contrast to emotional hunger, which has a profound detrimental effect on the growing child, real love sustains and nurtures. Genuine love may be operationally defined as those behaviors that enhance the well-being of children and assist them in reaching their full potential. Outward manifestations of love can be observed in people who make *real* emotional contact with another person; that is, they have frequent eye contact, display spontaneous, nonclinging physical affection, and take obvious pleasure in the other person's company. In an intimate relationship, love is expressed through direct, honest communication, mutual respect, acknowledgment of each other's boundaries, and a desire to share and cooperate.

Internally, a person who is capable of giving love generally feels warm and good toward the object of that love. He or she has a positive self-image and a healthy self-regard as well. Such a person maintains a sense of compassion for both the love object and the self and remains separate and distinct.

Love is not an emotion that exists in limited quantities; therefore it is not exclusive. Feelings of love and affection are intermittent and are affected by many variables. Therefore, statements of unconditional, constant, and enduring love are generally misleading.

The operations of love can be readily distinguished from those of emotional hunger by an outside observer, if not by the subject himself. In addition, these operations have an important differential effect on the love object and his or her sense of well-being.

Many people spend their entire lives in a futile pursuit of the love that never existed or that was withheld from them by their parents. They have internalized a strong negative image of themselves that they stubbornly refuse to change because the whole myth would crumble if they were to receive and accept positive responses or genuine recognition from another.

Parents have a stake in the pretense that they love their children because they can't bear to acknowledge that they are denying love to helpless creatures who remind them of their own painful childhood vulnerability. Their lack of a deep feeling of love makes them feel that they are bad people. They cannot tolerate knowledge of their own shallow, hungry nature. Focusing upon their children in a critical manner, parents attempt to find justification for not loving them. Their criticisms reinforce the children's belief that they are unworthy and unlovable. These negative accusations become part of the children's emotional identity, and as adults, they will later re-enact this same process with their own children.

HUNGER AND OVERPROTECTION

Many parents are not only incapable of genuine love or regard for their offspring, but unconsciously have a stake in their destruction—though this may be the farthest thing from their conscious desire or intent.

Immature individuals are anxious to have children primarily in order to gratify their own hunger. They want to form a bond or connection with them that will help to deaden their own emotional pain. However, forming this bond in fantasy causes them to lose any real sense of relationship with their children as individuals. These emotionally deprived parents use their children in order to maintain the illusion that they are never going to die. On some level, they believe that they will live on through their children, and in this way manage to allay their anxieties about death.

A child who is free and independent and has a strong sense of personal value is unlikely to maintain dependency on the parents. Therefore the parents must interfere with their offspring's emotional development or the child cannot be held on to. At the same time, the child's life must be protected, because if anything happened to the child, the parents would have to experience their own painful separateness. A strong stake in perpetuating the child's physical life is combined with an equally powerful need to render the son or daughter helpless and emotionally dependent so as to be manipulated and controlled. For example, many parents swear that they love their children and to prove it give evidence of their sacrifice and struggle to take care of their child's physical needs. "I would do anything for you." "I remember when I walked with you all night when you were sick and how I took you to the hospital and prayed that you would live." "You can always turn to me."

Parental overprotectiveness stems from two distinct sources: first, parents may fear for their child's safety and health as a reaction formation against underlying hostile feelings toward their offspring. Because they cannot accept these angry impulses in themselves, most parents repress them and act out their defense by placing unnecessary restrictions on their children. They actually stifle the child's natural curiosity and independence. Secondly, many parents focus on the negative aspects of life because they remember painful primal feelings from their own childhood. They overcompensate in an attempt to spare their child frustration and suffering. They tend to have an exaggerated notion of the helplessness of children based on the fears and doubts they experienced when *they* were very young. By their overprotectiveness, these parents foster unnecessary fear and dependency in their children. They are unable to appreciate the real maturity and capability of their children because they are maintaining fantasies of their own helplessness. Attempting to protect their children from feeling fear and sadness, they unwittingly inhibit their growth and development.

In conclusion, the concept of emotional hunger has not been sufficiently explored in the psychological literature, yet it is a primary factor in people's lives. It has a powerful negative effect on the child's development and subsequent adjustment. If parents realized that their children "belong" only to themselves and not to the parents, and both child and parent came to understand that they don't *have* to like or love one another all the time, there would be a chance for an honest relationship with genuine regard. Then it might be possible to break the cycle of unnecessary suffering incurred in the family when emotional hunger is acted out in the name of love.

Chapter 3

COUPLE AND FAMILY BONDS

The old way of love seemed a dreadful bondage. . . . The way they shut their doors, these married people, and shut themselves in to their own exclusive alliance with each other, even in love, disgusted him. It was a whole community of mistrustful couples insulated in private houses or private rooms, always in couples, and no further life . . . admitted: a kaleidoscope of couples, disjoined, separatist, meaningless entities of married couples.

D. H. Lawrence
Women In Love (p. 191)

The "fantasy bond" is the core defense, and as such is a fundamental part of the neurotic process. As stated earlier, the fantasy bond or fantasized connection with the mother helps to ease the anguish of emotional deprivation by providing partial gratification. The paradox of neurosis is that this imagined fusion that provided relief when we were young now severely limits our adult life. Most people attempt to replicate these primitive connections in their most important associations, using their loved ones as symbolic substitutes for the parental figures. They tend to relive the early experiences in their families with new people to the detriment of their present-day relationships.

The term *bond* is being used here to describe the transference of the original fantasized connection to a new person in the individual's adult life. Forming a bond, as I use the word, implies that one is substituting fantasy gratification for a real relationship based on authentic feelings of love and mutual respect.

Bonds—illusions of connectedness—are present to a large extent within the couple and in the traditional family. The process of forming bonds typically leads to a progressive deterioration in marital relationships and is responsible for much of the psychological damage sustained by children in the family. In the strictest sense, a bond exists only in one's imagination, i.e., obviously there is no real fusion; however, it manifests itself outwardly in a variety of behaviors that support one's fantasy of being connected or of belonging to another person. The man and woman who are in a bond avoid closeness and *real* affection and instead form strong dependency ties. Unable to accept the reality of their lack of feeling, they attempt to maintain a fantasy of enduring love.

Because of the anxiety inherent in being vulnerable and undefended in a new love relationship, an individual unconsciously attempts to merge and form a unit with the loved one. In forming a bond, the lover is able to alleviate anxiety and attain a false sense of security and safety by sustaining the illusion of being fused. The fantasy of being connected functions as a defense, for whenever this bond is broken, the underlying pain and fear of separation invariably surface.

The traditional nuclear family is structured in a manner that permits its members to avoid the real pain of separateness. However, the cost of this avoidance is a giving up of genuine experience and personal dignity for all its members. To the extent that couples live in bonds, they remain emotionally deadened to their own feelings and are insensitive to those of others, especially their children's. They must avoid or inhibit people who threaten to reawaken their repressed emotions. Their defended posture is passed on to succeeding generations.

THE DEVELOPMENT OF A COUPLE BOND

Men and women are most likely to form romantic attachments at a time when they are on the upgrade psychologically, often at the stage where they are breaking dependent emotional ties with their families. They are experiencing a strong sense of self and feel separate from the family bond. In this phase of development, the newly-independent person actively seeks friendships and new relationships. As one reaches out to other people and risks more of oneself emotionally, one attracts others with the resulting vitality and enthusiasm. One tends to feel exhilarated and spontaneous in personal interactions. In a new love relationship, one exists, for a while, in a relatively undefended and vulnerable state, typically referred to as the "honeymoon stage" of a relationship. Emotions are intensified and one savors the highs and lows of everyday experiences in a way reminiscent of childhood.

This state of being in love is volatile and exciting at the same time that it is frightening. Fear of loss or abandonment, a dread of being rejected, together with the poignancy and sadness that these new loving feelings evoke, sooner or later become intolerable, especially for those individuals who have suffered from a lack of love in their early lives. At the point that they begin to feel anxious or frightened, they retreat from feeling close and gradually give up the most valued parts of the relationship. It becomes very difficult for them to maintain a loving feeling or to feel that they are lovable once they have defended themselves against these sad or painful feelings.

This retreat from closeness and intimacy is an outgrowth of the adjustment that the child made in responding to the early environment. By the time they reach adulthood, most young people have solidified their defenses and have adapted to living on a certain emotional plateau. Generally they have arrived at a specific personal solution to the basic conflict between dependence and independence and live in a psychological equilibrium that they don't want to disturb. They may be relatively friendly with acquaintances because these relationships pose very little threat to their stability. However, there is a deterioration in friendly and respectful feelings as a relationship becomes more meaningful and intimate, because the new love object now threatens to disturb their equilibrium by penetrating their basic defenses. In their coupling, conflict develops because they strive to maintain their defenses, while at the same time, they wish to hold on to their initial feelings of closeness and affection. The two conditions tend to be mutually exclusive. In a relatively short time, either one or both members of the couple generally choose to sacrifice friendship and love in order to preserve their respective defended states.

SYMPTOMS OF A COUPLE BOND

When two people first become romantically involved, there are usually feelings of genuine companionship as well as a strong sexual attraction between them. Yet, when the affection and friendship in this new relationship stand in stark contrast to the unhappiness and rejection in their past, they unknowingly attempt to erase the difference.

As a couple's relationship "matures," symptoms of a destructive bond appear more frequently. For example, the man and woman who once spent hours talking to each other begin to be uninterested. They have less direct eye contact and stop noticing what the other person is feeling. They become less personal and less honest in their communication. A sense of obligation replaces their desire to be together. They begin to act according to roles; they behave more like a "husband" or a "wife," eventually a "mother" or a "father," than real people. One member of the couple or both begin to hold back their affectionate and sexual responses. Their sexual attraction for each other seems to diminish and their sex life becomes routine.

People strongly resist recognizing these negative trends in their relationships. They will literally obliterate themselves as independent, separate individuals to hold on to their bonds, imagining that they are holding on to real people. Often all that a couple has after years of being together is a fantasy of love which both partners protect by keeping the form of love—the roles, the routines, the accepted behaviors, the observation of birthdays and anniversaries. They maintain the fantasy that they love each other and that they love their children, long after they have stopped behaving in a loving and respectful manner.

At times when I have seen couples together for conjoint therapy sessions, this type of addicted or dependency relationship becomes obvious. Typically, the husband complains about his wife; e.g., she doesn't stay within the family budget, she won't discipline the children, she doesn't want to make love—the accumulation of years of criticisms and frustrations are revealed. The wife, in turn, defensively enumerates *his* faults. When I ask: "Why are you two together?" their answer is indignant: "Because we really love each other." However, it is difficult for me to see the love in these battle-scarred couples. The respect, concern, and caring that exist in a simple friendship are gone. In contrast, their behavior toward one another is made up of secrecy, distrust, deception, hostility, and indifference. The real explanation for remaining together in spite of their distress lies in the addictive nature of their relationship. They have become so dependent upon each other to preserve the illusion of connection that they cannot contemplate the thought of being separate.

Symptoms of a bond often appear following a commitment that at the time honestly reflected the partners' deep feelings toward each other. This commitment may be to marriage, to living together, or to starting a family. Yet, this commitment is often mistakenly accepted for a guarantee of continued love and security—external indications of a fantasy of connectedness. The sense of belonging to another person, of having proprietary rights over the other, of being loved "forever after," offers a reassurance, albeit false, that is difficult to resist, especially for those individuals with a poor self-image and strong dependency needs.

> When one patient began planning his wedding, a series of events occurred that clearly illustrates this process. The young man's fiancée decided to have her wedding ring made up from an antique ring that had been in *his* family for generations. The prospective groom was only too happy to have the necessary adjustment made, and the couple discussed the new design with the jeweler. The next week, however, the young woman became extremely irritable and unpleasant due to her obsessional worry over the wedding plans and her dissatisfaction with the design of the ring. Recognizing that her behavior could have serious implications for their future, the young man decided to confront her directly with his disillusionment.
>
> After the couple discussed the matter with the therapist, they realized that the ring had become a source of dissension and anxiety between them precisely *because* it symbolized a conventional guarantee of security. Although she was happy at first, it triggered in the woman catastrophic expectations from the past. Her desperate hunger for stability had driven her to interpret the ring as a visible symbol of connection and was followed by cynical thoughts which made her distrust and pick her fiancé apart. Once she had turned him into a source of security, she began to be irritated and dissatisfied with him.

Many couples, like the one described above, react negatively when they attempt to nail down their feelings or make promises that they will always feel loving. Given the nature of love—a feeling that is dependent upon a wide range of circumstances and fluctuates from weak to strong—pledges of continuing love are unrealistic. For emotionally mature individuals, on the other hand, a mutual commitment that expresses a desire to be associated with another person throughout life can be a positive expression of deep feeling rather than an attempt to find "ultimate" security.

Other Characteristics of a Bond

Each aspect of the defensive process can be observed operating within couple and family bonds. For instance, people who have formed this type of dependency relationship tend to idealize their mate as they did their own family; they usually have a poor self-image and are cynical toward people outside the immediate family circle. They often prefer to live an inward style of existence, exclusive of other meaningful "outside" friendships. Both partners tend to hold back outward expressions of affection from each other. Withholding is one of the more serious defensive patterns acted out between individuals in a bond and between parents and their children. (See Chapter 9, *Withholding*.)

In time, a bond becomes a pact of mutual protection wherein each partner implicitly agrees to honor the other's defenses. Each person avoids challenging the mate's self-destructive habits and behaviors, though these behaviors may cause great concern and worry. Instead, each partner complains ineffectually or indulges in the use of painkillers. Each wards off the other's deep feelings so that neither has to experience the sadness that genuine caring and tenderness would arouse.

Because one or both partners in a bond sacrifice their individuality to become one-half of a couple, their basic attraction to each other is jeopardized. People in a bond often experience themselves as an appendage of the other person, a condition that considerably diminishes their feelings of sexual attraction.

Faithfulness

Sexual fidelity can be symbolic of a connection or a destructive bond in a couple. Although it can be based on real desire or mutual agreement, pledges of "faithfulness" can be damaging if they are based on the false premise that people have proprietary rights over each other, more particularly over each other's bodies and sexuality. Monogamy imposed by external mores or standards routinely assumed by the individuals in a couple is very different from sexual fidelity based on freedom of choice and genuine personal commitment.

In a bond, the more intense the fantasy of connection, the more anxiety and pain are aroused whenever either person indicates sexual interest in someone else. Exaggerated need for reassurance that one's mate is always the first and only choice is symptomatic of a bond and necessary for its continuation.

> A therapy group for couples met for the first time, and the participants were beginning to get acquainted. One couple in their late forties were among the last members to talk. The husband spoke for both of them. Glancing first toward his wife, then at the other people, he gave his name, his wife's name, then announced, defensively, "We may not be in love, but we're faithful."

both. Every time a woman makes herself laugh at her husband's often-told jokes she betrays him. The man who looks to his woman and says, "What would I do without you?" is already destroyed. (p. 157)

Withdrawal of Desirable Qualities

In a couple bond, each partner attempts to regulate the flow of love and affection, that is, the amount of gratification the mate gives. By holding back qualities that are most admired or valued by the mate, one can turn a partner's love to anger or even hatred. By provoking a mate with a variety of childish manipulations one can diminish the partner's loving feelings and so maintain a more "comfortable" distance as well as keep one's defenses intact. Through withholding and manipulation, each individual is able to control and limit the other's positive feelings.

Some months after his wedding, one patient, who had initially admired his wife's intelligence, began to believe he had misjudged her. The man, a well-respected university professor, had recently married a young woman who was an interesting, independent person in her own right. Incidentally, she also held a teaching position in the English Department at the university where her husband lectured.

On the honeymoon, the patient had told his new wife that he enjoyed the way she openly voiced her opinions. He said that he was proud of her in conversations with his associates and friends because she was articulate and interesting. He reported that his wife had been deeply touched by his acknowledgment.

Several weeks later, however, this woman resigned her teaching position, claiming she needed more free time in which to furnish their new apartment. Later, her behavior at a faculty party literally made my patient's heart sink. She had spent the entire evening chatting with the faculty wives and had completely ignored her husband. When he finally managed to include her in a conversation with his colleagues, she participated in a desultory manner. She appeared bored and finally insisted they leave because she was tired.

With these actions and other similar behavior, my patient's wife had struck a damaging blow to the relationship. In effect, she had begun to hold back her most desirable qualities soon after her husband's acknowledgment of what they meant to him. However, her maneuvers had been unintentional and totally unconscious. In a session that she requested due to her own concern about the deterioration in the relationship, the young woman concurred with my patient's perception of these events. She was mystified by her behavior in hindsight, although resigning from her teaching position had *seemed* rational to her at the time. She gradually realized that her husband's compliments had made her feel like a lovable woman and had aroused considerable anxiety. In her words, "I saw myself as an attractive *and* intelligent woman who had something worthwhile to offer, an image far different from the way I saw myself while growing up." Her insights into the underlying dynamics of her withdrawal motivated her to take steps to reverse this destructive trend.

There are countless examples where people withdraw or begin to hold back their most desirable or lovable traits following a commitment or marriage. This withholding behavior, often subtle and difficult to identify, damages the relationship, sometimes irrevocably. Both parties become more inward and defended against each other once these patterns become well established. Indeed, the author has found that withholding plays a central role in marital disputes and is a major source of anger and disillusionment in long-standing relationships.

FAMILY BONDS

In forming a bond, a couple is under considerable pressure to prevent any rupture in their illusion of being connected or of belonging to each other. Each gives up more and more individuality in order to cling to the false security of this fantasized connection. In order to maintain their unreal ties, men and women must necessarily dull their real experiences and numb the aliveness of their own children. The psychological equilibrium of the couple must not be disturbed by the intrusion of a spontaneous, lively, loving, and affectionate child. Parents' efforts to defend themselves against a possible disruption in their bond begin very early in their child's life.

The infant is immediately drawn into the parents' world of illusion and pretense. Despite their concern with protecting and preserving the physical life of their offspring, the parents inadvertently begin to destroy the child's spirit. The baby, vulnerable and completely dependent on the parents, shows early signs of pain and struggle. The young child, too weak to combat people who have long protected their fantasy of love and defended themselves successfully against other intrusions on their bond, eventually gives up this struggle and fits into the family system. The tragedy is that the child is diverted from following a natural inclination to respond lovingly to the parents. He or she becomes, instead, self-protective and progressively more dependent on an illusion of being connected to them. The child's distress is eased to some degree and the struggle diminishes. The offspring becomes part of the parents' inward life style and learns to adopt their specific defensive maneuvers as strategies for coping with his or her expanding world.

Even after perceiving that their withholding, their inwardness, or their combative style is damaging to the child, parents still have great difficulty giving up their illusion of love and the kinds of destructive behavior that characterize a bond. If a choice is to be made between the child and the parents' fantasies and defenses, the child is usually expendable and parental defenses are maintained. Since every member of the family has to conform to the illusions of parental or family love, this process also demands that the child distort his or her sense of reality and of the self.

Family Labels

In a family where strong bonds exist, each child is given a definition or label. Children are categorized by their parents and carry these labels with them into adulthood, often without challenging their accuracy. Being known as the "quiet one," "the pretty one," "the wild one," "the smart one" limits one's sense of self. These evaluations and judgmental statements, correct or incorrect, are damaging because they suggest that people have static, unchanging identities. They reflect a deterministic view of human beings that militates against change and individual responsibility. The appeal of labels is that they offer a superficially stable identity to family members, which gives them a false sense of security and belonging.

In seriously disturbed families, one person, usually a child, is singled out as "abnormal" or deviant. This member becomes the identified patient if professional help is sought and attention is focused on his or her cure. Clinical studies have shown that this label and the diagnostic category in which the patient is placed often mask more serious dysfunctions in the family as well as covering up the parents' inadequacies. The patient, in many instances, has become ill in an attempt "to alleviate and absorb his parents' pain" (Satir, 1967, p. 2). In other words, in these families the child who is labeled the "patient" has distorted his or her own growth trying to preserve the family bond. The child's illness leaves the parents' fantasy of family solidarity intact in spite of the actual disharmony.

In most families, the attempt to categorize each other supports the illusion of connection between the parents.

> One patient revealed that his major problem had always been his struggle to control his rage and angry impulses. However, his fear of acting out physical aggression seemed out of proportion to the way he reported living his life on an everyday basis. I was puzzled by the discrepancy between this young man's seemingly stable temperament and his critical self-evaluation until his parents came in for a family session.
>
> The patient's mother, in describing her son's upbringing, told me that he had been an "angry infant, almost from the day he was born." She complained that he was an aggressive, unruly child, quite unlike herself or her husband. The young man persisted in accepting his mother's definition of him rather than perceiving that his parents' relationship was strained to the breaking point by feelings of suppressed anger and bitterness. It was obvious that the mother's facade of sweetness masked a good deal of covert hostility. In the session she totally controlled the speech of other family members through frequent interruptions and by speaking for them. Her need to define and control every movement within the family was obvious in the family interaction. My patient's misconception of himself as angry and incorrigible had served the function of obscuring the real disorganization and pathology in his family.

Parents also tend to define the character of the family as a whole. Usually family members attempt to maintain an image of being better than other families. Parents categorize their neighbors in much the same way that they pass on prejudicial attitudes to their children. Subtle or more obvious definitions of others are expressed in such well-worn clichés as "They're not our kind of people," or "You can only trust your own."

Parents generally want their children to reflect a superior family image by being better behaved, more outgoing, more athletic, or by getting better grades than the children of other families. Ironically, in trying to enforce good behavior in their children, parents often warn: "What would the neighbors think?" or exhort, "Why can't you be more like so-and-so?" One of the strongest, yet seemingly innocuous, signs of the family bond is the need for family members to defend themselves as "good and decent" people. These same people are capable of acting out hostile and disrespectful behavior on each other, all the while defending their good image.

COMMUNICATION IN COUPLE AND FAMILY BONDS

The dishonesty and pretense involved in maintaining a bond necessarily distort personal communication. Communication in the nuclear family is customarily restrictive and duplicitous. The flow of free speech limited, and verbal communication is manipulating and controlling. In fact, the members of a couple develop a style of talking with each other that is dishonest and misleading long before they have children.

Very early in my psychotherapy practice, I observed that men and women who were newly-acquainted, or were having affairs, or were consulting me unaccompanied by their spouses were, for the most part, honest and straightforward in their communication. This was generally not the case with the married couples I talked with. The unmarried couples acted as friends and made an effort not to deceive the other or play games with words. They didn't feel misunderstood or blaming of the other if they felt bad; they rarely projected their own problems onto the other and did not feel criticized and paranoid in relation to any information they received. They tried to communicate negative as well as positive emotions more honestly. Furthermore, their conversations were interesting and personal and drew me to them, whereas dialogues between the married individuals tended to be dull, repetitive, and blaming, and excluded me as a person or participant.

In analyzing communications between members of a couple, beyond the more obvious verbal abuse, sarcasm, hostile criticism and advice-giving that characterize the bond, I have noted subtle styles that help keep the illusion of connection intact; for example, the partners tend to talk *for* each other and often use "we" to describe themselves as a unit. In general, members of a couple lose the ability to articulate straightforwardly their wants in relation to each other and they progressively limit the sharing of important personal feelings. They are especially reluctant to challenge each other in their respective defensive areas by asking for and receiving (without retaliation) honest feedback. They lack the capacity for honestly and sensitively communicating negative feelings or perceptions they might have of one another.

Form vs. Substance in a Relationship

Communication between individuals in a bond is most often directed toward preserving the *form* of the relationship while disguising the fact that the *substance* is gone. The partners communicate with each other *as if* they are discussing real issues and expressing genuine emotions; however, their words only act to preserve the illusion that real feelings still exist. The conventional form of relating is made up of all the convenient habits and superficial conversation that partners depend upon to maintain their fantasy of being in love. For example, when a husband brings his wife flowers for their anniversary, both of them are reassured that their romantic feelings have not disappeared. Everyday routines, customs, and role-determined behaviors provide the structure and *form* of the relationship. More significantly, however, the style of communication, or even lack of communication, serves the purpose of maintaining distance while preserving the pretense of love.

Double Messages in Couple and Family Bonds

The "double message" is an important style of communication that supports the *form* while negating the *substance* of a relationship. It is a contradictory statement in which a person's nonverbal behavior and spoken words do not coincide.

It is composed of a spoken, manifest message and an opposite underlying latent meaning or action. Parents and family members continually give each other mixed messages to cover up their real sentiments. For example, a parent who tells a child, "It's time to go to bed; you need your rest," might be camouflaging a real desire to be free of the child for the evening, or might be attempting to hide a more general rejecting attitude. The child picks up the underlying message in the parent's tone of voice, body language, and expressive movements, but is confused by the words. The child realizes, on a deep level, that he or she is receiving two contradictory messages. However, because of the child's dependency on the parents and need to believe their words, the child must sacrifice his or her own sense of reality. Having one's sense of reality distorted can lead to serious psychological disturbance, particularly when rejection is denied consistently with double messages from one's parents.

In a couple bond, men and women give double messages far more often than they realize. If they honestly stated what they really thought or deeply felt, they would be breaking an implicit pact to maintain the pretense of love and therefore the form of their relationship. Believing the words of one's mate while ignoring the actions can lead to serious distortions of reality.

> One young couple had been deeply involved for several months when they began talking about the possibility of living together. In this instance, the man initiated the conversation fol-

lowing a particularly close, romantic evening. However, soon afterward, the young woman became uneasy when she realized that ·they had only spent one evening together over the previous week. When she asked her friend if he was pulling away from her for some reason, he became angry and acted insulted, denying the real message of his behavior, all the while insisting he still cared for her. The woman felt confused and depressed until she finally admitted to herself that her lover was trying to deceive her about his waning interest. She was still pained by the rejection, but regained her sense of perspective after she saw through his duplicity. She would have been less disturbed had she noticed sooner that his actions belied his reassurance of love.

Motivational Dishonesty

Many people delude themselves when they claim to want love and closeness in their lives. When they actually receive love, they generally react adversely. There is a vast difference between fantasizing about being loved and accepting genuine love in actuality. Real love threatens an individual's defenses and source of internal gratification and leaves the person feeling vulnerable. *Individuals generally react negatively or angrily to being chosen, to being seen as lovable, or to being preferred over others.* Personal acknowledgment and a sense of being valued by another person break into the fantasy bond. They cause one to become acutely aware of oneself as a separate person which, in turn, arouses anxiety.

Both partners pull back onto safer, more familiar ground, warding off closeness and increasing their dependency and fusion. Their anger at being chosen, which briefly exposed them to the anxiety of separateness and mortality, is typically repressed, yet it continues to undermine the relationship. Double messages and indirect communication serve the function of denying or covering up the hostility and the withdrawal of personal involvement.

CONCLUSION

Generally speaking, people never fulfill their natural destinies because they have adopted their parents' major defenses and typical response patterns. The process of forming bonds diverts them from seeking goals they might otherwise have freely chosen to pursue. Therapeutic intervention can help them recover some of what they have lost and therefore is a worthwhile endeavor. However, some children are so damaged by the time they are one or two years old that, even if they spent their entire adult existence working out their neurosis in good psychotherapy, they would never succeed in reclaiming all of themselves.

In forming a bond with our loved one, we deny the inevitability of our personal death and block out the terror of dying. The fantasy of being connected to another person gives us a sense of immortality, a feeling of living forever, but robs us of day-to-day life. In contrast, living in an undefended, non-fused state forces us to face our existential aloneness and separateness, which arouses anxiety. Indeed, the addictive and compelling nature of the bond lies in the fact that it denies death and relieves our anxiety about the future. The drawback is that it creates a powerful resistance to living a free, independent existence in harmony and genuine closeness with our loved ones.

Chapter 4

ORGANIZATION OF THE DEFENSIVE PROCESS

THE PRIMARY DEFENSE

The *primary defense* is the process of parenting oneself both internally in fantasy and externally by utilizing objects and persons from one's environment. It relates to an individual's reliance on internal fantasy for gratification (the fantasy bond) as well as the external manifestation of making connections (forming bonds) with other significant persons. A person who comes to depend on self-mothering through fantasy, together with self-nourishing habits and routines, develops an illusion of self-sufficiency, of needing nothing from the outside world in terms of love and care. Paradoxically, the more a person relies on this process, the less able one is to function in society and actually satisfy basic requirements for living.

SECONDARY DEFENSES

Secondary defenses are misconceptions about reality that keep the individual from yielding to the temptation to be open and vulnerable. They are systems of ideas and beliefs about the self and others that prevent one from taking a chance again on being gratified in reality.

These defenses act to justify, support, and confirm a person's retreat into an inward fantasy state. They protect the primary defense or fantasy of self-sufficiency from intrusion. This secondary line of defense keeps the primary defense intact.

Most people retain the specific patterns of thoughts, feelings, and actions that they used in childhood to protect the primary defense or self-mothering process. Once they have been hurt, people are quite reluctant to take a chance again and really come to trust another relationship. Often they will precipitate a rejection because the fantasy anticipation works as a real motivating force and can create anxiety in an interpersonal relationship. The end result is that the person becomes strengthened in the conviction that he or she is the only one who can take care of or love him or herself.

The degree to which a person depends upon fantasy for "nourishment" and psychological survival will determine the extent to which he or she will have to invent rejection where there is none. For example, a woman who falls in love, then finds herself suddenly disillusioned with her lover or imagines that he is rejecting her, is in all probability protecting the self-nourishing process. Because she cannot tolerate the intrusion of genuine love into her fantasy of self-sufficiency, she must eventually push her lover away.

A dominant characteristic of the schizophrenic patient is an aversion to any intrusion into his or her fantasy world. The patient often reacts with physical aggression when the therapist attempts to enter his or her world, whereas the neurotic pulls away in subtle maneuvers or mildly provokes hostility in others. All paranoia in the schizophrenic process is essentially related to the secondary defensive process and the system of thoughts whereby threats are seen as originating in others. Thus, all perceived "threats" from the outside world support and strengthen the self-mothering process.

People who are less disturbed psychologically also have periods of withdrawal from transactions with the outside world. Indeed, inwardness or a withdrawn state can be viewed on a continuum ranging from the mild introversion of a normal individual to the extremely withdrawn, regressive state of the schizophrenic patient. People in an inward state project their fears and anger onto others and so avoid contact with them.

In the secondary defensive process, there are two ways whereby the mechanism of projection works to justify the retreat to an inward state. First, the opportunity for positive gratification by other persons is minimized by *perceiving* the world as essentially negative, hostile, or even dangerous. Secondly, by acting angry or hostile while imagining that others are out to get him, the person provokes other people and pushes them away.

Thus, the male mental patient who physically attacks his therapist for tempting him with the attractions of reality is acting to protect his core defense, as is the woman who becomes defensively closed off from her lover and rejects him. Their methods and thought processes differ in terms of intensity and style but both serve a defensive solution. Psychotic aggression and neurotic distortions and maneuvers that keep distance between people are all manifestations of the secondary defensive process that preserve the primary defense of imagined self-sufficiency.

RECAPITULATING THE PAST

The neurotic individual achieves psychological equilibrium when he or she arrives at a particular solution to the basic conflict between reliance on an internal fantasy process for gratification and seeking satisfaction in the external world. When this equilibrium is threatened by events that contradict earliest childhood experiences, anxiety is aroused and the individual retreats to a more inward state of parenting the self. One's identity as the "bad" child is disrupted if one is valued or loved by a person who has significance in adult life. To defend against intrusions into this inner fantasy, the person utilizes three major modes of defense: (1) selection; (2) distortion; and (3) provocation. These defenses are behavioral operations that serve to protect the fantasy bond.

(1) Selection

Selection is a method whereby the neurotic person attempts to arrange present-day relationships in order to replicate the early family situation. This individual is resistant to forming associations with people who would behave toward him or her in a way that differs qualitatively from the treatment received as a child. He or she tends to choose a person for a friend or mate who is similar to the parent because this is the person to whom the defenses are appropriate. The neurotic individual externalizes the introjected parental image onto this new person and uses that person to keep the "good" parent/"bad" child system intact.

Thus, people may be attracted to someone who physically resembles their father or mother. A man may choose to marry a woman whose reactions to him are the same as his mother's. For example, one man who had an indulgent, possessive mother tended to repeat the pattern by gravitating toward controlling women of this type. Finding such a woman and marrying her served to re-establish his original fantasy bond or connection with a new, significant person in his adult life. In another instance, a woman who has a doting yet intrusive mother would probably *not* be attracted to a man who refused to cater to her whims or who was independent and free-wheeling. She would be more likely to marry a man who idolized her, gave in to her every wish, and who needed to possess her because of his own insecurities.

(2) *Distortion*

Distortion is another method that is used to protect the primary fantasy. The person who utilizes distortion as a defense alters perceptions of new objects in a direction that corresponds more closely to the members of the original family. Not all distortions are negative. Both positive and negative qualities may be attributed to significant people in the neurotic person's life. Admirable characteristics are exaggerated as well as undesirable traits, but the distortion generally functions to make new figures closely approximate the important people in the individual's childhood.

The child maintains an *idealized* image of the mother and projects her *real* qualities onto others. Later, the young person will focus a kind of selective attention on a significant person in his or her life, trying to prove that this new person has negative traits similar to those of the parent. Transference in psychotherapy is an obvious example of this type of distortion. A major task of the therapist is jointly to analyze the patient's misperceptions of the therapist. For this reason the psychoanalyst attempts to make him or herself into a blank screen in order for the patient freely to project distortions so they can be analyzed and understood.

Sullivan's (1953) concept of "parataxic distortion" describes altered perceptions as the basis of irrational behavioral responses and transference reactions to significant figures. He states that:

> There comes a time [in the therapy] when it is possible to *identify* one of the *parataxic concomitants* that have been permanent complicating factors in the patient's perceptions of significant other people. (p. 235)

As the therapist points out these distortions, the patient gradually "recalls vividly a series of highly significant events that occurred in interpersonal relations" (Sullivan, 1953, p. 236) with important people in the family.

People who make drastic changes in their relationships or in their life style often need to distort the new situation. Numerous case histories have been documented about children previously neglected or abused by their parents, who, when placed with loving foster parents, have distorted their new surroundings and therefore reacted adversely.

> One foster child, whose real mother's facial expression reflected her disturbed state and inner rage, had difficulty in his new, more positive environment. He mistakenly believed that his foster mother was angry toward him. He often misread her expressive movements and tone of voice, sensing irritation and tension even when she was feeling pleasant or relaxed. Continually misperceiving her as being hostile and threatening, he reacted in a fearful, guarded way. His silence and timidity made him unapproachable and unappealing to his foster parents.

It is characteristic of the damaged child to attempt to reproduce the circumstances of earlier environment, no matter how miserable they were. In the new situation, he or she may even try to provoke treatment similar to that received in the original family, if the child's use of distortion as a defense is insufficient.

(3) Provocation

Provocation is used by the neurotic person to manipulate others to respond toward him or her as the parent did. To a large extent, the individual will behave in ways that provoke angry, punishing parental reactions in others: employees provoke anger and cynicism in their bosses by unnecessary incompetence and inefficiency; students provoke their teachers to despair with unruly classroom behavior and their refusal to complete assignments; wives and husbands provoke each other to helpless feelings of rage by their forgetfulness, by being late for important engagements, etc. Most people are largely unaware of the fact that their behavior may have the specific purpose of provoking aggression in others.

> Several years ago my colleagues and I rented office space to a clinical psychologist. Within moments of meeting my associates, this man succeeded in irritating them to such a degree that his subsequent encounters with them became a standing joke. The

most astonishing fact about this man was that he was able to provoke one of my associates—a meek, somewhat passive man who had never been known to lose his temper—almost to the point of physical aggression.

Later, this man asked if he could participate in a series of therapy sessions with the author. In his therapeutic interaction, he revealed his warped, paranoid view of the world. He perceived people as being belligerent, threatening, and as trying to control him. In the sessions, he was condescending and contentious. It was obvious that this person elicited the kind of response that confirmed his distorted view of people. He did, in truth, live in a hostile world where people disliked him, but it was a world of his own making.

The neurotic tendency to recreate the past is particularly evident in couple relationships. Many marriages fail because each partner distorts his or her perception of the other and provokes angry responses in order to maintain a "safe" distance. In general, people have the most difficulty in their intimate relationships because the closeness, sexuality, and companionship threaten their internal methods of gratifying themselves. Instead of altering their defensive posture and allowing positive intrusion of friendship and love into their inner world, most people choose to distort their perceptions of their loved ones. The most tender moments in their relationships are followed by pulling back to a less vulnerable, more defended place.

All three maneuvers—selection, distortion, and provocation—work to preserve the internal parent that the person later projects onto new associations. A neurotic person anticipates that the destruction of the fantasy bond with the loved one would expose him or her once again to the anxiety, fear, and pain endured at a time in childhood when the person was helpless and dependent. Therefore, at the point where the individual begins to experience more closeness and feels more loving, he or she becomes anxious and retreats to a more familiar, less personal style of relating.

THE BASIC COMPONENTS OF THE DEFENSE SYSTEM

As stated earlier, the primary defense is one of substituting fantasy gratification for real relating. The secondary defense consists of negative hypotheses about the interpersonal environment that justify and support the primary defense.

There are several major aspects of the primary defensive process.

Characteristically the psychological defense mechanisms represent an adaptation to the home environment with all its deficiencies and pressures. They become abnormal because of their intensity or degree and the misapplication to new persons or situations.

The Primary Defensive Process

(1) IDEALIZATION OF PARENT, PARENTS, OR FAMILY	(2) NEGATIVE SELF-IMAGE, SELF-HATRED, "BAD ME"	(3) NEGATIVE DISPLACE-MENT OF FAMILY TRAITS ON INTER-PERSONAL ENVIRONMENT
(4) THE INWARD STATE AND LOSS OF FEELING FOR SELF	(5) WITHHOLDING	(6) SELF-NOURISHING HABITS AND ROUTINES

These six aspects are not discrete entities or specific defenses, but consist of readily observed patterns that tend to overlap to a considerable extent. Therapeutic intervention directed toward correcting one component challenges the entire defensive process. Thus the patient's resistance will be mobilized whenever he or she is threatened in any one area.

1. The idealization of parent, parents, or family, is a necessary part of the self-parenting system. Because of the extreme dependence during the early years, the child *must* see the parent as *"good"* or powerful rather than recognize parental weakness or rejection. The child feels that he or she could not survive with inadequate, weak, or hostile parents, and therefore denies their negative qualities and sees him or herself as bad. In order to parent oneself successfully in fantasy, one must maintain the idealized image of one's parent.

2. The negative self-image, the "bad" me, exists concomitantly with the idealized image of the parent. In perceiving the parent as good, the child has to think of him or herself as bad, unlovable, and undeserving. The child must interpret parental rejection as being his or her fault since the child needs to perceive the parents as being loving, competent people. The self-hatred inherent in the negative view of the self originates when the child incorporates the parent's negative attitudes toward him or her. These negative attitudes toward self become a prominent part of the self-concept and are at the center of the individual's self-hatred.

3. The displacement of negative parental traits onto the interpersonal environment is a result of the child's blocking from awareness the parents' weaknesses and their negative qualities. To keep the self-nourishing system intact by preserving the idealized parental image, the neurotic patient projects the parents' weaknesses and undesirable traits onto others.

4. A defended person experiences a progressive loss of feeling for the self as he or she relies more and more on fantasy gratification. Most of the time this individual exists in an inward state where he or she has very little compassion or self-love; rather there is self-hatred and loathing of the self and of others. In this withdrawn state, a person may feel very little emotional pain or anxiety. Indeed, some patients reported that, prior to therapy, they had felt somewhat content or comfortable in this state. They had succeeded in repressing much of their emotional distress and had only sought help after some sort of environmental stress had broken through their defenses.

5. Withholding is a holding back or a withdrawal of emotional and behavioral responses from others. When the child is hurt and frustrated, he or she withdraws the affection or the psychic energy invested in the parents or other objects—a kind of de-cathexis takes place. Extreme withholding reflects a basic fear of being drained and represents a pulling back from an exchange of psychonutritional products with objects in the real world. Theoretically, the self-parenting process can be understood as a psychonutritional system wherein the individual imagines that there are limited quantities of nourishment available. Withholding is a broad concept and is largely directed against *oneself* in the form of self-denial but is incidentally destructive to others. Because of the damage to close personal relationships, however unintentional, it increases self-hatred and guilt and also leads progressively to still more withholding, and completes a neurotic spiral.

6. The concept of "the self-mothering process" refers not exclusively to one's mother as an individual, but to the process of being a parent to oneself that began at an early stage in one's life (Firestone, 1957). It relates to the incorporation of the key person in the young child's life, not necessarily the mother; indeed, some fathers fulfill this function.

The methods and means of an inward style of self-nourishment begin early in life. As they mature, people substitute more refined techniques of satisfying themselves and alleviating pain and anxiety, e.g., overeating, excessive drinking, drug use, masturbating, and various compulsive behaviors. A person's degree of dependency on painkilling substances, habits, and routines clearly indicates neurotic dependence on the primary fantasy process. Emotional deprivation is at the core of neurotic addiction and abnormal dependency.

Processes that Break into the Primary Fantasy Bond

When one thinks of neurosis in terms of protecting the primary defense from intrusion, many perverse, puzzling behaviors can be better understood: for instance, people who become self-destructive following an important achievement, lovers who pull away from each other following a time of being very close and loving, children who are wary of trusting a friendly response after being abused. These reactive behaviors are typical responses to the anxiety that is aroused when bonds are broken.

During a person's life span, many circumstances arise that intrude on the strong sets, attitudes, and beliefs that characterize defenses. For example, the patient in therapy may progress to a point where the bond with the family is altered or broken. Specialized events catalyze changes in the patient's defense patterns and disrupt bonds. Developing a more realistic view of the family or learning to accept a more realistic perception of oneself—both threaten a fantasy of connection. Whenever these bonds are threatened, there is resulting tension and disequilibrium.

Anxiety occurs whenever the patient's state of psychological equilibrium is disturbed. Anxiety states may be described as having a bipolar causality. Because the neurotic person has achieved a stable balance between reliance on the self-mothering process and pursuit of gratification in the real world, *anxiety will be aroused by anything that threatens either the self-nourishing process or object dependency.* It is important for the therapist to differentiate between these two sources of anxiety.

Positive anxiety results from rewarding experiences, personal growth and achievement that threaten an individual's early view of the self and disturb the core of defense and secondary fantasies. Negative anxiety, on the other hand, results from personal failure or frustration in interpersonal relationships or object loss. It stems from situations and events similar to those that caused the person to become defended in the first place.

Negative events in everyday life predispose a person to go inward and attempt to reinstate the bond. Some of the factors responsible for arousing "negative" anxiety are: painful emotional experiences, excessive frustration, personal rejection and hurt, physical illness, separation or loss, and death anxiety.

On the other hand, positive experiences may also result in an elevated state of tension. These events include receiving special reward, regard, or acknowledgment of self by others. Love, generosity, and tenderness directed toward others, that is, responses that are not habitual or role-determined, also break into a bond. Reacting with genuine feeling or emotion typically draws a person out of an inward state. Realistic, goal-directed behavior, and planning intrude on the internal process of gratifying oneself in fantasy. Positive experiences that don't correspond to the person's image of him or herself in the family, such as promotion, success, new responsibility, power and authority, positive verbal feedback, and genuine love trigger anxiety states, which are often experienced as feelings of disorientation and fear. When these feelings are intense, there may be regression as the individual retreats to a more familiar defended posture.

Independence, creativity, and nonconformity challenge psychological defenses. In general, people find it difficult to tolerate the positive anxiety inherent in constructive change. Rather than challenging their defenses and actively pursuing their goals, most individuals spend their lives driven by the dictates of these defenses. Their actions are motivated, for the most part, by fantasies of rejection, which are monitored by an internal thought process that operates as a "voice." This inner voice or internal dialogue serves to regulate much of the self-nourishing, self-destructive behavior that is symptomatic of the defended state. The voice warns the individual against forming relationships or becoming too attached to others. It cautions him or her against taking another chance on being hurt again, and trusting other people. In effect, the *"voice"* is the language of the overall defensive process. The development of the concept of the voice plays an important part in the structure of our theory. We have directed specific attention to the application of this concept to therapeutic procedures as discussed later in the section on psychotherapy.

CONCLUSION

Many people become progressively maladapted because of their increased reliance on fantasy gratification. They arrange their lives to avoid anxiety, pain, and sadness, and thus they gradually become more defended, emotionally deadened, and alienated from their real selves.

The aim of psychotherapy with patients who are deeply involved in defending the internal fantasy process is twofold. In the case of the schizophrenic patient, the therapist (1) attempts to expose and attack the fantasy process through direct interpretations and other techniques which produce clear insights about the true state of the family, and (2) he or she encourages the patient to depend upon him or her for satisfaction and security. While somewhat different methods and techniques may be utilized with neurotic patients, the goals of therapy are similar.

Exposing the fantasy bond is a vital part of the therapy process with all patients, whether psychotic or neurotic. At the same time, therapy is an attempt to make reality more inviting. Each person is encouraged to leave the inward world and self-nourishing habits. The patient's energy and effort must be redirected toward taking another chance on finding satisfaction in the external world through goal-directed behavior.

Chapter 5

IDEALIZATION OF THE FAMILY

The primary defensive process consists of a fantasy of self-sufficiency and the externalization of this self-parenting process with new objects. A significant dimension of the fantasy bond is the idealization of the family and the protection of a "good" image of the parents, particularly the mother. In order for the fantasy bond to work, it is absolutely necessary to hold on to this idealization. The image of the parent must be positive because it would be impossible for the child to feel safe or secure with an internalized parent perceived as inadequate or destructive.

This idealization is difficult to alter or refute because, to a large extent, it is supported by society's belief in the sanctity of one's parents and family. Indeed, this cultural bias is an extension of individual defenses. Only in more blatant instances of child abuse and neglect does the collective idealization of the family break down. Furthermore, the image of parental strength and goodness always occurs in close conjunction with the development of a negative image of self. Patients who hate and blame themselves or perceive themselves as basically unlovable are defending and idealizing their parents.

Therapy that is directed toward disrupting the idealization of the parent generally diminishes the patient's self-hatred; however, changes of this nature create anxiety. For example, a patient who stops criticizing and belittling him or herself also begins to perceive the family more realistically. The patient stops blaming him or herself for being rejected and realizes that the parents, because of their own inadequacies, were unable to give much of what he or she wanted or needed as a child.

However, in giving up this idealization process, people also gradually lose the ability to gratify themselves with the image of the internalized parent. As the patient progresses in therapy, the internal system of self-parenting breaks down. The individual may suddenly perceive the self as being the same size and stature as the parents and can no longer lean on the now diminished parental image for support. The anxiety stems from two sources: one, feeling separated from the positive view of the parents, and two, giving up the corresponding image of oneself as the "bad" child. The person loses the lifelong hope of receiving love from the "good" parent, and often feels alone and despondent. Thus, maintaining a good image of the parent is mistakenly perceived by the patient as being essential to stability and security; yet, paradoxically, its preservation perpetuates self-hatred.

Origin of the Idealization of the Parents

In an attempt partially to alleviate the pain and anxiety of emotional deprivation in a climate where one's needs are not met, the child fantasizes an image of the parent or parents as good and loving. If the child were to form a more realistic mental picture of the parents with their shortcomings and weaknesses, his or her emotional world would fall apart. Therefore, the child creates an illusion that exaggerates the parents' good qualities. (One may even ascribe admirable traits to parents that contradict reality.) Generally, the degree to which the child is rejected or damaged determines the extent to which he or she overprotects and idealizes the parent.

The child who suffers because of contact with the rejecting parent, generally the mother, faces a desperate situation. The son or daughter clings to the image of the mother built during the first year of life, when the satisfaction of the offspring's needs was her sole responsibility. The young child finds it absolutely necessary to maintain the benevolent attitude due to total dependency. If in reality the mother is punishing and anxiety-provoking, it is not because she is malevolent but because oneself, the child, is bad. The child believes that the mother is right in being punitive, hungry, or intrusive. The child who is raised in this environment and wants to maintain an image of the mother's goodness tends therefore to accept her negative appraisal.

The preservation of the idealized image of the parent is made possible because the most unpleasant traits of the parent are blocked from the child's awareness. This removal from consciousness is made easier by the acceptance at face value of verbal protestations of love and concern. The child is deceived by the parent's professed love, and by a process of selective inattention remains unaware of hostile signs and rejecting behavior. Thus, the child retains two images of the parent: the good image, which is conscious, and the bad image, which remains largely unconscious and is projected onto other people in the interpersonal environment.

THE EFFECT OF CHALLENGING THE IDEALIZED IMAGE OF PARENTS AND FAMILY

In the process of formulating my concept of resistance in psychotherapy, I had occasion to deal with this process of parental idealization in two important areas: first with schizophrenic patients at a residential treatment center headed by Dr. John N. Rosen in Bucks County, Pennsylvania, and later with young patients with psychosomatic disorders at the Jewish National Home for Asthmatic Children. At Rosen's, my colleagues and I, applying the technique of "Direct Analysis," were able to encourage seriously disturbed patients to attack the image of parental love. "If they were really loved by their parents as children, why were they crazy now as adults? Why were they so angry and miserable if they were so loved?" We suggested that they express their angry feelings and supported the expression of negative ideas and critical comments about their families. We actively persuaded them to sing songs, limericks, etc., criticizing and attacking their mothers or fathers. Immediately after these sessions, which challenged unrealistic positive attitudes toward their parents, the patients would emerge from their withdrawn hallucinatory state and communicate more coherently with the therapist. Of course, this situation did not flow smoothly, as patients often resisted verbalizing these attacks because of their strong investment in maintaining the good parental image.

An important aspect of our therapy with schizophrenics was that since the patients preserved the image of their mothers as being "good and loving" at the expense of their own feelings of worth, the therapist had to expose these dynamics through direct intervention. The therapist needed to actively side with the patients and point out how "bad" and inadequte their mothers were and how they damaged them and made them "sick." Eventually, through verbalizing their own attacks and expressing their hostility about their mothers, the patients experienced significant relief from their psychotic symptoms and made better contact with reality.

The schizophrenic seemed to be the one person in the family who knew the family secret, but was both covering it up and exposing it through the symbolic metaphor of the illness. The author believed in and respected the integrity of the patients and felt that real events harmful to their psyche must have occurred to foster this level of regression and retreat. In other words, I took them at face value, which they themselves could not. I believed that their system of defenses was justified by their early set of circumstances. I was supportive of the fact that their symptoms made personal and logical sense. It gave the patients a sense of dignity to be approached in this manner. These sessions were more than a catharsis or the simple ventilating of attacks on parents; they were an important part of an overall personal support of the patients that helped them to understand and counter the dynamics of their illness.

Years later, during my treatment of a young asthmatic girl, I again observed the startling effect that exposing negative parental qualities had on symptoms.

When I first met Leora she was eleven years old. She had been diagnosed as an intractable asthmatic and had been sent to a research center in Denver that accepted only the most serious cases. The Jewish National Home for Asthmatic Children was successful in helping these children because of a unique and powerful medical and psychological approach. A primary part of the treatment was to separate the children from their parents for a 2-year period. During this time only two brief visits with the family were permitted. Generally, the separation and the diminution of psychological stress were very valuable and many of the children improved immediately upon separation, despite the loneliness and hardship of the drastic "parentectomy." This unique method, combined with good care and expert medical attention, seemed to turn the trick—but not for Leora. The staff was still unable to control her symptoms after a year and a half. In fact, Leora was frail and dying and the situation seemed totally hopeless. Everyone felt that the best thing was to send her home to her family to spend what little time was left to her in so-called normal familial surroundings.

Coincidentally, she and I were leaving the institution at about the same time. I had just finished my training there and was about to start private practice in Los Angeles. Leora was from that city, and the hospital referred her to me in order for her to continue psychotherapy when she arrived home.

I was chilled by the depths of her despair during those initial weeks.

There was little hope or desire in her to live. She really wanted to die and wished to be released from her psychological as well as physical suffering. "You'll follow me to the hospital and then to the grave," she had said at our first meeting.

Leora was very depressed and had learned to internalize her anger and develop physical symptoms instead. I knew that if she could begin to accept her anger she would ease up on her physical symptoms, as many of the children at the hospital had learned to do. I hoped that the early depression would give way to a defiant and angry stage and then the child would become freer of symptoms.

This is exactly what happened in the therapy with Leora. As the anger came out, she began to feel better. However, this was not a smooth and continuous process. There were periods of regression and anxiety followed by remorse and depression and sometimes serious attacks requiring hospitalization and emergency treatment. Once I was summoned to her side because she was failing rapidly. Her mother called me and begged me to hurry over. When I arrived Leora was very weak and frightened. I tried to get her to reaffirm her anger toward her mother, related to an incident of the previous week. I was scared of this approach at this time but it just came out of me. I voiced the anger that Leora was feeling toward her mother. Finally, I had to leave and I was not too encouraged by her reactions. There was only minor improvement.

I went back to my practice and got involved in my regular duties. The phone rang and it was Leora's mother. I was alarmed and anticipated bad news. I thought this was the end. She asked me, "What did you do with her?" I became more frightened, feeling that she was angry and critical of me, meaning that things must be pretty bad with Leora. But it was just the opposite. The news was good. She was feeling fine and the mother was thankful. Another crisis had been averted. The paradox was amazing to me at that time. What had I done with her daughter? I had helped her to face her hatred toward her mother and to see her mother realistically, so that she might live. Ironically, her mother was calling me to thank me for saving her child.

In looking over my notes at the time treatment began, I described Leora as having a strong negative image of herself. She was clinging desperately to this negative attitude toward herself and could not accept her hostile feelings toward her parents. She was very defensive about her family. She was especially reluctant to accept any inadequacies in her mother because her illness made her extremely dependent upon her mother for shots, medications, etc. Thus, if mother is "bad," Leora would surely die. However, in this emergency situation, merely listening to my verbal expression of her anger toward her mother, seeing her anger externalized, had been enough to break into her image of the "good" mother and cause a remission of life-threatening symptoms.

Protecting the ideal of family goodness and strength can take a less severe form than in the author's two experiences mentioned above. This protection is often expressed in a strong taboo against surpassing the parent of the same sex in the vital areas of life: professionally, intellectually, in athletics, in looks, in creating a happy marriage and family. Many people have difficulty after they have achieved success in areas where their parents failed or were incompetent. Surpassing one's parent breaks into one's feeling of safety and security and arouses considerable anxiety and guilt.

The Essential Division in Schizophrenia

On a schizophrenic level of regression, the incorporated idealized image of the parent is personified in feelings and delusions of omnipotence and grandiosity. This leads to expansive feelings and Godlike superiority, delusions of being God or Napoleon or other great figures. These feelings of superiority and power contrast sharply with the feeling of inadequacy and inferiority that is so apparent in these same patients. The omnipotent mother and weak child are both part of the system, and the split between these two parts of self leads to the thought disorganization that is characteristic of the illness. Aspects of each system are combined and there is much confusion and fragmentation in the regressed patient. One sees oneself as both entities and feels connected to the parent. One is at once the greatest and the lowest being, and contradicting attitudes and emotions exist side by side, causing considerable upheaval. These dynamics exemplify the split in the schizophrenic's intellectual and emotional organization, a division which severely impairs adjustment to the interpersonal environment.

Vanity in the neurotic is a diminished form of the grandiosity and omnipotence of the schizophrenic. It reflects a less serious split within the character structure of the patient and indicates the presence of the idealized parent. This vanity, an exaggerated fantasized image of the self, is tenaciously held on to. In less severe forms of psychological malfunction, the split is still present, but there is more functional integrity than in the schizophrenic. The dynamics, nonetheless, bear a close resemblance. It is a matter of degree rather than kind, with specific qualitative changes such as delusions and hallucinations occurring at the deeper levels of regression.

Feelings of vanity and superiority relate to images retained from childhood and are made up of the special traits that were praised and exaggerated by our parents. They attempt to combat feelings of self-doubt and inferiority. Thus a basic split in self-image exists in neurotic patients in subtle forms, creating an unstable view of self and others.

Very early in life, each individual sets up a dichotomy of superior and inferior qualities in relation to the idealized parental image. Within the system, the parents are clean, whereas the offspring is dirty; the parents are right and good, while the child is wrong, different, or peculiar; they are normal and the son or daughter is abnormal. The parents are prim and proper in their sexuality (the parent's sex life is hidden from the child), whereas the child is animalistic and sexual; they are powerful and the child is weak.

THE FALSE SUPERIORITY OF THE FAMILY

To compensate for the self-hatred inherent in the negative self-image, children take some satisfaction in identifying with the "good" parent, and their vanity is expressed in their pride about belonging to a "good" family. For a teenager, nothing could be worse than to be humiliated by a parent whose odd appearance or behavior points to a discrepancy between the idealized parental image and the real parent. This embarrassment can be viewed as an outward sign of the young person's strong resistance to having this idealization interfered with. Children resist hearing their parents criticized because they think it diminishes their own esteem. It makes them feel less worthwhile because they strongly identify with their families. The self-parenting fantasy, which offers strength and security, gains support through identification with parents, teachers, bosses, or other parent substitutes. For example, students may admire a popular professor or a well-known researcher and feel their own confidence shaken if the idol's work is attacked. This is especially true if the teacher is the student's mentor and the association has enhanced the young person's feelings of self-worth.

Partial gratification is gained from identifying with a superior family image, and the child is very reluctant to break away emotionally. A young adult may leave home physically, but rarely leaves emotionally, i.e., breaks this specific defense. Identification with the image of the family as strong and right is an attempt to alleviate deep feelings of worthlessness and "badness."

A physician who was a patient of mine told how as a youngster he had ambivalent feelings toward his father. In talking about his childhood, he described the incongruous wish he had that his father would be a hero and, at the same time, be killed in the war because he wanted him out of the way. He had this insight after remembering events from his painful adolescent years during a session where he experienced a release of deep feelings of sadness and rage. He recalled his sharp pang of disappointment when his father came back from the war as an ordinary man and not a hero. In spite of his death wishes toward his father, he regretted that he couldn't use him to aggrandize himself. Identifying himself with his father as a hero would have served to maintain his bond with him. Even if his father had, in fact, been killed, he would have held on to the connection with him and his image as a heroic figure.

Even people who criticize and blame their parents for their own unhappiness tend to mask an idealization process. They refuse to accept the limitations of their parents who, because of their own defenses, were unable to provide loving care and nurturance. Thus, the fact that an individual is critical of the parents may not necessarily indicate he or she has overcome an idealized view of them.

Mr. W., a management consultant, felt that he had put his unhappy childhood behind him and was free of his emotional ties to family and relatives. He believed that he clearly perceived the childishness and manipulations of his mother. In his therapy sessions, he talked at length about the methods his mother had used to control his life and keep him at odds with his father. He was sharply critical of his mother, and was objective about her faults. Yet, though he prided himself on being a self-made man who wielded some degree of influence in the business community, he was still unable to talk to his own mother on the phone without sinking into a depression because of her continuing intrusiveness into his life. In an effort to declare his independence of her, he had finally instructed his secretary to disregard calls from her. However, this acted as no real solution. It was an angry and rebellious maneuver and only served to inflame his mother's hunger and involvement.

Mr. W. was still idealizing his mother by giving her power over his life that he granted to no one else. Despite his claims of emancipation from his family, in relation to his mother he still was rendered helpless by her assaults. His mother had recently turned up at an important press conference, despite his pleas that she not come, and had deeply embarrassed him with displays of extravagant praise that were belittling and completely inappropriate to the occasion.

> Mr. W. was forced by this incident to realize that on some
> level he was still protecting an image of his mother as a powerful
> figure; otherwise he would have been able to break with her more
> effectively. He recognized that if he were more adult, he would
> have been better able to communicate and control her intrusive-
> ness. The fact that he was still not able to manage the situation was
> proof that he still deferred to her.

The fact that a person criticizes a parent or declares independence
from the family is not necessarily an indication that one has broken the
defense. In fact, exaggerated defiance or protest about one's independence may mask the presence of strong dependency drives and a refusal
to give up the idealization process.

THE IDEALIZATION OF SUBSTITUTE PARENTAL FIGURES

Emotionally deprived children find it impossible to see the parents'
faults; they cannot afford to do that because then their situation would
seem genuinely hopeless. To defend against their pain and despair, they
see themselves as bad and imagine that by performing, by trying to
please, or by doing the right thing, they can get their parents to love
them. The fallacy is that their parents cannot love them, because of their
own problems and their own inadequacies, and therefore, their children
can never get what they want from them. Yet they will go through their
entire lives trying in a symbolic form to get that love from parental
substitutes, going through maneuvers that they think will please, and
selling out on their own point of view to get approval. At the same time
they avoid and push away people who are not rejecting and appear
different from their parents. As long as the defense of protecting this
parental image is kept intact, these individuals feel that there is some
hope of being loved, so they are adamant about not having this idealization interfered with.

Most adults transfer the feelings and attitudes they had toward their
parents to other significant people in their lives, especially to their mates.
Husbands and wives tend to build each other up in their own minds so
they can gain a sense of security. Their idealization of the parent is
repeated with their mates. Concomitantly, feelings of childishness and
unworthiness (the "bad child" image) are internalized by each member
of the couple. At the same time, each has a great deal of anger and
resentment whenever his or her mate fails to live up to these high expectations.

This was the prevailing feeling that a patient expressed in his first therapy session. Mr. F., a successful thirty-four-year-old attorney, was referred to me by his physician for treatment of impotency. He was plagued, too, by a gradual worsening, over the past several months, of a chronic diabetic condition that he had suffered with since adolescence. It became evident to me after a number of sessions that Mr. F.'s sexuality, his health, and his emotional stability were being seriously undermined in his relationship with his wife and by his misconceptions about her.

Mr. F. blamed his sexual failure on himself, whereas the real cause of his impotence was later revealed to be his wife's sexual withholding. Fixing the blame on himself instead of his wife fit the same pattern that existed in relation to his mother. He denied any negative traits about his mother and was mostly unaware that she had held back her affections from him as a child. In one session, Mr. F. began to see his mother more realistically as he described the desperate maneuvers he had used in futile attempts to get attention and approval from her. Obviously, he was extremely angry toward his mother, but because of his guilt and his desire to protect her, he turned this rage against himself.

I was concerned by the state of Mr. F.'s health, both physical and psychological, at the time of his treatment. He was in such a depressed condition that the lack of control over his diet had become extremely self-destructive and reflected suicidal urges. He told me that recently he had found it necessary to increase significantly his dosage of insulin to balance his large intake of carbohydrates. His depression and self-destructive tendency reflected the same pattern with his wife and his mother. In both cases, he protected their images at his own expense.

Later on, when his wife came for sessions, her descriptions of the gradual deterioration in the couple's sexual life coincided with her husband's. It came out that Mr. F.'s impotency occurred whenever his wife was in conflict about *her* feelings toward him. This young woman was unable to tolerate feelings of intimacy and at unexpected moments would flare up in anger at Mr. F. She said that she tried to cover up her "meanness" and rejection toward him and would force herself to be affectionate or sexual when she was feeling quite the opposite. Her mixed signals left Mr. F. confused and self-hating, and he had fantasies of mutilating himself.

Mr. F. was being emotionally castrated by a woman whom he believed genuinely loved him, and as a result, he was slowly committing suicide. Without therapeutic intervention directed at this defense of idealizing his wife and mother, it is doubtful whether Mr. F. could have reversed this movement toward self-destruction.

In spite of his resistance, gradually, over a period of several months,

Mr. F. began to change his perception of the situation. He came to see that a large part of his sexual problem was in relation to his wife. His thinking became clear and he remembered how she would suddenly lash out at him with sarcasm and hatred. He came to understand his symptoms and reactions and felt relief from the savage feelings toward himself. He was no longer self-critical or confused, but still felt the pain of his wife's withholding.

An interesting side issue came to light during the course of Mr. F.'s therapy that is worth mentioning. In describing his evenings with his wife, Mr. F. revealed that the couple slept closely intertwined in each other's arms, though they rarely made love before falling asleep. This sleeping posture, with close physical contact while cutting off real feelings, was symbolic of their fantasy bond. When I pursued the subject of these sleeping patterns, Mr. F. said that "Whenever I fell asleep in my wife's arms, I pretended that she was in love with me and sexually attracted to me. Lying there close to her made me feel less anguished and frustrated about not being able to make love to her. I could forget for a while the pain caused by the deterioration in our sexual life. But in the morning, looking at her lying there in our bed, I would hate myself with a passion for being less than a man. Invariably, later in the day, I would eat the food absolutely forbidden on my diet."

Locked in each other's arms without being sexually close stood in sharp contrast to the intimacy of a genuine personal relationship; indeed, the compulsive pattern was part of a destructive bond; i.e., it strengthened a feeling of connection. Breaking into the idealized image of his wife left Mr. F. feeling alone and hungry, but it also left him stronger. His idealization of his wife had protected him from feeling the emptiness in the relationship. Only when he recognized her underlying hostility was he able to control his diet and limit his self-destructive habits.

THE GOOD MOTHER/BAD FATHER

The need to preserve the good image of the parent applies much more exclusively to the maternal image, because it is the mother in our culture who still plays the predominant role in raising the children. Indeed, the child who has blocked out the negative traits of the mother does *not* necessarily repress a bad image of the father. When the child is used by the mother as an ally in her battle against the father, the child may develop strong resentment toward the father and strong protective feelings toward the mother.

It has been my clinical experience that the idealization of the mother is more common and stronger than that of the father. Arieti (1955) agrees with this point of view. Preserving a good image of the mother prejudices the child against the father and against men in general. Men and women alike possess sexual stereotypes and attitudes in relation to men that are often incorrect. Both have cast the mother in the sacred role of being loving, feelingful, and competent in personal matters. In sharp contrast, they tend to see the father as "mean," overbearing, domineering, unfeeling, and generally uninterested in child-rearing.

These basic stereotypic misconceptions were clearly illustrated by a couple I saw together in therapy.

> Marilyn had been in individual therapy for several months when she requested a joint session for her husband and herself in order to discuss the problems she was experiencing with her two young sons. Her complaint was that the boys were almost uncontrollable. It seemed that neither she nor her husband were able to discipline them consistently in a way that was effective. The two boys, ages six and nine, had become the source of increased dissension between the parents.
>
> Watching this young couple interact in the session, I was aware that Marilyn's husband was being maneuvered into the role of the powerful, punishing father to wage his wife's battle with the children. The situation went against his basic character, as he appeared to be a basically reasonable, unassuming man who was unhappy with the troubled relationships in his household.
>
> Marilyn complained bitterly that her husband was inconsistent in disciplining; she demanded that he devote more time to her and to his children. Her face was distorted with hostility and resentment as she spoke. This was not too uncommon a situation, where the father was provoked into becoming punitive and harsh with his children as the mother abdicated the role of disciplinarian, threatening the children all day with warnings: "Just wait until your father gets home." Consequently, the older son was already so alienated from his father that he rarely spoke to him.
>
> Later, in an individual session with the patient's husband, the full extent of his assigned role of the "bad" or "mean" father was revealed. With tears in his eyes, he told of years of trying to get close to his children and of his failure, as he saw it, to be a father. He believed, on a deep level, that he was a hard man, with a mean streak, and unfit to be a parent.
>
> From my interaction with this man and my knowledge of Marilyn's childish manipulations, I knew that he had been provoked into accepting his wife's view of men and of himself as being angry and harsh. His boys were growing up to believe that because they were male, they, too, were mean and unfeeling.

RESISTANCE TO BREAKING THE IDEALIZATION OF THE PARENT

People are very resistant to having a positive image of their parents or parental substitutes challenged. This exposure can lead to angry, defensive reactions. Sometimes the person who provides a more realistic view of one's family is rejected outright. For instance, a husband may complain endlessly to his mate about his mother, yet if his wife dares to criticize his mother, she faces an onslaught of anger and righteous indignation from her husband. He can say things about *his* family, but she can't, and vice versa.

Some people complain about their families, then rush to explain their parents' motives in order to excuse their bad habits or weaknesses. Who has not heard these expressions: "My father was never home," or "he was an alcoholic," or "my mother lectured us continuously," or "she never paid attention to us," followed by "but he/she had a hard time; it was the depression; they had their own worries." Or "My father really loved us deep down, he just couldn't express it." These pathetic rationalizations protect both parent and child, and they serve to maintain the positive image of the parent. Even though these rationalizations contain some truth, they cannot undo the pain of being hurt or the awful reality of what actually happened in the family. People use these reasons as excuses for their parents' behavior and thereby attempt to cut off their own pain and hurt and deny their anger. It is psychologically harmful for people to protect their parents in this manner, but it *does* work to preserve the idealization of the family and on some level offers an illusion of security.

As a psychotherapist, I have encountered resistance in all phases of therapy, but one case stands out in my mind as a particularly stubborn expression of resistance. Interestingly enough, the patient's stubbornness revolved around the phenomenon of parental idealization.

> Several years ago I treated a young woman, Mrs. D., who with her eight year-old daughter had moved to Los Angeles from northern California. Mrs. D. had recently divorced her husband and was trying to start out again. Even in the initial sessions, she displayed a great deal of integrity despite the fact that she was quite fearful of being on her own for the first time in her life. She expressed a desire for help with her daughter, who was reacting intensely to the move.
>
> The daughter presented a serious behavior problem; she was secretive, sullen, and continually punished her mother by acting miserable. It seemed that she had been extremely upset after the separation. One of my associates began to see the little girl in therapy.

After approximately a year of therapy, Mrs. D. decided that she wanted to be more honest with her daughter about *her* part in the breakup of her marriage. She felt as if she had wrongly placed all the blame on her former husband. She knew that she had been indifferent, neglectful, and often hostile toward her daughter during those early years. She thought, too, of telling her about the ways she saw herself repeating this same pattern of aloofness with the girl's new stepfather. As a part of her overall plan to change these patterns of behavior, Mrs. D. wanted to be more explicit with her daughter regarding her past and present actions.

My associate had carefully prepared the child for this moment, and the four of us met together in my office. In the session, Mrs. D. was matter-of-factly honest and direct about herself, and at first her daughter seemed interested in the conversation. Toward the end, though, she appeared fidgety, even irritable, and when I asked about her reaction, she was strangely noncommittal. In her next session, the child was more openly angry toward her mother for exposing this information and contradicted it any way she could. She had absolutely no desire to see her mother realistically, because this new image threatened the strong bond between them.

The follow-up showed that the daughter, now thirteen, had recently increased her acting-out behaviors as a smoke screen to prove that she was bad and her mother was good. Her resistance had taken the form of intensifying her own self-hatred and the idealization of her mother. Despite her mother's exposure of her own inadequacies she was rejected for revealing the information. In effect, Mrs. D.'s daughter rejected a real relationship, a *friend-ship* with her mother, to hold on to the *bond* with her. Her strong need to defend herself with the primary fantasy of self-mothering required that she continue to build up her mother and deny any faults.

IMPLICATIONS FOR THERAPY

When a patient is able to accept a more realistic appraisal of the parent and becomes more tolerant of his or her ambivalent feelings, there is generally marked improvement. People who have experienced a deep emotional catharsis in Feeling Release Therapy[1] sessions often recover memories of painful episodes in their childhood where they were misunderstood or mistreated by their parents. By reliving the emotions that they repressed at the time of these traumas, they become acutely

---

[1]Chapter 17, *Psychotherapy Overview*, Part II, Feeling Release Therapy.

aware of their parents as real people with all their weaknesses, blemishes, mistakes, immaturities, and inadequacies.

Typically, the patients become more compassionate toward their parents and themselves, because, for the moment, they are not hating themselves. Their fantasized connection to the "good" mother is gone, as is their internal "bad" child. The patients are simply themselves without their usual overlay of defenses. They feel no need to build up the parent and disparage themselves. All too often, though, feelings of guilt gradually force patients to deny their new insights, and they begin to blame themselves once more for their parents' rejection of them.

Unless the patient is helped to sort out misconceptions about the parents and to develop a realistic picture, he or she will remain restricted by internalized images of them, and the self-concept will be significantly damaged. The perpetuation of an idealized image of parents and family often leads to a life of self-hatred, inwardness, and avoidance of close, satisfying relationships.

Chapter 6

THE NEGATIVE SELF-CONCEPT

Self-hate is the strongest human antitherapeutic agent in existence. Its potential for destructive possibility is almost limitless.

Theodore Rubin (1975)
Compassion and Self-Hate, (p. 5)

The idealization of the parent leads to converse feelings about the self. A system of negative thoughts, feelings, and attitudes about oneself is an integral part of the self-parenting process and is inextricably tied to the internalized idealized image of one's parents. The negative self-concept, an outgrowth of a "bad child" image, is an essential part of the patient's overall system of defenses.

The neurotic person hates him or herself as part of an ongoing, active process. The individual appears to be perverse in the strong need to hang on to self-hate, in the tendency toward self-denial and destruction, and in the refusal to change a negative self-image. Yet, viewed in the light of protecting the primary fantasy, these human characteristics become more understandable. Maintaining a negative self-concept protects against intrusions into the fantasy of self-sufficiency. The self-hating person predicts rejection by others because, on a deep level, he

99

or she experiences the self as unlovable. One anticipates and fantasizes about rejection to justify avoidance of close, personal relationships. One doesn't want to take another chance on being hurt again, and therefore tenaciously holds on to feelings of worthlessness.

People's resistance to changing their negative self-concept is due in part to the need to maintain an identity that reflects their parents' definition of them and includes the acceptance of their parents' rejecting attitudes. Changing one's basic identity by giving up negative self-evaluations would cause pain and anxiety because it would necessitate a disruption of the family bond and interfere with the process of gratifying the self with the image of powerful, all-knowing parents. For instance, if one stops defining oneself as the parents did, one also stops believing or accepting their negative evaluations. While one's own self-image is enhanced, theirs is diminished. For this reason, the process of changing one's image and the resulting improvement arouses a great deal of anxiety; however, there is no deep-seated therapeutic change without this accompanying anxiety.

Changing one's identity also involves a basic contradiction of one's earliest conception of reality and leaves the patient temporarily without a stable sense of identity. Throughout life, the person has had certain well-defined thoughts of the self as unlovable, and though these patterns of thought caused immense suffering, at least they provided an identity. Thus events that would lead to a positive change in basic self-concept are strenuously avoided because of the anxiety that this perceived loss of identity entails.

Psychotic states of melancholia as well as neurotic depressions are based on a loss of self-esteem that reflects a lack of love and the emotional deprivation experienced by the child. Fenichel (1945) describes the development of depression in which:

> . . . fear is felt not only lest something terrible occur within the personality but also lest there be a loss of certain pleasurable feelings, such as well-being, protection, and security, which were hitherto present. This feared loss may be characterized as a loss of self-esteem, the most extreme degree of which is a feeling of annihilation. (p. 134)

When this loss is severe, a process that is similar to mourning takes place, accompanied by a profound sense of guilt and strong tendencies to punish oneself for the loss. The child cannot afford to direct rage at the source of pain and risk destroying the only hope for love and security. Instead of expressing rage and sadness over a loss, the child accepts the blame for being rejected, and from that point on, relentlessly accuses him or herself of being unworthy of love from anyone. "No longer is the feeling of being loved the sole prerequisite for well-being, but the feeling of having done the right thing is now necessary." (Fenichel, 1945, p. 388)

Feelings of worthlessness, self-accusatory thoughts, and the erratic mood swings that characterize certain types of depressive states are controlled by an internal negative thought process or inner dialogue, the voice.

THE INNER VOICE—THE LANGUAGE OF THE DEFENSIVE PROCESS

Self-castigation, guilt, and distortions of the self are all regulated by an internal thought process, referred to here as "the voice." This partially conscious "voice" represents the introjection of the parents' rejecting attitudes toward the child, both spoken and unspoken. It is not generally experienced as one would hear an hallucination or an audible sound (Firestone & Catlett, 1981) (although it can be verbalized); it is more precisely a set of negative feelings and attitudes toward the self and incidentally toward others as well. *The "voice" may be described as the language of an insidious self-destructive process existing, to varying degrees, in every person. The voice represents an external point of view toward oneself initially derived from the parents' suppressed hostile feelings toward the child.*

The voice may be experienced as conscious thought, but more often it remains partially conscious or even totally unconscious. It is an ongoing internal dialogue that runs down the self and others and as such may be cynical or even paranoid in character. Most people are unaware of this dialogue, yet it is active on a subliminal level within them.

People sometimes *do* become aware of these critical thoughts when they are in stressful situations. For example, one who blames oneself for making a mistake may castigate him or herself with statements such as "Why did you do that, you stupid ass?" Or, "Can't you ever do *anything* right?" A person about to give an important speech may torment him or herself with thoughts like: "Suppose you forget your speech? Just look at your hands; they're shaking so much, the audience will be able to see that you're nervous."

This pattern of self-critical thoughts includes all the statements that are said to oneself in the process of self-parenting. This "voice" in effect tells the person that he or she is unlovable, worthless, and bad. In this way, it supports the preservation of the "bad child" image. The inner dialogue also "nourishes" the self by building up the person falsely with

exaggerated statements of praise, thereby setting the stage for subsequent self-attacks when the person fails to live up to this ideal. To the
extent that these self-nourishing and self-hating statements remain unchallenged, they become part of the person's self-concept.

A patient's self-attacks may or may not be the same specific criticisms
or abuses that the parents expressed toward him or her; however, the
style of attack and the underlying anger are characteristic of their destructive feelings. The child tends to take on the parents' distorted viewpoint toward him or herself, often the attitudes the parents held when
they felt the most rejecting and angry. The daughter or son incorporates feelings of loathing and degradation that lie behind their statements. The individual comes to believe that he or she is bad or unlovable
rather than perceiving that the parents are rejecting or inadequate.
Thus, this internal dialogue serves to protect the defensive process by
interpreting reality in such a way as to preserve the negative self-concept and the parental misconceptions of the child.

The voice has a tendency to generalize in that it extends specific
parental criticism of the child into other areas of life. For example, if a
parent tends to be compulsively neat and overly critical of a child's habits, that child will grow up to be self-attacking not only in relation to any
lack of neatness, but will tend to attack him or herself for other deficiencies or bad habits, such as smoking, overeating, or procrastinating. The
son or daughter will adopt the parent's particular style of ridicule, sarcasm, and derision as a global attitude toward the self and will generalize angry self-attacks to many personality traits.

A person's voice may become particularly active following success or
achievement. Thoughts such as the following are common: "Who do you
think you are? Now you've really got these guys fooled. Just wait till the
next project, though, you'll fall flat on your face, then they'll see your
true colors!" or "So what if you did okay in high school, just wait till you
get to college, that's a whole different story, you'll never make it" are
common. The voice insinuates that real accomplishments were a quirk
of fate, an accident, or somehow the result of others being deceived. It
warns that the person will never be able to sustain or repeat the performance. It tells him or her that pleasure over success is ridiculous because basically he or she is a phony and a fraud. This derisive aspect of
the voice contributes to the empty feeling or the sensation of being let
down that many people notice after they achieve an unusual success.

These more common self-attacks are easily recognized and are generally accompanied by agitation, irritability, or a slightly depressed
mood. It is important to note, however, that these critical, sarcastic
thoughts are merely isolated fragments of a more complete system of

destructive thoughts and derogatory attitudes that the person is aware of only a small fraction of the time.

THE VOICE AS DISTINGUISHED FROM A "CONSCIENCE"

It should be emphasized that the voice is not merely a conscience or set of values and moral attitudes, but a system of misconceptions about and negative attitudes toward the self. The author's conceptualization of the voice defines it as part of a self-destructive process, that is, an *overlay on the personality that is not natural.* I do not conceive of the voice as constructively directing the individual's morality or as being a function of the super-ego in the strict Freudian sense of the word. Rather, I see it as an essential element of a negative defensive process.

The voice does *not* function as a positive system of values; *rather it interprets and states an external system of values in a vicious manner of self-attack and castigation.* In that sense, the voice is not the basis of a decent, moral life or a conscience. It is often contradictory, both instigating actions and condemning them after the fact. In their most pathological form, self-attacks can lead to suicide, whereas the hostile voice toward others fosters aggressive or homicidal behavior. Often patients who are suicidal or homicidal report experiencing "voices" as actual hallucinations instructing them to act out destructive impulses.

Internalizing negative parental attitudes necessitates the adoption of an external value system (the parents') rather than a gradual development of one's own internal set of standards. Under close scrutiny, it appears that most people do not sufficiently develop their own morality or value system. Instead they judge themselves by external standards and maintain a feeling that they are "bad" in relation to these standards. For example, the author has observed that most children, when asked why they refrain from doing something they know is wrong, answer that they would get into trouble if they did it, rather than saying that the action would be wrong because it would hurt another person. The motivation of most people, first as children and then later as adults, is to avoid punishment by authorities, rather than to reflect a compassionate attitude toward oneself or one's fellow beings.

Though the voice represents an incorporation of parental values, its judgmental, punishing statements toward the self usually occur after the fact and are not helpful or useful to the person in guiding behavior. Even when the dialogue *appears* to reflect a value system, the tone of this voice is vindictive and tends to increase the person's self-hatred rather than motivate him or her to amend behavior. To one who knows oneself to be at fault, or feels that he or she has committed an error in judgment, the voice becomes self-righteous and punitive: "Look at what you did! They'll never forgive you!" Or, "You make great resolutions, but you're so weak-willed, you never live up to them." Or, "You're no damn good; this last mistake proves it!" These voice attacks are categorical and imply that the person will never change. The voice engenders hopelessness about gaining control over behaviors that the person wants to change. In this way, the voice demoralizes the individual who has "sinned;" it does not inspire the person to act differently, as in the case of a true sense of moral consciousness. When people do wrong or make mistakes, it serves no useful purpose to punish themselves or hate themselves. It is more appropriate and functional to change their behavior in the future.

The voice does *not* involve a rational consideration of alternatives. For example, a person trying to lose weight could engage in rational thinking about one's diet. In this case, he or she might be thinking, "I know I like to eat, but if I limit myself to 1,000 calories a day, I'll be able to maintain my weight loss." Dieters listening to the voice, on the other hand, alternately tempt themselves to indulge in overeating, then punish themselves viciously for yielding to temptation.

The voice condones and encourages self-denial; however, people who are self-sacrificing are usually destructive to themselves, and resentful of others whom they see as being selfish. Indeed, this seemingly "moral" aspect of the voice is not truly humanitarian in nature as it appears at first glance. To the contrary, it supports the person's tendency to give up his or her own wants and needs, which means, in effect, giving up significant parts of the identity.

How the "Voice" Contributes to the Formation of the Negative Self-Concept

When the voice is not challenged, but is listened to, accepted, and believed in a habitual manner, it is synonymous with the self-concept. People eventually become what the voice tells them they are; they develop the negative qualities that the voice tells them are theirs. For example, the woman whose voice tells her that she is unattractive compared with other women tends to look less attractive in reality. She may have been defined as "plain" as a child, and despite pleasing features, now presents an unappealing face to the world. Her self-consciousness about her appearance, her clothes, her hair, all militate against having a lively, spontaneous style that would actually make her more attractive.

Every time she tries to improve her looks, her voice tells her that it's hopeless, that that's just the way she is. She becomes dispirited and defeated from believing these self-attacks and hates herself even more. Similarly, the man who tells himself that he's cold and unresponsive in relation to women tends to be awkward and hesitant with them, thus confirming his opinion of himself.

Believing one's self-attacks predisposes behavior that, in turn, causes one's negative traits eventually to become a major part of one's style or approach to life. Children incorporate the parents' distorted definitions of them and later use these to categorize themselves. The voice, by labeling the person as the parents did, becomes the agent of a downward-spiraling, circular process. When an individual persists in believing the voice's categorizing statements such as "You're the dumb one, he's the smart one," or "You're always selfish or lazy," he or she will tend to act on these assumptions as if they are real. One will monitor one's behavior according to these internal statements. For example, one will actually *be* less intelligent than a sibling, or *become* lazy and selfish. Thus, these incorporated views, unchallenged, lead to a self-fulfilling prophecy.

The voice operates as if it comes from an external source like another person within the self. Although we may subjectively feel "I'm a bad person," this feeling obscures the external attack from the voice, saying *"You're* no good." The voice is not personal, compassionate or rational, but external, judgmental, and often irrational. When the voice becomes obsessional, it acts to block the emotional or feeling part of the personality, leaving the person in an emotionally deadened, depressed state, which makes one even more vulnerable to attack.

Even in its mildest forms, the voice interferes with a person's ability to cope with everyday living or to function adequately under certain circumstances. For example, the voice heard by a tennis player might be, "Here comes the ball, you're going to miss it; keep your eye on the ball! See, I knew you'd miss it." One recent book, *The Inner Game of Tennis* (Gallwey, 1974), instructs readers in techniques that help them identify this inner dialogue and thereby improve their game. The insights into the effect of the voice on the game of tennis can be generalized to all areas of personality functioning.

The male lover tells himself, "You're going to lose your erection; you won't be able to make her feel good." The wife or girlfriend thinks, "You're not feeling enough. You're not going to be able to have an orgasm." The voice runs down both partners with self-criticism and self-derision, causing them to become nervous and worried about their performance. Everyone has thousands of these critical thoughts in the course of one day; they take their toll on the person's efficiency, vitality, and basic feeling about oneself.

The process of listening to the voice also predisposes behaviors that lead to the avoidance of other people. Attacks on the self and on others are ridiculing and sarcastic in tone, even when the information used by the voice is correct. Patients who have felt free enough to give full verbal expression to these negative thoughts have been shocked at the viciousness and treachery of their voices, which often assume a quality and accent similar to that of their parent's actual speaking voice. Intonations and unusual words and phrases used by the parents are repeated by patients while verbalizing these thoughts.

> One patient took an extremely judgmental attitude toward himself and toward other people. In learning to verbalize his thoughts about himself, he became aware that for each action he took in his everyday life, he "heard" a sarcastic remark. It was almost as if an autonomous being existed within him who constantly observed him and commented on his behaviors. For example, following a recent promotion, as he entered his office in the morning, he "heard:" "Pretty neat set-up, eh? You're really in the big time now. Let's see what big deals you're going to make today." If he made a good decision, he would "hear:" "Think you're pretty smart, huh? Well, you're not the man you used to be. You got lucky this time."
>
> As he gave words to more and more of these mocking self-attacks, the patient realized that his tone of voice had become very much like that of his father. He recalled times when he was a child that his father had ridiculed and mocked him in the same sarcastic style with which he now tormented himself.

As in this man's case, it would seem that there is preserved within each of us an incorporated parental image that represents our real parents at their worst moments, when they were the most punitive toward us.

ORIGINS OF THE NEGATIVE SELF-IMAGE

The development of a negative self-image occurs early in life when the child suffers from emotional deprivation in the family. The self-esteem of the child is damaged by parents who are overtly or covertly rejecting. The absence of parental desire or capability of meeting the child's needs (love-food) obviously implies a corresponding rejection of the child as well.

A negative self-concept, together with feelings of self-hatred and depressive states, are multidetermined, yet they are basically a response to the *parents' deeply repressed desire to destroy the aliveness and spontaneity of the child whenever he or she intrudes on their defenses*. Indeed, the parent hates the child for this intrusion and on some level wishes him or her dead. These hostile wishes and destructive urges are even more profoundly effective in determining the child's self-concept than are parental inadequacies or a lack of love. In this sense, *the core of the voice, the critical thoughts about the self, is really directed toward the ultimate self-destruction of the individual.* The parent's unconscious desire to quiet the child, to put him or her to sleep, to suppress the child's feelings, arise because the *parent* is defended and emotionally deadened, and doesn't want to be awakened from this cut-off state by tender feelings for or from the offspring.

The parent who also was once a hurting child will do everything in his or her power to prevent these painful feelings from erupting into consciousness. Having sensitive, empathetic contact with one's own child threatens to arouse the parent's repressed pain, and so, by various means, the parent unintentionally sets out to destroy the spirit of the child. Genuine and spontaneous expressions are supplanted by socially designated feelings and the child is taught to adopt the defenses of the parents in order to protect them from unwanted stimulation of repressed feelings. The more defended the parent and the more rigid the system of defense, the more hostility will be felt toward the child, who is an innocent intruder. Of course, the parent feels guilty about this hostility and covers it up, often finding fault with the child and blaming the child for the "wrong crime."

The anger that the parent feels toward the child at these times is introjected in conjunction with the internalized parental image and turned against the self in the form of self-hatred. For example, patients who were abused verbally or physically as children invariably hate themselves and often repress memories of being punished or claim their parents were justified in being punitive. The child's pain, humiliation, and fear are repressed also, and feelings of blaming oneself for real or imagined wrongdoing take their place.

Similarly, anger felt by the child *toward* the punitive parent is not expressed because of the child's fear of losing the parent. Rather, the child turns the anger against himself as self-hatred. Anger turned against the self is a major cause of depressions, in both psychotic and neurotic depressive states.

Many examples of parents who openly revealed their destructive wishes toward their children have been documented in recent studies (Bowlby, 1973). In his research into children's school phobias, Bowlby states:

> [A colleague] who is studying mothers who are struggling to bring up children without a partner to help them, reports that a large proportion of them admit that, at times when they are more than usually anxious or depressed, they entertain ideas of getting rid of their children. . . . Unless she has very great confidence in an interviewer, however, a mother is most unlikely to admit to this. (p. 280)

My associates and I have similar experiences with a large number of patients in private practice. We, too, have found that mothers who learned to trust the therapist and realized that all kinds of thoughts and feelings were acceptable admitted outright destructive urges toward their children. This was particularly evident in women who had been abused by their own mothers. The destructive urges included murderous impulses, wishes to be rid of the child and a deep resentment of the child's dependency on them. These angry feelings were most often, but not exclusively, directed toward their daughters. In most cases, these hostile urges reflected the mother's repressed hostility toward herself.

Bowlby also writes that these hostile wishes may be far more common than clinicians would care to believe, because parents usually are too ashamed of them to report them, even to professional helpers. Children are too protective of the parents to reveal parental behaviors that seem in the least dangerous or abusive. Children's fears of the parents' conscious and unconscious wishes, even in the absence of verbal or physical abuse, may be expressed in their nightmares of monsters, witches, and other dangerous beings.

One indication of the murderous rage that the well-defended parent feels toward the child can be found in auditory hallucinations that occur in psychotic forms of depression. These patients may on occasion hear "voices" from the external world urging them to kill or mutilate themselves. This most pathological form of the internal dialogue is present in this severe type of depression where the person actually "hears" vicious attacks on oneself. These hallucinated "voices," which tend to have parental overtones, are an extreme manifestation of the self-attacks made by the depressed neurotic patient. This rage is preserved, with a great deal of functional integrity, in the internalized parent and exerts an enormous control over the neurotic patient's behaviors and affective states.

Under less extreme conditions, this rage is reflected in thoughts that urge a person to "be quiet, don't talk, who do you think you are anyway? No one is interested in what you have to say." The patient's voice may be directed against specific qualities or personality characteristics of the person; perhaps the attack is leveled against one's sexuality, or spontaneity. An individual may feel free in some areas of life, and yet very restricted in others, depending on whatever specific areas of functioning had intruded most directly on the parents' defenses.

Sometimes, unexpected thoughts or brief suicidal impulses may erupt into the conscious mind even in "normal" individuals; these are clearly indicative of this incorporated malignant thought process.

> One patient, a documentary film-maker who tended to be somewhat depressed, told of a time when he was filming Niagara Falls, standing close to the edge of the deep gorge. He "heard" a small, snide voice in his head saying, "You know, you could just jump off here—it's so easy, go ahead, you creep, just jump down there." The man was terrified at this strange, foreboding thought. There was only a low railing where he was standing, and he felt compelled to get away immediately.

Struggling against self-destructive and self-critical thoughts becomes very debilitating because defending oneself against the voice requires a great deal of energy. Often the seriously depressed patient is confused in identifying which is his or her own point of view and which is the voice's. Generally, the patient has such low self-esteem that he or she cannot "answer" the voice with positive, realistic statements about oneself. That is why depressions that contain suicidal thoughts and an extremely degrading view of the self so often leave the patient exhausted, listless, and defeated.

DETERMINANTS OF THE NEGATIVE SELF-CONCEPT

Parental characteristics that lend themselves to the formation of a negative self-concept are those that cause the child to feel guilty and self-hating. For example, the parent who experiences the needs and wants of the child as intrusions on the parent's own defense system will view the child as greedy, demanding, and "bad."

The disgust that some mothers feel toward their children's natural desires is transmitted to children by varied means. An infant senses its mother's rejection through her touch and facial expression long before it understands what her words mean. Consequently children develop guilt for wanting these basic necessities of life and later feel guilty any time they find themselves in a state of wanting. As adults, they may experience intense feelings of guilt and self-attacks by their voice as they pursue significant goals, whether professionally, financially, or in a satisfying relationship. Young children blame themselves for their parents' rejection and at the same time attempt to repress the anger and frustration they feel when their needs are not met.

Many parents, in denying undesirable traits in themselves, project these qualities onto their children and punish them for these qualities, real or imagined. In a sense they use the child as a "dumping ground" for traits they hate in themselves. The child's perception of the self is generally in complete agreement with his parents'; that is, the child sees him or herself through their eyes.

This image of being "bad" persists into adulthood; most people are reluctant to give it up because, ironically, feeling positive about themselves causes them pain. In sessions with children, as well as with adults, when I have encouraged them to say positive things about themselves with feeling, they generally experience strong feelings of sadness and pain as they begin to give themselves value and see themselves as lovable. Interfering with patients' negative self-concepts arouses painful feeling and tends to make them feel more compassionate toward themselves.

IMITATION OF NEGATIVE PARENTAL TRAITS

The child introjects the parents' negative qualities, as well as their rejecting attitudes especially at critical times when the parent is under considerable stress. This accounts for the fact that the worst qualities of the parents may be internalized by the child. It also explains why people continue to imitate their parents' negative mannerisms, behaviors, and attitudes more compulsively than they imitate their good qualities.

The child becomes sensitized to the worst side of the parent as it is the most hurtful.

> A father took his children away for a week's vacation and devoted himself to activities that they would enjoy. Everyone felt good during the week. On the drive home, he lost his temper with the kids when they were bickering in the back seat. His grown-up son recalled the vacation as a rotten experience where "dad was a real bastard." He isolated and fixated on the one time during the entire week that his father was rejecting. The event stood out in the mind of the son.

People focus on events that cause them pain and crystallize their defenses during times of stress. We seem to have a greater capacity to react to pain than to pleasure. For example, on a physiological level, a tiny cut on the finger can cause intense pain when it accidentally comes in contact with a piece of ice, but there is no comparable pleasure. In a similar manner we have a greater propensity for psychological pain than for pleasure or happiness.

Immediate and powerful learning of defenses takes place in the child during periods of emotional distress. For this reason, the voice reflects a selective incorporation of negative traits, feelings, and attitudes. An interesting sideline—the son in the story above developed as a carbon copy of his father in relation to his defenses, his inwardness, and a tendency toward irritability over small events. His "voice" was an exact replication of his father's defenses and it was reflected in his behavior.

The child takes on the characteristics of the punishing parent in order to relieve anxiety and gain some measure of security. In "identifying with the aggressor," in this case the parent, the child feels as if some mastery has been gained over stressful situations. At times, this internalized parent has been observed to "take over" the total personality of the individual under similar conditions of stress. R. D. Laing (1960/1969) describes this phenomenon:

> A most curious phenomenon of the personality, one which has been observed for centuries, but which has not yet received its full explanation, is that in which the individual seems to be the vehicle of a personality that is not his own. Someone else's personality seems to "possess" him and to be finding expression through his words and actions, whereas the individual's own personality is temporarily "lost" or "gone." This happens with all degrees of malignancy. There seem to be all degrees of the same basic process from the simple, benign observation that so-and-so "takes after his father," or "That's her mother's temper coming out in her," to the extreme distress of the person who finds himself under a compulsion to take on the characteristics of a personality he may hate and/or feel to be entirely alien to his own. (p. 62)

The explanation for this phenomenon lies in the fact that *human beings are capable of incorporating into themselves an image of their parents as the parents were when they were the most hated and feared by the child.* Throughout their lives, they attempt to deny that these qualities exist in their parents and preserve an idealized image of the parents by imitating their behavior patterns. This identification shows up the most in people's actions and attitudes toward *their own* children. By imitating the worst qualities of their parents, they obscure the fact that these undesirable traits were actually part of the *parents'* personality.

> The behavior of one of my patients, Helen, toward her child is illustrative of the strong compulsion to imitate negative behaviors of one's parents. Notes from a journal that Helen kept during the early phase of her therapy provide historical material and point out how she was mistreated by her mother when she was very young. Her memories and insights were valuable to her at that time in helping her break the strong fantasy bond she had with her family.
>
> "I remember my mother's impatience with me and the rage that she sometimes expressed toward me. One particularly vivid memory is of an incident that occurred when I was around four or five years old. I was standing in front of the bathroom sink—it was at my eye level—and I remember my mother starting to hit me with the hairbrush; she kept hitting me, and then suddenly she noticed that I was bleeding, and she stopped.
>
> "Another time, there was a typewriter sitting on the dining room table, and the keys were caught in the lace tablecloth, and my mother flew into a rage, yelling at me to untangle it. I remember I just froze with fear at her anger and tried to say to her 'Why don't you just help me get it untangled instead of getting so angry at me?' but I was almost paralyzed with fear and couldn't seem to get the cloth untangled as quickly as she wanted.
>
> "During the first months after I left home and moved to Los Angeles, I had to take a bus to the bank where I was working downtown. My strongest memory of those bus rides is that I would see middle-aged women riding the bus every day and I would feel intense anger at them. I felt confused by this anger because I didn't consider myself an angry person—but I was obsessed at times with those feelings. I think it was because of being physically separated from my mother by 3,000 miles that I could safely begin to feel the anger in me toward her, without the threat of really being able to kill her."
>
> Some years later, after Helen married and had a child, she returned for further therapy due to her concern over strongly ambivalent feelings she had begun to experience toward her two year-old son. Joey had recently begun to exhibit signs of a disturbance indicating a fear reaction that resembled, to a remarkable degree, some of Helen's early reactions to her own mother.
>
> Helen first noticed her son's unusual reactions when he was slightly over a year old. For example, when she attempted to put him to bed at night, he would scream and become stiff, arching

his back while crying in her arms. At first Helen rationalized this behavior as simple stubbornness and thought that Joey was going through a phase.

After months of this behavior and increased tantrums, Helen could not avoid seeing that *she* must be doing something to bring out these reactions in her son. One evening she was especially pained by the fear in her son's eyes when she insisted that he put his toys away. She was suddenly struck by the anger and impatience in her voice as she talked to him. She remembered that she had been spoken to in similar tones by her mother. A flood of emotions—guilt, self-hatred, shame—engulfed her as she picked Joey up and put him into his bed. The next day she had phoned me to ask for further therapy. For the next few months, Helen slowly and painfully revealed the extent to which she was reliving her own childhood through Joey.

It gradually developed that, for a long time, Helen had been stifling intense urges to be physically abusive to her son just as her mother had been with her. Joey had been able to pick up these deeply repressed feelings of rage in his mother and was reacting in much the same way that Helen had reacted to early stressful situations in her own life.

Helen was deeply affected by rereading the notes she had written during her earlier therapy. Over the intervening years between the time she kept her journal and the present, she had gradually lost track of the insights she previously had about the damage she had incurred in her family.

In protecting her mother's destructiveness Helen had imitated the very traits she hated in her. Realizing that her behavior had been a compulsive, unconscious imitation of her own mother's treatment of her was a first step in breaking the strong connection she had maintained with her since the birth of her son.

Compensation Perpetuates the Negative Self-Concept

When the voice goes unchallenged, an individual tends to maintain undesirable traits of which he or she is very much ashamed. In attempting to cover up real or imagined negative characteristics, the person compulsively acts out compensatory behavior designed to conceal these negative qualities.

An attractive female patient, who believed on a deep level that she was unattractive and ugly, attempted to compensate for this image with a variety of behaviors that seriously interfered with her life. She spent most of her spare time shopping for expensive clothes, going to the beauty parlor, reading fashion magazines, and trying out new cosmetics. These activities served the purpose of giving her some degree of satisfaction but the relief was only temporary. When asked why she spent so much money on clothes, shoes, and beauty aids, she became extremely defensive. She sensed that her cover-up was being exposed and she was desperate to keep it intact. She honestly believed that other people would find her unattractive and undesirable if she stopped these compensatory behaviors.

As she gave up these activities, her self-hatred and shame surfaced. It required many sessions for this woman to become aware of her specific derogatory self-attacks and to challenge her destructive view of herself.

RESISTANCE TO CHANGING THE NEGATIVE SELF-CONCEPT

Challenging distorted and exaggerated negative evaluations of the voice is absolutely necessary for a basic change in self-concept. Yet the process of identifying these self-attacks, in itself, separates the person from the internalized parent. The fear of losing this parental image and the guilt of symbolically leaving the real parent behind cause the patient to become very resistant at crucial points in therapy. The patient is, in a sense, losing or giving up an old self, and this causes emotional upheaval. One's sense of a static, stable identity cannot be shaken without arousing a multitude of unpleasant emotions. Usually the way a person was defined in the family serves as one's ongoing identity and the person becomes stubborn about changing it.

Avoiding the development of a negative self-concept and circumventing the formation of a punitive voice in the child is a major task of successful child-rearing. Similarly, the process of exposing the dynamics of the voice and identifying and making conscious all the aspects of this internal thought process is an integral part of the therapy process. Controlling the self-destructive behaviors that are dictated by the voice, that is, refusing to obey the voice's injunctions, is vital to the patient's progress. The patient is encouraged to behave in constructive ways that directly challenge the voice. These actions help the patient to separate from the negative traits and qualities in the parents or family. Challenging an individual's negative self-image and self-hatred and teaching the person to cope with the ensuing anxiety are primary tasks of an effective psychotherapy.

Chapter 7

DISPLACEMENT OF NEGATIVE PARENTAL CHARACTERISTICS AND THE DEVELOPMENT OF A VICTIMIZED OR PARANOID APPROACH TO LIFE

In preserving an idealized image of their parents, children must dispose of their parents' actual negative qualities. When they find it intolerable to perceive their parents realistically, they get rid of their parents' undesirable traits through the mechanisms of denial and displacement. Children block from awareness those parental characteristics that especially threaten them and project them onto persons outside the family. Thus, *by judging their parents as right or superior and others as wrong or inferior, children (and later, adults) preserve their illusions about the family.* Obviously, they must distort other people in order to maintain this unrealistic view of the parents and in doing so, tend to develop a disordered, cynical style of thinking and perceiving the world.

Negative attitudes and assumptions about other people originate as responses to traumatic events in childhood. In general, anticipations about the world are based on early experiences within the family, particularly interactions with the mother. If the general atmosphere at home was hostile and the mother inadequate or untrustworthy, the child's feeling reactions to these conditions will later be transferred to new situations and to the world at large. As an adult the person will distort events and other people and respond to them with negative or fearful expectations. At the same time, one will tend to be defensive of and oblivious to the weaknesses and faults in one's parents. Current fears will remain inexplicable if one does not connect them with early experiences and recognize the process of displacement.

In addition, the child has a tendency to deny and project angry reactions to parental rejection. Growing up in an atmosphere of criticism and neglect, one experiences considerable hurt and frustration. When the person becomes aware of this frustration and subsequent hostility, the anger is either directed inward or projected onto innocent outsiders. Denying hostility toward the parents allows the child to maintain the bond with them and, by redirecting aggressive impulses, to allay the fear of losing them. The process of projecting hostile feelings onto people outside the family also acts to preserve the myth of family love and solidarity and an image of the parents as being good and decent people.

Eventually adults come to provoke the treatment expected; usually they provoke negative responses very similar to those received in the original family. By acting on anticipations of rejection and hostility from others, the paranoid person actually elicits angry reactions and rejection in new associations. These negative responses in turn increase the individual's own aggressive or avoidance behaviors to counter the hostility directed toward him or her. A vicious circle is established and the paranoid ideation gradually becomes impervious to change.

THE DEVELOPMENT OF DISTORTED VIEWS OF OTHERS

People tend to perceive others in terms of certain strong sets or generalized misconceptions that they developed early in their lives. For example, a child raised by a harsh, critical mother will later tend to perceive a strong person as being overbearing and mean. However, the child will continue to block from awareness the perception of these qualities in the mother herself. By preserving an image of the mother as benevolent, the person is able to keep the good mother/bad child system intact, but must see other people in a negative light.

In general, a neurotic person sees the inadequacies and weaknesses of parents in other people and reacts to present-day events as he or she responded to the family situation. If raised by stingy parents, the person will perceive the world as an unrewarding place and see other people as tight and lacking in generosity. Similarly, an individual who was abused as a youngster will tend to perceive people as disrespectful and harsh and will react defensively, either submissively or with hostility.

In schizophrenic disorders, preconceived views of other people are especially impervious to reality-testing. The psychotic patient has beliefs that require little information to confirm them and are indeed very difficult to refute logically. They are appropriate only in the sense that they once *did* apply to the parents' behavior. These misconceptions cause overdramatic and totally inappropriate responses to present-day circumstances and interfere with an individual's ability to adapt.

In less extreme cases, neurotic individuals often behave in such a way as to make their critical or cynical view of people actually come true. They are adept at proving their negative allegations about people. The tragedy from the patients' viewpoint is that often, in order to rationalize and justify their negative perceptions of others, they increasingly damage their own lives and future relationships.

PASSIVITY AND THE PARANOID PROCESS

The tendency to play the victim is present in paranoid thinking and behavior and represents a form of perversion of normal anger responses. A victimized orientation to life is determined by two principal factors: first, by the child's denial and displacement of the negative characteristics of the parents, and second, by the repression and projection of the child's own negative, hostile, or aggressive impulses.

Paranoid thinking is a disorder of focus and perspective whereby the subjective world of the individual (feelings, reactions) is experienced as happening to him or her rather than originating in or being caused by the person. There is a tendency to dwell on unfavorable stimulus conditions instead of experiencing angry feelings in response. The person doesn't cope but rather complains and feels overwhelmed by the external situation. Thus anger that would be felt outwardly in reaction to not getting what one wants is perverted into a feeling of being hurt or wounded. This leads to a condition of chronic passivity in relation to events and to the expectation of harm from the outside. With this expectation and an abnormally high sensitivity to aggression in others, there is a tendency to distort and even to invent malice in other people. The person expects from others the anger and aggression—in a magnified version—that is denied in oneself.

Paranoia is a self-confirming system which precludes the awareness of conflicting perceptions. It is analogous to the work of a scientist who rigs the data to fit preconceptions. The tragedy is that paranoid individuals are virtually unconscious of the process and feel genuinely threatened from without. They see others as hostile or threatening and cannot see that their distorted perception of danger causes *them* to be the hostile ones.

People who tend to be paranoid feel that they have an inherent right to have their needs met. They believe they are entitled to good treatment from families, friends, and from their mates. Naturally, everyone has a right to need or want and, indeed, basic identity is defined in terms of wants. When needs are frustrated, there is inevitable anger that is a natural and basically healthy phenomenon. A person also has every right to *feel* angry and to consider constructive action directed toward changing circumstances. Yet, where reactions are tied to guilt, moral principles, or righteous indignation, paranoid feelings are inevitable. An individual who plays the role of victim deals in judgments and "shoulds" in interactions. This preoccupation with rights and shoulds is irrelevant to the actual problems faced and leads to inward brooding and vengeful feelings.

SEVERE PARANOID STATES

Paranoid reactions of serious proportions are often observed in schizophrenic patients. An important part of the schizophrenic process is that the negative qualities of the real mother are attributed readily to significant or transference figures, and sometimes may grow to include a large part of the social environment. The dangers and hostilities of the mother are at first transferred to substitute figures (authorities, etc.), often later to specific groups as in paranoid delusion, and eventually the patient comes to distrust all other persons. The strong sets and anticipations based upon early experiences with the "malevolent mother" can perpetuate a cycle of further withdrawal from the environment into self-nourishment through fantasy, which acts to incapacitate the person in social relationships.

Typically, after puberty, the preschizophrenic patient begins to conceptualize that the world is a bad place, particularly for him or herself. The schizophrenic also feels increasingly that *he* or *she* is bad or worthless. The patient imagines that:

> The malevolent authorities which populate the world are malevolent only toward him and with good reason. . . . The defense mechanisms become more and more incapable of coping with these situations. Anxiety is not covered any longer; on the contrary it is felt more and more and finally it is experienced with the same violence with which it was experienced in early childhood. Through generalization it spreads like fire to all situations which are similar to the original unpleasant situations. (Arieti, 1955, p. 69)

At some point in the schizophrenic regression, the patients' feelings of self-hatred become intolerable and they begin to project these feelings onto others. They imagine that other people hate them and anticipate hostility and rejection in social encounters. Their suffering is relieved to some extent by the projection of their own vicious self-attacks. Other people are now perceived as threatening or even dangerous. Expansive feelings of grandiosity and omnipotence are claimed by the patients according to their emotional need to protect themselves against these imagined enemies, whom they see as actually threatening their very survival.

THE ROLE OF THE VOICE IN PARANOID THINKING

Individuals anticipate rejection and aggression from others in two principal ways, based on what their "voice" is telling them: one, they use negative assumptions about themselves to justify their avoidance of other people; and two, they perceive *other people* as having undesirable traits or anger and so they avoid close contact with them. Either orientation fits in with the patients' predisposition to limit their contact with other people and thus maintain their negative self-image and their idealization of the family.

In the former case, the voice warns the individuals that they themselves are deficient or different from others: "You're not as smart as they are," or in derisive, sneering tones, it asks: "Why should they be interested in *you?*" Or, in predicting future rejection, it warns: "Sure, they like you now, but just wait until they get to know you better." Each self-denigrating thought leads the person to believe that he or she won't be liked or accepted by others. In effect, the voice persuades one to avoid meaningful relationships and is therefore functionally maladaptive. By "listening" to the voice and acting on feelings of inferiority, a person fails to develop relationships with others beyond a certain level of superficiality.

In the latter case, negative sets and anticipations about other people lead to the same maladaptive actions as those that are motivated by inferiority feelings. Cynicism and distrust of others play a prominent role in paranoid thinking. The paranoid person has a continuous internal voice that subliminally runs down other people or distorts their motives. The patient may think, for example, that "People are selfish and self-centered;" "He's really two-faced;" "These so-called friends of yours are out to exploit you and take advantage of you;" or "How do you know they're not all crooks? Don't make any business deals with them, you'll get taken."

A person who feels misunderstood and misperceived by other people attempts to justify the anger and disappointment. In situations where he or she feels victimized or wounded, the voice says: "Nobody understands you." "You're such a sucker, always doing things for them, what did they ever do for *you*?" "You deserve better than this." "You're much too good for them." "They don't treat you right."

People who assume a self-righteous stance are playing an adult version of the child-victim or martyr role. The adult who continues to act out victimized feelings fails to develop appropriate reality testing, mature coping behavior, or mastery in overcoming problems. In playing this role, such people have a strong need to be "right" in order to justify their feelings of martyrdom. For example, a woman finds herself thinking: "Your husband *should* be home on time for dinner;" "Your children *should* call you more often." The disgruntled employee's voice assures him: "You *should* have gotten the promotion. Management is *unfair!*" Stressing the fairness or unfairness of an issue is less functional than directly expressing an angry reaction.

The voice can lead individuals to exaggerate the real irritation and anger they see in other people. They may misinterpret momentary outbursts of temper as deep expressions of hostility and often mistakenly feel that they are directed toward *them*. For these reasons a paranoid person tends to overreact to variations in other people's moods and takes them too personally.

Delusions of reference are more serious manifestations of these distortions. Schizophrenic patients, who have very little sense of boundaries between themselves and others, over-react to subtle nuances in other people's emotional responses. Everything appears to revolve around them. More severe paranoid states can also result from these victimized ruminations. In general, any patient who has a history of feeling wronged by others and who isolates him or herself because of this distrust is approaching serious pathology. Out of a distorted sense of self-protection, which these patients see as necessary in order to live in the harsh, dangerous world that they have created, they will on occasion become aggressive and explosive. In unusual cases they may come to act out criminal activities with an absence of guilt because they believe the world somehow owes them what they missed in childhood.

The absence of moral considerations or poorly developed conscience seen in character disorders, delinquent, and criminal individuals follows from this type of victimized thinking:

A teen-age shoplifter, who also stole money from her closest friends, asserted her right to take from people whom she felt "had so much money that they probably wouldn't even miss it." Her ability to rationalize her behavior stemmed from a victimized orientation. When she verbalized her inner thoughts in therapy sessions, they were as follows: "You deserve something better." "Look at your friends, they have everything and you have nothing." "They've always snubbed you, this is your chance to get even."

This young girl felt no remorse in relation to her delinquent acts. Her lack of conscience was a direct result of a distorted view of people, expecting them to make up to her for what she missed in her upbringing. Her initial reactions to the neglect and rejection by her parents were an angry rebellion against their values and a paranoid expectation that the world owed her something. Feelings of martyrdom and bitter disappointment were recurrent themes in her therapy sessions. She used these powerful, primal feelings of being wronged and the convictions of her voice to justify her delinquent behavior.

From interviews with the patient's parents, it was clear that they also had a diminished sense of loyalty or feeling for other people. The patient's father especially had been malicious and abusive in his treatment of his daughter. These circumstances established her pattern of reacting out of vengeful feelings and with total disregard for the feelings of her peers.

When acting on the warnings of their voice, paranoid individuals eventually provoke the treatment that this negative thought process leads them to expect. In manipulating other people to reject them, they escalate their own hostility, establishing a vicious circle where their paranoid system is strongly reinforced.

A negative view of others is fostered by the voice which helps to maintain the idealized picture of the family. The patient is strongly resistant to perceiving the family accurately and to changing the negative perceptions of others. This resistance stems from the patient's fear of trusting again after once having been hurt. Psychotic paranoid states with elaborate and complicated systems of logic are particularly difficult to treat clinically. Similarly, less severe forms of paranoid ideation, such as various manifestations of stereotyping and prejudice, are defenses that stubbornly persist in the face of logic and contrary evidence. Indeed, *routine biases, stereotypes, and prejudices are all examples of the negative voice toward others.* These views tend to be supported by conventional attitudes that are very prevalent in our society and, for this reason, they are very difficult to challenge.

<h2 style="text-align:center">STEREOTYPIC THINKING</h2>

A person's cynical view of the world is also determined by the assimilation in childhood of the parents' distorted perceptions of other people. Through the process of introjection, the neurotic child takes on the parents' negative attitudes toward the child *and* their set of beliefs about the world outside the family unit. Raimy (1975), in writing about the importance of introjection in the formation of a person's basic misconceptions about the world, states:

> In *introjection* the individual adopts wholesale the complex patterns of behavior of others without integrating them into himself. Even though unintegrated, these patterns are perceived by the individual as valid aspects of himself. (p. 163)

Thus, the parents' mistaken perceptions of the external world breed the misconceptions that their children will carry with them throughout *their* lifetimes.

Most children emulate their parents with regard to the formation of attitudes toward minority groups. For example, a child who learns to dislike and avoid black people on the assumption that they are inferior or dangerous is reacting to the biases of the family. The parents may call attention to headlines featuring crimes committed by blacks and ignore information to the contrary. Through a process of selective inattention, constructive and humanitarian acts by blacks are either passed over or are seen by the parents as atypical. In this manner, prejudicial attitudes and stereotyping are handed down from one generation to the next. Deeply held beliefs about racial or ethnic superiority are merely extensions of a conviction that one's family is special and superior to other families. Thus, the prejudicial attitudes subscribed to by many members of our society contribute to and validate each person's idealization of the family and help maintain family bonds.

Idiosyncratic family views about people or groups of people are no different from prejudice or stereotyping and have the same effect. "Politicians and people in power must be corrupt!" "Doctors, lawyers, psychiatrists are only in business for the money, not for humanitarian motives." "The poor should be able to pull themselves up by their bootstraps." These cliches are a part of the voice that acts to separate people from one another according to categories and status.

Most patients who seek therapy bring with them a myriad of false notions, ideas, or beliefs about other people that they learned in their family and that they need to relinquish in order to expand their personal lives. These learned misconceptions protect the family bond in two ways: first, they predispose children to avoid certain groups of people so that the children rarely receive correct information which would contradict their distortions; and second, by denigrating others, their family is upheld as being special and superior.

Each family has its own peculiarities, systems of belief, and remedies for the world's problems. Each has its particular slant or bias in its perception of specific groups of people. Family members are tenacious in their adherence to their prejudices and false beliefs, as exemplified by the following case history:

> One of my patients, a young woman, was married to a talented and successful computer scientist. The couple was reasonably happy when the young woman's parents moved to a nearby city. In her attempt to re-establish contact with her family following the years of separation, the young woman invited her parents for a visit to her spacious new home. During the visit, she noticed her father's obvious discomfort and coolness. When she asked him what was bothering him, he bluntly said: "Well, if you really want to know the truth, I can't stand your money, your home, your cars, and your expensive clothes. You know how I've always felt about wealthy people: 'The rich don't get where they are without stepping on others.'"
>
> Raised in a comfortable, though frugal, middle-class home, this young woman had listened to her father's lectures about the corrupt values and disregard for humanity that he believed characterized wealthy people. Soon she was able to identify the source of her guilt, which was activated whenever she went shopping for clothes for herself or for her children. Indeed, one of the most troublesome areas of her relationship with her husband was her inability to accept his generosity. Instead of bringing her happiness, her new possessions and beautiful home caused her anxiety and distress. They actually led to considerable problems in the marriage and caused dissension within the couple.
>
> This young woman had unconsciously adopted many of her father's attitudes toward success. Her father's pseudoliberal views were really an outlet for his aggression and hostility. These patterns of resenting and disparaging others were now incorporated parts of the patient's personality make-up. When she became suc-

cessful herself and reaped the rewards her father had disparaged, she was, in a sense, opposed to herself. Her guilt caused her to turn against herself and her own best interests.

In idealizing one's family, an individual adopts the parents' biases and idiosyncratic beliefs and imitates their negative responses toward other people. In this manner, cynical views held by members of one's family and their prejudicial attitudes toward specific groups of people and individuals are passed on from generation to generation.

CONCLUSION

The interrelated dimensions of an individual's defensive process—made up of an idealization of parents and family, a negative self-concept, and the displacement of negative parental traits onto other people—all injure an individual's ability to function in the real world. They act to keep him or her alienated and distant from others and prevent the person from finding satisfaction in close relationships. The resulting self-protective style predisposes an inward state of nonfeeling. To varying degrees, all people suffer from emotional deprivation as children. To the extent that they generalize their reactions to new situations, they are reluctant to trust again and instead tend to move toward an isolated and inward state.

Chapter 8

INWARDNESS AND THE LOSS OF FEELING

As individuals develop a negative self-concept and a cynical view of other people, they progressively lose feeling for themselves and others. They gradually retreat into a defended state of nonfeeling characterized by varying degrees of withdrawal of interest and affect from objects in the outside world. A person in an inward, withdrawn state guides his or her life primarily according to the dictates of the "voice." He or she believes, based on the warnings of this negative thought process, that people cannot be trusted.

All people move in and out of this inward state, and they are almost two distinct and separate personalities from one state to the other. Many people live suspended in a cut-off state, feeling little compassion or love, or indeed any genuine emotion, for long periods of time. The times that they do feel sensitive, loving, and close to their feelings are notable exceptions.

Essentially, the concept of the *"inward state"* is used here to describe the dimensions of being that characterize a neurotic style of life. This *inward, defended state* and its opposite, *a feelingful state,* represent end points on a continuum. Between these extremes lies a gray area in which most people live. "Average" or so-called "normal" individuals are continually contending with the voice. They are neither totally possessed by a critical point of view toward themselves, nor are they completely removed from their feelings. However, their spirit and sensitivity are

125

dulled considerably. They are capable of unconsciously acting out destructive behavior toward themselves or others. The internal dialogue between the individual and the voice consumes a great deal of energy and leaves the person with diminished vitality. Often, over a long period of time, this inner conflict will lead to a mild neurasthenic condition of fatigue and psychosomatic complaints.

Most people will not tolerate the kind of life they say they desire because expanding their boundaries and finding love or warmth trigger painful sadness and revive the emptiness of past hurts. They cling to a familiar negative image of themselves because to think of themselves as genuinely good or kind or generous would rekindle their repressed pain. They are averse to reawakening primitive feelings left over from childhood and, in numbing themselves to these negative emotions, block out positive emotions as well. They can remain suspended for long periods of time in this cut-off state. If they were to embrace their true feelings and experience them fully, they would have to recognize their own innocence and feel their vulnerability. They would become aware that they were hurt or rejected through no fault of their own.

Positive experiences, that is, being treated respectfully with love, tenderness, and real recognition, can cause much discomfort. If individuals had not been hurt originally and had not been damaged in their basic feeling for themselves, this would not be the case. Unable to escape a punishing or hurtful home situation, *a child gradually disengages from the self as a hurting person and becomes, in a sense, someone other than him or herself.* In doing so, one severs the feelings of compassion one might have had for oneself or others.

In a defensive posture, the growing child gradually becomes more dependent on fantasy gratification and imagines that he or she needs nothing from the outside world to sustain him or herself. One ceases to identify with oneself or give oneself much value and instead builds a kind of facade. This facade or social image is a self-protective response to the incorporated parent's hostile feelings toward the child (the voice) and represents a vain attempt to fight back and deny the allegations of the voice. Role-determined emotions and conventional perceptions of the world gradually replace real feelings and clear, rational thinking. Growing older, the child becomes progressively more inward, and appears one step removed from directly experiencing the world around him.

THE VOICE'S ROLE IN CUTTING OFF FEELINGS

The voice, in promoting a state of chronic passivity and feelings of self-hatred, sets the patient up to be defensive and withdrawn. As described earlier, neurotic individuals often "hear" their own critical voices in the statements of others and feel denigrated or punished. Excessive concern over what other people are thinking about them represents an attempt to externalize self-attacks and is indicative of underlying feelings of self-hatred. The obsessional quality of self-attacks is antithetical to maintaining an ongoing state of feeling. Genuine emotional responses are destroyed in the process of listening to the voice and its projection onto others. Ideation gradually replaces feeling and the individual becomes even more withdrawn and isolated. A pathological condition in which the voice becomes the dominant part of the personality gradually develops. If "negative" feelings such as anger, hostility, or competitiveness arise, the voice judges them as wrong or bad, causing the individual to suppress the feelings. Loving feelings are also judged and censored.

Defense mechanisms that act to repress spontaneous emotions keep us from feeling fully alive to present-day events. Our reactions become more automatic and cerebral and less emotional or attached to our bodies. Feelings originate in the body, but, as the voice becomes more prominent, we become increasingly removed from our bodily sensations and our deepest feelings. We spend most of our lives trying to keep one step ahead of our pain and fear and can no longer experience the richness of our inner life.

SUPPRESSION OF PAIN AND THE PROTECTION OF THE FAMILY

The conventional view of psychological pain is that it is unacceptable and that people who are in emotional pain are sick or abnormal. This is a typical misconception of the nature of feeling. The reality is that repressed pain eventually finds expression through neurotic acting out, withdrawal into fantasy, or psychosomatic illnesses.

The author's theoretical approach to the dynamics of inwardness and emotional deadness is parallel to Arthur Janov's (1970) position as described in *The Primal Scream* in that its major focus is on how an individual deals with the primitive pain and trauma of childhood. The author believes in the reality of the painful episodes described by disturbed individuals and accepts the concept of emotional trauma occurring within the nuclear family caused by the exigencies of fate in an interpersonal environment that often lacked sensitivity or warmth or other necessary ingredients for comfort and security. In the context of the typical family situation, the child must not show pain because it would betray the family secret. Revealing unhappiness would point up the parents' inadequacies. Instead, the child turns these feelings of rage, sadness, and hatred on the self and becomes more inward and secretive about how he or she really feels. The child learns to go underground with feelings that aren't "acceptable," intuitively knowing that to show these feelings would make the parents feel angry or guilty.

Many a child has been injured by the vacillations of the parents as they move in and out of feeling for themselves. When they feel good temporarily, parents respond with feeling and are more sensitive to their offspring. For a short time they feel and express the love that they normally withhold. The child responds to this condition with love and affection. However, when the parents, for whatever reason, revert to a more inward state, they are blocked in their sensitivity and concern for their child. This withdrawal causes considerable hurt. The child is particularly distressed when this occurs at critical times following unusually positive experiences.

The same situation arises in the dynamic interaction within the couple. When a mate or loved one withdraws into an inward, defended state, personal feelings are withheld, a process that hurts those dearest to them. When an individual is in a defended state, he or she will choose to protect the self over any real concern for a relationship. Many times, without intention, one causes a great deal of harm. There is no way for a person to be innocently defended or inward without causing damage, particularly to those who are open or vulnerable.

The unconscious aspect of becoming inward and recapitulating one's past as an adult has pervasive and far-reaching destructive consequences. The very process of repressing painful episodes causes their inevitable repetition through succeeding generations. This outcome is predictable despite the best intentions of people who originally were victims themselves but who now are acting as agents or perpetrators.

The Effects of Suppressing Pain

Feelings arise involuntarily and are felt as sensations in the body. They cannot be forced; neither can they be successfully legislated against or suppressed. Feelings cannot be consciously controlled, while actions based on feelings are fully controllable. Feelings may be pictured as flowing through the person the way the wind blows through a tree, freely, without purpose or intent. When this rhythmic flow of feelings is interfered with, when "bad," painful, or sad feelings are blocked, a person becomes suspended in a cut-off state. By not experiencing the painful feelings that arise in the course of life, one causes oneself a great deal of harm. In this cut-off state, one acts out behavior that is profoundly detrimental to one's well-being.

It is the nature of emotional pain that if it is suppressed instead of experienced, it does not dissipate, but retains a bodily component, while a conscious awareness of the pain is repressed or forgotten. Pain that is not fully experienced at the time continues to exert its damaging effect on the person and finds symbolic expression through patterns of neurotic and self-destructive behavior. The avoidance of pain leads to compulsive reliving and repetition. The defended person continually manipulates the environment so that this repressed pain from the past will not surface. Primitive pains and longings are stored in layers in the body and cause tension and psychosomatic illnesses as well as depression and anxiety. Nevertheless, if one enters a psychotherapy where the atmosphere is conducive to the expression of these painful feelings, one can retrieve this pain and experience it, which results in a reduction of rigidity and bodily tension. The expression of these painful repressed feelings is usually accompanied by clear memories and intellectual insights.

THE INWARD STATE AND FANTASY

An inward person tends to spend a large part of his or her waking life in a fantasy state. This state is far more extensive and inclusive than the simple daydreams and imaginary companions of our childhood. In this condition, ideation takes precedence over feeling and fantasy gratification precludes genuine involvement with objects in the external world. This fantasy world is completely under the child's control. One can escape from a frustrating emotional climate by going into fantasy whenever one feels the need. It is obviously far more reliable than depending on one's mother, whose attention or lack of attention is influenced by so many outside variables.

Both the child and later the adult attempt to hide their fantasizing and develop a strong sense of guilt about seeking internal gratification while rejecting people. A person who feels guilty for pulling away from other people must necessarily distort their real qualities and become critical of them in order to justify isolating oneself. To avoid becoming "too attached" to the people one is closest to, one misperceives them and holds on to a negative view. In losing compassion and sensitivity for others, one turns away from feelings for oneself as well. The entire process leads to a state of existential guilt, which adds to the person's self-hatred and feeling of isolation.

To preserve this inner world, the neurotic person must protect illusions about the self and resist exposure. So one pretends, to oneself and others, that one is still pursuing realistic goals—love, material success, a rewarding career—while in fact maintaining self-denial and sabotaging one's life. To complicate matters further, one rationalizes failure and frustration and complains that one has been defeated by other people or circumstances.

The degree to which a person is withdrawn or in fantasy can be expressed on a continuum ranging from the completely withdrawn schizophrenic to the healthy person who typically uses fantasy and withdrawal only as a temporary means of amusement or pleasure, planning action, or as a rehearsal for creative work. Shyness, unsociability, and introspective qualities are associated with symptoms of a withdrawal into fantasy. However, these qualities are not the only signs of inwardness. Indeed, people who appear extroverted or outgoing on the surface may be acting out roles while investing little real affect in their relationships.

When the cluster of symptoms reflecting an inward state becomes the dominant mode of existence, we have a truly schizoid personality. The presence of flat affect, a sense of being removed from the mainstream of life, the absence of appropriate emotional reactions, obsessional ruminations about the past, a lack of interest in concrete goals, all point to the fact that the patient has become seriously withdrawn and inward in life style.

The inward person may appear indifferent to significant events in life, while reacting melodramatically to other, less important events. The individual focuses on playing the victim, overreacting to everyday situations with intense recriminations and blame. A person who exists in a cut-off state is generally not spontaneous or flexible. Everyday activities become very routinized and are determined more by playing out social roles than by genuine inclinations. One may be passive and undemonstrative toward other people, and often become parental and judgmental when involved in a position of authority. The man or woman makes an unusually close identification with the parent of the same sex, as well as with other family members that he or she is protecting. Often the individual acts, moves, and speaks like the parent of the same gender. The inward person tends to display many of the same negative parental characteristics resented and disparaged in his or her own upbringing.

BREAKING BONDS—DISTURBING THE EQUILIBRIUM OF AN INWARD LIFE STYLE

Much of human behavior is directed toward the avoidance of feeling—the painful, primal feelings from childhood as well as sad and hurtful feelings in the present. Existing in an inward state provides an escape in a sense. Moreover, this condition may not feel all that unhappy; it can even be a seemingly comfortable way of life for people who have cut off their feelings. Many patients have reported that until an unexpected crisis caused a major disruption in their lives, they seemed reasonably content and satisfied. They had succeeded in using routines and rituals to dull the anxiety and pain of their daily lives.

Separation, divorce, illness, unusual positive experiences, geographic or financial movement can disrupt the equilibrium of an inward life style. In a sense, anything that breaks into the fantasy bond or external bond can be disruptive.

One patient, a thirty-five year-old dentist, graphically portrayed his placid way of life as he told me of events leading up to his initial sessions with a family counselor who later referred him to me for individual psychotherapy:

> My life was stable and very well planned from the time I was a youngster. I knew that I was going to become a dentist; my parents knew it and encouraged me every step of the way. I married my wife when I was in my first year of dental school. She worked to help support me and exactly one year after I set up my practice, we decided to start trying to have a baby. Everything was perfect and went according to my fantasies and the plan I always had for the way my life should progress.
>
> When the baby was born, we moved into a very nice house in a good neighborhood, and I felt my life was complete. I had a rapidly expanding practice and my wife seemed to be the perfect mate. Though we didn't feel as romantic as we did when we first met, we weren't unhappy; we never argued. Then my wife got pregnant again—it was too soon, according to our time schedule, but I wasn't worried.
>
> After our second daughter was born, life seemed a little more hectic. Soon I noticed that I was irritable and at times had moments of uncontrollable rage toward the children, which I couldn't explain. Then last week, my wife dropped a bombshell. She had gone to see a counselor; she said she couldn't stand to see what was happening to the kids; she thought that they were in bad shape. She was terribly worried about their crying and tantrums.
>
> I was stunned and humiliated. I was furious that my wife had consulted someone professionally. The counselor who saw the children at the clinic felt that there were serious problems and recommended therapy for the children and for my wife and myself as well. I felt deeply resentful of this interruption in my life. I haven't been able to sleep; my nerves are raw, and I feel like I'm falling apart.

Breaking into his illusion of having a loving, happy home life caused this man a tremendous amount of pain and anxiety. Facing the problems in his family life put him in touch with emotions he had not felt since early childhood. The inward life style he had achieved had been directed by his wish to avoid the painful feelings and hurt he had experienced in his original family. His defended way of living caused him little outward suffering, yet had led to the avoidance of real contact with his wife and children. Finally their problems did intrude on his inward state and caused him considerable discomfort.

This man might well have succeeded in stifling all feelings of distress in himself if his wife had not been alarmed by the obvious signs of suffering in their children and sought help. In counseling sessions, she revealed specific behaviors of the children that were symptomatic of serious psychological disturbance, especially in the older girl who had frequent and uncontrollable temper tantrums. Both children displayed signs of impoverished affect and symptoms of depression. She tried to communicate her concern to her husband, but she said he had usually cut her short with reassurances that, "It's a phase they'll outgrow." She sensed, rightly, that this was not correct.

Despite her guilt and her fear of finding out things she did not want to face about herself or her marriage, the patient's wife sought help for her children. Her action had broken into her husband's fantasy world and destroyed this couple's pact of noncommunication and mutual protection. It disrupted their bond and the inward state they had lived in since they were first married. By including their offspring in their life of make-believe and their isolated, inward life style, the couple had inadvertently destroyed their daughters' spirit and vitality, which gave rise to a serious psychological disturbance.

IMPERSONAL VS. PERSONAL RELATING

The child who is hurt or rejected gives up being him or herself in exchange for a fantasy connection with the rejecting parent. In doing this, the child cuts off genuine emotional attachment to the parents and substitutes an imagined connection with them. As stated earlier, one gives up identifying with oneself as a hurt individual and develops a superficial and protective facade. This false front reflects the person's withdrawal of a genuine investment in others, *and in oneself*. One no longer reflects one's own point of view, but conforms instead to other people's opinions. The person loses or never develops a sense of identity and personal values and instead seeks approval or criticism from the significant people in his or her life. As an adult, the individual continues to make a parent out of other people and attempts to seek fusion through identification. As one forms a fantasy bond one progressively gives up real feelings. *It is this withdrawal of personal feelings from the people in important relationships that most characterizes an inward state.*

In this withholding posture, the child and later the adult loses a sense of meaning in life. This condition appears to be a major neurotic symptom of our time. Viktor Frankl (1967) has written extensively about this phenomenon. In *Psychotherapy and Existentialism,* he describes

> . . . students who complain about the meaninglessness of life, who are beset by that inner void which I have termed the 'existential vacuum.' Moreover, not a few instances of suicide among students are attributable to this state of affairs. (p. 17)

Life and the external world have no inherent meaning, in and of themselves. There is no hidden significance to life that may be discovered, rather it is only the person's investment of the self, of feelings, his or her interest in life, in other people, in objects, in activities that give life its *particular* meaning for the person. For example, when a man falls in love, his loved one's personality, physical being, thoughts, and feelings hold a great deal of personal meaning and value for him. If, later, for whatever reason, he withdraws his love and interest from this person, he loses excitement about his own life as well. Subsequently, he tends to relate to his loved one in an impersonal fashion. The lack of genuine involvement can be observed in his style of communication; for instance, he doesn't appear to stand solidly behind his statements, and there is a discrepancy between his affect and his verbal expression. The absence of personal feelings, eye contact, etc., give an observer the strange impression that this person is not totally present in his own body. This quality of dissociation is an important symptom of an "impersonal" style of relating that is typical of the inward person.

A bond is an unspoken agreement between two people not to intrude on each other's defenses or inward style. Both persons are afraid to break this pact because they are reluctant to be independent themselves and tend to be restrictive of the other. Therefore, both individuals operate out of guilt, fear, and obligation to maintain their inward state. In a bond, a person plays either a submissive or a domineering role, both of which are unequal and childlike. The antithesis of this mutually shared inward state is a friendship in which the individuals are neither superior nor inferior and where they act out of free choice, not obligation. This style of interacting is personal and feelingful, and genuine companionship exists.

Any interaction between two people can be analyzed in terms of whether it is conducive to the expression of personal feelings or whether it serves to cut off or obscure them. Communications that are glib, sarcastic, condescending, or a plea for approval ward off closeness and promote inwardness. On the other hand, an open dialogue, characterized by compassion, which is candid and straight-forward, intrudes on a withdrawn state.

In the author's opinion, the process of turning inward begins very early in life, perhaps as early as the first few months of infancy. It is reinforced during childhood, and it is reactivated by crucial events during adulthood.

All people exist, to varying degrees, in a state of fantasy. They have the choice at any given moment of satisfying themselves in reality or through the imagination. This choice is mutually exclusive. An individual who is being personal in a close, intimate relationship experiences genuine feelings toward the other person and expresses these feelings outwardly. By contrast, in a more impersonal mode, the individual is merely *fantasizing* feeling for the other person. Trying to rationalize the guilt one feels about an incapacity to care deeply for another individual, one may claim, "I love you but I just have a hard time expressing it." Or a person may be quite unaware that he or she only loves in fantasy and is blocking the outward expression of love, which accounts for the fact that he or she is not reaching the other person.

A man complained to his wife that she had been very distant during the last week. She responded with surprise and said that she had been thinking loving thoughts about him all along and had even been daydreaming about having great sex with him. In this example, both partners spoke in good faith, but it pointed up how the inward component of loving can be mistaken for acting on or externalizing the expression of positive feelings. Indeed, the woman felt gratified in her fantasy of loving her husband while in reality she was avoiding and rejecting him.

In the most extreme form of inwardness, the schizophrenic patient has withdrawn the libido from environmental objects; that is, has given up vitality and feeling toward persons in the outer world, because he or she can no longer cope with the stress of an interpersonal world and its attendant state of anxiety. Schizophrenic patients exist almost totally in an inward state where they are feeding themselves and taking care of themselves in fantasy. They have cut off all personal associations and exist in a state where they even "talk" to themselves.

The schizophrenic's withdrawal from real life is an exaggeration of

the kind of impersonal relating that constitutes many "normal" relationships. Initially, there is genuine interest and emotional involvement until
one or both parties become afraid of the closeness. When threatened in
an intimate relationship, each partner may withdraw emotional investment in the other person, even though outward behavior may appear to
continue as before. Many people who relate to each other in an inward,
cut-off style actually increase the amount of time they spend with each
other and develop a false togetherness to reassure themselves that
they're being personal. These compensations just confuse the issue, and
often all that remains in this kind of relationship is the fantasy of being
in love.

From my experience with a wide range of patients in psychotherapy,
I have concluded that the vulnerability of the human infant and its
capacity for pain in its undefended state is great. It seems that no one
comes through childhood without being scarred to some extent. The
suppression of intense feelings and the subsequent formation of symptoms act as a powerful limitation throughout life.

Many people, both professionals in the field and lay people, are not
fully aware of the extent to which human beings are directed and controlled by primal feelings. They underestimate the pain that is aroused
by positive experiences in life. They cannot understand a person's resistance to positive or corrective experiences and the negative reactions
caused by genuine caring or concern. They do not recognize the fact that
when people are responded to in a new, more positive way, it severs their
bonds and cuts them off from their past. It makes them aware objectively
that they were not loved or treated respectfully, that they were not
listened to or responded to realistically or compassionately when they
were young.

In a sense, a positive experience or nice treatment separates one
from one's old identity, from one's place in the family, and makes one
feel more alone. Indeed, the fundamental resistance in therapy is based
on the terror of facing separation from one's family and from one's
voice, and ultimately against facing death anxiety (Firestone, 1984).

INWARDNESS AND ITS CONTRIBUTION TO WITHHOLDING

In the context of the overall defensive process, the *voice* represents
the patient's self-destructive and critical *thoughts*; the *inward state* reflects
the *suppression of feelings* and the choice of fantasy gratification; and
patterns of withholding represent the *behavioral component* of the neurosis.

On a behavioral level, the patient who exists in an inward state drastically reduces emotional transactions and holds back responses from people in the interpersonal environment. Active strivings are replaced by a passive fantasy life and the inward individual becomes crippled in efforts to cope with the everyday realities of life.

Ernest Becker (1964), writing in *Revolution in Psychiatry*, accurately portrays the human conflict between action and fantasy, and the human ability to inhibit actions whenever one chooses to be inward and withdrawn. He states:

> Of all animals . . . [man] is the best equipped for action in the external world. But his supreme uniqueness lies not only in this. Of all animals, paradoxically, he is at the same time alone in *being able to stop external action completely, and to keep activity going in controlled inner thought processes alone*. Thus the same mechanism that enables him to find an external world more rich than any other animal, permits him to lose the capacity to act in it. (p. 73)

In losing feeling for ourselves, we lose the ability to respond spontaneously out of our own desires. We become locked into compulsively imitating our parents' life style of self-denial and withholding. Personal destiny is no longer of our own making, but is diverted onto another path—one that we would not have followed had we been allowed to develop in a healthy, growth-enhancing environment.

Chapter 9

WITHHOLDING

> You can hold yourself back from the sufferings of the world;
> this is something you are free to do and is in accord with your
> nature, but perhaps precisely this holding back is the only suffer-
> ing that you might be able to avoid.
>
> Franz Kafka
> (quoted in R. D. Laing,
> 1960/1969)

Withholding is an important aspect of the primary defensive process. This basic holding back of pleasure or fulfillment from the self
reflects the neurotic process on a behavioral level. Withholding also
involves a withdrawal of emotional and behavioral responses from
others. When hurt and frustrated, a child withdraws the emotional investment or the psychic energy invested in parents or other objects; i.e.,
a process of de-cathexis occurs. At a certain point in development many
children begin to hold back spontaneous expressions of affection and
interest in the people closest to them. Later they may withhold abilities
and special talents.

Passive aggression due to suppressed anger is only one form of withholding. This form of withholding, characterized by the presence of contrary, negativistic traits, seriously impedes an individual's performance and productivity. Withholding, however, is a broader concept and is largely directed against *oneself* in the form of self-denial and is only incidentally destructive to others. Because of the damage to close personal relationships, however unintentional, it increases self-hatred and guilt and leads progressively to still more withholding.

Withholding is the mechanism that maintains the primary fantasy of self-sufficiency. By reducing the responses of both giving to, and taking from, objects in the external world, the child limits emotional transactions with others. The underlying feeling is one of not needing anything from others and especially of not wanting to give anything of oneself, out of a deep-seated fear of being drained or depleted. Theoretically, the self-parenting process can be understood as a psychonutritional system wherein the person imagines that there are limited quantities of nourishment available in the interpersonal environment. The individual unconsciously rejects real gratification and gives up goal-directed activities in order to hold on to the safety of a fantasy world over which he or she has complete control.

WITHHOLDING AND FANTASY GRATIFICATION

Feeling close to one's feelings and existing in a state of genuine wanting lends excitement and vitality to one's life. It creates a strong sense of personal identity. A psychologically damaged child learns to stop wanting real affection, that is, becomes *self-denying*, and also abrogates natural feelings of love and affection *for* or toward parents; i.e., he becomes *withholding*. The child learns first to arrest the flow of natural feelings, then to substitute fantasy and a defensive structure.

The ultimate extreme of withholding can be seen in mental hospitals where maximum care is needed by those patients who delude themselves that they are omnipotent and need nothing from anyone. In these disturbed individuals the fantasy of self-sufficiency has become all-encompassing, and the patient withholds almost all natural responses. One schizophrenic patient I treated was so withholding that he refused to urinate in a toilet. He had been incontinent for over a year and was terrified to part with any product of his body. In his delusions he perceived his urine as nourishment, which was a vital part of his self-parenting fantasy (Firestone, 1957).

An extreme state of the passive-aggressive type of withholding can also be observed in the rigid, immovable stance of the catatonic schizophrenic. In this condition, rage has reached such proportions that patients feel they must exert absolute control over their angry impulses. Their rigidity is a desperate attempt to contain their anger and avoid action. Negativism and stubbornness are very evident. When one tries to move this type of patient in one direction, he moves oppositionally.

Control is all-important to withholding individuals. They regulate their inner fantasy world, composed of idealized parental images and their own negative self-image, so that it remains stable, predictable, and under their control. By contrast, they see spontaneous responses and free-flowing interactions with their environment as risky, potentially painful, and not under their control. As stated earlier, they feel that they must limit their generosity and giving to others out of a primitive, deep-seated fear of being drained. People's natural tendency to avoid fear and pain is understandable, yet paradoxically, the very act of holding back to avoid being hurt can seriously jeopardize their adjustment. Whenever they unconsciously inhibit loving and affectionate responses that have previously been part of their behavioral repertoire, they are, in a sense, negating their basic nature, their basic self. By withholding these responses and turning to fantasy for security and partial satisfaction, they go against themselves and experience a great deal of guilt.

HOSTILE WITHHOLDING

Hostile withholding patterns are typified by the presence of negativistic trends in the personality. Passivity and indirect hostility are maladaptive attempts on the part of the child to cope with the damaging aspects of the home environment. When feelings are suppressed in the home, the child finds a way of "getting under the parents' skin" while concealing more direct feelings. This use of negative power is more effective than a direct power play against a stronger or more powerful opponent.

Traits in parents that arouse the child's rage and fear contribute to the development of hostile, self-defeating patterns of behavior. They include: parental dependency, intrusiveness, domineering attitudes, lack of respect for the child's boundaries, and inconsistent behavior. These parental behaviors and attitudes have a devastating effect on the child's capacity to respond spontaneously and positively. The child reacts with intense anger when intruded upon or emotionally drained by the parent, and has a strong desire to retaliate. The intensity of this rage is overwhelming and terrifying because its object is the very person on whom the child is dependent for survival. Hence, the rage is repressed, which subsequently leads to a basically hostile attitude that is expressed through patterns of withholding.

The child soon discovers that by *not* performing, by *not* doing what the parents want, he or she is able to exert a considerable influence. When the child indirectly acts out anger toward the parent, there is some measure of release. The withholding has a stubborn quality; precursors of this attitude can be observed at that stage of development when the child repeatedly states an emphatic "No!" to most, if not all, parental requests.

Children who are stubborn about being toilet-trained, or who obstinately refuse to eat, outgrow these specific behaviors, yet as adults, they develop more sophisticated equivalents of childish stubbornness. Children who hold back talents and abilities, who refuse, for example, to function or perform at the level of their abilities in school, later have difficulty living up to their potential in their chosen careers. They have adopted a certain set, an overall style of holding back, that now operates even in areas where they themselves want to excel. As such, withholding is a learned response that is difficult to alter once it has become well established.

Although the child's early stubbornness (during the second year of life) arises partly from the desire to express independence and separation from the maternal figure, nevertheless, the continued routine refusal of parental requests beyond a certain age is symptomatic of a more general withholding. Parents who feel guilty for not loving their children allow these withholding behaviors to continue without much interference.

Whenever the child succeeds in efforts to engage the parents in an ongoing battle of wits over these issues, he or she fails in basic ways to complete important developmental tasks. In the attempt to get even with the parents for their own withholding and their insensitive treatment, the child significantly restricts his or her own potential. Children may eventually become so accustomed to withholding that they believe they are unable to perform certain tasks that are, in reality, within their capabilities.

Camouflaged reactions to parental intrusiveness often come to light when a patient is encouraged to experience a deep release of feelings in therapy sessions. Many people, in the midst of an intense reliving of events from their childhood, have screamed out their protests: "Leave me alone," or "No," or "Get away from me." Patients' primitive emotional reactions to their parents' excessive demands indicate the presence of deeply repressed rage. This submerged anger is the motivating force behind this type of withholding behavior.

Because withholding is an unconscious process and is manifested primarily in passive behaviors, it is difficult to confront this defense directly or to pinpoint which specific behaviors are being withheld. The person who is made aware of negativism tends to act wounded and misunderstood, and becomes very defensive when passive-aggressive techniques are exposed. The adult will transfer these reactions to new figures in life, especially authority figures. This person may lose the ability to function adequately or appropriately in situations where he or she has intense transference reactions to individuals in positions of power.

Patterns of withholding that include passive-aggressive components are prevalent between employee and employer. Both men and women characteristically hold back from authority figures whose superior positions they resent. This particular type of withholding tends to be resorted to especially when there is no outlet for anger or hostility. In business situations, in industry, at school, and in formal situations in general, anger is little tolerated or accepted; therefore, angry feelings come out in passive ways. Withholding is often expressed through procrastination, fatigue, lack of concentration, disorganized or nonproductive working styles, complaining and acting overwhelmed, forgetfulness, and errors that could otherwise easily be avoided. The cost to industry and business of withholding on the part of employees is immense.

The Role of the "Voice" in Withholding

Both self-denial and withholding from others are regulated by a negative subliminal thought process, i.e., the "voice." Behavior that would otherwise be expressed is held back because of a person's critical attacks on the self. When parents are unable to meet a child's needs, the child tends to turn against those wants as though they were bad. Parents will accuse a child of "selfishness" when they are threatened by the child's wants. Children are often told: "You don't deserve the things you get;" or, "You're greedy, always thinking of yourself;" or, "You always want things your own way." By distorting and attacking the child's desires in this way, the parents and later the incorporated "voice" effectively stop the child from expressing genuine responses that would otherwise be a natural part of personal interactions.

As a consequence, children often become painfully self-conscious whenever they feel like acting natural or with unrestrained spirit. The voice warns about exuberance in the same style that the parents cautioned: "Don't get so excited;" "Don't make a fool of yourself;" "What's the big deal anyway?"

Later, as an adult, if one feels generous one tells oneself: "They don't want (need) anything from *you!*" If the generosity takes the form of wanting to give a gift to a loved one, he or she thinks: "It's not good enough;" or, "She won't like it;" or, "What did he ever do for you?" The resulting posture is one of insulation and self-deprivation whereby the individual, in denying the self pleasure and happiness, also denies others warmth.

In listening to the voice and following its injunctions, people deny themselves the excitement and enjoyment they *could* feel in their work and in their personal lives. They appear to have lost the child's natural capacity for joy and enthusiasm. Some people make a virtue of self-denial and see it as constructive. Actually, they create negative social pressure and their self-righteous attitudes and self-denying patterns hurt others, especially their children. A withholding posture is obvious in people who have learned to be stingy and ungenerous. Tight personality traits, rigid styles of relating, and sullen facial expressions reflect the tightness or constriction that has become an integral part of their character structures.

It is important to emphasize that self-denial and withholding are, for the most part, unconscious phenomena and that, over time, the holding back of responses that are pleasurable can become automatic and involuntary. At this point, the voice that attacks the individual's spontaneity and wants typically exists on a subliminal level. For example, a woman who is unable to experience a full sexual response is withholding on an unconscious level. Her inability to attain orgasm has become an automatic reaction of a physical nature and is no longer under her control. Thus, she is denying herself this pleasure even though her conscious desire is to be fully responsive. Because of withholding, many men become passive, ineffective dreamers who rarely achieve success in their professional lives.

People can and do withhold their responses in many situations of everyday life in response to the dictates of the voice: housewives hold back their ability to create a pleasant home environment; husbands withhold companionship and communication from their wives; employees become incompetent and can't seem to follow directions; children procrastinate in doing their homework; and so on in infinite variety. These everyday manifestations of withholding are so commonplace that they tend to be accepted by many people as "normal;" nevertheless, they have a powerful undermining effect on the family.

AN ANALYSIS OF THE DYNAMICS OF WITHHOLDING

Withholding is a defensive posture that exists on a continuum.

There is a wide range of withholding responses, with variations in the intensity, persistence, and strength of these behaviors. Withholding parents have a drastic effect on their offspring, but the key figure in the situation is most often the mother, as she is usually the central figure involved in child-rearing.[1] The crying of her infant may activate deep painful feelings in her that have heretofore been successfully repressed, and she may come to hate her child for this intrusion into her defended state. The father generally remains more distant at this stage of his child's life and may be more successful at blocking out the infant's cry; however, both parents may come to resent the child if its responses threaten their respective defenses.

A withholding mother is well-defended against emotional experiences that might cause her to feel anxious or that would arouse painful emotions. She denies herself happiness and fulfillment in areas of life that would hold the most meaning for her. She tends to hold back affection and sexual pleasure from herself and her husband and love from her children. Nor can she easily accept her child's spontaneous expressions of love and affection directed toward her. Damaged emotionally in her own childhood, she now can offer little to her needy, dependent child. She typically has a negative self-image and feels unlovable and inadequate.

Initially, a mother may feel genuinely tender and loving toward her newborn infant, but these feelings sooner or later become threatening to a woman who has experienced deprivation in her own childhood. A few mothers are withholding toward their offspring even from the moment they are born. In most instances, women are unaware of this process and do not realize they have begun to limit the expression of affectionate, tender feelings toward their infant. Others who are more sensitive to their responses date the onset of their withholding feelings at approximately two months after birth, when studies (Hainline, 1978) have shown that infants first begin to recognize their mothers.

> In talking with the author, one patient, a young mother, said she remembered when she had suddenly decided to stop breast-feeding her three-month-old baby daughter, rationalizing that her baby seemed "uncomfortable" when held to the breast for feeding. As she described to me what she meant by "uncomfortable," this mother realized that it was *she* who had felt awkward and tense in the situation. As she described it, she said she felt nervous and very uncomfortable when her baby looked up at her

---

[1]In cases where the mother is not the principal caretaker and there is a substitute, either another woman or a man, we have observed the same dynamics.

with a feeling of special recognition in her eyes. "I had the urge to put her down immediately. I always managed to think of something important that *had* to be done right then." Prior to her baby's recognition of her and its ability to engage in direct eye contact, this mother reported that she had felt more at ease breast-feeding her baby.

Holding back a response implies that the feeling really exists and is now being withheld. If a child were unaware of the love and affection potentially available, he or she would probably not develop such a strong longing for it. The fact of first being loved and cared for, and then not being responded to, or being inconsistently responded to, creates a pull on the child that has a strong addictive quality. The child is compelled to try, by whatever means are at his or her disposal, to recapture the love once experienced, and this emotional hunger will tend to persist into adult life.

WOMEN'S COMPULSION TO IMITATE THE WITHHOLDING MOTHER

In my experience, I have found that most individuals suffer considerable pain and emotional deprivation in their early interactions with their mothers. Part of this pain is unavoidable, as no person can successfully anticipate or be in harmony with the needs of another at all times. Therefore, frustration is inevitable to a certain degree, but is compounded by immature or rejecting mothering. Infantile frustration leads to a combination of intense rage and hunger, which has no acceptable outlet. These negative feelings manifest themselves in withholding or holding back from the mother desired responses.

In the case of female offspring, where the identification with the mother is strong, the daughter's angry response is transformed into a style of holding back that resembles the mother's own style. *Strangely enough, the more the daughter resents the mother and suffers at her hands, the more she imitates her and attempts to form an imaginary connection or bond with her.*

Initially the baby girl has a natural, loving response to her mother and feels physically affectionate toward her. In her frustration, however, this early love turns to anger, and eventually she no longer allows herself to feel affectionate. She begins to renounce the original feelings for her mother or keep them inside. She eventually comes to hate and resent the most important person in her life at the time. Since a daughter strongly identifies with her mother, and uses her as a role model, if she can't like or admire her mother, neither can she like herself.

Often, a young girl learns, by imitation, to be like the mother, toward whom she feels hatred. She observes her mother's behaviors, and then later unconsciously acts in similar ways when *she* becomes a mother. Because she feels compelled to imitate her mother's behaviors and finds it difficult to tolerate the guilt or anxiety of being different from her, she is locked into a posture of hating herself.

As she matures, a young woman's withholding leads to childlike behaviors and manipulation through weakness. She may break down in tears very easily (and childishly) or merely threaten to break down. She may play the martyr and make her family feel guilty about her self-sacrifice, or she may be self-indulgent, competing with her children for her husband's attention. On the other hand, she may seek to dominate the family, becoming more parental and punitive, though this pattern is less common. A significant characteristic of withholding is a lack of independence or a strong point of view. For example, many married women exhibit a passive, resentful acquiescence to their husbands' opinions. Either orientation, whether it be submissive or domineering, reflects an unequal, childish attitude.

The role of wife and mother offers many opportunities for a woman to hold back adult behavior in practical matters: forgetting to drop off an important letter that she offered to mail, acting overwhelmed by housework and care of the children, being unable to balance the checkbook, being habitually late, not serving dinner on time, refusing to carry her own load, e.g., suitcase or packages, and pretending to be unable to discipline the children.

A woman withholds her affection and companionship in ways that show up in countless everyday situations: by rarely joining in conversation with her husband's friends or business associates; by tearing him down behind his back yet building him up to his face; by talking to him about *her* problems and rarely listening to his. On the other hand, she may act soothing and baby him, play up to him, and yet not share equally in planning family projects or vacations. All of these are typical forms of rejecting behavior on the part of the withholding woman. Most people are unaware that these routine withholding behaviors are anything but innocent, somewhat endearing, traits that reflect the "feminine nature." On the contrary, these habitual responses have a devastating effect on husbands and children and are in no way representative of mature womanhood.

THE EFFECT OF WITHHOLDING ON MALE CHILDREN

The effects of maternal withholding on men are every bit as devastating as on women. The male may become desperate, dependent, and clinging to his mother and later tends to become possessive of his mate. Many men maintain attitudes of hostility both toward women and toward themselves. Their anger at being withheld from persists into adulthood and seriously affects their relationships with women.

In families where the mother manipulates and controls through weakness, the son tends to take her side and develops angry feelings toward his father, and against men in general. The small boy develops an acute sensitivity to his mother's moods and is able to read her expressive movements. Later, in his adult relationships, he is tuned in to his mate's variations in emotional responses and any withholding on her part causes him a great deal of distress.

The young boy tends to repress his original affectionate feelings for his mother and later becomes cynical and distrustful toward women. He internalizes his anger and becomes self-hating and guilty about his hunger.

To summarize, both men and women develop strong fantasized connections with their mothers based on their unrequited longing for maternal love and care. They hope that some day this hunger will be satisfied or fulfilled, and they feel resentful when their mates fail to fill the void in their lives caused by maternal withholding.

SEXUAL WITHHOLDING

Sexual withholding refers to holding back natural sexual desire and its expressions: physical affection, touching, physical attractiveness, and all other aspects of one's natural, healthy sexuality. Although this particular form of self-denial and holding back takes place primarily in the privacy of the bedroom, its damaging effects are not contained there. They are widespread and affect every aspect of family life.

We have found sex differences in the manifestations of withholding. The core of a woman's withholding is related to sexual withholding. Whenever a woman holds herself back from her mature sexuality, for whatever reason, she becomes more childish emotionally. On the surface, she may appear to be very adult and mature, talk logically and rationally, yet on an interpersonal level with her husband and family, she reverts to immaturity. She becomes, as it were, her mother's daughter—guilty about her own sexuality, distrustful of men and generally self-hating. Nancy Friday (1977), in her book, *My Mother, My Self*, makes this point succinctly:

> Whether we want our mother's life or not, we never escape the image of how she was. Nowhere is this more true than in our sexual lives.... When men seem bright and alluring, we momentarily ally with them against mother's antisexual rules. But men cannot be trusted.... Marriage, instead of ending our childish alliance with her, ironically becomes the biggest reunion of our lives. (p. 4)

Sexual withholding may take place at any point before or during love-making. For example, a sexually aggressive, overly-seductive woman who initiates sexual contact may not be genuinely wanting. She may be acting as if she wants to be sexual to cover her withholding on a deeper level. Some women become rejecting of a man even before making love. They complain of headaches or fatigue or avoid coordinating bedtimes, thus avoiding the likelihood of sex. During love-making, a woman may become critical of the way a man touches her, and may imply subtly, or not so subtly, that he is stupid, inept, or insensitive. Some women become coy when undressing or are ashamed of their bodies. Others will act totally uninterested in being sexual when, in fact, they *are* interested. Women often report that they become tense or fearful as they approach orgasm. One patient was puzzled by her method of ending the close contact with her husband after love-making. She told me that she invariably turned her back to her husband in bed and slept inwardly after being fully responsive.

Women's views about their bodies often prevent them from feeling sexual. On some level, a man picks up the woman's distorted view of herself and becomes less attracted. For example, one woman believed that her breasts were too small. Her husband was put off by his wife's negative feeling toward that part of her body and so never thought of caressing her breasts. Many women think that their vaginas are too large, their hips and thighs too heavy, or that they have unpleasant odors. These negative feelings may be barely conscious and the woman may be unaware that she thinks she is repulsive in these specific areas; yet a man can generally sense her feelings and stays away. Some women have learned from their mothers that a man's penis is not "nice." Unconsciously they believe that a penis is dangerous and potentially harmful. Because of this feeling, they tend to become fearful and tense at the moment of penetration.

The woman who withholds her love and sexuality ironically complains that her man doesn't love her any more, or she constantly seeks reassurances of his love. She may become extremely jealous of any interest he shows in other women; she criticizes him or is self-deprecating;

she no longer greets him with enthusiasm and happiness at the end of the day; she no longer wants to share the activities that she cherished early in the relationship. The good times of the past seem remote to her, sometimes even unreal, and she experiences her mate's desire to be with her as a demand or an expectation.

Both men and women are predisposed to becoming sexually withholding if their mothers had ambivalent feelings about sex. The daughter's tendency to hold back her natural interest in sex is usually more pronounced than the son's. She identifies with the mother, who is, to some degree, nonsexual or hides her interest in sex. The daughter is expected to grow up to be like her mother, while the son isn't. Thus, roles and gender-identification play a significant part in determining the extent to which a woman becomes sexually withholding as compared with a man.

Sexual Withholding in Men

Men can be withholding and manipulate through weakness as a form of retaliation, as many women do. Many of these fearful men become controlling and dominating. They may attempt to buy women with gifts, or they may be withdrawn and noncommunicative generally, then expect to have a sexual relationship. Others become distrustful or critical of women who are sexually responsive and avoid forming relationships with them. Some men, out of fear, may reject a woman immediately after a close personal relationship.

A man who has become sexually withholding as a result of his early experiences with a rejecting mother tends to feel hesitant in approaching women. Underlying his hesitancy is a tremendous amount of repressed anger that, as described earlier, is part of both men's and women's responses to a withholding mother. This rage may break through to consciousness if the man is sufficiently provoked by a woman's withholding behaviors. In general, however, he tends to be somewhat passive and defers to a woman's wishes. Symbolically he is still trying to placate his mother by being submissive.

The most significant factor in these cases is that the man has incorporated his mother's view of himself and of men in general as being mean and unfeeling. His attitude and approach toward women usually reflect that view. If his affection was rejected by his mother, he may come to feel that there is something unpleasant or even repulsive about his physical nature. This feeling about himself will interfere with his establishing a satisfactory sexual relationship as an adult. The man who denies his natural sexuality unconsciously adopts his mother's attitude toward himself and other men. He sees his masculinity in the same negative light that his mother saw men in general. Thus, he is at odds both with himself and with other men and cannot relate to them beyond a superficial level. This hostile point of view toward himself and toward other men damages his capacity to sustain long-lasting friendships with either sex.

Incidentally, women who choose this type of man over men who are truly strong and confident often falsely equate meanness with strength and mistakenly perceive passivity as sensitivity or kindness. As a matter of fact, these passive men generally have a cynical and superior attitude toward women.

THE EFFECT OF SEXUAL WITHHOLDING ON THE MAN

In the beginning stages of a romance, a woman generally feels very attracted to her partner, yet later she may withdraw her sexual responses and lose her enthusiasm. The process of first being responded to sexually, then having it held back bewilders the man. He begins to lose self-confidence and the sex act starts to feel less natural or spontaneous than it once did. The woman's withholding makes him feel increasingly inadequate and inferior and reawakens suppressed rage from earlier experiences with a withholding mother.

In his clinical experience and observational study of the experimental community, the author has found that in most cases *a man's ability successfully to perform the sex act principally depends on the woman's genuine desire for sex.*[2] When a woman consciously or unconsciously denies her sexual wanting, the man is, more often than not, physically affected. He can sustain an erection only by either resorting to sexual fantasies or by working hard to stimulate enough physical contact to cause orgasm. To complicate matters, many men who find themselves fantasizing about another woman during love-making or utilizing other, more elaborate sexual fantasies report considerable guilt. Often, men turn to fantasy as a method of disposing of feelings of rage and frustration. Nancy Friday (1980), in her analysis of hundreds of men's sexual fantasies, states the case for the male dilemma in her book, *Men In Love:*

---

[2] Although men's sexual performance tends to depend heavily on the woman's desire and responsiveness, of course there are some men who have been so damaged in their early experiences that they are unable to enjoy a satisfying sexual relationship. In these cases, the man himself is predisposed to being withholding due to his own self-denial, fear, and hostility.

> Inside every adult male is a denied little boy ... when he approaches women, he carries with him all his unconscious memories of mother's awesome powers of retaliation and rejection.
>
> How can he handle the fear and rage that sex means for a man under these conditions? He can't stop, doesn't want to stop, being a man.... Maybe the best thing to do is turn your back on ... [women] and forget the whole problem. In the end, it is the man's relentless desire for women that keeps him from this surrender. Fantasies are invented. At least for a sexual moment, magic is called in, reality altered, the perceived nature of women changed; the conflict is healed. Fantasies are the triumph of love over rage. (p. 526–527)

In resorting to fantasy as a method of overcoming these primitive emotions, a man's genuine affectional and sexual feelings toward the woman in his life are diminished to a considerable degree. In addition, because the man is not in emotional contact with his partner during this cut-off way of love-making, he may feel confused and hungry toward the woman following the experience.

The extent to which a healthy man is sexually attracted to a woman is proportional to her honest wanting. He can feel his full attraction only toward a woman who genuinely desires sexual relations, that is, a woman who has not given up her sexuality and emotional involvement with men to maintain her tie with her mother. Further, an independent and mature woman has energy and a vitality that adds to her physical attractiveness.

By contrast, when a woman is withholding in her responses, she relates to the man on an *impersonal* level and the sex act lacks tenderness and compassion. Sex becomes more like a feeding experience, wherein the woman wants to be fed symbolically by the man instead of allowing herself to feel equal and adult in the act. During this more impersonal kind of love-making, the woman is attempting to replicate the type of relationship she found herself in as an infant: an unfeeling connection with the mother, where the maternal behaviors were often mechanical and lacking in emotional involvement. In retreating from an adult sexual response, a woman tends to gravitate toward a form of sexuality in which she becomes more inward and childlike and at the same time more controlling and manipulative.

A relationship in which the partners' desire for sexual contact isn't equal tends to create hungry, desperate feelings in one of the partners. Usually, but not exclusively, it is the woman who wants to be sexual less frequently than the man. This lack of desire on the woman's part creates hunger in her mate. The partner who is sexually withholding maintains control in other areas of the relationship by doling out sex as a manipulation. Because most men are generally desirous of being sexual, the woman's response or lack of response has tremendous leverage in their relationship.

When he becomes chronically hungry toward a woman, a man acts weak, becoming more passive, desperate, and unattractive. His mate, in turn, becomes further alienated from him, because she now finds him less appealing or even uninteresting. She now has justification for rejecting him.

JEALOUSY AND WITHHOLDING

Jealousy often occurs or is intensified as a reaction to a person's own withholding. When an individual holds back sexual responses toward a loved one, he or she tends to focus on what a rival is getting and feels cheated. Jealous feelings cover the fact that it is one's own self-denial that prevents one from achieving one's goals, not the presence of a rival or competitor.

Men and women are very possessive and controlling of their mates in an attempt to compensate for their feelings of inadequacy and fears of being competitive. They are excessively concerned about their mate's fidelity when they hold back their own feelings. They are very manipulative and act on the assumption that people "belong" to each other and have proprietary rights over their mates. Conventional views of monogamy support defensive maneuvers in relation to these "rights," while making it extremely difficult for individual men and women to decide on the basis of their own, undefended, free choice whether or not to have an exclusive sexual relationship. This possessiveness and control extend well beyond sexual fidelity into other areas of functioning.

DYNAMICS OF WITHHOLDING IN RELATIONSHIPS

The unconscious choice of each partner in an ongoing relationship is, more often than not, to limit pleasure and enjoyment so that he or she won't be vulnerable again as was the case in childhood. Withholding is ultimately suicidal in that the person, in attempting to gain control over potential loss or separation, kills the self off in small ways each day. Nowhere is this more true than in relationships that offer the most opportunity for closeness and intimacy. In a sense, to be in love and respond fully during the sex act is similar to experiencing "la petite mort." The fear of momentary loss of control and conscious thought during orgasm is on the edge of awakening deeply repressed anxieties about dying. The intensity of the feelings, the excitement of being with the loved one, the wanting and the aliveness, make us subliminally aware of just how much we could lose through rejection, separation, and eventual death. The poignancy of these powerful emotions often saddens and frightens us.

The style of sexual relating commonly found in a couple bond is characterized by the gradual development of a number of symptoms that are directly or indirectly related to sexual withholding. (1) One or both partners tend to retreat to a more restricted or immature level of sexual functioning. (2) The woman generally becomes less responsive sexually. (3) The man reacts to his mate's withholding in a manner similar to the way he initially responded to his mother's rejection. (4) The woman expects to be taken care of by the man. (5) A pattern of immature sexual relating develops, and the sex act itself is characterized by a greater degree of inwardness and takes on a more impersonal, masturbatory quality. The focus turns more to self-gratification with a great deal of dependence upon fantasy to intensify excitement and a concomitant decrease in genuine emotional contact.

Women who become withholding need to distort the man in their lives in order to maintain this defense. When regression occurs, that is, when a woman retreats from relating sexually with her mate on an adult level, she symbolically equates the man with her mother and involves him in her survival. She needs to hold on to a fantasy of being connected to the man and tends to distort the relationship. For example, many times women who are superior to the man in their lives both intellectually and in their ability to cope with the world relate to men in a passive and dependent mode. They cater to male vanity and defer to the man's wishes, setting up a situation that has a serious impact on both the man's and woman's sense of reality. Despite the current emphasis on equality of the sexes, there still exists a strong social pressure for women to build up a man's vanity and there may be negative consequences and recriminations from her mate if she does not comply. Whenever a woman surrenders her individuality and gives up her dignity out of guilt and fear, the result is a tragic personal loss for herself, her mate, and her family.

Furthermore, a woman who has become withholding needs to maintain the illusion that she is loving and that her man is unfeeling because she feels intense guilt if her withholding is exposed and she becomes aware that she is causing pain to the people closest to her. She strives to keep the entire process unconscious and to avoid knowing that she is withholding.

The author has observed that men also are generally reluctant to explore the possibility that their mates are withholding. As the process of withholding is uncovered in marital or conjoint therapy, usually at a point where the woman begins to reveal her specific patterns of holding back or where she becomes more open about her anger and resentment, most men react angrily. Accustomed to blaming themselves for sexual failure and familiar with being defined as harsh and unfeeling, they are resistant to receiving information to the contrary. Some angry men use the new insights into this process to support their cynicism and hostility toward women. Both men and women are strongly resistant to becoming aware of their patterns of withholding. Although there is considerable guilt, people are very reluctant to alter their defensive patterns and become vulnerable once again.

The dynamics of withholding in a long-standing relationship that has developed into a destructive bond can become very complicated and difficult to unravel. The fact remains, however, that *both* partners are living out a repetition of the rejection they suffered as children at the hands of a withholding individual, generally the mother—the woman typically imitating her mother's withholding behaviors and the man reliving his primitive longing for his mother's attention and love. Withholding is a defensive posture that consists of unique patterns of self-denial determined very early in the person's life. For this reason therapeutic intervention needs to be directed more toward individual therapy than marital counseling or analysis of couple interactions.

CONCLUSION

The effect of chronic patterns of withholding is an ultimate shutting down, a paralysis, of that part of the individual that strives for emotional health and growth—the part that contributes to feelings of self-esteem. Self-denial and withholding lead to the obliteration of a person's most desirable qualities due to the efforts to ward off loving responses from other people. In restricting qualities in the self that he or she especially values and those that are admired by the loved one, an individual relieves the unbearable anguish felt in relation to potential separation and object loss. Withholding involves a progressive elimination of the self and goal-directed activity that serves the purpose of insulating the person against potential loss. The retreat from self and self-pursuits mitigates death anxiety.

On an existential level, the couple bond, therefore, becomes a death pact in which each partner alters behavior and withholds admirable traits to such an extent that he constantly hates himself. In the process of destroying oneself as a lovable person, one is inadvertently destroying the love and affection of one's mate. In developing hostility toward his mate and himself, a person dulls himself to life and in some sense triumphs over death, having eliminated, through withholding, both the self and the other, whom he loves and would feel anguished to lose.

An understanding of the existential issues underlying withholding elucidates the reason that real acknowledgment and love so often trigger negative reactions. Genuine love makes an individual feel open and lovable, a state of vulnerability that becomes unbearable past a certain point due to the fear of potential loss through separation or death. Through withholding, many people effectively commit a slow suicide, systematically ridding themselves of all that is most valued until, in a sense, they have nothing left to lose.

Withholding and self-denial are regulated by the destructive thought processes of the voice. From a developmental perspective, the voice represents the parents' wishes to destroy that part of the child which is the most threatening to the parents' defenses. In most cases, it is the child's natural capabilities, enthusiasm, spontaneous attraction to the parent, lovability, liveliness, exuberance, humor, that break into the parent's well-defended state of emotional deadness. The parent must stifle these qualities in the child in order to maintain his or her own psychological equilibrium.

Karen Horney (1945) has written extensively concerning these parental reactions:

> Usually . . . there is a combination of cramping factors . . . out in the open or quite hidden, so that in analysis one can only gradually recognize these influences on the child's development. Harassed by these disturbing conditions, the child gropes for ways to keep going, ways to cope with this menacing world. Despite his own weakness and fears he unconsciously shapes his tactics to meet the particular forces operating in his environment. In doing so, he develops not only *ad hoc* strategies but lasting character trends which become part of his personality. (p. 42)

The author's conceptualization of the child's predicament is that *because* of weakness and fear, he or she resorts to the only tactic available, that of *not* responding, of *not* expressing what he or she feels at a given moment. This is especially exemplified by passive forms of withholding and withdrawal of affect. The child transforms the initial strivings toward life into an opposite drive toward destruction and self-denial, and the entire process, which is only partly conscious, may come to light only in deep analysis.

The child's early strategies of holding back from the people who are the most significant, at a period in life when the child is the most vulnerable, eventually evolve into the major character defenses of later life. Because these specific traits are unconsciously determined and because they are closely tied to the self-nourishing fantasy or core defense, withholding is extremely resistant to change. Progress in therapy requires that the patient become aware of his or her typical methods of manipulating the environment through withholding responses. The patient must learn to correct this withholding life style through challenging the voice and altering behavior. One needs to learn both how to be generous to others and how to accept love and friendship. Finally, one needs support in overcoming the urge to obliterate the self as a person in the desperate attempt to gain control or mastery over death anxiety. The aim of therapy is to interfere with each patient's tendency toward gradual self-destruction and help alter the balance in the direction of live pursuits.

Chapter 10

SELF-NOURISHING HABITS AND PAINKILLERS

Self-nourishing habits fulfill the function of parenting oneself and thereby establish a pseudo-independence. They also serve the purpose of cutting off painful feelings. In denying oneself fulfillment and satisfaction from objects in the outside world, a person comes to rely more on self-nourishing behaviors as substitutes. In order to ease their suffering, people learn to block out painful episodes and emotions. Unfortunately, they simultaneously limit feelings of joy and exhilaration as well. Psychological methods and means used to dull pain generally become addictive. Like drugs, they reduce anxiety and lead to feeling better temporarily. However, because these habits are closely tied to the destructive process of self-denial, people who rely on painkilling habits become increasingly crippled in their ability to function and find satisfaction in personal relationships. They tend to limit their pursuit of actual goals and become progressively more involved in an inward life style of fantasy and substance dependency.

Self-nourishing habits include a wide range of behaviors beginning with thumb-sucking, then progressing to masturbation, excessive television viewing, compulsive eating, drinking, drug use, addiction to routines, and mechanical, impersonal sex. These habits temporarily satisfy emotional hunger and primitive longings left over from infancy or early childhood, giving the individual some measure of control over the internal state. They function to support the illusion of self-sufficiency, the fantasy that one can take care of oneself without the need for others. A self-nourishing life style emerges that shuts off personal feelings and is primarily defensive and self-protective (Firestone & Catlett, 1981).

Breaking a compulsive habit pattern or an addiction can be the most difficult task that a patient undertakes in therapy. Anxiety and other painful symptoms generally accompany this withdrawal. The patient's dependence obviously involves more than would a simple physiological addiction.

In psychoanalytic terms, self-nourishing habits are categorized as "ego-syntonic," that is, they arouse little conflict with normal ego functioning. Evidently, until their use becomes obviously self-destructive or potentially dangerous, they are "in consonance with the person's ego" (Freud, 1916–17/1961). These habits tend to be acceptable to the self and do not cause deep inner conflicts until they become quite serious.

Eventually, well-established self-nourishing habits usually become self-destructive because they progressively limit the person's capacity to cope with everyday experiences. They tend to foster an inward, isolated life style. When these habits do become associated with a more generalized retreat from the real world, they no longer feel acceptable to the self and cause the person considerable guilt.

The more a person has been emotionally deprived and frustrated in early life, the more he or she tends to rely on self-feeding defenses that give the illusion of self-sufficiency and ease the pain. As in all other aspects of the defensive process, the "voice" plays an important role in supporting addictive tendencies: first, by seducing the person into indulging the "habit," then by punishing him or her. For example, first it encourages the person who drinks excessively to "take one more drink—what's the harm?" then it accuses the drinker of "having no will power" or of "being a hopeless alcoholic." These self-accusations in turn lead to more self-hatred. In attempting to alleviate these secondary reactions of guilt and pain, a person invariably resorts to more "painkillers," and the vicious cycle continues. In some cases of long-standing addictions to harmful physical substances, these self-nourishing habits lead to ultimate self-destruction.

DEVELOPMENT OF HABITUAL SELF-FEEDING PATTERNS

Self-nourishing or self-mothering habits come into play early as infants expand their repertoire of behaviors. Some of these habits develop out of natural predispositions, such as the sucking reflex.

Healthy infants exhibit a certain amount of sucking beyond what they engage in while taking the bottle or nursing. For this reason, it is difficult to determine exactly when sucking begins to function more as a substitute for parental love. Nevertheless, thumb-sucking and the use of the pacifier can become prolonged and habitual, and beyond the age of approximately two years, these patterns may be symptomatic of emotional deprivation.

These primitive self-nourishing behaviors become associated in the infant's mind with the fantasized image of the mother (the fantasy bond), and they act to reduce the baby's tension and partially satisfy its hunger. Later, in times of emotional stress, the child retreats into an inner world of fantasy and utilizes these same techniques to soothe and comfort itself. As children become older, these behaviors proliferate, and they develop new habits and techniques with which to parent or symbolically feed themselves. Nail biting, smoking, excessive drinking, masturbation, or drug use are some of the activities that come to be relied upon for pleasant sensations and relief of tension.

There are three general categories of painkillers that can become associated with a self-nourishing life style: (1) addiction to physical substances; (2) addiction to ritualistic behavior and routines; and (3) the use of private, isolated time to fantasize and maintain one's self-hatred.

ADDICTION TO PHYSICAL SUBSTANCES

Food as an Addictive Substance

Many children eventually learn to substitute eating for the love and companionship that is missing in the family situation. Food then becomes their major focus and overeating may become a well-established habit. Later, as an adult, a person's attempt to cope with obesity can become as destructive as the original eating disorder. A cycle of overeating, then dieting, compulsively acted out during the course of a lifetime, affects not only one's physical health, but it can also become extremely detrimental to one's emotional well-being. When they become part of a self-gratifying, inward process, both concern with dieting and overeating are functionally maladaptive.

> Some years ago, a physician referred a patient to me whose problem with overweight was complicated by a long-standing dependency on prescription diet pills. When Mrs. R., thirty-one, finally sought professional help, she had been struggling for

many years to break her addiction to several types of diet-related drugs, an addiction that started when she was twelve years old.

Although Mrs. R. was a well-respected instructor at a local college and a woman of exceptional intelligence, she was rarely able to go through a full day of teaching without a large number of amphetamines. Terrified by a close call with death after ingesting a combination of amphetamines and alcohol, the patient decided to seek professional help and was eventually referred for psychotherapy.

Mrs. R.'s history revealed a lifelong focus on dieting. Commencing at three years old when her mother placed her on a strict diet to qualify her as a model for a baby commercial, through puberty when a doctor prescribed diuretics in response to her mother's concern about her "unusual" metabolism, the young woman became dependent on diet drugs and developed an image of herself as different from other girls her age. The nightmare continued in college and graduate school where Mrs. R., still striving for perfection and some sign of approval from her parents, was forced to live furtively, obtaining pills where she could.

Mrs. R.'s therapy included elimination of all diet drugs, identification and separation from the attacks of her destructive "voice," and use of a dieting method that broke into her inward, self-nourishing style.

In her sessions, the patient focused on her deceptively seductive "voice" that urged her to eat her favorite foods and then savagely attacked her after the indulgence. Her insights into the myriad self-attacks with which she tormented herself dispelled some of her hopelessness and motivated her to lose weight in a sensible manner. During the therapy, as Mrs. R. approached her ideal weight, this "voice" became even more active. In one session she enumerated her attacks on herself and discovered that each one could be traced to a distorted image she had of herself as a woman. She found herself thinking, "You may be losing weight, but nobody notices, especially men." "You're still unattractive; your clothes just hang on you." "You're ugly anyway, so why bother to lose weight."

The end result of this series of attacks was an almost overpowering urge to cheat on her diet. Mrs. R.'s voice effectively supported her self-nourishing habits as well as her negative self-image. Traditional methods of controlling her food intake had not worked for her because of her inward style of self-parenting. Her stubborn habit patterns originally developed because of severe emotional deprivation during early childhood. These defense patterns were preserved and administered by her destructive voice.

To combat this inward, self-nourishing style of dieting, I suggested to Mrs. R. that she utilize a technique that appears to interfere with long-standing eating disorders by breaking into the patient's illusion of being self-sufficient. This technique, described in the literature as *The Love Diet* (Jansen & Catlett, 1978), involves the dieter including a friend in her diet. The friend plans the entire menu for the dieter, the dieter eating only what is given by the friend. In this way, inward secretive methods are interrupted and contact with another person replaces preoccupation with food and dieting. A real friendship is substituted for internal self-feeding.

At the other extreme in the category of eating disorders, anorexia nervosa is also associated with self-feeding. The patient (generally a female) may alternate between self-starvation and bulimia (gorging and self-induced vomiting). In this situation, the patient exercises total control over her food intake. Often, the process of not eating has become the sole focus of the anorexic patient's struggle to find some sense of identity. These patients often have little sense of what they feel, physically or emotionally; and they lack a clear awareness of the sensation of hunger.

Dr. Hilde Bruch (1973), writing about the anorexic patient in *Eating Disorders*, states that:

> If . . . a mother's reaction [in feeding the infant] is continuously inappropriate, be it neglectful, oversolicitous, inhibiting, or indiscriminately permissive, the outcome for the child will be a perplexing confusion. When he is older he will not be able to discriminate between being hungry or sated, or between nutritional need and some other discomfort or tension. (p. 56)

Very early, children raised by mothers with the characteristics described above realize, on some level, that they cannot trust their mother adequately to feed or nourish them. They attempt to take control of this basic process and "nourish themselves." However, their disturbed perception of their internal state makes even this primitive adjustment tenuous. The anorexic patient's methods of taking care of herself are desperate attempts to ward off extreme anxiety and panic or to escape emotional involvement with a controlling, intrusive mother. These maneuvers may lead to bizarre eating behavior and destructive fasting. The patient usually reports feeling terrified of "taking the first bite of food, for fear that I'll never be able to stop eating."

Anorexia nervosa and obesity are conditions that reflect the use of food for purposes other than sustenance; these disorders indicate that food has taken on a separate, specialized meaning. The anorexic patient refuses food in order to have some semblance of control over her life. It can also represent a defiant oppositional gesture toward the parent who wants her to eat.

The most significant factor is that both habits, overeating and self-starvation, preserve the patients' illusion that they can take care of themselves, because they temporarily alleviate anxiety. Indeed, the strict regulation that the anorexic patient exerts over food intake serves in some cases to avert further regression into a psychotic state. In summary, as is so often the case in other self-nourishing habits, the dynamics revolve around the central issue of control and self-parenting.

Dependence on Alcohol

A compulsive need for self-nourishment and control is also characteristic of an individual's addiction to alcohol, cigarettes, and drugs of various kinds. Anxiety that is allayed by these substances will come to the foreground when the "drug" is given up by the patient. The perceived loss of control that accompanies withdrawal leaves the person in a disoriented state, feeling helpless and at the mercy of outside forces. Regression to childish behaviors and angry outbursts of temper are common.

The compulsive eater, the drug-user, the alcoholic, all deny their dependency on other persons and have pseudo-independent attitudes— "I can feed myself, I have my own bottle."

> One patient, an alcoholic man, a professor at a nearby university, was very meek and self-depreciating in manner. Yet in relation to stopping his drinking, he was extremely defiant and hostile, saying to his therapist, "Don't tell me what to do." In his dependency on alcohol, he had succeeded in denying his need for real people. His stubborn refusal to break his addiction to this self-nourishing habit caused him to terminate therapy after a few months, precluding any progress he might have made in other areas of his life.

The determinants of substance addiction—alcoholism, drug abuse, and eating disorders—are varied, yet each behavior or habit is an attempt on the part of the patient to numb primal pain from the past as well as suffering due to present-day frustration and stress. In every case, the patients' addiction supports the fantasy that they can somehow "feed" and care for themselves. However, in repeatedly turning to these habits for relief and for a sense of control over their pain, the person progressively blocks out important emotional reactions. In this manner, they become more incapacitated in their ability to work productively or to function adequately in social situations. They come to exist in a dazed, cut-off state for long periods of time and damage their personal relationships. Friends and family experience considerable suffering and become increasingly alienated as this process spirals downward.

ADDICTION TO ROUTINES AND HABITUAL RESPONSES

Almost any repetitive behavior or ritual may be used to dull one's sensitivity to painful feelings and can be said to have addictive qualities. A person who suffers from a high degree of emotional stress in life may easily fall prey to habits that are tension reducing. Once these patterns are formed, any behavior seems preferable to the anxiety that the person would experience if these routines were to be interrupted.

Early childhood compulsions illustrate the compelling nature of ritualistic behaviors. Everyone remembers certain favorite phrases they repeated over and over as children. "Step on a crack, break your grandmother's back," and other magical slogans are traditionally chanted over and over by children. Youngsters will repeatedly count up to a certain number or sing a favorite song over and over again. Some adults make elaborate lists, over-planning every detail of their day. Many people insist on having their ritual morning cup of coffee before they can function adequately. Some people who live alone go through nightly rituals of looking under their beds, inside their closets, and compulsively checking the locks on the doors many times before retiring. Family observations of holidays, birthdays, and reunions are often ritualistic in nature, and are characterized by much formality and role-playing. Religious rituals are observed to ease pain and grief. They provide needed structure to relieve the anxiety inherent in the issues of life and death.

Ritualistic activities take an enormous importance in severely disturbed children. A colleague who worked at a residential children's treatment center told of her young patients' insistence that things always be kept the same—the daily routines as well as each piece of furniture in the room. In an attempt systematically to desensitize these autistic and schizophrenic children to gradual changes in their environment, it was decided that the tables, chairs, easels, and desks would be rearranged each morning in the children's classroom. Additional teachers and therapists were on hand to handle the ensuing panic and anxiety in the children, which were immediately aroused when they entered the room.

The children were "contained" physically, held and reassured, and gradually their panic abated. Each day their anxiety eased somewhat and gradual changes were also made each day in the furnishings of the day-room in the cottage where the children lived. This program had the incidental effect of intruding into these patients' fantasy world and, to some degree, decreased their autistic self-stimulatory behaviors. The significant feature in this experiment was the amount of anxiety and panic that was aroused in the children during the first few days. This phenomenon was evidence of the fact that rigidity and routines served the purpose of keeping the children's anxiety and panic from becoming conscious or out of control. Similarly, neurotic patients often unknowingly adhere to strict schedules and daily routines in order to avoid anxiety. Routines offer a false sense of permanence and a feeling of certainty, yet their negative side effect is to deaden the individual as a feeling person.

Many destructive habits and routines are generally seen as acceptable, even desirable. Children and adults both spend countless hours viewing television; men and women spend large blocks of time jogging, working out, and exercising, and though physical-fitness routines are beneficial to one's health, they nonetheless can become largely self-involved and narcissistic activities.

> A young man whom I saw in therapy during his late teens had become totally dedicated to body-building exercises and physical fitness programs. As a young boy, he had been mercilessly teased and ridiculed by his father and older brothers for his slight build and sickly appearance. Now as a seventeen year-old, he spent his free time each day working out with weights, jogging, and taking karate lessons. As a result, he had no social life to speak of and led an isolated existence.
>
> Running and working out had become an obsession for him. Although he bore no physical resemblance to the weak, sickly boy he had once been, these habits still persisted. This patient had never really faced his inner feelings about himself or his body. He had compensated for feeling weak and inadequate by developing his physique together with an exaggerated image of his power. His routines of exercise and jogging kept him one step removed from painful feelings of inferiority. He was using his fantasy of having a strong body (now a reality) to nourish himself and feed his vanity. Still, his underlying pain and poor self-image remained. He was only able to deal with these underlying emotions after he had stopped acting out the compensatory behavior.

Masturbation as Self-Gratification

Early in his or her development, the child learns that thumb-sucking yields pleasure and satisfaction. Later the child discovers that touching the genitals leads to pleasant sensations as well as relief from tensions. This activity gradually becomes a soothing, isolated method of taking care of oneself. If the child is found masturbating and reprimanded, he or she learns to be secretive and ashamed of the habit. Later the child creates sexual fantasies while gratifying him or herself, and will become inward and secretive about sexual thoughts as well.

The continuation of habitual masturbation, after the person is mature and there are sexual partners available, is symbolic of the self-feeding process and a rejection of one's need for love and sex from outside. As such, it reflects a pseudo-independent posture and is indicative of a fantasy bond or connection with the mother.

Seriously disturbed children often masturbate compulsively and this behavior is partly a compensation for serious deprivation as an infant. In one residential facility an experiment was carried out with an eight year-old boy suffering from a schizoid disorder of childhood. He masturbated for prolonged periods each night before falling asleep. He was offered a glass of milk at bedtime, and a glass of milk was also placed by his bed before he went to sleep. As a result, there was a dramatic reduction in masturbatory activity. It appeared that this willingness to accept real nourishment from the nurses or technicians freed him from his fixation on his own method of satisfying himself.

In another case, a twenty-nine year-old male patient was struggling to break long-time habitual patterns of sexual self-gratification. He routinely attended pornographic movies and masturbated, while at the same time ostensibly deploring the lack of female companionship in his life and his inability to maintain an ongoing relationship with a woman.

As he progressed in breaking with these habit patterns, this man was able to develop a romantic attachment to a woman and began to date her on a regular basis. However, as the relationship continued, he reported anxiety and a compulsion to return to self-gratification. He was contemplating the possibility of their living together when he once again slipped back into his old patterns of behavior. Later, as he succeeded in controlling the impulse to masturbate, his relationship with the woman showed significant improvement. As his tolerance for positive gratification and the attendant anxiety increased, he was able to hold on to the progress he had made in therapy. There was a clear relationship between the breakdown of this patient's self-nourishing, fantasy-oriented defense system and his ability to seek and maintain real gratification from the outside world.

Addiction to Compulsive Work

People often use what might otherwise be constructive work activities to cut off feelings and soothe pain. The "workaholic" is an individual who has developed compulsive and routine habit patterns of work to ease anxiety in a manner that is not only accepted but encouraged by society. To block out their personal lives, isolated workers, such as bookkeepers, accountants, computer programmers, engineers, etc., have a unique opportunity to reduce their anxiety because these activities are harmonious with an inward life style.

The interruption of routine and habitual working patterns which occurs sometimes, for example, on a vacation, often generates a temporary happy and "alive" feeling in the individual. The person seems to experience a sense of renewed energy that is released by breaking the deadening routines that had previously dulled excitement as well as pain. Often the specific conditions and limited duration of a vacation seem to allow an individual temporarily to break with routines and "enjoy life." It is likely that a permanent break from such routines would cause anxiety in the same individual. Indeed, some people are unable to break their chains and confinement for even a short period of time, and find vacations intolerable.

The workday world usually includes activities that are routine or habitual. Work generally provides only superficial contact with other people. Interpersonal relations are complicated by role-playing, cliché exchanges, hostility, and politicking. The work environment in most cases serves to alienate people from themselves and their feelings. They return to their homes in an insulated state and find it difficult to relax and make personal contact with their families.

Routinized Sexual Experiences as Pain Relievers and Tension Reducers

A person who is blocking out a large part of his or her emotional experience finds it difficult to have close and loving sexual contact. Such a person may, in fact, use sexual experiences as a defense against feeling and closeness.

Couples often develop a routine and mechanical style of lovemaking that includes withholding of affection and tenderness and a dulling of sexual responses. Their "voice attacks" create self-consciousness and a feeling of being "spaced out" or removed from the real situation. Symptomatic of this type of cut-off contact is the reaction of feeling depleted following the experience. The partner may feel especially hungry or thirsty or may fall into an unusually deep, but not necessarily restful, sleep.

> A male patient, while alone on a business trip for several days, experienced deep insights about the lovemaking between himself and his wife. He was afflicted with anxiety and insomnia while on the business trip, which he attributed to the tensions of his work day. He realized that at home he used routine and unfeeling sex with his wife as a narcotic to repress these feelings of anxiety. He shared this insight with his wife and this encouraged the couple to attempt to recapture their early spontaneous feelings of excitement and close contact while making love.

SELF-DESTRUCTIVE USE OF PRIVATE, ISOLATED TIME

There are both positive and negative uses of private time. Sometimes, individuals use their time alone for creating, planning, or constructive introspection. However, private time is often used as an opportunity for losing oneself in fantasy, indulging in self-nourishing habits, and hating oneself.

Put to such use, lengthy periods of time alone are not only unnecessary to an individual's well-being but are often destructive. It has been my experience that reducing the amount of time spent alone in isolated activities can have an extremely positive impact on psychological development.

In a wide variety of settings, I have observed a correlation between the reduction of private, inward time spent by disturbed individuals and their development of a sense of vitality, optimism, and enthusiasm. *I have concluded that an increase in time spent alone, unless utilized for concentrated work, creativity, or relaxation, generally leads to an increase in depression and self-hatred.* This hypothesis has apparent validity in a large number of cases.

> One such case involved a young woman who was deteriorating physically, including serious weight loss, as a result of a long-standing alcoholic problem. Cynthia, thirty, led an extremely reclusive life and had convinced herself that she would never marry and have children.

An essential element of her therapy involved suggesting she take practical steps to make acquaintances and engage in social activities. As she complied with these suggestions, Cynthia felt compelled to set aside more and more time to be alone to "replenish herself." The development of friendships created the inevitable anxiety caused by interference with her self-protective defenses.

To cope with this anxiety Cynthia felt the need to retreat to her apartment to "revitalize" herself. She felt secure in this private world where no one would intrude. However, as she developed in therapy, she gradually realized that the time she spent alone was really used to strengthen her defenses and avoid her new friends.

Cynthia also noted that she fell prey to significant attacks from her "voice" during her time in isolation. She felt that this was reminiscent of her childhood when she found seclusion alone in the bathroom, away from the stormy arguments and hostility between members of her family. As a child, she had had to share a bedroom with her brothers, so her time alone had become a precious commodity. As an adult, she habitually used her time alone to reinstate the authority of her voice and to fantasize. The solitude that may well have preserved her sanity as a child had now become a self-destructive and self-hating time that prevented her from making progress in therapy. It was only by gradually weaning herself from the hours of isolation that Cynthia was able to develop and sustain personal relationships and alter her defenses to permit real gratification and freedom of movement.

RATIONALIZING SELF-NOURISHING HABIT PATTERNS

It seems clear that people develop and utilize numerous habit patterns and routines in an effort to blunt feelings from the past as well as in the present. Since these techniques not only diminish or repress painful feelings but also destroy the ability to feel love, closeness, happiness, and excitement, they create a condition that is simply wasteful of the human potential for a richer life. These deadening habits, routines, and techniques are often rationalized in everyday life.

Drug users often insist that the substances give them a feeling of self-confidence and additional enthusiasm to perform well or be creative. They frequently declare that the consumption of a few drinks or a joint, etc., makes it possible for them to be less inhibited sexually or more relaxed in a social situation. Overweight people rave about the joy of eating and the necessity for eating and drinking as part of job-related entertaining. However, all of these rationalizations seem perverse in light of the self-destructive effect of the excesses.

These methods can become important elements in the neurotic individual's attempt to deaden his or her life. In a drugged or cut-off state, people are easily capable of acting against their best interests. They are more likely to behave in ways that deviate from their stated goals and damage their most important relationships. In any event, people need all of their consciousness and sensitivity to cope with real-life stresses. It is extremely dangerous to rationalize the use of self-destructive substances. Even where the pattern does not lead to actual life-threatening activities, the negative effects of these techniques should never be minimized.

One of the most destructive processes found in couple relationships is the acting out, by either partner, of subtle suicidal impulses through indulgence in self-destructive or self-limiting activities. A wife urging her husband to diet because she is concerned that his excess weight will have a damaging effect on his health is, in a sense, asking him to stop committing suicide. His refusal to comply and the resulting fear and "nagging" on her part become part of a negative dependency that is symptomatic of a bond.

A Bond as an Addiction to Another Person

Becoming dependent on another person out of a desire for security is one of the most prevalent forms of human addiction and plays a prominent role in the deterioration of couple and family relationships. The process of forming addictive bonds that takes place in most families in conventional society contributes to practically every condition of unhappiness in human beings: neurosis, psychosis, juvenile delinquency, psychosomatic illness, to mention only a few.

The loss of feeling in individuals in our society has been accompanied by anxiety and has led to the alienation of people one from the other. Indications of this contemporary anomie and isolation have increasingly come to the surface in the form of divorces and a partial breakdown of the family and the church. These symptoms of anxiety and alienation have mistakenly been considered to be the causes of emotional distress and neurosis. The *real* cause, however, lies in the defensive process which characterizes the conventional family. Parental dishonesty, role-playing, and suppression of spontaneity (the symptoms of a bond between parents), are the most significant causes of the damage sustained by our young people.

Conclusion

There are specific types of therapeutic intervention for patients who are strongly addicted to self-nourishing habits. The patient's lack of self-direction and self-control, combined with an unusually self-protective, self-nourishing style, points to one important prerequisite for this type of therapy: it is generally necessary for the patient to give up addictions to particular substances or routines before any real therapy takes place.

The difficulty with this approach is that it obviously meets with strong resistance. Patients often project their own desire to change and their original wish to break these destructive habits onto the therapist, and then perceive the therapist as trying to get them to change. Patients thus engage in what they think is a battle of wills and imagine that they are defying the therapist's demands. To counter this resistance, the therapist must not join in this battle of wills but be firm and matter-of-fact and *not* assume a proprietary responsibility for a patient's development.

There are other character traits of seriously "addicted patients" that influence the general direction and form for effective psychotherapy. Their compulsive need for control, their emotional immaturity, their intolerance of pain and anxiety, their extreme dependency on substances *and on other people,* their tendency to be passive and to rely on fantasy, their intense hunger for love and approval, must be dealt with in the ongoing transference relationship with the therapist. The primary aim of psychotherapy with these patients is to control the acting out. Without this discipline, the therapy will certainly fail. Secondarily, the underlying dynamics must be exposed as they recur in the present context. The therapist must help the patient re-experience the painful feelings and deep frustration that originally caused the person to seek gratification inwardly. The initial deprivation began at the oral stage of development, when the patient was totally dependent on the mother for survival and environmental support. As an adult the patient still believes on a deep level that he or she would not survive if ever again to experience these primitive wants and the anticipated rejection.

These patients must become aware of their ongoing needs and desires and use the therapeutic situation to ask symbolically for what they want, to learn to tolerate the resulting frustration, and to discover that they can survive without environmental support. In the course of facing their anger in the transference situation, they strengthen their independence and become separated from the bond with the mother or family. They begin to perceive the possibility of relating to the therapist on a more equal basis. By recognizing that they can never obtain the gratification they so desperately needed as children, that, in fact, these needs are no longer vital to survival nor even to happiness, they can progress to a point in their development where they are able to tolerate, even enjoy, their separateness and independence.

PART II

THEORETICAL ISSUES

Chapter 11

SEPARATION, REGRESSION, AND FUSION

Death and birth resemble each other, say the Rabbis. Suppose a child in its mother's womb to know that after a lapse of time it will leave the place it occupies. That would seem to it the most grievous thing that could happen. It is so comfortable in the element that surrounds it and protects it against outside influences. However, the time of separation approaches, with terror it sees the protecting envelopes torn asunder and it believes the hour of death has arrived.

From the *Talmud* in Otto Rank's *Will Therapy and Truth and Reality* (1936/1972, p. 184)

The process of individuation, whereby a person increasingly differentiates oneself from the mother, occurs naturally throughout one's lifetime. It is obvious, however, that psychological growth and increasing independence never proceed smoothly nor is the child's development consistently directed toward progressive differentiation. Each successive stage of maturity confronts the child and later, the adult, with the basic facts of personal existence—aloneness and separateness, as well as the vulnerability to death. Each step forward is accompanied by reminders of the terror of being abandoned as a totally dependent infant. Each phase is also marked by guilt at leaving the mother behind, and by anger and resentment at having to face the world alone. Whenever this fear becomes overwhelming or when the individual is unable to bear the guilt or face the anger at separation, he or she once again reverts to self-nourishing methods of defense. Generally speaking, there is regression to a previous level of development, with the accompanying tendency to form a bond or imaginary connection with significant others. Regression to an earlier stage of relating, where there appeared to be more security, tends to fixate behavior at that level and leads to the perseveration of a childlike immaturity.

As stated earlier, neurosis is a response, in part, to a natural fear—the terror and anxiety that surround our awareness of death. However, a maladaptive fear reaction and dread of separation occur long before the child learns about death. These are the infant's responses to the all-encompassing pain and anxiety which is felt in experiencing frustration. The anticipatory dread of abandonment and fearful reaction to separation are related to the infant's total dependency on the mother to gratify its needs. Beyond a certain age, both fears—fear of separation from objects and fear of death—affect the child as he or she moves from complete dependence and symbiosis to independence and self-support.

In his conceptualization of the neurotic process, Otto Rank defined life as a succession of weaning experiences that create anxiety. His description of an individual's reactions to progressive separations from the maternal figure is analogous to my theoretical approach to regression. I conceive of *regression as the defense mechanism that is used to heal the fracture in the original fantasy bond with the mother caused by indications of separation.* Regression represents an unconscious decision to return to a state of imaginary fusion with the mother or parents. This fantasized connection or bond exists internally in the patient's imagination, and is expressed externally by acting out in a passive or dependent mode in relation to the real world.

Rank (1936/1972) emphasized that the anticipation of separating from the therapist has a powerful impact on the patient. He wrote that "the authentic meaning of the therapeutic process . . . comes to expression only in the end phase," that is, in the termination of therapy when the patient must separate from the therapist. Rank made the dynamics of the ending of therapy his focal point from the beginning in the hope that his patients would learn to deal with the problem of separation. Their reactions to this crucial central issue of separation revealed the core conflict. Rank recognized the danger that regression would take place at this crucial separation, which he viewed as symbolically representing birth. He was well aware of the patient's desire to remain ill and dependent on the therapist, a wish which expressed itself in the patient's repeated efforts to prolong the therapeutic process by reverting to old symptoms and by bringing up material that had previously been worked through.

It has been my experience that the patient who is approaching termination of therapy reverts to symptom formation because of the fear of breaking the bond with the therapist. It can be said that the patient is reacting adversely to the positive event of getting well. Paradoxically, good feelings about change and improvement lead into the inevitable problem of separation, which the person dreads.

Psychosis is a more extreme manifestation of this regression and imagined reconnection. Hospitalized psychotic patients have typically regressed to an infantile level in many areas of their lives. In their attempts to find safety and connectedness in fantasy, they are progressively debilitated in reality. Their regressive behaviors are supported by similar patterns in fellow patients and fostered by institutional life to such an extent that they often become fixated at a lower level of functioning.

On the other hand, regression in the normal or neurotic individual, though not as maladaptive as in psychosis, also represents an attempt to elicit parental responses from others in order to create the illusion of being taken care of. Thus, both neurosis and psychosis are characterized by the patient's desperate attempt to recapture the security and the sense of oneness with the parent. The longing to merge with the parental figure is an individual's most basic response to fear of separation and anxiety about death.

SEPARATION

Separation is a vital part of the human life process. It begins at birth with the actual physical separation from the mother, referred to by many authors as the birth trauma. The severing of the infant's connection to the mother's body, the cutting of the umbilical cord, marks the first step in a lifelong process of individuation. At a later stage, the infant's psychological birth is marked by a dawning awareness that it is not a part of its mother's body, that it is not the center of the universe, and that its desires and needs are not always immediately gratified. The realization about this basic condition of separateness is, in some sense, an emotional shock from which the individual never fully recovers. The child copes with the fear and frustration brought about by this new awareness of separateness by using the emerging powers of imagination to create an internal image of the mother's breast. These fears are somewhat relieved as the child becomes more adept at calling this image to mind whenever hungry or afraid. This primitive fantasy connection to the mother is used by the child to mend the first break in its blissful union with her.

Human beings face dramatic events that originate from two basic sources. First, there are the inevitable traumas of life: poverty, injustices, inequalities, illness, and eventual death. These negative experiences are beyond our control. The second category of trauma is the unnecessary damage caused by parental deficiencies. The parent's inadequacies and defenses lead to insensitive treatment which injures the child and causes unnecessary feelings of isolation and pain. Children who suffer this type of trauma suffer more intensely because of residual primal feelings, and react more negatively to the inevitable separations that occur at normal developmental stages in their lives. The fact of separation alone is not necessarily traumatic. Separation is painful to the degree that the child reacts to the new situation with primitive emotional reactions from the past and therefore experiences unnecessary dread in response to the current situation. In other words, the child who is deprived or rejected will tend to over-react to successive separations throughout life.

DEVELOPMENTAL STAGES OF INDIVIDUATION AND SEPARATION

The growing child passes through a succession of stages beginning with the earliest phase when it still believes that it is connected to or is a part of the mother's body. At the time of weaning, there is unusual frustration, which leads to an expanding awareness of being separate yet still dependent. In this fear, the child partially shifts dependency from the breast or bottle to a dependence on thumb-sucking and other self-gratifying mechanisms combined with imagination and fantasy. It pretends that it can feed itself and develops a fantasy bond of imagined self-sufficiency. Following regression to this primitive level, the child gradually adapts to the new condition of being separate and learns that even though the mother may go away temporarily, she still returns. In the new phase, the child learns to trust in the constancy of the mother's presence through periods of her absence.

When the infant is weaned, when the toddler learns to walk, when the child starts school, when the adolescent graduates, when the young person goes away to college, and when the adult marries and has children, he or she is forced to recognize that there is movement farther and farther away from the mother and father and other members of the family. Each event creates new situations that are potentially traumatic because they signify the loss of parental support. Each separation, whether symbolic or real, is capable of causing the person to regress to a time period before he or she was aware of the new quality of separateness. Individually, each person retreats to the specific level of functioning that immediately preceded the experiencing of a particularly painful point of separation in life.

Primitive reactions to separations are common in adult life. Many individuals seek professional help at this time because they experience emotional distress when their bonds are broken.

> A patient, whose wife had divorced him some months previously, was troubled by anxiety attacks. In the process of experiencing an emotionally intense reliving of a scene from his past, the basic pain of his childhood flashed before him:
>
> "I pictured myself sitting in something small, a sandbox, in back of my house. Without even seeing them, I knew that my parents were there. I knew the ways they had been destructive to me from what I'd learned in therapy and how much I had counted on the things that they said they would do for me but which they never did. But it was so important that they were there, the whole image of them and me, together. It's a part of me. All the rest of it didn't matter as long as I could have them and everything that goes with them in the past. All the images that made up my life as a child: the street, my sister, my aunts and uncles, the car, the dog, all of the things that are me. When I think about walking away from that and that I could never go back, I just know that something terrible would happen if I would walk away. There's nobody there, there's nothing. I just don't have anybody, at all. It's this past, these people, and that world that somehow defines me. I can't imagine what I would be like if I wasn't like I am. It's really like stepping off into nothingness."

This man, who was approaching middle age, still held on to an old image of himself as helpless, which was symbolic of his bond with his family. Since the divorce he had become increasingly incompetent and passive in his work. His longing for the past was a desire to return to a point in his life before he was aware of himself as an independent person, separate from his family. It was interesting to note that the patient's anxiety diminished subsequent to this line of interpretation. He realized that his unrealistic hope for a reconciliation with his wife was connected to his desire to keep the memory of his family and home alive. The fear of breaking his bond with his wife, despite the poor relationship in actuality, is typical of separation anxiety. Once he faced the hopelessness of reconciliation and further severed his ties with his wife, he began to improve.

EMOTIONAL REACTIONS TO SEPARATION

The great source of terror in infancy is solitude.
William James (1890)

Psychoanalytic theory has attempted to explain behavior associated with specific developmental periods and has increasingly emphasized specific infantile and childhood experiences and their derivative behaviors found in the adult personality (Katz, 1981). It is evident from observing the developing child that powerful emotions accompany each crucial step in the process of individuation. Of particular importance in understanding regression is an analysis of the child's feeling reactions to separation, both symbolic and real, that mark the transition from one developmental stage to the next.

Anxiety

Proposed theories about the psychodynamics of children's emotional responses to separation are numerous and diverse. Bowlby's (1973) review of the literature summarizes a number of important hypotheses ranging from Freud's first writings to more recent theories. In *Three Essays On The Theory of Sexuality,* Freud (1905/1953) states that: "Anxiety in children is originally nothing other than an expression of the fact that they are feeling the loss of the person they love" (p. 224).

Melanie Klein's (1948/1964) theory of "depressive anxiety" indicates that separation anxiety stems from the young child's belief that when the mother disappears, the child has eaten her or otherwise destroyed her. This belief, she says, arises from the ambivalent feelings a child has for the mother.

> Along with a certain proportion of libidinal impulses, [the child has] very large quantities of aggressive ones. . . . He perceives his anxiety arising from his aggressive instincts as fear of an external object. . . . The infant has, incidentally, some real grounds for fearing its mother, since it becomes growingly aware that she has the power to grant or withhold the gratification of its needs. (p. 269)

This theory would imply the development of guilt in the child as a consequence of entertaining such beliefs. Feelings of sadness generally accompany the melancholy described by Klein. However, other theorists question the ability of the young infant to directly experience feelings of grief or mourning.

The concept of "frustrated attachment" describes the "child's pleasure in his mother's presence as being as primary as his pleasure in food and warmth" (Bowlby, 1973). This concept emphasizes "separation of a young child from an attachment figure as in itself distressing and also as providing a condition in which intense fear is readily aroused. As a result, when a child senses any further prospect of separation some measure of anxiety is aroused in him" (p. 376-377).

The author believes that the infant's attachment to the mother develops naturally as a result of having its need for love-food adequately met. However, to the extent that the care the child receives is inadequate or inconsistent, unnecessary anxiety and frustration are aroused. Then the anxiety that the infant experiences at the realization of separateness is compounded by the pain and anxiety of not having its basic needs satisfied. When emotional pain is very intense, the child's attachment shifts to a powerful fantasy bond with the mother. It is important to emphasize that anxiety reactions do *not* necessarily diminish in intensity as the child matures. In anticipating the breaking of bonds, the adult at times still anticipates being overwhelmed by separation anxiety.

At a specific developmental stage, separation anxiety becomes associated with the knowledge and dread of death. After this critical point, whenever individuals progress to a new stage of individuation, they are struck simultaneously with an awareness of *both* existential conditions, their aloneness and eventual death. It is this connecting link that ties together the personality dynamics of the psychoanalyst and the more philosophic beliefs of the existentialist. The two theories overlap in noting the importance of both separation anxiety and death anxiety, and each attempts to explain this phenomenon.

Anger

One of the most profound effects a parent can have on a child is to threaten abandonment. On one hand a child is enraged and terrified by parental threats of desertion, while on the other hand, the child dare not express this anger because he or she fears the actual loss of the parent. Anger at the parent is usually repressed and directed at other targets. Periods of separation, threats of separation, and other forms of rejection are capable of arousing both anxiety and dysfunctional anger. A child may be furiously angry at one moment with a parent, while at the next moment seeking reassurance and contact.

Bowlby (1973), in noting the frequency with which anger is aroused after a loss, raised the question of its biological function.

> The answer proposed is that whenever separation is only temporary, . . . it [anger] has the following two functions: first, it may assist in overcoming such obstacles as there may be to re-union; second, it may discourage the loved person from going away again. (p. 247)

He concludes that "Angry coercive behaviour, acting in the service of an affectional bond, is not uncommon."

Angry manipulations on the part of children elicit feelings of guilt and obligation in parents, thereby strengthening the fantasy bond. On the other hand, this process works both ways. When an older child or adolescent indicates movement toward increased independence or sepa-rateness, many parents display a wide range of angry, pleading, guilt-provoking behaviors to bring the youngster back into line. It is obvious that insecure parents often have a stake in keeping their children more helpless and dependent on them than is necessary at every develop-mental stage.

Guilt

Children's guilt in relation to hostile fantasies of destroying the parental figure has been assumed by some clinicians to be a principal cause of the anxiety that they experience during actual separation. How-ever, there may be a more parsimonious explanation for the child's and adolescent's guilt at separating from the parental figure. For example, many of the events that lead to separation are initiated by the child. Bonds or fantasies of connection between parents and children are pow-erful agents of security, often far more important than the realistic se-curity in the actual functioning relationship. Breaking a bond is analog-ous to letting the other person die, because an individual has difficulty maintaining a bond or fantasy connection without the cooperation of the other.

The child feels considerable guilt as he or she experiences the par-ents' distress at the child's growing freedom and independence. If the parents are very immature and dependent, these feelings are exagger-ated and the child will come to feel that movement toward adulthood and personal power is mean or destructive. Later he or she will feel the same guilt in the new bond with a mate. In many instances, there is so much guilt at leaving one's parents that symbolic acts distinguishing oneself from the parent of the same sex, or surpassing the level of the parent's ability or education, or being successful in personal relationships where a parent has failed, lead to considerable remorse and symptom formation.

> In a tentative step toward independence, a six year-old boy asked to visit his relatives in the country. On the drive there, he became very nervous and began to whine and complain. When questioned about his change of mind, the boy, with tears in his eyes, responded with, "My mommy said she would die if something happened to me. I want to go back home so she won't die, so she can see I'm not hurt." Soon after saying this, he relaxed and fell asleep. The boy spent the remaining time alternating between happy times spent in outdoor activity, followed by regressive behavior and nervous inquiries about his mother. It appeared that on the trip, the boy was reminded of his mother's unintentionally destructive statement about her concern for his safety. He felt guilty for enjoying being away from her for an extended period of time.

Overprotectiveness toward children is an important symptom of a strong fantasy bond in the family. It is an outward expression of the illusion of connection and not only damages the child's self-esteem but seriously cramps his or her style and limits the child's freedom.

Threats of desertion or warnings to children that they will be sent away if they are not "good," together with subtle or direct threats of parental suicide, illness, or insanity, occur in families more often than is commonly thought. Chronic statements by parents to the effect that "You'll be the death of me," or that "You're driving me crazy," are all too often taken literally by very young children. However, these parental remarks constitute only a small part of manipulative styles of communication that arouse guilt feelings in children.

Parents who act out self-destructive behaviors, as well as those who deny themselves happiness and enjoyment, arouse tremendous feelings of guilt in their children. This guilt becomes more evident as young people take tentative steps toward breaking emotional ties with their parents. People seldom recognize this guilt fully on a conscious level, yet it manifests itself in a variety of symptomatic behaviors that are maladaptive. For instance, people tend to withhold their capabilities and talents in those areas where their parents were failures. Because of their feelings of guilt, they seriously restrict their active pursuit of personal goals and achievement.

Both real and imagined losses precipitate symptoms of separation anxiety. The necessary and sufficient condition for successful maturation is the availability of the kind of mothering that will enhance the ego capacities vital for psychological growth. Unfortunately, few adults arrive at maturity without experiencing considerable distress. The degree of regression that occurs and its longevity are a function of many variables. The most significant predisposing factor is the amount of emotional deprivation and unnecessary frustration caused by inadequate or insensitive mothering. The more deprivation, the more an individual will become dependent on a fantasy bond and the greater will be the detrimental effect of separation.

REGRESSION AND FUSION

Regression is defined here as a psychological retreat to a prior stage of development in order to reduce fear and foster an illusion of security. Regression acts to obscure the knowledge of separateness through the process of forming a bond, an imaginary connection with another person. Whenever separation anxiety becomes intolerable, an individual unconsciously reverts to a lower level of functioning and represses much affect and richness of feeling in the present.

In describing the dynamics of regression, Freud (1905/1953) wrote:

> An adult who has become neurotic owing to his libido being unsatisfied behaves in his anxiety like a child: he begins to be frightened when he is alone . . . and he seeks to assuage this fear by the most childish measures. (p. 224)

Thus, Freud indirectly associated *regression* and childish behaviors with separation anxiety due to loss of the love object.

The purpose of regression is to relieve the emotional distress and anxiety that accompany separation or loss by denying, on a deep level, the reality of one's existence as a separate person. This denial is accomplished by forming a bond, that is, a dependency relationship where feelings of connection, possessiveness, and belonging prevail. The fantasized connection with persons or substitute symbols is represented in the imagination as well as acted out in actual relationships with other people. The tendency of human beings to revert to a type of thinking and style of behaving that support this illusion is universal and occurs whenever the fear of separateness, aloneness, and death becomes too great. The basic defensive solution to human "primary existential anxiety" is the formation of bonds or illusions of fusion (Fierman, 1965).

Helmuth Kaiser—Fusion-Delusion

Helmuth Kaiser's concept of a delusion of fusion as the universal symptom of neurotic disturbance is analogous to the author's concept of a bond as the core defense. Kaiser postulated that the human being is subject to a basic need for contact with another person, and that "the psychic derivative of this need may be conceptualized as a universal wish or fantasy of fusion" (Fierman, 1965, p. 208). This human propensity was originally described by Kaiser as regressive, but he later abandoned the psychoanalytic approach and terminology for a more empirically-based theory of psychotherapy.

Fierman (1965), in describing Kaiser's theoretical orientation, wrote that:

> The individual blunts and distorts his own awareness of separateness, creates the illusion of fusion, and is precariously gratified on an imaginary basis in a fusion relationship with the other person. . . . The individual is impelled throughout his life by this dual psychological phenomenon: the need for contact and the aversion to awareness of separateness. . . . The universal psychopathology is defined as the attempt to create in real life by behavior and communication the illusion of fusion. (p. 208–209)

Kaiser limited his study to the patient in therapy, who, unable to tolerate his individuality after some point in the therapeutic process, attempts to fuse his personality with that of the therapist. In describing the typical patient, Kaiser remarked, "As his adult intellect does not allow him to maintain an illusion of unity he does something which is a compromise between fusion and mature relationship: Namely, he behaves either submissively or domineeringly." (Fierman, 1965, p. xix) In other words, the regressed individual either defers to authority or acts out a critical, parental role, neither of which represents a genuine *adult* response.

Symptoms of Regression and the Fused State

On a behavioral level, regressed individuals appear to seek environmental support and direction. They give up autonomy and authority over their own lives and desperately try to elicit parental responses. In general, they tend to experience themselves as incomplete, and seek a mate with character traits that they hope will complement their own deficiencies. They attempt to fill the spaces in their personalities by merging their identity with someone else. The dependency relationships that they form tend to have many elements of the early symbiotic infant-maternal relationship. They may alternate between an extremely dependent posture on one hand, and an authoritarian stance when they are in the parental mode.

Self-esteem in a regressed state is regulated by either submission to or defiance of external standards of behavior and moral codes. Emotional well-being appears to depend on the expression of approval or disapproval from significant others. The individual reverts to a repetitive use of the defense mechanisms developed at an earlier stage of growth or at the time of a particularly traumatic separation.

In reverting to childlike behaviors, there is a strong desire to imagine or even provoke rejection from love objects. The regressed patient appears to suffer unnecessarily from imagined and real rejection. Overreactions to slights, pleas for reassurances of love, withholding of personal responses and affection, and overdependent behavior all provoke rejection. Regressive trends also manifest themselves in self-destructive and careless actions that elicit concern and worry from loved ones.

In regressing, the individual attempts to block out genuine feeling reactions appropriate to the present, while at the same time, childish feelings or states of dramatic or heightened emotionality may prevail. The regressed individual usually moves toward an inward existence and often reverts to a state of passivity and confusion. In more serious cases, there can be a remarkable change in looks and deterioration in personal appearance and hygiene. At times, the regressed individual becomes dependent to such an extent as to demand control and regulation.

REGRESSIONS TYPICAL OF SPECIFIC DEVELOPMENTAL STAGES

Regression to infantile or childish behavior may occur at any one of a number of crucial stages in the developmental process. For example, many young children of two and three years of age display a combination of angry temper tantrums and fearful, clinging behavior that is more appropriate to infancy. Regressive traits often manifest themselves during the child's toilet-training experiences. Obstinate withholding behaviors alternating with helpless, more infantile activities such as thumb-sucking are characteristic of this phase of a child's development. Both types of behavior draw the parent into caretaking functions appropriate to an earlier stage. The child is usually successful at manipulating the parents into fulfilling their part of the bond, that is, catering to the child's dependency and presumed helplessness.

Parents mistakenly encourage this type of regression in their children by accepting infantile, acting-out behaviors as part of a "normal" phase. They retreat from the function of properly socializing their child because all too often they refuse to adopt a powerful adult posture in their own lives. Immature parents are too guilty to stop regressive, infantile behaviors in their own children while maintaining childish acting out in their own lives.

Countless examples of regressive trends can be observed in everyday family interaction, as, for instance, when the infant clings possessively to the mother following a temporary separation or when the child starts wetting the bed following the birth of a sibling. The four year-old who has temper tantrums following the parents' divorce, the child who develops school phobia, the young girl whose severe asthma attacks draw exaggerated care and attention from her rejecting mother, and the youngster who refuses to eat or to clean his or her room—all are examples of efforts to manipulate parents or other authority figures to behave in a manner that supports the child's illusion of safety and perpetual care and attention.

Throughout the latency period and into adolescence, regressive behavior is commonplace. Episodes of sleepwalking, facial tics, an inability to concentrate on schoolwork, and simple forgetfulness are indicative of this pattern. Self-destructive habits, ranging in severity from mild forms of self-abuse such as habitual nail-biting, picking at one's skin, and running oneself down, through more serious manifestations such as drug and alcohol abuse, running away, delinquent acts, and suicide attempts, are all examples of regressive behavior. These actions serve two primary purposes; namely, that of reducing the intensity of the anxiety accompanying this turbulent developmental phase and that of eliciting parental, controlling responses.

The unifying concept that explains the secondary rewards of these regressive behaviors and childish tendencies is that of the fantasy bond or imagined state of fusion. These behaviors act to cement the bond by manipulating other persons or institutions into a parental role. The resulting parental responses, in turn, support the illusion of connection.

THE BIPOLAR CAUSALITY OF REGRESSION

Regression has long been recognized by clinicians as being caused by environmental and interpersonal stress and by events that remind the patient of trauma in the past. *Positive events* are also important causative factors, yet their significance has not been sufficiently emphasized heretofore. Regression can be described in terms of a bipolar causality—that is, it is just as likely to be activated by important *positive* events in an individual's life as the opposite. For instance, an unusual success or achievement will, in many cases, trigger a retreat from the kinds of adult activity that led to the accomplishment.

Regression may occur as an after-reaction to experiencing unusually deep personal feelings. As has been noted, members of a couple often pull away from each other after sharing a close, emotional interaction. Usually one partner or the other initiates a childish or provoking ploy in order to draw the other into a parental role. Family life is often characterized by patterns of closeness, followed by emotional withholding, disrespectful interactions, or even hostile exchanges.

Nonconforming behavior or the act of expressing a strong point of view in the face of controversy may generate fear in a person, which in turn can cause one to regress. A heightened sense of individuality can make one feel self-conscious and more aware of separateness. The person who develops a deep friendship or who begins a romantic love affair is taking an emotional risk. One's sense of being vulnerable can arouse considerable anxiety and may influence a return to a more isolated, pseudo-independent posture. Reaching sexual maturity can also lead to regression. A woman who experiences orgasm for the first time after struggling with this problem for a long time often has a tendency to regress.

At the other extreme, the inevitable unpleasant and painful aspects of life are capable of causing regression. *Negative* events such as financial loss, academic failure, and personal rejection arouse levels of anxiety and psychological pain that are difficult to tolerate. Illness, accidents, and the subsequent physical pain often act to precipitate regressive behavior. Hospitalized patients tend to revert to immature attitudes and responses and, in fact, are often treated like children by hospital personnel. Nurses are known for their style of talking to patients in a condescending tone of voice, reminiscent of the manner of a mother addressing her young child. This treatment, together with the patient's weakened condition, supports regressive trends and encourages feelings of helplessness.

A reunion with one's family or mate following a separation is frequently the cause of a return to dependency and passivity. These trends can be clearly seen when a college student, who has been the model of neatness and reliability at school, reverts to slovenliness and immaturity on returning home. Within the typical couple, individuals gradually give up their independence and revert to being one-half of a partnership when reunited following separations. Varying degrees of regression always accompany the surrender of one's sense of separateness and independence.

REGRESSION DUE TO ACHIEVEMENT OR SUCCESS

Serious, long-term regression can occur in reasonably well-adjusted individuals when they experience unusual success or achievement. For instance, well-documented examples of incompetency and inadequate performance often follow promotion and the assumption of executive positions.

> Some years ago, a patient of mine had just achieved an unusual success in the business world. At that time, Mr. R. was a brilliant trial lawyer who decided to expand his avocation of business consulting into a full-time career. After successfully revitalizing one company that had been on the verge of bankruptcy, this man was hired by a rapidly-expanding corporation to manage its expenses and control its growth. The corporation subsequently went public and Mr. R. was appointed its president. Several months later, Mr. R.'s father, who had been ill for many years, died at home. From this point on, Mr. R.'s career appeared to disintegrate.
>
> The most notable change during this time period occurred in Mr. R.'s attitude toward his work. Prior to his appointment as president, he had approached each day as an exciting challenge and had enjoyed a particularly good rapport with associates and employees alike because of his personal warmth and interest. Following his assumption of this leadership position and even prior to his father's death, there had been a noticeable change in Mr. R.'s demeanor. His associates observed that he appeared to be playing the role of president more than actually carrying out the everyday functions of managing the company. He became careless in selecting new personnel for management positions and delegated work and responsibilities to new employees without properly determining their level of knowledge or competency. Following his father's death, Mr. R. became increasingly dependent on his associates and employees.
>
> The death of Mr. R.'s father, occurring when it did, undoubtedly accentuated the regressive trends already present following Mr. R.'s appointment as company head. Both events, one positive, the other negative, acted as catalysts for intense anxiety states. Both symbolized separation: the first effectively sym-

bolized Mr. R's rise to maturity and independence. By assuming leadership he no longer had a "parent" to look to for direction, support, or guidance. The second, the actual death of his father, was experienced as a real loss of dependency and support. Incidentally, for a year following his father's death, Mr. R. could not erase the image of his father's dead body being carried out of his house and into the waiting ambulance. This picture tormented him in recurring nightmares in which he himself felt in danger of death.

Regressions such as the one described above are not uncommon in individuals who reach certain levels of maturity, achieve leadership positions, or pass specific symbolic and actual milestones, such as marriage and parenthood. It is difficult to convince a withholding person of his or her retreat from power and responsibility because he or she still tends to go through the motions of leadership. In this case, it required many months of working through the underlying causes of his regression with a therapist before Mr. R. could assimilate, on an emotional level, the drastic effects of his retreat and, from there, begin a steady movement toward recovery.

Holding on to the "Inner Child"

Regressive behavior in adults indicates the presence of unintegrated parts of the ego that have become fixated at certain points or stages during the child's development. It has been my experience that most individuals retain childish modes of responding to the interpersonal environment. Under certain anxiety-provoking circumstances, whether positive or negative, these immature levels of functioning come to the foreground.

Many people appear to have preserved in their imaginations representations or images of themselves as small children. The adult tends to hold on to this mental image of the self as a "noble, misunderstood" child as if it were a necessary part of the personality, and seems unwilling to part with it. The grown person has an illusion that one can maintain this child-self, and it is this image that one protects, caters to, feels sorry for, and otherwise parents as part of the self-nourishing process.

People attempt to preserve the world of the child and move in that direction whenever they become too frightened to live in the adult world. Under stressful conditions, they are capable of reverting instantaneously to childlike behaviors and communications. In this way, they reassure themselves that their "inner child" is still alive, an illusion which gives them a feeling of being suspended in life and contributes to a false sense of immortality.

BECOMING A PARENT AND SUBSEQUENT REGRESSION

Whenever an individual senses that the time has come to renounce behavior and personality characteristics appropriate to a previous stage, separation anxiety will be aroused. Having a child of one's own, though in itself a positive experience, nevertheless implies a *separation from or a letting go of one's fantasized child-self*. It has the symbolic meaning, too, of killing the parent. The destruction of both internalized images is tantamount to giving up the self-parenting process on which one has become so dependent. In addition, becoming a parent symbolizes an end to the hope of ever receiving the love and attention that one was denied as a child.

This critical transition has a symbolic and a real meaning far deeper than that of merely fulfilling the new role of "parent:" it denotes a natural progression that takes a person one step closer to the end of life. It puts the individual in touch with the inevitability of personal death, an unpleasant thought that has been repressed on many levels. Starting a new family signals the end of one's own childhood, yet many new parents desperately hold on to remnants of their pasts by retaining behaviors and attitudes more characteristic of childhood and adolescence than of adulthood.

> In talking about this important crisis of transition in her own life, one patient insightfully stated her aversion to knowing that her life was steadily progressing through its various stages. In one session, she voiced her reluctance to growing up: "When I was a child, I knew that the next logical step was to be an adult. When I turned twenty-one, I thought, 'Now the next logical step is old age and death.' I absolutely didn't want that next step, so I rejected the step of being an adult. I thought of myself as much younger than I was to avoid knowing that I was really an adult."
>
> This woman was unusually sensitive at this particular time in her life to the symbolic meaning of reaching adulthood. Earlier, she had developed hypochondriacal symptoms during her pregnancy. Her attempts to elicit sympathy with physical complaints contrasted to such an extent with her previous disregard of minor discomforts that her husband had urged her to see a psychologist. Prior to this insight, she had been defensive about her "condition"

and the special attention she seemed to require. Her argument
had been that because she was pregnant, she deserved, in her
words, "extra consideration." Her rationalization was no different
than that of many prospective mothers who regress to more childish reactions because of the frightening prospect of perceiving
themselves as adult women. They tend to return to more childlike
postures, where they expect to be taken care of.

Conventional views of pregnancy generally support a woman's return to dependency and self-indulgence during this period. This basic
attitude, generally unchallenged in our society, fosters a wide range of
regressive behaviors in many expectant mothers.

This particular type of regression generally continues uninter-
rupted until delivery, at which time either movement toward recovery or
a more pronounced regression takes place. Indeed, the dynamics of
postpartum depression indicate the presence of highly-charged emotional reactions to this sudden shift from a childlike mode of being taken
care of to the reality and responsibilities of being a parent, of having to
take care of one's own child. This is a difficult transition to make, especially if the woman's imagined dependency needs were catered to during
her pregnancy.

As stated earlier, a woman who becomes a mother herself is, in one
sense, letting her own mother die. Her mourning over this symbolic loss
as well as the loss of actual dependency and care during her pregnancy
can cause a depressive reaction which sometimes reaches psychotic proportions.

CONCLUSION

The bipolar causality of regression becomes explicable when viewed
in the light of the individual's reaction to the trauma of separation—the
original separation from the parent at weaning and later the anticipation
of the final separation from the self that occurs at death. The seemingly
paradoxical adverse effect of positive events on the developing individual becomes more understandable when the universal human propensity to deny death is taken into account. Positive or fortunate
circumstances—success, genuine experiences of mature love and
sexuality—shatter bonds and fantasies and make us keenly aware of
valuing our lives. We feel that our experiences are precious, and this
feeling is tinged with poignancy when we contemplate our limitations in
time. Good feelings and good times are frequently followed by moments

of unusual clarity and a powerful awareness of separation and impending personal death. In this manner, positive experiences threaten the *unconscious* illusion in all of us that we are somehow immortal.

The human being takes a contradictory view of his or her own personal death. This contradiction was early recognized by Freud (1915/ 1957), who wrote:

> Our unconscious, then, does not believe in its own death; it behaves as if it were immortal. What we call our 'unconscious'— the deepest strata of our minds, made up of instinctual impulses—knows nothing that is negative, and no negation; in it contradictories coincide. For that reason, it does not know its own death. (p. 296)

It may well be that positive events strike terror at this unconscious level, disrupting bonds and upsetting our disbelief in the inevitability of death. The entire process takes place below the level of awareness. Negative events, on the other hand, by their very nature, fit in with the conscious lip service we pay to the obvious fact that people die. Their causal relationship to regression has always been more predictable and straightforward.

Regression as a defense in the service of denying death on an unconscious level is one dimension of the individual's resistance to progress in psychotherapy. As the therapist becomes acquainted with specific events, whether positive or negative, in each patient's life that have symbolic meaning for him or her in relation to the trauma of separation and eventual death, patterns of resistance are revealed, with resultant understanding and insight.

Chapter 12

PSYCHOSIS

Psychosis represents the culmination of a pathological retreat into fantasy. The psychotic patient is one who has withdrawn from the outside world and regressed to an inward state of withholding and "nonfeeling." This process is analogous to the psychoanalytic formulation that the schizophrenic withdraws the libido from environmental objects because they are too threatening, and retreats into narcissism. This state becomes preferred because the pain, frustration, anxiety, and fear involved in interpersonal relations have become intolerable. Negative experiences are compensated for in the fantasy process. When it is no longer possible for the person to gratify the need for satisfaction and security in the external environment because of inability to cope successfully with interpersonal situations, he or she resorts to self-gratification through fantasy.

> The schizophrenic process is an attempt to withdraw from socialization and preserve some integrity. It is a solution in the sense that the psychotic delusions, hallucinations, and fantasies seem to alleviate the intense anxiety and panic, and in the patient's eyes, act to protect and preserve his life. (Firestone, 1957, p. 132)

STAGES IN THE DEVELOPMENT OF SCHIZOPHRENIA

Progressive Involvement in Fantasy

Developmentally, *"schizophrenia is a specific reaction to an extremely severe state of anxiety, originated in childhood, reactivated later in life"* (Arieti, 1955, p. 43). In infancy and early childhood, the consequences of severe maternal rejection and emotional deprivation set up the conditions necessary for the child's dependence on fantasy gratification.

For example, when certain physiological needs are activated, it is thought that they precipitate tension states in the infant, which are discharged when the need gratification sequence is terminated. The good mother helps the infant to maintain its equilibrium because she is sensitive to its needs and promptly relieves tensions and anxieties related to her infant's helplessness in the face of instinctual demands. Fantasy can act as self-mothering in the sense that it provides partial gratification of needs that are operating and may reduce tensions and produce affects similar to the actual maternal responses, *but only within the personality.*

As described earlier, under conditions of considerable deprivation, the infant is able to form an image of the mother in its mind, one that has a private symbolic meaning. In this highly individualistic inner world, it imagines that it is once more connected to her. It fantasizes that it has total control of her comings and goings and its anxiety is significantly reduced. Later, the child elaborates this inner world, entering it at will whenever feeling threatened by potentially hurtful interpersonal situations.

The process of fantasy gratification and inner control, while having the advantage of alleviating anxiety and partially gratifying strong needs, nevertheless has serious disadvantages. Relying on fantasy progressively debilitates the person in a capacity to cope with the *real* world; that is, it impairs ability for reality testing. It also arouses strong feelings of guilt that originate from two major sources: from society and from within. Guilt plays an important role in the individual's progressive retreat into fantasy. The process is circular, with secrecy and guilt leading to a progressive retreat into fantasy and desocialization, which, in turn, tends to create new feelings of guilt.

Guilt from Society

There are strong sanctions in society against self-gratification. For example, children suffer a great deal of embarrassment when caught daydreaming in class or when their performance in team sports is less than adequate due to their being lost in reverie. They become the brunt of jokes from their peers when habitually involved in fantasy and become known as peculiar or strange.

The school-age child who is isolated and nonsocial, as well as the hyperactive or overly aggressive child, comes under the scrutiny of teachers and counselors. The shy, inward child is encouraged to become more involved in group activities. Pressures from authority figures and ridicule from schoolmates create a sense of guilt in the child each time he or she retreats into a secret fantasy world.

Often children reserve the privacy of their bedroom for fantasizing, while attempting to appear more outward in social situations. One patient recalled that as a young girl, she bitterly resented sharing a bedroom with her sister because it interfered with her inwardness and isolation. Before falling asleep each night, she fantasized extensively and required absolute quiet for this activity. Whenever her sister attempted to carry on a conversation with her or made the slightest sound, she would become angry. This girl grew up to become an extremely isolated, secretive young woman who had great difficulty allowing anyone to get close to her. In her therapy, she was strongly resistant to revealing the simple facts about her life in initial interviews. She was extremely guilty about her lack of social skills and her secretiveness.

Internal Guilt

Because of external pressures to pursue actual goals in the real world, people become increasingly devious in their attempts to seek satisfactions in fantasy. They attempt to deny the fact that they are merely fantasizing about their goals and future accomplishments. Meanwhile they become more passive about taking concrete steps toward achievement. Their dishonesty about not pursuing real goals creates an internal guilt and causes a lowering of self-esteem. They sense their own lack of integrity and are ashamed of their hypocrisy. For example, one is demoralized whenever one makes a strong resolution to reach a specific goal and does not follow through with concrete action. One experiences a great deal of inner guilt and becomes paranoid in relation to others, fearing *they* will discover this duplicity. These feelings, aside from damaging the individual's emotional well-being, only strengthen the sense of alienation and increase self-hatred. The person's verbalizations are directed more toward preserving a facade or pretense in front of others, rather than reflecting a genuine point of view. Beyond a certain point in this process, people are no longer aware of their own duplicity: they live in fantasy, but lack insight into their condition. The stage is thus set for more serious psychological disturbance.

Because of the need to distort one's perceptions, the disturbed person's inner world becomes very different phenomenologically from the world of reality. The inner world no longer matches the agreed-upon view of the world shared by normal individuals. Intrusions from the real world must be kept to a minimum because real experiences and genuine contact with others threaten the fantasy world. The patient chooses to give up broad areas of competence and achievement to protect the inner world. Academic failure, inability to succeed at one's chosen career, repeated failures in interpersonal relationships are symptomatic of an insidious retreat into fantasy.

In removing oneself from social interactions, the patient develops even more guilt because of the need to distort others to justify this isolation.

> He projects to the world, or to society at large, the feelings
> that he had for his family, but he is not aware of this projection.
> ... He also feels that the world is going to be bad, and bad for
> *him only*. (Arieti, 1955, p. 68)

Or he guards against becoming dependent on others out of a primitive fear of being overpowered or losing identity. The patient creates a negative picture of people to support deep feelings of basic mistrust. In losing empathy and feeling for others, one no longer feels compassion toward oneself. This condition arouses a profound sense of existential guilt that only adds to the feelings of self-hatred and isolation.

Loss of Meaning in Common Symbols

As the illness begins to manifest itself in obvious clinical forms, prepsychotic patients lose the ability to use the common symbols of the society in which they live. It is not that they have lost their intellectual understanding of the meaning of these common symbols; the symbols have simply become emotionally remote and no longer arouse the strong reactions in these individuals that their own private symbols do. In losing this attachment of meaning to objects and events in the outside world, these patients experience a general impoverishment of the personality.

In becoming indifferent to, or losing interest in, external objects, these individuals also lose a part of themselves. No matter how rich their fantasy life had been, it cannot begin to compensate for the bleak emptiness that the real world now presents to their eyes. When they lose the ability to interact in the interpersonal environment, they are profoundly and terribly lonely, for they are not only without others, they also have less of themselves. In this precarious and weakened state of inwardness, a single traumatic event or a stressful interpersonal situation can create a panic or confused state that catapults the person into an acute psychotic episode. In the regression to a previous level of ego development, the patient's attempts to stabilize and integrate the personality at intermediate stages fail, until finally a very primitive level of equilibrium is reached.

HISTORICAL DEVELOPMENT OF THE AUTHOR'S CONCEPTION OF THE SCHIZOPHRENIC PROCESS

Early Ideas

In attempting to understand the paradoxical nature of human behavior, I became interested in the conflict between assertion and dependence. I observed that people were torn between their desire for separation and independence and the desire for submission and fusion. They wanted to be strong and adult, yet commonly reverted to a childish regression.

Later, in working with a seriously disturbed patient in an outpatient clinic, I learned more about this polarity in people. The young woman, Lynn S., was tremendously anxious, paranoid, and tortured without knowing why. She led a dramatic, fantasized existence, was emotionally dishonest, and had a pattern of lying. She was given to hallucinating and there was a basic schizophrenic pattern to her thinking. In talking with Lynn, I was partially able to understand her life in terms of the basic conflict between her wish to be strong and independent and her desire to be taken care of. I could see that she was holding on to being a child in a fundamental way. Her immaturity, continually making a parent out of people and being at the same time the naughty child, was a way of holding on to something out of her past, a pattern that was long established.

What impressed me the most was that in Lynn's hallucinations, there was a parental quality. Voices would tell her to do things, how to behave, or they would criticize her behavior or judge it in moral terms. Her hallucinations, her feelings, and the voices she heard, sounded very much like her descriptions of her parents. It was almost as though she were both the parent to herself and the pathetic child she once was. She was the powerful parent who is critical and judgmental, and the infantile child who is helpless, bad, and condemned by the parental side. Both parts were alive and at odds in her. In her hallucinations, the parental aspect came across. This was the process of her schizophrenia. She was in a self-parenting kind of retreat, a retreat from real life into a self-parenting process. Later on in my dissertation on schizophrenia (Firestone, 1957), I referred to it as the "self-mothering" process. I began to understand that this process was not just something related to schizophrenia but had implications for myself and for other people and was a part of a human condition that affected us all.

Rosen's Treatment Program

While I was working with Lynn, a friend of mine, Jack Rosberg, had taken a job working with Dr. John N. Rosen, a renowned psychiatrist who had begun to apply psychotherapy in a systematic way to schizophrenic patients. He had achieved fame for his work and his contributions to the treatment of schizophrenia. Rosen's work was referred to as "Direct Analysis," which was, in his terms, a direct application of psychoanalytic theory to the productions of schizophrenic patients. Rosen's (1953) book, entitled *Direct Analysis*, impressed me with his courage in attempting to work in a field that was seen at that time as unacceptable (even foolhardy) by his psychiatric colleagues. Schizophrenics were known to respond poorly to psychoanalytic types of therapy. That was the prevailing opinion at the time, and yet Rosen was going to hospitals and demonstrating that he could make contact with these patients. He communicated with them in a way that led to demonstrable change in their psychotic mode of adjustment, especially when he worked with patients who were in the early stages of schizophrenia. He helped these people to change very serious conditions, for example, states of extreme catatonic excitement when the patients would normally develop high fevers and die.

When I learned that there was an opportunity for me to work at Rosen's, I interrupted graduate school in order to work on this project. When I arrived there, I was presented with a unique opportunity to develop and expand my own ideas. What I had learned earlier from Lynn played an important part in my almost immediate understanding of the patients with whom I became involved. Furthermore, I had a chance to work independently in this new environment. I relished this opportunity, though it was emotionally painful to be living with patients, surrounded by this illness and with the threat of violence.

Rosen's treatment of patients in a noninstitutional atmosphere where they actually lived their everyday lives with their therapists, as well as the wealth of information about the patients gathered in this setting, left a lasting impression on me. My current work, which involves observing and interacting with people in a new form of social environment as contrasted with office or laboratory conditions, has reconfirmed the importance of this type of unique psychological laboratory.

The material in the remainder of this chapter relates primarily to a discussion of a theoretical position that I developed some 27 years ago when I was working with schizophrenic patients, and applies to that syndrome. I believe, however, that the basic concepts also apply to neurosis or the process of maladjustment in individuals who are not psychotic or severely disturbed. The ideas presented are based on my doctoral dissertation, which was completed in 1957, and indicate the nature and course of an historical development or evolution of ideas that has become refined and generalized over the ensuing years.

THE ROLE OF FANTASY IN SCHIZOPHRENIA

The importance of the role of fantasy in the development of the psychoses has long been emphasized by theorists and students of the illness. The concept of fantasy as described here is multidimensional and is composed of many important variables. Fantasies act to "nourish" the ego in the form of a partial gratification and thus can contribute to psychological equilibrium when security or satisfaction from the real environment is lacking. Freud has emphasized that fantasies and dreams always represent a wish fulfillment. The fantasy structure is central and plays a vital part in the formation and maintenance of self attitudes.

The "primary fantasy" acts to maintain psychological equilibrium, that is, to reduce abnormal tension states by providing self-"nourishment" when the environmental gratification is insufficient. Thus, deprivation of love and care in interpersonal relations results in anxiety states which disturb the psychological equilibrium and this tension may be relieved by the process of fantasy. The primary fantasy, therefore, is the "self-mothering" process or the incorporation of the maternal image within the self as a "nourishing" and controlling agent.

It is hypothesized that the degree of neurotic or psychotic regression is a function of the degree to which the person depends upon fantasy for "nourishment" and psychological survival, which is, in turn, related to the degree of early deprivation and parental rejection. Psychotics will do everything in their power to stay "sick" and to maintain their solution. It is no wonder that they refuse to take a chance again on object relationships in which they have experienced such overwhelming anxiety. If their solution breaks down because of external interference in the autistic processes, they experience considerable anxiety and their aggression is mobilized to defend their system. This reaction substantiates the importance of the fantasy process in psychosis, a process which acts to reduce anxiety and maintain the psychological equilibrium (homeostasis).

An observation related to this was the experience with a catatonic man who was presented with a glass of milk and a glass filled with some of his own urine. When asked what came out of his penis, he answered that it was milk. At this stage in therapy, when presented with the choice, he invariably chose "the milk from his penis," that is, his own urine. Actually, he preferred the fantasy gratification of his "self-mothering" to the therapist's food. He would promptly drink the urine, and we persisted in interpreting to him the significance of his behavior (i.e., in terms of the preceding theoretical presentation he was acting as his own mother.) Finally, one day, (when it is assumed that he had appreciated the significance of his own self-deception), he spat the urine out in the face of the therapist. Eventually he began to accept milk from the therapist.

It is hypothesized that our experiment and interpretations interfered with the patient's self-gratification through fantasy. He first became angry at the therapist, then when the appropriate interpretations were made, and he was treated with affection, he was able to rely upon the therapist for gratification. In a sense, our interpretations of his psychotic solution may have made the fantasy less rewarding and our love and affection induced him to take a chance once again on object gratification. He gradually began to emerge from the schizophrenic process.

Dimensions of the Self-Mothering Process

The idealization of the mother or parenting figure is a necessary part of the self-mothering process that the schizophrenic patient turns to for gratification under these adverse conditions. At the same time, the mother's covertly rejecting evaluation is introjected by the patient and forms the core of the individual's self reactions. In simpler language, the schizophrenic feels basically worthless, low, dirty, unlovable, and that the mother is good, pure, wonderful, affectionate, and kind.

An interesting phase of this process of incorporating the ideal image of the mother is the essential contradiction found in many paranoid reactions, especially in delusions of grandeur. For example, the patient who describes himself as God or "the infinite being" may refer to himself as being worthless and insignificant at another point in the conversation. By the same token, he may cry out for his mother when he feels danger, despite the fact that he is an omnipotent figure who controls the world. These patients are at the same time the highest and the lowest members of humankind for in some way they have identified with their omnipotent mothers, and simultaneously regard themselves as the dirty, evil, unlovable child. In this sense they are the good mother and the bad child all in one person.

Another significant part of the schizophrenic process is that the negative qualities of the real mother are attributed readily to significant or transference figures, and sometimes may grow to include a large part of the bio-social environment. The patient becomes suspicious and wary of all people who come into contact with him.

In the schizophrenic regression, patients become again at one with the idealized mother and see her real qualities in other persons. It is hypothesized that the strong sets and anticipations based upon early experiences with the malevolent mother can perpetuate a cycle of further withdrawal from the environment into self-nourishment through fantasy. The incorporated ideal mother image serves to nourish the ego as a substitute for real gratification. Patients, by fantasizing about being their own mother, make themselves completely independent of others in their autistic thinking. For example, a paranoid man described how he often imagined the possibility of having breasts. When asked how this would help him he replied that he would not need others and that he could meet his own needs. He could both feed and get sexual satisfaction from himself and in that way, there would be no need for relationships.

THE SELF-PARENTING ASPECT OF HALLUCINATION

In working with a schizophrenic patient, the therapist feels as if he or she is dealing with a closed or exclusive situation, a mother and child in the same person. Many patients refer to themselves in the third person almost as if they were doting mothers. They may reply when asked how they feel, "Oh, he feels all right," or they may say in reference to themselves that "She wants this or that." Others have stated that they are their own mothers and that the only time they have been fed properly was when they took care of it.

Frequently, auditory hallucinations take the form of mothering or controlling statements. These hallucinations are a pathological, exaggerated manifestation of an ongoing, self-critical thought process, the "voice," [1] that is also present in the "normal" and neurotic person. In the final phases of the schizophrenic regression, however, these internal self-attacks, which are the sources of the patient's self-hatred, are disowned by the self and projected onto the outside world. Psychotic patients, in imagining that others hate them and accuse them, similarly imagine that they hear voices degrading them or ordering them to perform self-destructive acts. These hallucinated voices may be heard as commands to perform certain actions, or the patients may hear voices saying "shame on you" when they are masturbating. Often it may be ascertained from the patients that the voices remind them of parental reprimands or orders. In delusions of influence, there is still another example of this controlling mechanism.

It is suggested that the "split personality" in schizophrenia relates to the infant and incorporated mother division, or it could be formulated in terms of a split between the id (infant) and super-ego (mother), each one approaching a separate personality and having some functional autonomy in the schizoid process. This "split" exists in the neurotic person as well as the psychotic, although to a far lesser degree. The "super-ego," in this sense, *refers to the incorporated ideal mother rather than being restricted to the introjected values of the parental figures.* What *is* introjected are the parents' rejecting, hostile attitudes toward the child, preserved as an internal thought process in the adult patient.

THE CONCEPT OF THE PERVERSE MOTHER IN SCHIZOPHRENIA

As described above, the child learns to evaluate the self as the rejecting parents did. Since the concept of self is learned in a social context, a child who is not accepted by the mother, or the most significant person in early life, will tend to feel unworthy and unlovable. This is what is meant by the concept of the "bad me." The child needs to feel that the parent is good, and if in fact she appears punitive or anxiety-provoking, it is not because she is malevolent, but because the child is bad. The question is why the child needs to preserve the positive image of the mother at his or her own expense, so to speak. The answer points up how important the mother is to the child at this stage of life. The mother represents the world to the child, who must accept her in order to fulfill its inborn potentialities toward full maturation and socialization. The schizophrenic preserves the ideal image of the mother in the hope that

---

[1] The "voice" referred to here is the language of a self-destructive process existing, to varying degrees, in every person (Chapter 6).

she will some day accept and love, or at least approve of him or her. If these patients accept the truth about the origins of her rejecting evaluation, they must deny the possibility of ever getting the gratification which was denied them in their childhood.

If it is the child who is bad, then it is possible that if he or she changes behavior in various ways, the mother might love him or her. To preserve this hope the schizophrenic will accept the negative evaluation and attempt to modify his or her behavior. The patient will literally try everything to win her, and in this full-blown psychosis much sacrificial behavior is an unconscious attempt to attain her love. For example, a paranoid schizophrenic man burnt holes in his hands and feet in order to purify himself and remove the bad spirits. Although he was Jewish, he wore two crosses and embraced Catholicism (the maternal church) and the Virgin Mary. In the course of therapy, he would suddenly make resolutions to deny himself food and sex. When it was interpreted to him that these behaviors represented personal sacrifices with the hope of winning his mother's love, he no longer continued these responses. He later came to understand that he accepted himself as "bad" because he needed to believe in his mother as "good." As therapy progressed still further, he was able to accept the fact that she was incapable of loving him and caring for him, and that this represented her inadequacy as a mother, rather than indicating that he was worthless or unlovable.

CHARACTERISTICS OF THE "MALEVOLENT" MOTHER

The mother of the schizophrenic child is a mother whose child serves an important part in her psychological life. As such the child is used as a wastebasket into which she can pour those wishes, characteristics, and impulses that are unacceptable to her ego. Furthermore, she capitalizes upon those productions of her own child which she finds socially acceptable and admirable, such as intellect, mechanical skill, etc. These she takes credit for as if they were her own.

A paranoid schizophrenic man complained to me that he wished his mother would not always show off his paintings, because they were his, not hers. His mother actually spent a great deal of time telling others in the environment about the remarkable achievements of her son. She did this in a way which made him exceedingly uncomfortable, and he inhibited his productivity. In a sense, this type of mother is dependent upon her child whom she needs to provide her with products as well as to be an outlet for her psychological wastes. She takes over what is good as if it were her own and projects onto him her negative qualities or failings.

Her child is required to meet the demands of the mother rather than the reverse; the child is called upon to "feed" her (emotionally) and she is unable to "feed" him.

She regards her child in terms of her own body image or self-concept and shows the same attitude toward her child which is characteristically directed toward her other productions. If she feels that her products are evil or dirty, etc., she will tend to regard her child in this manner. If she is customarily retentive and stingy about her products, she may refuse to give up her child despite her negative attitude and may thereby actively inhibit the child's growth.

The mother's hostile and rejecting attitudes are rendered unconscious to her as these feelings are not acceptable to her ego. They are often projected onto the child in the form of: "You don't love me;" "Why don't you confide in your mother?" "You must tell me everything so I can help you;" "You have no feeling for me;" etc.

The schizophrenogenic mother is exceptionally intolerant of ambivalent feelings toward her child. Therefore, she attributes her hostile feelings to her offspring and thus exaggerates any expression of aggression by her child. The child comes to feel basically evil if he or she has resentment toward the mother, and will subsequently tend to repress hostility or turn it upon the self. Fear of repressed impulses leads to unpleasant anxiety and damages self-esteem and interpersonal relations. This type of mother acts out behavioral dynamics through her child that assure her psychological survival, as discussed above. She sees her child as a rival in the sense that by the very nature of the child's biological immaturity and helplessness, he or she is entitled to the unqualified loving care and nourishment that she, the mother, feels she needs so desperately. She "devours" her child's products, leading to inhibition of his creative output and spontaneity, and is intolerant of his aggression.

Rosen (1954), in a paper on transference, described how the psychotic person has been tremendously frustrated and deprived in the early relationship with the mother. He describes how the psychotic has had to incorporate the mother and has to recreate or hallucinate the mother in order to survive. Rosen stresses the concept of the psychosis as a "survival mechanism." He explains "survival" in terms of a reduction of severe anxiety states and, to some extent, as the preservation of feelings of worth and self-esteem. The absence of anxiety attests to the diabolical efficiency of the process. The patient is schizophrenic because he or she desperately wishes to be and is not kindly disposed to having the sickness interfered with.

In schizophrenic patients, the fantasy of self-sufficiency has become all-encompassing, yet paradoxically, the more they imagine that they need no one and that they can survive through mothering themselves, the more dependent they are on others for care. Occasionally patients may feel too threatened by their hallucinated "voices" to allow themselves even to carry on the activities necessary for actual physical survival.

For example, a young patient described by the French psychoanalyst, M. Sechehaye (1951), was in a desperate condition of near-starvation because her "voices" ordered her not to eat. At a crucial point in therapy, M. Sechehaye assumed the role of the "good" mother in reality, thereby replacing her patient's fantasized images that had warned her against accepting food. She began by feeding the sixteen year-old girl an apple while holding her like a small child. Later, she placed two apples, symbolizing the maternal breasts, on a table where they would always be in her patient's view. With these therapeutic maneuvers, because of the strong rapport already established with her patient, Sechehaye was able to restore her patient to a peaceful state where she was no longer disturbed by hallucinations or imagined threats of destruction. Gradually, the young girl was "weaned" and brought to higher levels of integration by successive steps of separation and individuation carefully planned by the therapist. In psychodynamic terms, the patient's self-nourishing fantasy, consisting of the good mother/bad child image, was drastically interfered with by the therapist's direct offering of love-food. Thereafter, progress was made by building on the patient's more realistic and positive self-concept. Concomitantly, the patient verbalized coherent, clear insights concerning the extreme deprivation she had suffered early in her life because of the inadequacies of her mother.

In conclusion, the mother-child dynamics that were formulated throughout this section are those relationship variables which the author feels to be most conducive to producing schizophrenia. They need not all be present to produce this disorder and furthermore, one must consider the entire developmental matrix in order to thoroughly understand the illness. Substitute object relations can protect the child from developing schizophrenia when confronted with maternal deprivation and covert rejection. In some cases, it is also possible that the father may play the most important role in the etiology of schizophrenia.

A further problem related to these dynamics involves the consideration of a biological or constitutional predisposition for schizophrenia. Some theorists have emphasized that the illness is strictly somatic, while others have considered it to be purely psychological. The author feels that all illnesses are psychosomatic, that is, have a psychological and a somatic component; that, indeed, human beings are "psychosomatic." It is my belief, however, that in the vast majority of cases the causes of schizophrenia are principally psychological. One possible somatic component may be that preschizophrenic individuals have an unusual or exaggerated reaction to stress. Indeed, individuals demonstrate varying degrees of tolerance for anxiety and emotional deprivation, as is the case with tolerance for physical deprivation. For this reason, one must be concerned with the total biosocial background in order to explain the disease process. Considering the multitude of factors operating it is surprising that we find so much consistency in research studies and theories concerning predisposing factors related to intrafamily dynamics.

THE CONCEPT OF LOVE-FOOD

In this discussion, considerable attention has been devoted to the relationship between the mother and child. Defects in this form of experience are considerably important in the development of the schizophrenic reaction. The question arises as to what the good mother (mother of a healthy child) provides that the schizophrenogenic mother is incapable of providing. The answer may be contained in the concept of love-food. The good mother must be able to provide affection and warmth as well to control the child and provide physical nourishment. She must furnish security and satisfaction, and she is the person (agent) through which the child must learn to achieve successful socialization. In this sense the concept of love-food is a product-relationship variable referring to the psychonutritional exchange between the mother and her child.

Anyone who has had the experience of working or coming into contact with schizophrenics has been impressed with the amount of preoccupation with food that these patients indicate. The classical Freudian position is, of course, that the schizophrenic has regressed to the oral phase of psychosexual development. Often they suspect that their food has been poisoned or tampered with. Many times there is considerable ritual concerning the partaking of meals. Sometimes they will starve themselves and frequently they complain about pains around the mouth or stomach. The patient has come to equate food and love in the psychotic regression, for during infancy the concept of love and tenderness is derived from the omnipotent mother's prompt gratification of the infant's needs and relief of its tension. It is the deprivation of this need for love-food that leads to the production of fantasy and self-mothering.

The process of self-mothering, even in normal personality development, includes the concept of self-control or self-regulation as well as self-nourishment, for the mother is also the vehicle of the child's socialization. The child needs parental regulation as well as love in order to adjust to the social milieu. Love-food is a special combination of control and affection. Both are necessary for successful adaptation to the environment. If there is both love and control, the parent will not only have the ability to provide for the child's satisfaction but will also have the desire, that is, the parent must be both strong and loving. Love alone from a weak parent is not enough, nor is control without love from a strong parent.

ANXIETY AND THE CENTRAL CONFLICT

According to the theoretical position presented here, a person exists in a state of psychological equilibrium between self-mothering and external object gratification when not undergoing intense or unpleasant anxiety states. In the healthy person these processes are of approximately the same importance and he or she remains both a creative individual and a social being. The person is able to give and receive love-food and retains a high level of spontaneity. However, a person can maintain psychological equilibrium (that is, avoid serious tension states) and still be very sick psychologically. The schizoid adjustment is highly efficient in alleviating anxiety, but there is, as mentioned previously, undue dependence upon the internal, self-mothering process, which progressively incapacitates the person's adjustment to the real world. The individual is completely unable to form rewarding interpersonal relationships and has created a world based on autistic fantasy. Equilibrium has been established but it is not what would be called a healthy one.

Anxiety is the result of any threat to a person's equilibrium with reference to the central conflict. For example, a man who has been very shy and withdrawn in his relationships with the opposite sex may experience anxiety when he is tempted to approach or enter into a relationship with a woman to whom he is attracted, or he may develop anxiety when he experiences the threat or actual loss of an object relationship upon which he has grown to depend.

Anxiety may result from anything that threatens either object dependency or the self-mothering processes. Object loss or frustration in interpersonal relationships leads to anxiety and to the necessary formation of a new psychological equilibrium. This is achieved by compensation either through real action or by fantasy activity. Aggression also arises when there is disequilibrium and is directed toward either the interfering agent or expressed indirectly in some form.

The end product of the schizophrenic regression is a form of psychological equilibrium at the expense of object relationships and dependence. Schizophrenics literally shut people out of their life and become their own mothers, psychologically. Now in this situation, anxiety is experienced when there is external interference with either the self-mothering process or the psychotic dream. Thus, when the therapist succeeds in creating anxiety in the schizophrenic through exposing to the patient the meaning of his or her productions, this is looked upon as a favorable prognostic sign. It is an indication that the therapist has succeeded in breaking through the autism and, if capitalized upon, can be a beginning of a reversal of the entire process.

QUALITATIVE CHANGES IN THE SCHIZOPHRENIC REGRESSION

The author sees the process of schizophrenia as existing as part of a continuum ranging from normal, healthy functioning to chronic psychotic states with severe decompensation. However, as one progresses through the continuum and there is more extensive damage, there are qualitative changes, such as delusions, hallucinations, and peculiar thought disturbances. Thus, in different stages of the continuum, qualitative symptomatic changes appear.

Chances in Intellectual Processes

One of the most important symptoms or signs of this illness is the change that occurs in intellectual processes. "Emotions . . . have the power to distort the intellectual processes, and this type of distortion has its most typical example in schizophrenia" (Arieti, 1955, p. 185). *Rationalizations* are among the most common distortions and are found in normal people and neurotics as well as in psychotics. These are attempts to explain plausibly or justify actions or ideas that in reality are directed, not by reason, but by an emotional need. They can still be supported, however, by Aristotelian logic.

Arieti (1955) proposes that the need for rationality is as powerful as the need to gratify the irrational emotions. He suggests the principal that:

> *If, in a situation of severe anxiety, behavior at a certain level of intellectual integration cannot take place or does not bring about the desired results, a strong tendency exists toward behavior of lower levels of integration in order to effect those results.* (p. 191)

He refers to this process as "the principle of *Teleologic Regression*" because less advanced levels of mental integration are used, and the process is purposeful—namely to avoid anxiety. Patients adopt a more primitive type of logic, i.e., paleologic, that permits them to see reality as they want to, one which offers them a pseudo-fulfillment of their wishes. For example, the patient may assume that, having one characteristic in common with another person, he or she *is* identical to that person in every other respect.

Other intellectual distortions closely related to paleologic and reflecting the oral level of development are overgeneralizations; confusion of sexual symbols with feeding symbols; identifying two objects that engender the same feeling in the patient; and forming inappropriate associations despite evidence to the contrary, for example, associating the messenger with the message. In one instance, a schizophrenic woman was informed that her husband had decided to divorce her; whereupon she became very aggressive toward the therapist, calling him a Hitler and a tyrant, fat and evil. She accused him of a variety of crimes and refused to accept the information as correct. In an attempt to deny certain information that was very threatening to her, she attacked the source. Intellectual distortion helped her to deny what would have produced excessive anxiety.

In summary, as individuals progressively withdraw into the fantasy or defensive process, there are characteristic changes in the intellectual organization. They can no longer rely upon Aristotelian logic to explain their behavior since their responses are the result of intense emotional disturbance. They cannot adapt to a painful reality that creates severe anxiety. Their intellectual functioning and organization based upon Aristotelian principles are not flexible enough to fit in with their urgent needs. Because of this, they must rely upon a less organized rational base for their behavior. It is important to realize that their intellectual distortion is in the direction of need gratification and the avoidance of severe anxiety states. It is integrally bound up with the defensive process and directly related to the specific mechanisms of defense. The patient is always attempting to preserve equilibrium and in all his or her productions and responses, some form of rationality or intellectual organization is involved.

Hallucinations

The person who thinks paleologically tends to live in a world of distorted perception rather than in a world of conception. As the process of paleologic thinking progresses, there will be more and more "concrete elements, representing reality as it appears to the senses, rather than to the intellect. . . . Perceptual elements finally completely eliminate higher thought processes" (Arieti, 1955, p. 244), as exemplified in dreams and in hallucinations. Patients do not *think* that they hear voices, they actually hear them. Often the perceptual quality of the person's thoughts is so pronounced that he is afraid other people will hear them. "When the process is more advanced, he still recognizes that the thoughts are his own, but on account of their perceptual character, he feels that people are repeating them verbally." (p. 249) In later stages of the illness, the patient no longer recognizes his thoughts as his own, and projects them completely onto other people. Psychotherapy with schizophrenics attempts to reverse this insidious process. When schizophrenic patients begin to recover, they question the reality of their hallucinations, in the same way that the dreamer in the process of waking up starts to realize that the dream was a dream.

PSYCHOTHERAPY WITH SCHIZOPHRENIC PATIENTS

The therapy process designed to alleviate the psychosis consists of two distinct kinds of activities. One, the therapist must counteract and attack the psychotic dream solution, thereby disturbing the psychological equilibrium and creating anxiety; and two, he or she must encourage the patient to "take a chance" again on interpersonal relations, through the provision of love and care. These two processes, of course, occur simultaneously in the therapy of schizophrenics.

In successful therapy patients will be forced to relinquish the self-mothering process due to the therapist's intrusion upon this system. As this process continues and develops patients will tend to rely less upon fantasy gratification and more upon gratification of their needs by the therapist. In this way they form a very deep relationship with the therapist who is in essence nothing more than the "good mother" that the infant was denied. This "good mother" now provides the patient—to the best of the therapist's ability and circumstance—with the love and care and understanding that was needed during early life.

It is important to note that the patients are constantly testing the relationship and there there is very considerable resistance and aggression manifested in this process. They do not take lightly the intrusion upon their psychological equilibrium and will do everything in their power to stay sick. As has been said earlier, they have developed strong beliefs that their new "mother" (the therapist) is every bit as bad as their real mother was. The therapist points out evidences of this type of distortion to the patients when they occur. Schizophrenic patients will try anything to provoke rejection or duplication of the behavior of the real mother. In this way, they protect themselves from taking the big chance and reinforce their psychotic solution. The therapist, for this reason, must always be alert and must maintain control over the situation. If such is not the case and the patients succeed in controlling the therapist's feelings and actions, the therapy will result in failure. Another important aspect of control is that it points out to the patients that they can once again safely feel the emotions they repressed in childhood. When the therapist is affectionate and takes good care of them, they learn that they are lovable. They are again, in a sense, given the opportunity for love which only the young baby received.

An important therapy technique conducive to growth in the schizophrenic patient is the use of restriction or control over the patient's life. For example, the patient may show certain external manifestations of the psychotic process such as making peculiar signs, or performing certain ritualistic or stereotyped behaviors. The therapist can forbid the patient to act out these dynamics or can actually physically interfere with these expressions by using restraint or force. Such restrictions, if handled adequately, can precipitate anxiety in the patient and focus aggression on the therapist. This technique may act to stimulate the patient to produce material that can then be subject to interpretation. Another aspect of control over the patient is that it is conducive to transference to the therapist as a parental figure.

It is important to control manifestations of the patient's illness, that is, the acting out of antisocial, aggressive impulses which the patient may be unable to control himself. The therapist needs to assure the patient that he (the therapist) can control and master these urges which often threaten to overwhelm the patient's ego. Sometimes the therapist may choose to demonstrate his power over the patient's self-destructive and aggressive actions by the use of constraints and other environmental controls. Both control and affection are necessary to counteract the effects of an inadequate emotional environment created by the schizophrenogenic parent or parents.

In a sense, the therapist is forcing the patient into a situation that is analogous to that of the young child in the home. The patient is given another chance to develop and mature in a new parental environment. (It is obvious that, in advocating this kind of environmental control, the author is in disagreement with psychotherapeutic techniques wherein regressive behaviors and acting out are allowed and even considered to be a necessary part of the movement toward health.)

As described earlier, these patients preserve the image of the mother as being "good and loving" at the expense of their own feelings of worth, and the therapist must attack the dynamics of this idealization. The patients must also learn to express their hostile feelings to others. They must come to see how they have needed to recreate the maternal relationship within their own personality because of the severe deprivations in their early life and how they have used fantasy and withdrawal to compensate for frustrations in the interpersonal environment. Finally they must build a relationship with the therapist that is comparatively free of transference elements or parataxic distortion. They must come to trust and be able to give and receive love and affection from the therapist in a "real" as opposed to a transference relationship. They must come to face the facts about their illness and its cause and must learn to feel worthwhile and lovable. At the end of this difficult and arduous process they should be able to transfer their learning to other persons in the social environment and be able to make the necessary adjustment for living in the larger world.

In the process of counteracting the schizophrenic solution every attempt should be made to mobilize the environment in attacking the psychotic solution. The primary tool of the therapist in affecting change in the psychotic dream is the procedure of interpreting directly the productions of the patient. These interpretations are geared to the patient's level of awareness and formulated in the language of the self-mothering process. Psychic energy is thereby freed and affect is focused on the therapist conducive to the beginning of a transference relationship. Direct interpretations facilitate the psychonutritional exchanges from the self-mothering process to the acceptance of the therapist's "mothering" and in a relatively short time the therapist is accepted as a significant figure in the patient's psychological life.

Therapy with psychotics, as emphasized by Rosen (1953), Fromm-Reichmann (1939), Sullivan (1953), and others, focuses on the patient's relationship to the therapist. Psychotic patients form a very sensitive transference relationship to the therapist and their feelings are exceptionally intense. The transference interpretations are central to the process of psychotherapy, and should be handled carefully and with a great deal of skill and sensitivity on the part of the therapist.

The therapist must actively point out the distortions that the patient imposes upon the relationship and must demonstrate in a variety of ways that he or she loves the patient. The therapist should openly demonstrate affection and love and should take over, insofar as possible, the function of nourishing the patient in both the physical and psychological sense. At the same time, as the patient matures, the therapist must be prepared to relinquish control over the patient and allow more autonomy. Overgratification of the infantile demands of the patient can be just as crippling to the therapy process as a deficiency of "maternal" responses on the part of the therapist. Such overemphasis acts to make the sickness rewarding and prevents the development of more mature social behavior in the patient.

The therapy process is an attack upon the internal source of gratification through fantasy while at the same time it is an attempt to make reality more inviting. The patient is encouraged to leave the autistic world and to become involved again with real objects. The therapist becomes a substitute parent who helps the patient to readjust to the interpersonal environment.

CONCLUSION

Research in the area of psychotherapy and in the more general area of personality theory has been criticized for its preponderance of theory without experimental validation. In the current work, a system of hypotheses was established in the attempt to put forward a consistent explanation of the schizophrenic process. It is suggested that the concepts employed in this system lend themselves to operational definition and to experimental investigation in a treatment situation for these patients. It is only with this type of effort that we can evaluate psychotherapy for schizophrenia on a sound scientific basis. Despite the problems involved in isolating the relevant variables and in making objective measurements of the patient-therapist interaction, the author feels this approach is a useful point of departure for more rigorous experimental studies of schizophrenia. If this discussion stimulates more precise research into the psychodynamics of schizophrenia or assists the therapist in working with patients suffering from this disorder, its major purpose will have been served.

Finally, I do not believe, despite all of the problems involved in treating schizophrenics with psychotherapy, that the condition of schizophrenia is incurable. I feel that in certain instances, with the proper kind of treatment, dramatic and powerful results can be achieved. From a theoretical standpoint, working with these patients adds vastly to a clinician's knowledge of symbolism, theory, and research about the self-mothering process. It is valuable as a research tool and provides an unusual opportunity for training and experience. Though costly in terms of time and effort, it is helpful even if it benefits a small number of patients.

Chapter 13

SEXUALITY

> It was sex that turned a man into a broken half of a couple, the woman into the other broken half. . . . He wanted so much to be free, not under the compulsion of any need for unification, or tortured by unsatisfied desire.
>
> D. H. Lawrence
> *Women In Love,* (p. 191)

Sex is one of the strongest motivating forces in life. It has the potential for creating intense pleasure and fulfillment or causing considerable pain and suffering. The effect of a natural expression of sexuality on one's sense of well-being and overall enjoyment of life cannot be overemphasized. The way people feel about themselves as men and women, the feelings they have about their bodies, and their attitudes toward sex contribute more to a sense of self and feeling of happiness than any other area of experience.

A "healthy" orientation to sex is reflected in a person's overall appearance and attractiveness, ability to be tender and generous to others, sensitivity to children, and general level of vitality. The combination of loving, sexual contact and genuine friendship in a stable, long-lasting relationship is conducive to good mental health and is a highly regarded ideal for most people.

On the other hand, disturbances in one's sexual life can have serious negative consequences: jealousy leads to passive brooding and low-grade anger, denying oneself sexual pleasure and fulfillment causes irritability and tenseness, and sexual withholding activates regressive or childlike feelings of inadequacy in oneself and rage and desperation in one's partner. An individual's basic attitudes, thoughts, and feelings about sex determine, to a large extent, the extent to which he or she relies on inward and self-protective mechanisms. Relegating sex to a completely separate and distinct area of life also contributes to a basic distortion of human sexuality. It compartmentalizes sex and takes it out of the realm of a natural human function. On a societal level, sexual incompatibility is seen as a major cause of divorce and broken families.

Most intimate couple relationships start out with the individuals spontaneously expressing their sexual feelings, but tend to degenerate into destructive bonds typified by sexual withholding and other maladaptive responses. Resistance to change or progress toward a better life finds its most direct expression in this bond and more particularly, in the form that an individual's sexuality takes within the couple bond. People who are involved in long-term intimate relationships are, for the most part, deeply affected by the declining quality in their sexual relating. However, unless they are troubled by a specific sexual problem, they may be unaware of the extent of the damage they sustain in the privacy of their bedrooms.

Most people view their mutual patterns of withholding and their diminished sexual attraction to each other as the normal course of events and mistakenly place the blame on the familiarity, the routine, and the daily contact that marriage entails. Once people have been damaged in their basic feelings about themselves in their early lives, they react against experiencing themselves as being lovable and capable of offering real love and companionship. They are reluctant to change or give up their negative self-image and thereby risk incurring anxiety and subsequent disappointment.

In a bond, dramatic changes tend to occur in the sexual part of the relationship as well as in the couple's feelings about themselves as men and women. These have a profound impact on other areas of functioning. The problem can be traced back to disturbances in the original mother-infant dyad. Beyond a certain point in the early phases of a new relationship, most people gradually stop responding to each other according to present-day reality. Instead, regressive, childlike feelings and reactions gradually replace adult responses. One's original feelings toward one's parents are transferred onto the person of the loved one. This process is an extended view of the concept of the transference relationship in psychoanalysis.

In light of this maladaptive process, marital relationships are generally characterized by limited sexual responses and/or distorted views of sex based on the past. These are now acted out in the course of the couple's everyday interactions. These inappropriate responses vary in intensity and become compulsive to the extent that the individual experienced deprivation and rejection in early life.

In reverting to a more childlike level of sexuality, individuals are denying their need for another person or for anything outside the self-mothering system. They fantasize on some level that they can really meet their own needs, that they can feed themselves. To understand where patients stand in relation to this defensive process, it is valuable to examine their sexual life and sexual fantasies because they symbolically express the individuals' attitudes toward the giving and taking of love in relation to other persons. This analysis also reveals the manner and the extent to which they have retreated to an inward style of self-feeding in order to gratify themselves.

THE ORAL BASIS OF SEXUALITY

An individual's sexual orientation may be represented on a continuum, ranging from total fantasized self-sufficiency as in the psychotic patient, to a healthy interdependence with another person in meeting one's needs. The stages of psychosexual development as described by Freud (1940/1964) can be conceptualized as corresponding to points on this continuum, ranging from the oral phase to mature genital sexuality. At one extreme are psychotic productions in which the patient tends directly to confuse oral symbols with sexual symbols. In schizophrenic regression, there is a retreat from object relations into an autistic self-mothering process. Because of trauma that occurred at the oral stage of development, the patient is focused to an enormous degree on feeding symbols.

When there has been considerable anxiety and deprivation related to early feeding experiences there will generally be subsequent sexual maladjustment. Actual sexual relationships and bodily contact with other persons may become too threatening. Such a person is generally too immature to experience satisfactory sexual relations with other persons and tends to resort to a great deal of fantasy concerning sex. The fantasies often conceal themes which are basically oral in nature pertaining more directly to the giving and taking of nutritional products. Often the overt sexual content of schizophrenic productions is analogous to the manifest content of the dream; it merely acts as a screen to hide the unconscious oral cravings. Because of the symbolic psychonutritional exchange involved in sexuality, it is useful at this time to look into the process of schizophrenia where this symbolism is more direct and apparent.

In becoming familiar with the productions of many schizophrenics, one is impressed with the importance of incestuous thought content encountered in these patients (Firestone, 1957). It is interesting to question why schizophrenic patients are so preoccupied with incestuous thoughts and ideas. It is also interesting to investigate whether these incestuous thoughts, expressions, etc., are truly sexual in nature, or whether the sexual content conceals more basic motivations.

It is conjectured that the reason for the preoccupation with incestuous thought content in the schizophrenic is that the productions conceal an abnormal hunger to be loved and fed by the parental figure, i.e., in order to obtain love-food. It is because the schizophrenic child is rejected and deprived that he or she must fantasize about being close to the parents. These early fantasies come to have a sexual overlay as the child develops to maturity, and, because of the social taboos and restrictions, contribute to a great deal of anxiety. Thus, incestuous feelings are heightened because the emotional deprivation in the child's early environment fosters exaggerated need and dependency.

A schizophrenic man plagued by hallucinations of a breast and a penis and by considerable incestuous thought content was relieved of these symptoms when it was interpreted that the breast and the penis which he saw represented his wish to be nourished by his mother and father; that he was like a baby, who wanted to suck and be fed by the maternal breast; but that when this was denied, he turned to the paternal penis as a substitute. Both the penis and the breast that he hallucinated manifested his wish to be fed. This same patient at a later stage of his analysis described how he used to pray for his mother's love and affection and how he used to imagine sucking her breast.

For many female patients, the wish to be impregnated by the father may symbolize the need to be fed and for the stomach to be filled. It is basically an outgrowth of maternal deprivation and results from the symbolic substitution of penis for breast and semen for milk.

From these examples, one can see that often sexual symbolism in schizophrenic patients is related to feeding manifestations. Furthermore, interpretations when geared to this level seem to be effective in alleviating psychotic symptoms. Thus, the preponderance of incestuous thought and fantasy in schizophrenia is hypothesized to be an outgrowth of oral deprivation and an attempt to seek gratification in a fantasy outlet which protects the individual from further rejection in terms of interpersonal objects.

HOMOSEXUALITY AND CONFUSED SEXUAL IDENTIFICATION IN SCHIZOPHRENIA

It is suggested that in the development of schizophrenia, there is first a retreat from heterosexuality into the homosexual phase, and when this is unrewarding or threatening, there is a depersonalization or withdrawal from all objects. The importance of latent or hidden homosexual tendencies has long been emphasized in the study of paranoia, but it is suggested here that it is a distinct phase in every type of schizophrenic process. Paranoid schizophrenia apparently represents a stage between the homosexual phase and the complete depersonalization process. Because of the threatening nature of homosexual impulses, they are projected onto other persons, leading to paranoid suspicions and fears. The fact that the homosexual impulse operates and is strong indicates that the regression and self-mothering process are not yet complete.

The schizophrenic child is prone to develop strong fantasies about being close to the parent of the opposite sex. As a result of the threatening quality of these thought processes, there is considerable anxiety that operates in the relationship with persons of the opposite sex. That is, sexual fantasies become associated with the guilt and punishment related to the strong incest taboo. The fears and guilt associated with these activities become so overwhelming that the person is forced to retreat from heterosexuality.

Another important dynamic in the development of schizophrenia associated with homosexuality and confused sexual identification is that the patient characteristically manifests the wish to be of the opposite sex. Children rejected early in life by the important figure in their adjustment may develop the belief that perhaps if they were of the opposite sex, their mother would love them. This may then be translated into a deep wish and longing to be of the opposite sex in the hope that maternal love will ensue. This dynamic is especially true when the patient has a sibling of the opposite sex who appears to him or her to be more loved by the parent. One catatonic boy, when asked whether he would prefer to be a male or a female, replied that he would rather be a girl. The question, "Why would you rather be a girl?" was answered, "Because Ann [his sister] got more food."

A further complicating factor in the problem of sexual identification is the wish to be self-sufficient, that is, to possess the genitals of both sexes at the same time. Often patients are preoccupied with thoughts about the possibility of having the genitals of the other sex, or having operations whereby a man can have breasts and a vagina and a woman could acquire the male penis. When subjected to depth analysis, these fantasies reveal hidden wishes on the part of patients to be able to feed themselves sexually without ever having to be deprived. In this way, symbolically, they would never have to depend on others as before and, therefore, do not have to run the risk of incurring anxiety and painful rejection.

The Oral Basis of Sexuality in the Neurotic or "Normal" Person

The oral basis of sexuality and the symbolic confusion of sexual and feeding symbols is not restricted to psychopathology. It is fundamental to our understanding of the general subject of sexuality in normal individuals. People who are not psychotic or severely disturbed, but who are avoiding sex and closeness, are, in effect, turning away from seeking gratification outside themselves. The avoidance (whether it is through sexual symptoms in the male of premature ejaculation or delayed or retarded ejaculation, or through impotence, or in the woman of being frigid or unresponsive and withholding) represents a movement away from closeness and from an emotional exchange between two people. A woman who is avoiding sex or who is sexually withholding may also be saying in effect, "I don't need to be fed." She does not want to be thrown back to that infantile dependence which led to so much pain earlier in life. In a sense, she doesn't want to become addicted to the man, that is, to being satisfied by someone outside the self-nourishing system. Thus, she will not allow the man to give her that gratification. Her sexual withholding is a denial of the wish to be fed from the external environment, and is a symbolic statement of her pseudo-independence, "I can feed myself."

The same is true with men in relation to sex. A man may compulsively masturbate and avoid closeness to a woman or he may become defiant and hostile in relation to women. At the same time, he sustains the infantile fantasy that he can take care of himself, that he does not need a woman. A man may have the fear that a woman, the mouth or the vagina, will drain him, will take everything from him, as his parents did when they were emotionally hungry, wanting something from him rather than giving *him* what he needed. He may feel that he is not able to care for a woman, and may avoid her sexually when he feels her sexual demands or her own hunger toward him.

On the other hand, when the woman is sexually withholding, the man feels unloved and cannot feel himself in the sex act. Any time the woman retreats from the spontaneity and natural expression of her sexuality, this acts as a provocation to the man. As described earlier, the man, when provoked to anger, feels guilty, self-blaming, and confused in relation to his mate's sexual withholding. This is especially true when he is unaware that she is holding back her responses. In almost all cases, he will tend to blame himself for the woman's lack of interest. The subtle, unconscious aspects of her nonresponse confuse him, and if they significantly affect his sexual performance, he feels self-critical. Men also expect that they should feel sexual under all circumstances. These factors contribute to a man's feeling uncomfortable during lovemaking. He comes to feel anxious about giving satisfaction (symbolically, successfully feeding the woman), and may retreat from being active or assertive sexually.

In conclusion, the way people relate to the opposite sex reveals a great deal about where they are in their development psychologically, in their growth and independence. Men's and women's attitudes toward sex as well as the nature of their sexual relationships clearly indicate the extent to which they are defending themselves against being adult. Mature sexuality, in combination with feelings of friendship in a long-lasting relationship, tends to arouse anxiety because it represents a powerful intrusion into the primary fantasy or self-mothering process.

THE DEVELOPMENT OF SEXUAL IDENTITY IN THE NORMAL INDIVIDUAL

Attachment—The Child's Natural Attraction to the Mother

> Love has its origins in attachment to the satisfied need for nourishment.
>
> Sigmund Freud (1940/1964)

Psychoanalysts have for a long time been in agreement in recognizing a child's first human relationship as the "foundation stone of his personality," but there is as yet no agreement on the nature and origin of that relationship (Bowlby, 1969).

It is suggested here that in the earliest stages of development, children of both sexes are attracted to their mothers and that this attraction has a sexual component. This physical attraction expresses itself in a desire to look at and touch the mother's body. The impulse to touch reflects the child's natural curiosity about the mother's physical nature.

These affectional and sexual impulses are accompanied by strong affect. Sometimes patients in therapy are able to recall instances when, as children, they followed these urges with actions, and were discouraged or even punished and ridiculed. Evidently they were allowed to be physically close to the mother until a certain age when their touching and curiosity were prohibited or, at the least, discouraged. The origins of this intense attraction and interest may be found in the infant's early recognition of the mother as the source of satisfaction (reduction of tension states).

In *Three Essays on The Theory of Sexuality,* Freud (1905/1953), expressed his views on the dynamics of the infant's choice of its first love object.

> At a time at which the first beginnings of sexual satisfaction are still linked with the taking of nourishment, the sexual instinct has a sexual object outside the infant's own body in the shape of his mother's breast.
>
> But even after sexual activity has become detached from the taking of nourishment, an important part of this first and most significant of all sexual relations is left over. . . . All through the period of latency children learn to feel for other people who help them in their helplessness and satisfy their needs a love which is on the model of, and a continuation of, their relation as sucklings to their nursing mother. . . . A child's intercourse with anyone responsible for his care affords him an unending source of sexual excitation and satisfaction from his erotogenic zones. . . . Children themselves behave from an early age as though their dependence on the people looking after them were in the nature of sexual love. (p. 222-224)

In Freud's (1940/1964) later writings (*An Outline of Psycho-Analysis*), there is a dramatic description of the child's relationship to the mother as being "unique, without parallel, established unalterably for a whole lifetime as the first and strongest love-object and as the prototype for all later love-relations—for both sexes" (p. 188).

Although there is disagreement and controversy in the field of psychology over Freud's powerful linking of early feeding experiences to the subsequent sexuality of the individual, nevertheless, there is much empirical evidence for this connection as well as support and agreement from other theorists and clinicians (Deutsch, 1944; Klein, Heimann, Isaacs, & Riviere, 1952). Some theorists regard attachment behavior and sexual behavior as two distinct behavioral systems (Harlow & Harlow, 1965), while conceding their unusually close connections. It is believed that overlaps between attachment and sexual behavior are commonplace and each impinges on the other and influences the development of each other (Bowlby, 1969).

I have concluded that the child's natural attraction to the mother grows out of the satisfaction of the child's needs and from the pleasure of being stimulated in erotogenic zones, especially those areas involved in the feeding experiences. The drive to be physically close to the mother is one of the earliest determinants of an appropriate sexual identification for both male and female offspring.

Frustration of the Child's Natural Attraction to the Mother

The young child's initial attraction to the mother may be frustrated early in the relationship. If a mother is uncomfortable with physical contact in general, if she dislikes her body, if she is hungry and trying to extract love *from* her child, if she is intolerant of the feeling of interest and affection coming from her baby, she will necessarily reject its attempts to achieve close physical contact. Some researchers believe that the social taboos against a baby daughter's expressions of affection are stronger than against the son's. This taboo also operates to keep the mother's physical contact with her daughter to a minimum:

> . . . [women's] feelings for their baby daughters may frighten them if they label them sexual. This can lead mothers to limit their physical contacts with their young daughters severely. (Caplan, 1981, p. 59)

It has been observed that many mothers are also more reluctant about expressing affection *to* their daughters then toward their sons and that this hesitancy has serious implications for the girl's later sexual development.

Dr. Sirgay Sanger, quoted in Nancy Friday's (1977) *My Mother, My Self*, says that:

> The subtle deprivation of physical demonstrations of affection that little girls often suffer from their mothers makes women more vulnerable to fear and the loss of attachment. . . . It makes women greedy to hold on even to men who treat them badly, more possessive and competitive for whatever crumbs of love may be available to them. (p. 58)

Mothers who are intolerant of accepting love *from* their young children create a feeling in the child that his or her physical touch is unacceptable or even repulsive. This deep-seated belief is one of the reasons why a young person develops feelings of being unlovable. In adolescence, the young person transfers these early feelings to current relationships and sees him or herself as being undesirable or unattractive to the opposite sex.

Intense rage is also aroused by a mother's rejection of her child's proffered love and affectionate embraces. Sons and daughters alike are damaged in their sexuality by rejection of their specific physical expressions of love. The reaction of rage due to the frustration of their desire for physical contact can lead to subsequent perversions and sexual disturbances. This intense anger is resolved in different ways according to the sex of the child. During the process of gender identification that spans several years of childhood, the young woman moves closer to her mother, represses her anger, and becomes sexually withholding in her adult relationships. The young man, in identifying with his father, attempts to overcome his anger, and tends to cater or sell out to a woman in his sexual relationships.

ADULT EXPRESSIONS OF SEXUALITY

Two Kinds of Sexuality

In general, *any* adult sexual relationship provides the opportunity for experiencing two distinct modes of sexual expression: an inward, more masturbatory style and an outward form of genuine contact that is a natural extension of the affection and companionship between two people. The basic *characteristics of an inward style of sexuality center around the issue of control and reflect the degree to which the man or woman is sexually withholding.* Sexual desire is toned down or diminished for the individual who is more inward. Habitual patterns of self-denial have a blunting effect on the excitement and wanting usually experienced at the beginning of a relationship. In holding back one's original desire for sex, a person transforms the act of lovemaking into a contest between the attempt to control the mate's feelings and the desire to be genuinely close.

Inward sex is characterized by the presence of self-attacks and a distorted view of the other person. In other words, the person's "voice" becomes active during the sex act. It manifests itself in the form of worry, embarrassment, self-consciousness, and a focus on the other person's satisfaction. Critical thoughts about oneself interfere with the free flow of feelings and serve to inhibit sexual responses. For example, women may have thoughts such as: "Don't let him touch you there;" "How can he like to do that?" "Don't move around so much, he'll think you're a whore." A man's "voice" might say: "You're not going to be able to satisfy her;" "Your penis is too small."

A man or woman may hold back responses or have negative thoughts ("voices") at critical points before and during lovemaking. For example, a woman may unconsciously alter her appearance or inhibit her general attractiveness if she is fearful of a sexual situation. In talking about sex or in anticipating the possibility of making love, people often become anxious about their performance and uncertain about the outcome of their experience together. The change from a conventional social situation to a sexual one can be a tense transition. When affectionate gestures become more overtly sexual, both partners may feel awkward and hesitant. Two people making love for the first time often become self-conscious upon entering the bedroom or when they undress. Negative attitudes toward the body and about nudity will tend to come to the foreground at this point.

During foreplay, negative views about certain parts of the body are picked up, on some level, by one's mate, who may avoid touching these areas. When penetration occurs, there is a transformation in the quality and meaning of the whole lovemaking experience. Intimacy is greatest at this time; symbolically, the woman is being intruded on (in a good sense) by the man. Many women become fearful during actual intercourse, and their tenseness is somehow communicated to the man, causing his excitement to diminish.

Both men and women tend to worry inwardly about their performance relating to orgasm. Their self-attacks are especially strong in this area where they are so vulnerable to "failure." Many men worry about holding out until the woman is satisfied. Others at times find it difficult to complete the sexual act, whereas women are generally concerned about their ability to achieve orgasm. Some women have difficulty at the moment of penetration because of an unconscious apprehension or fear of the penis being hurtful or dangerous. These women may also have a fear of "letting go," or of the loss of control that orgasm implies. Thus, each stage of lovemaking can present complications if either partner's anxiety or tension interrupts the smooth progression of feelings.

To summarize, two distinct kinds of sex can be described: one in which real feelings are held back and where there is a fantasized impersonal connection used to relieve primitive feelings of emotional hunger. This type of inward sex generally characterizes the couple bond and is used to avoid the emotional impact of inevitable separation that takes place when the sex act is over. By contrast, sexual experiences that are emotionally fulfilling involve genuine affection, tenderness, and sensitivity, followed by adult regard, independence, and separation.

Two Views of Sex

Concomitant with the two kinds of sexuality are two widely differing points of view about sex. There is no question that virtually all of us have developed a negative point of view about our bodies: those parts that are sexual have especially been imbued with a dirty connotation. On an intellectual level, most people would agree that sexual functions are a simple and natural part of human nature and that a "dirty" point of view must have been a learned response. Learning to feel guilty or restrictive about sex has made it an area that is fraught with anxiety and pain, and most people still have negative attitudes toward their sexuality in spite of recent movements toward sexual freedom.

Clean sex can be defined as being a natural extension of affectionate feelings. It is not seen as an activity separate from other aspects of a relationship. A clean view of sex is usually associated with the more personal, outward type of sexuality described above. Clean sex includes affection and emotional closeness. By contrast, a dirty view of sex sees it as an activity that should be kept hidden, remain a secret, be thought of as separate from other normal, daily activities. This conception of sex sees it as a subject unfit for social conversation and definitely one not to be discussed with children. It is obvious that a person who views sex in this way would be inward and secretive about sexual activities, even with people closest.

An indication of how people feel about sex is how they feel about their bodies. Since many individuals have been damaged by parents' attitudes about nudity, their attitudes toward sex are similarly affected. Children come to confuse sexual functions with anal functions at the stage of toilet training. On some level, they assimilate the verbal and nonverbal cues that communicate the disgust and displeasure that some parents feel to an inordinate degree while changing diapers. Later, many children associate the functions of the genital area with the anal region and perceive sex as "dirty." For example, in grammar school, "bathroom" jokes are often the predecessors of the "dirty" sexual joke.

Sex assumes a dirty connotation when fantasy develops and active masturbation begins. Early traumatic experiences of being "caught" by the parents in the act of masturbating cause the child a great deal of shame. There is also a sense of guilt about the specific content of sexual fantasies which may have incestuous or other forbidden components. In the adult relationship, a person may feel particularly guilty if he or she fantasizes about a person other than the sex partner during the actual sex act.

Conventional Views of Sex

Despite the advances achieved by the sexual revolution, society's attitudes about sex still reflect, for the most part, the "dirty" point of view. Conventional views are expressed in contradictory messages that cause people confusion and a great deal of misery. For example, sex outside marriage is secretly conceived of as more romantic and exciting, yet it is sneered at as illicit or labelled as "cheating." Married love and sex are seen as dull and routine, but "clean" because sanctioned by society.

Sexism creeps into many of the so-called "lessons" about sex that boys and girls learn while growing up. The clichés and language describing these activities illustrate the dirty view of sex as being "bad." A man supposedly has to "talk a woman into sex," while a woman "gives in to a man" or is an "easy mark," if sex does occur. A man has "scored," or "made it," or "triumphs" over the woman if they have sex together, whereas a woman "has fallen for his line."

In the area of sex education, most people would support the idea that children should learn healthy attitudes about sex, yet very few parents discuss this matter personally and openly with their own children. Sex education classes offered by the schools are still opposed by some parents, who refuse to let their children attend, or even prevent these classes from being taught.

CONCLUSION

Restrictions on people's sexuality, whether internally imposed through guilt and fear or externally by moral code, custom, or distorted views, serve to impoverish them in later life and interfere with fulfillment and sexual maturity. Defensive patterns of sexual expression, i.e., sexual withholding, depersonalized sex, and unusual dependence on sexual fantasies, represent a retreat from mature, natural sexuality. There is considerable resistance to forming adult relationships which would alter people's conception of themselves in a positive direction, because these changes would symbolize a movement away from the original bond with the mother and later the family.

Conventional views of sexuality support the fantasy bond by placing limitations on sexual expression, by seeing sex as dirty and the naked human body as unacceptable, by perceiving the destructive bond within the couple as "normal," and by encouraging people to act out of "shoulds," form, and obligation. As such, conventions are behavioral guidelines that restrict or damage healthy natural attitudes and creative sexual functioning. Sexist views about the difference between men and women add to the battle of the sexes, lead to distortions and misinformation about men is and women's sexual nature, and perpetuate myths that support neurotic dependency and/or alienation between men and women.

In socializing their children, parents are operating under tremendous pressure from society to inculcate restrictive values and narrow views of sexuality in their offspring. These conventional attitudes, in conjunction with the parents' own personal limitations and defenses, act to damage the child in sexual development. Taboos against physical closeness between members of a family effectively limit parents in their ability to accept the child's first tentative expressions of love for them. As we have described, the child's sexual identity and later success in forming sexual relationships are profoundly affected by the parents' reactions and defenses. Neurotic symptoms and problems in the sexual area play a significant role in limiting each person's sense of happiness and well-being. In addition, these problems bear a direct relationship to the individual's overall defensive posture and are therefore important factors in establishing diagnosis and prognosis.

Chapter 14

SOCIETY AND CONVENTIONALITY

> The family's function is to repress Eros; to induce a false
> consciousness of security; to deny death by avoiding life; to cut off
> transcendence; to believe in God, not to experience the Void; to
> create, in short, one-dimensional man; to promote respect, con-
> formity, obedience. . . .
>
> R. D. Laing (1967)
> *The Politics of Experience,* (p. 65)

Defended individuals limit themselves as thinking and feeling people. Because one does not exist in isolation, one will necessarily hurt
other people, especially those closest. A person cannot be innocently
defended; one must become defensive, even abusive or hostile, and does
the greatest harm within the family. Parents who are self-denying and
who cannot love themselves, unintentionally injure their children psychologically and emotionally. However, this destructiveness doesn't end with
the nuclear family; it extends to society at large.

Collective individual defenses exert a powerful effect on society
through social pressure. Both implicit and explicit social mores act to
limit the individual in the pursuit of life. Social pressure is a strong pull
from important people in one's family and from society in general to

imitate the behavior of other people. In this way, people are influenced more by the actions of other people than by their spoken words. Social pressure has a profound effect because there is a strong tendency in people toward conformity. Self-denying and self-hating people activate guilty feelings in others, particularly members of their own families. They cannot place restrictions on themselves without constraining those in close contact with them. They cannot remain emotionally deadened against feeling without also punishing those who inadvertently cause them to feel their pain and sadness. They cannot avoid the honest pursuit of goals without exerting a powerful pull on others to give up what they have, out of guilt. Furthermore, a defended individual confuses other people by acting with duplicity and offering double messages that attempt to conceal the true extent of his or her self-denial.

On a deep unconscious level, neurotic individuals cling to a fantasy of pseudo-independence. They hold on to feelings of self-hatred and to the bond with the family, which they continue to idealize. Yet on a more conscious level, they strive to maintain a compensatory image of themselves as decent, respectable people who want love and success and who love their spouse and their children. It is this basic split in people that misleads others in their sense of reality and cumulatively adds to the destructive effect of social pressure.

Guilt in relation to other people who are self-denying takes the joy out of achievement and diminishes one's sense of healthy competitiveness. For example, one patient, a woman, told of being reluctant to share her excitement about finding a new man to whom she was attracted with her roommate who made herself unappealing and showed little interest in men. On the other hand, she wished she knew another woman to talk to who was herself pursuing a relationship with a man. Then she would have felt supported.

Many people hold back feelings of happiness and excitement and hide their successes in order to shield friends who are more passive and self-denying. Withholding these feelings in relation to one's accomplishments can be a first step in a negative progression toward increased self-denial. An assertive person may eventually give up the pursuit of priorities and realistic goals and retreat into passivity. Indeed, most people unconsciously deprive themselves of much of what they value in life because they fear going beyond a significant person in their background, particularly the parent of the same sex or a symbolic substitute for this parental figure.

Most people in society are suspicious and cynical about other people and about relationships in general. When there are multitudes of people defending themselves in this manner, trust in human relationships is severely undermined. Conventional attitudes toward marriage and toward the opposite sex reflect this cynicism. The commonly accepted expectation that romance is destined to fade after marriage is a self-fulfilling prophecy for many people.

Eventually, some conventions, however shortsighted, become formalized into written laws. Even when they remain unwritten and implicit, they still become the accepted standards by which people measure their behavior and attitudes. Much of what people accept as standard, routine, or normal is damaging psychologically. Indeed, people living by conventional standards are unconsciously and unknowingly limiting their choices and personal freedom, which in turn will impair their emotional health.

The author sees society and social mores as a pooling of combined defenses of all its members. Conventionality and conformity support the individual's defense system. Both act in concert to oppose the natural striving of the individual. Indeed, an objective observer coming to view the existing social order, catching a glimpse of the paradoxes of conventional life, would be stunned by these observations. He or she would become aware that the things that one was expected to believe about oneself and about society were frequently the opposite of the way things *really* were. From an outside point of view, this observer would perceive that most members of the social community were unwittingly working together to maintain a dishonest way of living. He or she would note the lies, the double messages, the delusions that most people in society accept as self-evident truths.

Through social pressure, implicit and explicit value systems perpetuate the very destructiveness that they were originally set up to control in primitive communities. Because people tend to conform to external standards and norms, society is able to place prohibitions on spontaneity and sexuality, which in turn creates hostility and tension. By reinforcing moral lessons learned in the family, social institutions help to maintain and perpetuate the toxic effects of neurotic family interactions. Children and, later, adults are bound by conventional thinking and conformity which influences them to act out of "shoulds," form, and obligation, generally denying their real preferences, due to feelings of guilt.

Distortions of Conventional Values as Rationalizations for Self-Denial

The question arises as to why most individuals feel so much guilt in relation to their values and mores, many of which are inherently good and ethically sound. Unfortunately, they are taught to be selfless, to conform to senseless and unnecessary prohibitions at the expense of self. People who are self-denying and selfless have little to offer others. *When people become self-hating and self-destructive they use conventions as justifications and rationalizations for their self-denial.* In other words, they utilize values and value systems in the service of their self-destructive "voice."

The concept of being bad does not originate with moral training; it comes from being unloved and not wanting to see one's parents as inadequate. This feeling of being bad becomes a core self-concept when there is emotional deprivation. It comes from not being loved and from blaming oneself for this condition. Later, the child assigns the feeling of badness to real behavior that conflicts with moral values. In other words, when one feels that one is bad, one will do "bad" things and actually get into trouble. One tends to attach one's "badness" to objective criteria to obscure the real source of feelings of unworthiness in the family.

Children are taught moral precepts at the same time that they are also internalizing their parents' rejecting attitudes. They come to use these learned values in conjunction with the destructive thought processes of the "voice." They misconstrue ideals and mores, distort their meaning and use them against themselves. Their self-hatred is intensified when they take a moralistic, judgmental attitude toward themselves.

It is not just the exceptional child or a small minority that feel that they are "bad." These dynamics apply to the vast majority of children and later become the core self-concept for adults as well. The internalized value systems of many adults and the conventions of society work together to remind people to be self-denying, to make negative choices that are against their own self-interest. With a logic that appears to be quite rational and consistent, people deny themselves the things they want most in life and then feel guilty about their self-denial. When they *do* attempt to fulfill their wants and goals in a straightforward manner, and others close to them are self-denying, they feel guilty and alone, even selfish. The process is circular, with these individuals giving up more and more of their lives and justifying this behavior with moral imperatives.

THE IMPROBABILITY OF PARENTS LOVING THEIR CHILDREN DESPITE THEIR GOOD INTENTIONS

In order to place the question of parental love in proper perspective, the author would define this love as behavior that enhances the well-being and development of children. In this context, the majority of parents are unlikely to love their children because they themselves grow up with an incorporated negative self-image. If they do not love themselves, have a negative view of their bodies, and have become ashamed of their productions, they cannot pass on love and tenderness to their children. People who do not really like themselves are incapable of genuinely loving others. In fact, they are more likely to dump their negative feelings on others and act out their hurt.

As an illustration, one of my patients, Andy P., continuously doubted his own masculinity. In the course of his therapy it became clear that his father had pronounced latent homosexual tendencies. Unwilling to see these impulses and fantasies in himself, he projected them onto Andy, developing the fear that his son would be effeminate. Andy's father overemphasized sports and physical prowess, and his son felt the pressure and tension to prove he was a man. Although Andy did not develop overt homosexual traits, he did come to doubt his masculinity.

Perhaps the single most important reason that parents fail in their desire to provide love and care for their offspring is that the parental defense system must be kept intact to avoid pain and anxiety. Most people have turned their backs on their child-selves many years ago because they were in so much emotional pain. Now, as parents, for their own protection they must remain insensitive to their children in those areas which threaten to arouse those powerful repressed feelings. For example, a man who cannot bear to be reminded of his own childhood sadness may be vindictive or punishing to his children when they cry. A mother may suppress her children's pain in just the opposite way—by overcomforting and overprotecting them. The more self-protective a person is, the more he or she will act out these defenses on the child and progressively fail to understand and encourage healthy development. In other words, *the child is always more expendable than the parent's defense system.*

Parental good intentions are not a substitute for nourishing love, which could only be provided by a psychologically healthy and independent adult. It is both the *intention and the capability (love-food)* that is necessary to sustain a small person in growth toward maturity. Parental mistreatment, that is, the absence of parental love, causes the child psychic pain. These traumatic episodes are later partially or totally repressed, but the scars of these early wounds play a significant part in the everyday life of the adult individual.

Children find many methods to defend themselves in order to deaden their pain and relieve feelings of frustration when their needs are not met. They begin to act and respond in terms of roles rather than expressing their real selves. Their actions are geared to manipulating their parents and other people and in this process they lose themselves.

> For example, a woman who was in therapy some years ago tended to smile at inappropriate times, both in her individual sessions and when participating in groups. Her smile seemed disconcerting when she was saying something angry or sad. She was embarrassed when this was pointed out to her. But, as she began to refrain from smiling at these times, she felt a great sadness.
>
> The woman realized, then, that her parents had conditioned her, in a sense, to smile by ridiculing her "seriousness" and by cautioning her not to frown or look unhappy. So she smiled to placate them and later unconsciously smiled in difficult situations to please other people. More significantly, her sadness as a child had been a rebuke to her parents, an outward sign that they were not good parents or mature people. She was implicitly trained to stifle any symptom that might point to the fact that her parents had caused her unhappiness. Her inappropriate smiling also served to block out her own awareness of her genuine feelings of sadness. This woman had a fragile hold on her own identity because of her parents' inability to fulfill her needs and because she had been made to feel ashamed any time she expressed a desire for something that she really wanted. Her reactions of sadness and depression were "not allowed." Her sense of self was diminished even more as she learned to present a false front of cheerfulness.

CONVENTIONS AND INSTITUTIONS THAT SUPPORT THE "VOICE"

Social institutions that propagate judgmental values have an important effect on our lives because they are similar to the injunctions of the individual's "voice." The voice utilizes morals and ethical values as rationalizations for self-denial. Certain social institutions more than others foster this destructive propensity of human beings to be self-denying. Traditional religion's dogma of selflessness is essentially an externalization of the individual's voice and therefore has a powerful negative influence on behavior. The haranguing voice of the fundamentalist minister castigating sinners and urging them to seek redemption directly resembles the self-critical "voices" of the members of his congregation. The content of the sermon closely corresponds to specific internal self-attacks. Sacred teachings in the hands of neurotic and misguided religious leaders have had a profound negative effect on all areas of human affairs, but most particularly on human sexuality. Our conventional views of sex are steeped in the Judeo-Christian tradition that teaches self-denial and selflessness.

TRADITIONAL RELIGIOUS VIEWS OF THE BODY AND SEXUALITY

Faced with the agonizing awareness that the body would not live on after death, humankind postulated the concept of a soul that would survive the death of the body, opening up the possibility of imagining an eternal life. To preserve this illusion, people were willing to renounce earthly desires, principally sexual desires. In turning away from so-called pleasures of the flesh and in turning against the body and giving it a dirty connotation, human beings paid a painful price.

The creation myth, as recorded in the Bible and other ancient writings, is one of many legends used by traditional religion to support people's tendencies to renounce aspects of their physical nature in return for the hope of living forever. Misinterpretations of the concept of original sin have served to alienate people from their own bodies with their sensations and feelings. Feelings occur in the body, thus any philosophy that is anti-body is also anti-feelings. Many religious ideologies are immoral because they cause unnecessary suffering to human beings in the area of their sexuality. The view that sex is animalistic and that the human body is corrupt and unclean has had tragic consequences in terms of an extensive crippling effect on sexuality and on human relationships in general.

Many religious ideologies are immoral because they support a collective self-destructive process. A philosophy of self-sacrifice and self-denial that equates thoughts with actions is an insidious form of thought control or brainwashing. The suppression of our physical nature and the unnecessary limitations imposed on other aspects of human life have only succeeded in arousing human hostility and destructiveness. Thus the suppressive effects of the church paradoxically have contributed to the occurrence of the very crimes and immoral acts that religious leaders have sought to avoid.

The concept of "original sin" has been distorted by clergy and laity alike to mean that people are "born bad," a condition that children accept when they incorporate their parents' negative feelings toward them. This "bad" image of the self leads the individual to seek atonement through self-denial. "Original sin" has been interpreted to mean that the naked body is somehow sinful and dirty. This mistaken notion supports feelings of shame that originate in the child's earliest experiences of the family. In traditional families, most children grow up with considerable guilt about their bodies and their bodily functions. Abnormal guilt reactions introjected by the child from defended parents lead to serious limitations in adult relationships.

CONVENTIONAL VIEWS ABOUT THE FAMILY THAT SUPPORT DEFENSES

Conventions stand solidly behind the family, right or wrong; society idealizes parents and supports the myth of unconditional love; its institutions support destructive coupling and family bonds. Traditional marriage vows preserve the exclusiveness of the married couple and form the core of the family's isolation and attitudes of superiority and distrust. Restrictive conventional standards often have tragic consequences because they place limitations on how much a person who is struggling to develop him or herself can actually change or progress. The individual who successfully challenges deeply ingrained defenses through psychotherapy must still contend with the daily frustration and pain imposed by other members of society and social institutions.

The Myth of Unconditional Family Love

The precept of unconditional parental love is a fundamental part of society's morality and the core of family life. It leads to considerable guilt feelings in parents. These feelings of guilt further contaminate the picture for those individuals who have difficulty in, or are incapable of, loving their offspring. The alternative to facing this painful lack in oneself is to act as though one is loving whether or not one happens to be. Most parents who have come for psychotherapy over the years have found it difficult to admit to not loving their children. The author has spent considerable time and effort to convince obviously unloving parents that they do not love their children and that this fact is innocent. They could not be otherwise, given their own parental environment and personal make-up. This admission is a fundamental step in changing the situation in the family. As long as the fantasy of love is maintained, there will be no real change.

It serves no constructive purpose for people to conceal their inadequacies from the child. Indeed, an honest acceptance of this fact would enable both parties to cope with reality without the additional defensive pressure. With a diminution of this pressure and the subsequent relaxation for both parent and child, they may even come to have genuine regard and loving feelings toward one another. On the other hand, the tension introduced by covering up the absence of love further injures the child. Because they cannot bear to know that they are rejecting of their children, many parents systematically cut off the children's opportunity to develop and cure themselves of their pain.

Many books on childrearing which counsel parents how to "act" or "talk" with their children encourage role-determined behavior that only increases the tension and dishonesty within the family. In a moral sense they are destructive and harmful to the families they profess to help. The immorality lies in the act of willfully deceiving the child through jargonized speech or other techniques of manipulation. There can be little doubt that this deception is injurious to the child's psyche. There is absolutely no circumstance where misleading the child or making a show of being loving or of loving each child equally, etc., is justified.

Parents in their dishonesty manipulate their children and hide their real feelings, and of course their children learn early to manipulate back. The parent uses force and becomes arbitrary and judgmental, and the child learns passive-aggression and how to control through weakness. This sets the stage for years of conflict between them, and this basic acting out on the child's part becomes the core of further manipulation in later life. Once the child's defenses are formed, these bad habits interfere with the parents loving him or her and later ward off other people as well.

The Proprietary Rights of Parents and Their Idealized Image

Society strongly supports the belief that children belong to their parents and that the parent is always right. The assumption that parents have proprietary rights over their children has its source in the illusion of connection between parent and child. This belief is closely related to the misconception that people who are married to each other also "belong" to each other. Within this context, parents are assumed to have the best interests of the child at heart, and to be mature and capable of raising their own children without interference.

Many parents express the attitude that because they gave life to their offspring and have spent much time, energy, and money on their upbringing, their children belong to them, much as any other possession. They establish an "exclusive" emotional tie with their baby that is different from a natural attachment characterized by genuine loving feelings.

This enveloping, constraining interest reflects the parents' feeling that the child is "theirs," a part of them, to do with what they will, to raise in whatever way they see fit. Parents with strong dependency needs of their own focus their feelings of emotional hunger on their child and are overly concerned with his or her performance. These parents see the child as an extension of themselves and there is a general blurring of the boundaries between them.

Except in cases of blatant child abuse or neglect, parents' rights over their children's lives and destinies are held sacred and inviolable in most courts of law. This lack of acknowledgment of the child's separateness and inherent rights as a person goes hand in hand with society's idealization of the family and the belief that parents know best. The truth is that many parents are adults physically, but still children emotionally. To the extent that they have been malformed in their own development, they will act out their neurosis on all persons who come into close contact with them, especially their children, who are helpless and cannot escape.

One of the sacred beliefs that is taken for granted by most members of society is the assumption that the members of a family love one another. The nuclear family is regarded as the bulwark of society and its image must be protected at all costs. Again, the child is expendable in the face of this collective defense. Individual rights are sacrificed and ignored by most social institutions, including those dealing with mental health problems in the family. In one extreme case that attracted national attention, society's neglect of serious warning signs in a "nice" family led to a tragic patricide. The son, sixteen, killed his father in a last desperate attempt to put an end to the physical abuse he had suffered and to protect his younger sister from continued sexual assaults by the father. The fact that this tragedy could have been averted if certain preconceptions about the family had been set aside was revealed in a news story of the crime:

> Most social agencies are reluctant to intervene in troubled families before the tragedies occur. That was certainly the case with Richard Jahnke [the boy who killed his father]. When he approached local authorities for help, he reports, "They treated me like a rebellious teen-ager." A case-worker dropped by, chatted amiably with the family, then left—unable to believe that the violence . . . reported could take place in such a comfortable middle-class home. The beatings grew worse. (*Newsweek,* June 27, 1983)

The popular notion that parents deserve respect simply because they are parents undoubtedly influenced the social worker's judgment, which led to the tragic consequence only a few days later.

Few family conflicts reach the murderous proportions of the one described above; nevertheless, the same dynamics apply to less serious crimes against children: verbal abuse, deception, overprotection, exploitation, to mention a few. In summary, conventional thinking validates the sanctity of the family and supports the protection of parents' rights over their children. These beliefs are part of a collective defense that often unwittingly condones the harm done to children "for their own good."[1] All these beliefs act to support the sense of "badness" that is instilled in most children by their righteous and powerful parents.

THE MIXED MESSAGES OF SOCIETY

Society's ideals conflict with everyday life experience in a way that confuses people's sense of reality. An accurate perception of reality is central to a person's well-being and is vital to sanity. Having one's sense of reality distorted or denied can be a shattering blow to the psyche. To mislead other individuals or confuse their perception of the world around them is extremely destructive, yet mixed messages characterize the traditional family. In seriously disturbed families, double messages are an important factor in causing mental illness.

The Double Bind in Schizophrenic Families

The "double bind" has been studied extensively by Gregory Bateson and his colleagues. In Bateson's analysis of communications in families of schizophrenics (Bateson, Jackson, Haley, & Weakland, 1956), he has concluded that in these families, the mother consistently sends contradictory messages to the child. The child is prevented from commenting on the discrepancy between these double messages by the fear of losing the relationship with the mother. Generally, the schizophrenogenic mother has intense ambivalent feelings toward her child; she cannot face her own hostile feelings in relation to the child, nor can she tolerate feelings of affection and close contact. Given these family dynamics, whenever this mother experiences affectionate feelings toward her child, she begins to feel threatened and must withdraw from him or her. However, she cannot accept the hostility implied by her withdrawal, and to deny its existence, she must pretend to be affectionate and must simulate closeness with her child.

Bateson (1972) describes the prepsychotic child as growing up "unskilled in determining what people really mean and unskilled in expres-

---

[1] The reader is referred to *For Your Own Good*, translation of *Am Anfang war Erziehung*, by Alice Miller (1980/1983), a Swiss psychoanalyst, for an elaboration of this point.

sing what he really means, which is essential for normal relationships."
He suggests that this situation occurs in normal relationships as well.
When a person is caught in a double-bind situation, he will respond
defensively in a manner similar to the schizophrenic, though less intensely.

Thus, when children are given two opposing messages or are
expected to act in contradictory ways without being able to comment on
the discrepancy, they tend to develop serious behavior and thought disturbances. Other studies have shown that in families where there is an
identified schizophrenic patient, these double messages occur at a sub-
stantially higher frequency than in families of "normal" or neurotic children. On a larger scale, double messages permeate our society to such an
extent that one can predict similar effects on a social level.

Society's Double Messages About Marriage

The stated ideals about marriage and the reality of the divorce rate
present many people with a basic contradiction that leads to cynicism
and feelings of futility about the future of their relationships. For example, most people in society profess strong support for close, enduring relationships between men and women, yet the reality is that most
couples are alienated from one another. Indeed, a man and woman who
have been married for a long time and who still act romantically or express affection in public will be teased or even made fun of. Stereotypic
attitudes about the opposite sex learned in the family and later through
other social institutions also prevent people from being close. Thus,
young people are taught, in this instance, two divergent views of marriage and relationships. On one hand, they are told to look forward to
marriage as providing a high potential for personal happiness. At the
same time, they are taught conventional sexist attitudes about each other
that are as discriminatory as racial prejudice and create a cynical view
of marriage.

Because marriage vows and conventional attitudes support the
guarantee of enduring love between two people, romance inevitably
dies, to be replaced with a fantasy of love. When people attempt to freeze
their feelings of love in time, the feeling eludes them and disappears
from their lives. Often, all that is left is the pretense, the form, and the
dishonesty necessary to maintain the fantasy of love and connection. As
in the double bind, if one partner, in a moment of clarity, comments
about the real situation, the couple bond is disrupted. This step is generally too threatening for either partner because, on a deep level, both
feel that if the bond were broken, the relationship would be over. Thus,

fear of loss and separation helps to maintain the bond and discourages personal honesty and integrity.

CONCLUSION

The duplicity or dishonesty of defended individuals is reflected in the contradiction between the stated values of society and objective reality. On an individual level, we seek a fantasy bond that denies our interdependence and need for others. Then, there is an illusion of connection within the couple that denies the reality of human separateness. At a later stage, there are the intentional and unintentional lies that are told to children by parents who are protecting the family bond and the myth of family love.

Each specific manifestation of dishonesty is also expressed in society's value systems and its social institutions. Generally speaking, people remain unaware of the duplicity in themselves and in others. They mask their perceptions and fail to comment on the discrepancies that they perceive. Members of society are accustomed to living with these mixed messages and accept them as normal and proper. In this sense, social mores and conventions support the individual's self-destructiveness. These act to protect an habitually defensive life style and provide the person with justifications for self-denial.

Conventionality supports the bonds and fantasies of connection that give an individual a false sense of security and an illusion of immortality. In this manner, social mores and conventions play a significant role in individual defenses against death anxiety. The universal fear of death is generally repressed in our society or is well-hidden under elaborate belief systems. In blocking out the awareness of death and denying anxiety about dying, a person also tends to limit present-day experience. This progressive self-denial cuts into one's vitality and diminishes emotional investment in life-affirming activity.

Chapter 15

THE DEVELOPMENT OF INDIVIDUAL DEFENSES AGAINST DEATH ANXIETY

It is indeed impossible to imagine our own death; and whenever we attempt to do so we can perceive that we are in fact still present as spectators. Hence the psycho-analytic school could venture on the assertion that at bottom no one believes in his own death, or, to put the same thing in another way, that in the unconscious every one of us is convinced of his own immortality.

Sigmund Freud (1915/1957)
Thoughts for the Times on War and Death, (p. 289)

After children reach the awareness that death is inevitable, the core of their defense systems center around their anxiety about death. Many human endeavors and behaviors are shaped by a desperate attempt to avoid the reality of this limitation in time, yet the fear of death cannot be quieted or dismissed. On a conscious level, people are aware of their personal end; they know, intellectually, that they will die someday. Yet on an emotional level, most people deny this knowledge.

The basic framework for an individual's denial of death can be found in the system of defenses built at the stage in development that preceded the understanding of death. In the first weeks and months of life, an infant is often faced with feelings of frustration and pain that occasionally reach intolerable proportions. In this situation, the baby

241

lacks the capability to control the world that threatens it. The infant cannot even control its own physical reactions to the intrusions from its environment. It is, quite literally, completely helpless and dependent on the good will and abilities of its parents. It is this feeling of absolute helplessness and fear of possible annihilation that becomes unbearable to the infant.

To cope with this overwhelming feeling, *the young child builds a fantasy of omnipotence, imagining that it has a permanent connection to its mother,* that it is at one with her. This illusion of self-sufficiency, of being its own mother, of being able to meet its own needs without going outside itself, is a desperate attempt on the child's part to deny its true state of vulnerability. As we noted earlier, children who suffer from rejection and emotional deprivation in their early development come to prefer this solution over reality testing and an active mastery of their expanding world.

By the time children come to the realization that their parents are vulnerable to death, they already have at their disposal a well-developed system of defenses. To avoid this new threat to their security, they tend to return to a prior stage of development. They generally regress to the stage where they were unaware of this fracture or separation. They use their illusion of pseudo-independence to reassure themselves that even in the event of their parents' death, they can take care of themselves. Soon, however, they learn that they too must die and discover that they cannot sustain their own lives, that is, they become aware of their ultimate helplessness in relation to life itself. At this critical "point of futility," their sense of omnipotence is deeply wounded.

People rarely recover from this final blow. They deny death by strengthening their defenses, that is, by returning to the fantasy of connectedness with the mother, an illusion that alleviates their sense of helplessness. They form bonds with new significant figures in their lives and become childish, defended, and defensive. In believing that they can somehow cheat death, they hold on to remnants of their infantile feelings of omnipotence. Helplessness in the face of severe frustration necessitated the formation of their original defenses; later these defenses are intensified when they become aware that they are helpless to insure their ultimate survival. In this sense, neurosis can be said to be a maladaptive response to a very realistic fear—the terror and anxiety that accompany direct confrontation and awareness of the fact of death.

This interrelationship between the psychoanalytic view of the defense system and the existentialist's attempt to deal phenomenologically with the problem of death brings the two systems of thought into juxtaposition. Both views offer important insights into individual and societal defenses against death anxiety. The concept of the Fantasy Bond unifies the two theoretical positions in relation to the issue of death.

It is the author's view that denying death leads to a progressive giving up of life-affirming activities and pursuits for the security of an imagined fusion with another person. Renouncing one's destiny or instinctual life creates existential guilt because it goes against one's nature to avoid fulfilling oneself in the world. However, any real movement *toward* life and an independent existence leads in turn to a fuller awareness of death and intensifies the fear of dying.

It appears that we are caught in an unresolvable dilemma. On the one hand, if, free of our customary defenses, we contend with the full emotional awareness of death, with its attendant feelings of fear, despair, and dread, the impact of this awareness threatens to overwhelm us. On the other hand, we will bear the pain of existential guilt if we deny death's reality by employing defensive maneuvers that cut into our real experience while protecting our illusion of immortality.

THE RELATIONSHIP BETWEEN SEPARATION ANXIETY AND DEATH ANXIETY

> Anxiety is the ego's incapacity to accept death.
> Anxiety is a response to experiences of separation, individuality, and death.
>
> Norman O. Brown (1959)

> For behind the sense of insecurity in the face of danger, behind the sense of discouragement and depression, there always lurks the basic fear of death.
>
> G. Zilboorg (1943)

The fantasy bond initially protects the infant against the ravages of its reactions to temporary separations from its mother, separations which it interprets phenomenologically as permanent loss. *Temporary separations from the mother and tentative moves toward autonomy evoke a form of deep anxiety and dread that are the precursors of the unbearable emotional response that is aroused somewhat later by the full awareness of one's death.*

Separation anxiety is a primitive form of anxiety, described by Freud (1925/1959) as "a reaction to the felt loss of the object." It is a broad conceptual term, encompassing a wide range of experiences and reactions, and is not meant exclusively to describe reactions to separation from the parental figure, per se. In fact, theorists tend to discuss the infant's initial fear responses in a variety of terms and attribute their appearance in the child's primitive emotional life to any number of causes. For example, Anna Freud (1965) postulates a sequence of forms of early anxious reactions, including "archaic fears of complete annihilation, to separation anxiety, castration anxiety, fear of loss of love" (p. 231). Mahler (1968) theorizes that, at very early stages in his development, an infant fears most the annihilation of the self due to the "loss of the symbiotic object" (p. 220). She believes that separation anxiety, per se, develops at a later phase "after the beginning of object constancy has been achieved" (p. 222). At this point, "among children whose basic trust has been less than optimal, an abrupt change to acute stranger anxiety may make its appearance. . . . This inverse relation between basic confidence and stranger anxiety deserves to be emphasized" (Mahler, 1974, p. 96).

It is the author's view that failure on the part of the parents to provide "love-food" arouses considerable emotional distress in children and plunges them into a state of agitation and deep anxiety. This form of intense anxiety, together with the inevitable anxiety engendered by the normal comings and goings of the mother, breaks into the infant's primitive sense of oneness with the mother and destroys the infantile illusion of omnipotence. When the child is older and discovers death as a fact of existence, he or she is once again subjected to a similar state of helplessness, anxiety, and dread.

The Primary Fantasy Bond, in conjunction with primitive self-nourishing behaviors such as thumb-sucking, prevent the infant and young child from being overwhelmed by the intensity of their reactions to disturbing events in early life, because it allows them to conjure up their mother's presence whenever they are under stress. This imagined connection guarantees an endless source of gratification. In the child's inner world of fantasy, time has no meaning, there are no separations, and everything is permanent and secure, including one's life and the lives of one's loved ones.

The formation of the Fantasy Bond and the child's increasing dependence on it may well be the most significant developmental process of early childhood. The essence of this core defense lies in the child's deeply-held belief in his or her own powers, a conviction that was described by Freud (1925/1959) as "the over-estimation of the importance of psychical reality—the belief in 'the omnipotence of thoughts'—which lies at the root of magic as well" (p. 66). The sequence of events in an infant's life is such that this illusion of power is actually reinforced by reality. Because their needs and wants are met frequently enough, young babies are conditioned to associate their desires with their mothers' act in satisfying those desires. This association of needs and their subsequent satisfaction—even though sometimes delayed—sets up the conditions necessary to further affirm these fantasies of invincibility and self-containment. It verifies their illusion that they are capable of controlling their physical environment; especially, it reassures them that they can control their mother.

Due to the prolonged period of infantile dependency, there is a tendency on the part of the very young child to believe that what is wished for and demanded will become reality. Only as language develops is this conviction gradually abandoned. However, remnants of this infantile fantasy exist within each adult and, indeed, most people are reluctant to give up the unconscious notion that they can achieve immortality through a connection with significant people in their lives.

Whenever events occur that make it impossible for older children or adults to avoid the full impact of death's inevitability, they tend to return to the false safety and security of the bond. At these critical times, they attempt to form a connection with a significant person whom they believe can guarantee them immortality in the same sense their mother did. In this manner, the fantasy of being merged with another person provides people with the false assurance that they will live forever. *The Fantasy Bond that was formed originally to cope with separation anxiety becomes the primary defense against death anxiety.*

STAGES IN THE CHILD'S DISCOVERY OF DEATH

> Ben . . ., [aged eleven] in his mother's bed for a minute or two
> before breakfast, talking about measles, said happily: "I'd like to
> die." "Why?" "Because I'd like to be in the same grave as you."
> Sylvia Anthony (1971/1972)
> *The Discovery of Death in Childhood and After*, (p. 150).

In our clinical experience with a number of children, my associates and I have noted several stages through which children progress in their discovery of death. These stages appear to be associated with the successive steps that children take in differentiating themselves from their mother, and in separating from the original symbiotic relationship with her. A rough analysis of these stages of a child's increasing awareness of death may be described as follows:

1. In early infancy (birth to six months), a child's denial of separateness from the mother is achieved through the subjective feeling of being at one with the mother's breast—the Primary Fantasy Bond.

2. At the next stage (six months to two years), there is a gradual accommodation to reality, to an awareness of being separate from the

mother. However, under pressure or stress, children still tend to regress to the earlier phase when they imagine that they and their mother are one. At this stage of development, the infant experiences intense episodes of separation anxiety and a terror of annihilation or loss of self, though there is as yet no structured concept of death.

3.   At a critical point in growing up (three to six years), children begin to be aware that their parents are vulnerable to death. Again, children tend to regress to a prior stage when they imagine that they can control their mother's movements in relation to themselves and consequently believe that they can control her life or death by their wishes (infantile narcissism). In this phase, the Fantasy Bond becomes strengthened as children incorporate traits and attitudes of both parents and develop secondary defenses, including the "voice." Children are now connected to an *internalized image of the mother.* They imagine that they can survive on their own and that they can feed and take care of themselves.

4.   Eventually children come to the realization that they cannot even sustain their own lives. Some researchers believe that this awareness develops between the ages of five and nine years (Nagy, 1948). Others place it at an earlier age (Rochlin, 1967). This discovery effectively destroys children's illusions of self-sufficiency. They are unable to bear the prospect of losing themselves through death. Their well-regulated world is literally turned upside down by their dawning awareness that people, parents, and even they must die. They are completely demoralized by this new awareness and cannot come to terms with it. On an unconscious level, they deny the reality of their personal death by regressing to a previous stage of development and to the bond with the parental image. At the same time, they accept the *idea of death* on an intellectual level.

Children become aware of their own vulnerability to death right after they discover that they can lose their parents through death. Frequently, however, there is a partial repression of this knowledge; for instance, children may accept the fact that their parents can die, yet deny that death applies directly to themselves. In these cases, their logic follows their earlier, magical mode of thinking. They believe that even though their parents are mortal, they can still take care of themselves, they can "feed themselves." In their desperation to escape a situation that they see as hopeless and futile, they cling more tenaciously to this familiar solution. As a result, the self-mothering process is strengthened, becoming more deeply entrenched as a core defense *after* the child becomes acquainted with the concept of death.

Symptoms of Denial and Repression of an Awareness of Death in Children

Denial of the knowledge about death may be immediate—or it may be slow to develop. Sylvia Anthony (1971/1972), in her study of children's understanding of death, cites cases that illustrate the defense mechanisms employed by children and their parents to avoid the anguish of this discovery. In one straitforward account given by a mother of a conversa-versation with her three-year-old daughter, she writes:

> [My daughter, Jane,] said, "I don't want Nan [the child's nursemaid] to . . . change and grow old." Then, "Will Nan die? Shall I die too, does everyone die?" On my saying yes, she broke into really heartbreaking tears and kept on saying, "But I don't want to die, I don't want to die." This rather upset me and I stupidly tried to console her by hedging—a fatal thing with a child as I know if I had not been wrought up myself. I tried to make things better by saying everyone and everything died, when they were old and tired and therefore glad to do so. (p. 139)

In other cases, Anthony noted the tendency to defend against the knowledge of death by imagining a union with the loved one after death. She states:

> In all these instances, anxiety is clearly about death as separa-tion from the love-object, and the defence has taken the form of a belief or hope of union in death; indeed unconsciously of a closer union in death than was possible in life. (p. 151)

Anthony's research indicates underlying fantasies on the part of many children that a reunion with the mother, in a deep sense, brings with it immortality. Her findings tend to agree with the author's hypothesis that the unconscious, fantasized connection with the mother is associated with a general sense of immortality in children. Further, the child's advancement through the stages of intellectual development does not necessarily result in a permanent abandonment of the primitive thinking that was characteristic of earlier stages, especially in relation to ideas about death.

The desire to remain a child rather than grow up quickly was also found in a large number of children interviewed by Anthony. This wish was associated with a belief that one dies only when one is older. If children equate maturity and old age with dying, then it follows that they would attempt to remain childish, that is, to engage in immature, even infantile, behaviors as a defense against death anxiety.

In his work with children, the author has found that fears and anxieties about death and old age are prominent throughout childhood. Children's responses upon discovering death typically include a denial through regression to immature behaviors, as suggested above. Frequently, children withdraw from close personal contact with their parents when they begin to think in terms of their own death or when they comprehend that their parents are vulnerable to death. They strengthen an imaginary connection or bond with their parents but relinquish real closeness and affection for them. For example, a four-year-old girl appeared despondent following a conversation with her father about the possibility of his growing old and dying. She expressed hostility toward him for talking with her about the subject even though she had spontaneously initiated the conversation. In the succeeding days, the little girl was not at all her usual joyful, carefree self. She tended to ignore both her parents, treating them rather coolly and matter-of-factly. It was obvious from her behavior that she had pulled away sharply from the close, affectional contact that she ordinarily enjoyed with them. The phase passed and she was no longer distant, but it is likely to return at other times when she feels afraid of separation or death.

SYMPTOMS OF CHILDREN'S UNDERLYING CONCERN ABOUT DEATH

Otto Rank (1968) perceived that sexual conflict is universal because the body presents an insurmountable problem to a creature who must die. He believed that children feel guilty about their bodies because they are aware that their bodies are fallible. This guilt leads to anxious questions about sex and reproduction that may really be questions about the meaning of the body, the terror of living in a body that can grow old and die. Children's revulsion at the thought of their parents having sexual intercourse, that is, the trauma of the "primal scene," may be due simply to their rejection of the undeniable physicalness of an act performed by people who they believe to be immortal and invulnerable and therefore "above" things of the body.

Many children report nightmares filled with themes indicating a deep-seated preoccupation with death and with the vulnerability of their bodies. These terrifying dreams appear more frequently in those children who have not successfully repressed their emotional reactions to the knowledge of death. These nightmares decrease in frequency during later childhood and early adolescence, a fact that may indicate the child's increased ability to deny death on an unconscious level. Studies have shown that adults who had experienced the demise of relatives or close friends in their early years, especially before the age of ten, have significantly more nightmares involving themes of death (Feldman & Hersen, 1967).

Other researchers have noted a greater incidence of deaths in mothers of schizophrenic patients (Hilgard, Newman, & Fisk, 1960) and depressives (Beck, Sethi, & Tuthill, 1963) than in matched samples from the "normal" population. It was hypothesized that these early losses through death of relatives, friends, or parents aroused emotions of mourning and melancholy that the children could not successfully handle through the normal processes of grief. It is likely that, in these cases, the blow to the children's narcissistic sense of omnipotence is so great that their subsequent regression into fantasy is more severe and longer-lasting than those experienced by children who have no early acquaintance with death. Even where there is no death experience in the child's early family life, there is a gradual loss of spontaneity and joy with a progressive, habitual denying of the pleasures of life after children find out about death and begin to apply the concept to their own lives.

HOW THE DEFENSIVE PROCESS WORKS AS A PROTECTION AGAINST DEATH ANXIETY

> Kierkegaard understood that the lie of character is built up because the child needs to adjust to the world, to the parents, and to his own existential dilemmas. It is built up before the child has a chance to learn about himself in an open or free way, and thus character defenses are automatic and unconscious. The problem is that the child becomes dependent on them and comes to be encased in his own character armor, unable to see freely beyond his own prison or into himself, into the defenses he is using, the things that are determining his unfreedom. . . .
>
> Ernest Becker (1973)
> *The Denial of Death*, (p. 73).

Withholding and Death Anxiety

The infant defends itself from feelings of annihilation and separation in its initial struggle for survival; later, this same protection becomes disabling as the child extends these defenses to include more and more areas of psychological functioning. Seeking gratification in fantasy limits the possibility of finding actual satisfaction in relationships and is a denial of the natural human need for affiliation with other people. Self-denial or withholding, especially when acted out in an ongoing sexual relationship, is a negation of all that is alive, pleasurable, or spontaneous. People become sexually withholding partly in order to escape an awareness of being connected to their body which is vulnerable to illness, aging, and death.

In addition, people who feel guilty about being self-denying or withholding become progressively more self-hating; their guilt about hurting others and their shame about their inward style of gratifying themselves merely affirm the "bad child" image which is a vital part of the internalized fantasy bond with the "good parent." On an unconscious level, such people believe that their lives will go on forever, because they are still connected, in their imagination, to their critical, powerful parent. Their thoughts, time, and energies are consumed by self-attacks, dramatic fantasies of being rejected and victimized by life, or by efforts to find justifications for their self-denial. They are focused primarily on themselves and on their self-critical thoughts and become indifferent to some extent to events in the external world and to other people. In this way, self-hatred serves the purpose of narrowing down or trivializing life experience so that individuals can escape the full awareness of their existence and their mortality. In continuing to act out the "bad child" role, they often feel a sense of being younger than their years; their lack of maturity on an emotional level obscures a view of themselves as adults who must grow old and die.

In a bond, both partners progressively withhold their lovable qualities, the ones especially admired by their lover. Symptoms of this insidious process of self-obliteration emerge as both reinstate their defenses and give up genuine caring and love for the other. Why does this process appear to be almost universal in intimate, long-standing relationships? It is because the experience of being loved and valued makes individuals acutely aware of their existence. It arouses an intense fear of loss—loss of the loved one through rejection or death and loss of the self through death. By systematically eliminating one's desirable characteristics and loving responses, one rids oneself of the special qualities that were valued and loved by both one's partner and oneself. Ultimately one has very little left to lose through death. In a sense, one has triumphed over death by giving up one's uniqueness and individuality out of an anticipatory fear or grief in relation to an inevitable loss. The entire process takes place primarily on an unconscious level, and the person generally remains unaware of the underlying causes of the deterioration in the relationship and in the self.

In effect, both partners commit psychological suicide through withholding. Consequently, they are tortured by the existential guilt of going against their own natures. In this self-hating, guilty state, they lose interest in life and become oblivious to death. In this manner, withholding, as it manifests itself in a bond, can become a powerful defense against death anxiety.

How Self-Nourishing Habits Act to Relieve Death Anxiety

The addictive power of self-nourishing habits and routines lies in their ability to block out the highs and lows of our life experiences. The various methods of parenting ourselves are psychologically debilitating and dull us to the realities of our existence. They diminish our awareness of a limitation in time by giving us a sense of being suspended at a certain stage or process. Whenever we encounter positive events that cause us to value our lives and make us aware of how much we stand to lose through death, we often become anxious and tend to withdraw into a more isolated, inward state and increase our use of addictive substances.

To the extent that individuals parent themselves, they also maintain the fears they learned from their parents. Furthermore, they have incorporated their compensatory maneuvers in relation to these fears. In other words, self-feeding or taking care of oneself is associated with the tendency to protect oneself in the same manner as one's parents. Parents initially warn their children of dangers in an attempt to preserve their physical lives. They warn them not to run into the street, to be careful, to be wary of strangers—to mention only a few warnings. Many adults tend to maintain an exaggerated control and watchfulness over themselves, and these patterns form a vital part of their self-nourishing, self-protecting style of living. It is doubtful, however, that people would need compulsively to overprotect themselves had they been raised in the best of circumstances by loving parents.

People who defend themselves in a fearful style against a perceived harsh world use obsessional thinking, i.e., the voice, to block their spontaneity and restrict their actions. They imagine they can control death by guarding and protecting themselves and anticipating all contingencies. Their denied fear of death, displaced from its source, can become transformed into specific phobias or compulsive, ritualistic behavior.

Anticipatory Fantasies that Support Self-Denial

Superstitions about death are common as evidenced by the belief that good times are inevitably followed by bad in the overall scheme of things. People feel that "good luck" can never last and that the "axe is bound to fall sooner or later," or that "fate" intervenes at the moment they least expect it. This deep-seated anticipation of unfortunate events is used as justification for not giving their joy and exuberance full rein. Instead, people restrain their enthusiasm considerably. They have been told by parents, "Don't get so excited," so they habitually and unconsciously stifle outward expressions of excitement.

Expectations about misfortune, illness, and death arise in part because as children we learned that good times with our parents were usually followed by withdrawal or punitive behavior. In this manner many children are systematically trained to expect the worst after enjoying particularly good times with their families.

Another related phenomenon that tends to arouse the dread of death generally occurs when a person feels unusually fulfilled in life, is especially happy, or is on the upgrade psychologically. Nightmares about dying that feel very realistic are more frequent at these times. A chance reminder of the inevitability of death can become agonizing to a person who is living life to the fullest.

One patient, after years of struggling to build a career for herself, had succeeded in becoming a highly successful dress designer. She had recently married a man whom she loved very much, and the couple was planning to start a family in the near future. Her lifelong fantasy of having a family of her own with the man she loved, as well as her dreams of success in her chosen career, were being fulfilled. Furthermore, she was nearing the end of her therapy that had covered a period of 3 years, during which time she had shown considerable improvement.

Therefore I was puzzled when this patient arrived for her session one day in a state of indifference and lethargy that did not at all fit her previous exuberance and happiness about her life. As she talked about the events of the previous week, she seemed dispirited and listless.

When I mentioned my impression of her emotional state, she was surprised. Later in the session she remembered an incident that appeared to have some bearing on her deterioration. She had been driving home one evening from a business appointment in a nearby town when she had come upon a traffic jam that slowed her progress to a crawl. In the patient's words:

> I was driving along the freeway one evening near sunset. I don't remember ever feeling so alive as I did at that moment. I loved feeling the sensation of the cool wind on my face; the scenery, even from that dull stretch of freeway, looked beautiful to me. I was elated by the success of my meeting with a potential

buyer and I was looking forward to seeing Dan as soon as I got home.

I actually ached with happiness. I didn't mind the delay in traffic until the thought occurred to me that there might be an accident ahead. My heart started beating furiously. Moments later I was passed by a speeding ambulance. As I slowly approached a curve in the freeway I could see an overturned car by the side of the road. Two attendants were covering someone who was lying on a stretcher. I couldn't tell if he was dead or alive, but I immediately thought of Dan—what if it had been him? I started shaking uncontrollably. I felt that I couldn't stand the thought of Dan lying there, dead in the road. The scene was too stark, too real, to forget. I kept seeing it before me as I drove the rest of the way home.

An hour later, I arrived at our apartment and Dan was waiting for me. I was very shaken and cried as I told him what had happened that evening. Dan was very sweet and understanding and by the next day I had practically forgotten the whole incident. But since that night, Dan and I haven't made love—I just haven't felt like being close to him. I didn't understand why until just now. It's hard to believe that I stopped feeling attracted to him because I happened to see a traffic accident, but it's really true. It's as if my feelings went dead, so I wouldn't have to keep picturing that scene on the freeway.

The patient's recounting of this frightening experience was accompanied by a great deal of emotional affect and the catharsis appeared to be beneficial to her. She seemed closer to her feelings after realizing that she had lost, in a sense, almost an entire week in her life with her husband. This insight also aroused her regret and sadness because the reaction was characteristic of the way in which she had defended herself against close attachments ever since she was a child. Her objective had always been to avoid unpleasant situations and thoughts of illness or death.

Until the patient met her husband, she had been extremely hesitant about deep involvements, keeping an air of aloofness that put off many potential friends. Through therapy, she had overcome many of her distancing behaviors and was really enjoying her life when this reminder of life's fragile quality caused her to retrench her position and reinstate her defensive pattern of withholding from loved ones. In being made aware of the possibility of losing her husband, she had given up feeling for him.

The behavior of this patient is not at all unusual; many people return to outmoded patterns of self-denial, withholding, or to self-nourishing habits following progress in therapy or unusual success and achievement in their personal lives. Sometimes there is no need of a conscious reminder of death such as was experienced by this patient. Merely enjoying a full life is enough to arouse a wide range of negative anticipations. Unusual happiness is often followed by anxiety and subsequent regression. In essence, happiness and fulfillment make one aware of valuing one's life and separateness. However, people are reluctant to feel that they exist as separate entities because then they must recognize that they face life and death alone, unconnected, and can no longer maintain illusions of immortality.

CONCLUSION

It is the author's hypothesis that the most powerful and effective denial of death is to be found in the imaginary connection with the mother, the Fantasy Bond. In learning how to protect oneself against impending separations and possible abandonment in the early fight for survival, the young child constructs a defensive structure and a fantasy world in which he or she becomes increasingly imprisoned. By avoiding gratification in the external world and withholding the most precious and lively parts of one's personality, an individual actually hastens deterioration into old age and death, the very fate one is attempting to escape. By denying oneself real experience and meaningful activity, one commits a gradual suicide, because one cannot bear the thought of losing a self that is fully alive and vital. This suicide is a pathetic and futile attempt to master death anxiety.

Chapter 16

CONVENTIONAL DEFENSES AGAINST
DEATH ANXIETY

> . . . Everything that man does in his symbolic world is an attempt to deny and overcome his grotesque fate. He literally drives himself into a blind obliviousness with social games, psychological tricks, personal preoccupations so far removed from the reality of his situation that they are forms of madness— agreed madness, shared madness, disguised and dignified madness, but madness all the same.
>
> Ernest Becker (1973)
> *The Denial of Death,* (p. 27)

The curse of awareness and imagination is that the human being functions as a self-conscious animal; we are able to ponder our beginning and our end and, in turn, are continually trying to avoid the anxiety this awareness causes us through some form of denial. The capacity to conceptualize and imagine is at once a strength and a weakness. Our ability to conceive of our own death makes our experience different from that of other animals. It sets us above and apart with unusual artistic sensitivity and power, yet we are the only creatures who are obsessed and tortured by the prospect of our eventual death.

In our "flight from death," we attempt solutions that bring our imaginations into play. As described earlier, we seek illusory connections with others, hoping to recapture our infantile sense of omnipotence. Furthermore, we seek oneness with God and a hope of life after death; we search for immortality through our creative powers or through our children; or we long to sacrifice ourselves for a cause. More significantly, however, we *attempt to gain control over death through a process of progressive self-denial*; that is, we deny ourselves experiences that would enhance our lives and give them value. The thought of losing one's life, losing all consciousness, losing all ego through death is so intolerable that the process of giving up offers relief from the anguish.

An analogy can be made to the convict on death row who commits suicide in his cell before he can be executed. Perversely, in taking his own life, he is regaining some degree of mastery over his death and his future. As people give up their lives slowly through self-denial and self-destructive behavior, they maintain a false sense of omnipotence, as if they retained some power or control over life and death. For this reason, we find that people proudly display a stubbornness about an unrewarding life style and self-destructive habits. In withdrawing feeling or affect from personal pursuits and goal-directed activity, they reduce their vulnerability to hurt, rejection, or loss. On a symbolic level, they are achieving mastery over death.

I.   "MATURITY"—ULTIMATE SELF-DENIAL OR PARTIAL SUICIDE

> The freeing of instinct from repressions causes fear because life and experience increase the fear of death; while, on the other side, renunciation of instinct increases guilt. . . . From the life fear, a direct path leads to consciousness of guilt, or better, to conscience fear, which can be understood always as regret for the possibility of life that has been neglected, but its full expression, on the other hand, creates death fear.
>> Otto Rank (1972)
>> *Will Therapy and Truth and Reality,* (p. 133)

"Maturity"—as it is defined in our society—is in actuality an insidious form of self-denial that becomes progressively worse as a person grows older. Because a life that is fully lived is more agonizing to contemplate losing through death, most people prevent themselves from realizing their full potential, and avoid becoming deeply involved with other people. Their anxiety about death is relieved by this process, but it is transformed into a fear of living or of becoming too attached to life. It is ironic that in accommodating to death in this way, people barely notice the transition.

Aided and abetted by the consensually validated attitudes on the part of most members of society about age-appropriate behavior, people tend to give up life-affirming activities, relationships, friendships, and adventure. These individual defensive maneuvers are a part of the collective illusion and large-scale denial of death in the social system. How is this defense of self-denial so easily maintained? How is it possible for people to give up meaningful activities without noticing their loss?

The Fantasy Process and Progressive Self-Denial

> There is no real difference between a childish impossibility and an adult one; the only thing that the person achieves is a practiced self-deceit—what we call the "mature" character.
> Ernest Becker (1973)
> *The Denial of Death,* (p. 46)

In order to see how the mechanism of fantasy contributes to this self-deception, it is important to clearly distinguish between constructive use of fantasy and its destructive use as a substitute for action and satisfaction in the real world. Without the capacity for imagining future events and activities, we could not create or plan ahead and would, of course, be very limited in our accomplishments. Yet, this ability to create in fantasy an image of ourselves and the fulfillment of our goals also sets the stage for psychological disturbances.

A number of factors contribute to the development of an individual's "practiced self-deception." First, people who live primarily in fantasy confuse fantasy images with real, goal-directed action. They believe that they are actively pursuing their goals, when in fact they are not taking the steps necessary for success. For example, an executive in the business world may only perform the functions that enhance an *image* of himself as the "boss," and leave essential management tasks unattended. The distinction between the image of success and its actual achievement is blurred. Retreat from action-oriented behavior is masked by the person's focus on superficial signs and activities that preserve vanity and the fantasy image.

Secondly, involvement in fantasy distorts one's perception of reality, making self-deception more possible. Kierkegaard (1849/1954) alluded to this power of fantasy to attract and deceive when he observed:

> Sometimes the inventiveness of the human imagination suffices to procure possibility. Instead of summoning back possibility into necessity, the man pursues the possibility—and at last cannot find his way back to himself. (p. 77, 79)

Thirdly, through its assigned roles and its rules for role-designated behavior, including age-appropriate activities, our culture actively supports people's tendencies to give themselves up to more and more passivity and fantasy as they move through the life process. In addition, the discrepancy between society's professed values on the one hand, and how society actually operates, on the other, tends to distort a person's perceptions of reality, further confusing the difference between idealistic fantasies and actual accomplishments. The general level of pretense, duplicity, and deception existing in our society contributes to everyone's disillusionment, cynicism, resignation, and passivity. The pooling of the individual defenses and fantasies of all society's members makes it possible for each person to practice self-delusion under the guise of normalcy. Thus chronic self-denial becomes a socially acceptable defense against death anxiety.

Author's View of Death Anxiety

Any evidence that heightens our awareness that we are leading a separate existence, are free agents, or any event that reminds us that we possess strength and power, that we alone are responsible for our decisions, causes us to be acutely conscious of our life and of its eventual loss. It has been my experience that people tend to be *more* aware of death when they are really alive to their existence, and *less* aware of it and less caring about it when they are leading a restricted, deadened life.

Many existential thinkers hypothesize that the fear of death is greater in people who do *not* live up to their potential than in those who fulfill themselves (Yalom, 1980). This thesis leads to the conclusion that therapeutic interventions which free patients from their repressions, so that they will be better able to actualize themselves, will also reduce their fears about dying. For instance, Norman O. Brown (1959), in his comprehensive work, *Life Against Death*, in pleading for a return to unrepressed living and the primary pleasure of the body, writes that "The horror of death is the horror of dying with what Rilke called unlived lines in our bodies. . . . The hard truth which psychoanalysis must insist upon is that the acceptance of death . . . cannot be accomplished by the discipline of philosophy or the seduction of art, but only by the abolition of repression" (p. 108-109).

In the author's view, on the other hand, there is a *real* fear of death that is intensified when life is experienced fully. I have concluded that because individuals feel more vulnerable to the fear of death when they have *more* to lose, they often choose to give up what they value about life rather than be deprived by external forces in the end. This process is analogous to the defenses people use to avoid falling deeply in love. Who wants to become so attached to someone when we know that the relationship might end for one reason or another some time in the future? All relationships end—eventually. This analogy extends to the situation of life itself; why commit oneself fully to life when one knows that it is finite and restricted? The dilemma created by this unavoidable limitation in time is difficult to face. People attempt to resolve the problem by refusing to involve themselves emotionally or by giving up parts of their lives through self-denial. Like actual suicide, this partial suicide gives the individual a false sense of power over dying.

Existential Guilt and Conventional Guilt

> The neurotic must punish himself. . . . This is not merely because he can only grant himself this or that pleasure satisfaction thus, but because he must bribe life itself, for which, according to Schopenhauer's deep insight, we all pay with death. . . . The neurotic then is a man whom extreme fear keeps from accepting this payment as a basis of life, and who accordingly seeks in his own way to buy himself free from his guilt. He does this through a constant restriction of life (restraint through fear); that is, he refuses the loan (life) in order thus to escape the payment of the debt (death).
>
> Otto Rank (1972)
> *Will Therapy and Truth and Reality,* (p. 126)

There are two separate and qualitatively different types of guilt reactions that need to be distinguished. The first type we refer to as existential guilt, which is the guilt and self-hatred we feel when we retreat from real life, pursuit of goals, and the people we feel closest to. It is a kind of turning against one's natural desires and self-expression, which leads to feeling empty and futile about life with accompanying thoughts of self-condemnation.

The second form of guilt reaction, termed conventional guilt, arises when a person chooses self-actualization. In pursuing a full life, one avoids the basic existential guilt of denying oneself instinctual satisfaction; however, in choosing to affirm life and free experience, an individual deviates from the cultural pattern.

For instance, if we chose to go against our inhibitions and spontaneously embrace life, we would then have to deal with the fear and guilt aroused by our affirmation of individuality and personal power. We would experience anxiety from having separated ourselves from our bonds with others and would be vulnerable to guilt for surpassing our parents and contemporaries. We would feel painfully separate, choosing to live while others are choosing to destroy themselves. We would feel guilty and self-conscious, standing out from the crowd and being nonconformists. In maintaining our aliveness, our excitement, wanting, and spontaneous sexuality, we would break with the traditional mode of behavior in our surroundings. Many people, when they are feeling less defended than usual, become aware that they are thinking self-condemning thoughts for enjoying life or for faring better than others. When combined with an intensified sense of vulnerability, the anxious and guilt-ridden thoughts of the "voice" may feel unbearable.

This form of self-blame and guilt is graphically portrayed in William Styron's (1979) novel *Sophie's Choice*. Styron recounts the brutal facts of Sophie's experiences in a German concentration camp, and in flashback, he tells of the terrible choice the young Polish mother was forced to make in trying to survive her ordeal. On the day of her internment, an SS guard forces her to choose which of her two children should die immediately and which should be spared. The alternative is death for both children and most likely death for her. Sophie chooses to give her elder child, a boy, the chance to live and sacrifices her daughter. Basically, she chooses life for herself, and from that point on, she is never free from the guilt of being a survivor. Released from the camp following the war, she makes her way to the United States where, with her last remaining strength, she makes a feeble attempt at suicide.

After the attempt fails, Sophie meets Nathan, who takes care of her as she begins to recover from the ravages of the camp. Fearful and guilty about life, she uses Nathan's sadism and paranoia as a tool in her own self-destruction. Nathan's drugged, paranoid rages are directed toward Sophie's guilty secret.

At one point, he questions Sophie: "How did you get out of Auschwitz?" Nathan's accusations echo Sophie's own condemnation of herself. In a sense, she has projected her self-destructive voice on to Nathan and uses him to punish herself. But evidently, in her eyes, the punishment is not severe enough to equal her crime—that of being alive.

Finally, the couple is found dead, victims of a double suicide. Sophie, too guilty to live any longer with the memory of the horrendous consequences of her choice to save her own life, has ended her life by submitting to Nathan's psychotic plan for them to die together.

The significance of this novel is that conventional guilt relates to every person's experience. Most people are able, on some level, to identify with this extreme example of self-destruction in a bond.

To feel one's guilt about surviving, simply living, or valuing one's life is painful. For this reason, it typically is repressed, surfacing at times as feelings of self-consciousness or in apologetic gestures toward others who are less fortunate. While it is true that people who restrict their lives experience annoying feelings of boredom, emptiness, and existential guilt, they do minimize or avoid painful feelings relating to death anxiety that would follow from investing in a full life. Most are willing to pay the price of living a defended, self-hating existence and choose a conventional, self-limiting life style.

Symptoms of a Progressive Accommodation to Death

The tendency to give up one's interest in and excitement about life is built into the defense system and manifests itself early in life. People do not wait until they are middle-aged or elderly to constrict their lives and limit their experiences; they become self-denying when they are made to feel guilty by their defended parents for having "selfish" wants or needs.

Slowly and almost imperceptibly, such people's orientation to life changes. They gradually become more passive and retiring rather than remaining active and striving to achieve concrete goals. They rationalize their slow withdrawal from important activities by claiming that they are "not as young as they used to be." They shift the problem of death to the periphery of their consciousness, as does society as a whole, by isolating the phenomenon and not acknowledging its impact. Thus, death passes almost unnoticed instead of being a discrete event in most people's lives.

When death comes, most individuals have already unknowingly disengaged themselves from living, that is, from the people, the work, the play that once gave them pleasure. They are essentially deadened to life, but are still physically in this world. Their apparent acceptance of life and fate is considered "mature" and "well-adjusted," and they appear to accept sickness, deterioration, and death, with "good sportsmanship." They are "good" patients. However, their so-called "maturity" merely reflects their cut-off emotional state and lack of feeling for themselves. The conventions of our society also tend to support this early retirement from living.

> A physician whom I was treating for depression had guided his life by traditional rules and conformed to the roles he felt he was expected to play in life. He had learned at an early age to submerge his own desires as he tried to earn approval and love from his parents. His father, especially, had expressed definite ideas about the career his son should pursue and essentially had planned his son's life.
>
> In doing everything "right," in becoming what his parents wanted, this man had never developed a strong identity of his own. In retrospect, it seemed to him that he had spent the major part of his life giving up activities at the "appropriate age." For instance, he had been a fine athlete and had loved sports, yet he had stopped actively participating in his late twenties and was now only a spectator. He and his wife kept close watch over each other's health and physical endeavors by helpful reminders such as, "Remember your back, dear."
>
> The couple had once been avid theatergoers, but lately were content to "stay at home and watch television." Whenever he threatened to step out of this mold and become more involved in a project that was physically taxing, he became anxious about the possible consequences and frequently discontinued the activity. At forty-eight, this man looked 10 years older than his actual age and had successfully deadened himself to most of the activities that had once excited him. His friends and associates supported his withdrawal from life by their own retreat. They, too, had stopped doing many of the things they had once enjoyed, yet they all accepted this condition as the normal course of events.

Conventions about "mature" behavior effectively disguise the process of self-denial, and people are able inadvertently to ease themselves out of the mainstream of life. It appears that there are well-defined stages in the life cycle where it is implicitly expected that a person will restrict behavior. For example, unabashed joy and spontaneity are expected in a child, acceptable in an adolescent, somewhat unacceptable in an adult, and in an older person are often seen as signs of senility or symptoms of the onset of "second childhood."

Since specific behaviors are deemed appropriate for different developmental stages, a decrease in a person's activity level is not generally viewed as abnormal or unusual. No one questions the fact that most people, as they grow older, tend to lose interest in being physically active; it is assumed that this is due to a normal reduction in their physical stamina and energy levels. Very few people wonder why they lose enthusiasm for the pursuits they enjoyed so much when they were younger. They rationalize the loss with well-known clichés, e.g., "Act your age," "Grow old gracefully," "No fool like an old fool," etc. Society's conventions and norms for the "appropriate" level of one's participation in sports, sex, romantic relationships, work, and activities in general make a neurotic, self-denying life style appear normal.

Despite progressive thought relating to pursuing physical activity and exercise, there are implicit restrictive taboos operating in our culture against active participation in sports as an individual ages. Society conceptualizes vigorous, competitive sports as being exclusively for youth and sees mature adults more or less as spectators. The "mature" person's concern about health or possible physical injury is the major rationalization for limiting active involvement in team sports, e.g., football, baseball, and basketball. Most men give up their male friendships and stop participating in athletics when they marry, often using wife and family as excuses for their lack of interest. Occasionally one encounters an exception to this general trend.

> A colleague, forty-five, who plays hardball on a semiprofessional team, mentioned to a friend the fact that he played baseball once a week. His friend was shocked and exclaimed: "What are you trying to prove? You must be out of your mind playing hardball at your age!" My colleague realized that even he attacked himself about the issue. He tortured himself with constant admonishments: "You're really breathing hard; feel that pain in your left shoulder? It could be more serious than simple muscle cramps. One of these days you're going to have a heart attack while running to first base." It is noteworthy that the attacks of my colleague's voice, which seemed on the surface to be concerned or self-protective, fit in exactly with his friend's attack.

Although many misconceptions about sex have been challenged by the sexual revolution, stereotypic attitudes toward age-appropriate sexual behaviors persist. Many people use these outmoded ideas to explain or rationalize their self-denying behaviors. Excitement about life and about sexuality is accepted in young people as being appropriate and even enviable. However, after marriage, many sexual relationships tend to become routine and lose this sense of excitement. Indeed, romance is not expected to last long past the wedding ceremony.

Sexual withholding between men and women is so widespread that it is considered to be a natural result of the familiarity of marriage. A high level of personal interest and romantic feeling after years of married life is unusual, despite the fact that it is a professed desire.

On the other hand, men and women who continue to be sexually active well into life may feel out of step with the majority. Although more liberal views about women's sexuality have succeeded in breaking down many artificial boundaries to women's sexual responses, there is still a great deal of bias, misinformation, and even outright prejudice in this area.

> A woman in her early forties, who had come to her gynecologist for a routine checkup, was asked by the doctor, "How often do you *still* have intercourse?" His inquiry, which had seemed innocuous at the time, implied that he expected her level of sexual activity to be on the wane. In the succeeding weeks, she noticed a significant decrease in her sexual desire. When she talked with her husband about her lack of interest, she suddenly recalled the gynecologist's question and realized that the doctor's attitude had done its damage on an unconscious level by making her feel self-conscious about her sexuality. She had begun to think that she was too interested in sex and became convinced that having sex frequently and feeling enthusiastic about making love were signs of immaturity.

Many men and women give up a good part of their former interest in sex due to fears relating to sexual performance or because they are no longer as attracted to their wives or husbands. Others pursue extramarital affairs to compensate for doubts about their sexual identity.

Although generally given superficial approval, a lively interest in sex on the part of older people is, in fact, often reacted to as odd or eccentric. The prospect of an elderly couple having sexual intercourse is sometimes even joked about or ridiculed. This bias contradicts studies that show people's sexual desire continuing well into their seventies and eighties.

Being forced into retirement at an arbitrary age arouses feelings of resignation in many men and women. The stimulation of going to work every day and remaining aggressive and competitive, accomplishing concrete goals, usually has a stabilizing and invigorating influence. Men especially tend to sink into apathy after retiring. Accustomed to choosing passivity over goal-directed behavior in their leisure time, they don't have adequate means at their disposal for struggling against the inactivity of retirement.

A general sense of boredom and stagnation plagues many people as early as their middle years. If they are dissatisfied with their career, they feel that it is too late to begin again. In fact, some people resent the possibility of change. Life becomes tedious and meaningless for people with rigid and unchanging concepts of themselves.

Society has many myths about aging that people use to rationalize their self-denial. One myth surrounding the aging process is the conviction that "older people generally become 'senile.'" "Senility" is used extensively by doctors and lay people alike to explain the behavior of senior citizens (Butler & Lewis, 1983). Another myth is that old people are necessarily unproductive. It is assumed that elderly people are no longer capable of being productive in their work and lack creative energy. There is actual discrimination against older individuals based on these misconceptions. For the most part, these prejudices are blatantly incorrect, yet they militate against older people feeling useful and functional.

Dynamics of the "Voice" in Fostering Progressive Self-Denial or Partial Suicide

The well-documented "mid-life crisis" (Sheehy, 1974), characterized by a wide range of behaviors including withdrawal into isolation, frantic activity, new sexual liaisons, paranoid reactions, and an increase in self-denying behaviors, is related to a more immediate awareness of the life process and death anxiety. When one believes one has arrived at the midpoint in life, one becomes keenly aware of time passing. Fear and apprehension are aroused when people begin to notice physical signs of aging.

During this stage, an individual's "voice" may become more dominant. This destructive thought process exerts increasing influence by first instigating and then rationalizing self-denying behaviors. In general all of our psychological defenses become more strongly entrenched when there is a resurgence of fear.

As people go through life, they imitate more and more the behavioral characteristics of their parents. In looks, body structure, and man-nerisms, most middle-aged people begin strongly to resemble their par-ent of the same sex. They develop styles of behavior and idiosyncracies that seem to replicate their parents' characteristics. Often friends and relatives tell them: "You look more like your mother every day," or "You're getting to be just like your father." These incorporated person-ality characteristics of our parents, many times the qualities we dislike the most, persist and grow more prominent within our own personalities as we enter middle age. As we take on these negative characteristics we become demoralized because we are looking more and more like the people who caused us pain and anger when we were young. A great deal of self-criticism and self-hatred is generated by this process of imitation.

As a person matures, raises one's own family, especially after one's own parent or parents die, the internalized parental image may take precedence over other facets of one's personality. Indeed, the death of the parent of the same sex often triggers a severe regression charac-terized by the assimilating or taking on of the personal qualities of the dead parent. The closer a person draws to the end of life, the more he or she tends to form a union with the parent.

Many people steadily reduce their activity level because they follow the dictates of their voice; yet they remain unaware that they are going against their own best interests. The voice has two principal ways of encouraging progressive self-denial: (1) self-criticism, and (2) self-indulgent attitudes.

(1) Self-criticism inhibits action because it feeds a person's fear of failure, rejection, and loss. People may stop initiating new projects by thinking cynical thoughts, such as: "Why start something you can't finish?" A man may decide not to build the home he's always wanted, even though he is financially able to carry out his plans, because he has been thinking things like: "You're too old to take on such an ambitious project. Besides, you would probably have only a few years left to enjoy it."

Some people progressively stop themselves from wanting things they used to feel were important to them and block their desires before they are translated into action. For example, a woman in her mid-thirties gave up wanting to have a baby, telling herself that she was too "set in her ways" to begin having a family. In going against her desire to have a child, she was denying a basic biological urge that persists throughout life. Though she may for practical reasons have ultimately decided *not* to have a child, she would have been better off if she had done justice to her *feeling* of wanting. If a woman denies something as natural as wanting to have a baby, she often becomes more confused and childish in her other responses and less self-directed and adult.

People who turn their backs on their wants are tampering with a basic part of their identity. To the extent that they repeat the self-denying patterns of the parent of the same sex, they lose a basic sense of self.

(2)   The pattern of giving up real activities generally coincides with an *increase* in self-indulgent behaviors. Older people usually focus more attention on taking care of themselves in a childish, self-parenting style. They tell themselves, "You can afford a little extra weight at your age; so stop worrying about your diet, go on and have some dessert," or "You need your rest, so why go out tonight?" This subtle self-indulgent form of the voice nevertheless has the same effect as self-critical thoughts, that is, it encourages inertia and passivity.

As a person grows older, self-destructive thinking takes precedence over rational, constructive thoughts. For instance, the middle-aged man who worries about his sex drive diminishing tells himself: "You're not going to be able to keep your erection. You're getting to the age where men become impotent. Better slow down, you're not the man you used to be." If he listens to the voice and its predictions of humiliating failure, his nervousness and concern will actually have a damaging effect on his sexual performance.

The voice tells the "mature" person to "take it easy," "don't overdo," "don't be undignified," "leave it up to someone younger with more energy," "you've had *your* day, it's time to hand the responsibility over to a younger person." This seemingly reasonable advice is self-defeating and psychologically damaging.

Fears that seemed appropriate in childhood and adolescence, but persisted into adulthood and middle age, often cause older people embarrassment and shame. When they were younger, they imagined that they would overcome their fears as they got older. When this fails to happen, they become more and more demoralized and may finally give in to their fears. Self-attacks, such as "How can you still be so self-conscious and nervous about speaking in public at *your* age?" or "How can you possibly be shy at parties after all these years?" intensify their feelings of self-hatred and cause them to depend more on a facade.

An analysis of these destructive thoughts indicates that the *majority of the voice's injunctions, predictions, and rationalizations are attempts to annihilate life by gradually limiting exciting and spontaneous pursuits.* The fear of death mobilizes the voice. An individual relies on this incorporated parental image and these negative attitudes to protect and insulate him or herself against this fear. Very few people recognize the extent to which they limit their involvement in the activities and relationships that give their life value. For this reason, the process of progressive self-denial has not been accorded the importance it deserves as a pervasive defense against death anxiety.

II. RELIGION—HOPE OF LIFE AFTER DEATH

> Religion and nationalism, as well as any custom and any be-
> lief however absurd and degrading, if it only connects the indi-
> vidual with others, are refuges from what man most dreads: isola-
> tion.
>
> Erich Fromm (1941)
> *Escape From Freedom,* (p. 34-35)

Religious ideologies contribute to a self-destructive collective defense by validating man's tendency to be self-denying and self-sacrificing. Doctrines based on self-sacrifice and original sin support each person's voice. Acting as external validation, they intensify self-criticism and self-destructiveness, helping one to deny one's physical life, sexuality, and happiness, and contributing to a passive orientation to life.

Traditional religious ideologies offer protection against death anxiety through a fantasized connection with an all-powerful figure and emphasize the submission of the believer's will to that of a god. People who cling to belief in a punitive yet forgiving god use this ideology to feel unworthy and powerless in their own right. On the other hand, they are able to feel righteous and powerful when they believe that they are connected to their god or doing god's work. Thus, the bond represented by religion is directly analogous to the good parent/bad child dichotomy of the primary bond with the mother. The process of investing someone outside oneself with strength and goodness to the detriment of one's own sense of worth is the same in both cases. Both connections provide relief from one's existential fears by offering a sense of immortality. The belief in a life after death based on the immortality of the "soul" is a more sophisticated version of the child's earliest fantasies of omnipotence and control over events in the external world, including control over death.

The doctrine that only a "chosen" few will find eternal life through belief in their god fosters the perception that the rest of humankind is basically evil and therefore doomed. This is an extension of the child's attempt to enhance the self-image and thereby allay self-hatred and feelings of helplessness by identifying with the all-powerful idealized parent. It also parallels the displacement of negative parental qualities onto people outside the immediate family.

Some ministers imagine that they personify God and are "on God's side," and separate themselves from the "evil" congregation and their own internal image of themselves as "bad" or "sinful." Their condemning, sermonizing life style is often a reaction formation against aggressive and sexual impulses, which are severely repressed and threatening. Their lives have a compulsive quality, because they must be continually on guard against the eruption of emotions that they consider as reprehensible. This style of preaching and of accusing the congregation of sinful behavior is acceptable to the members because of their own sense of guilt and an immature need for punishment.

As a defense, religion preserves the image of the all-powerful parent, as in the original bond, and it offers hope for surviving death through oneness with a god. The psychological damage incurred by clinging to these beliefs as a defense is enormous, despite the comfort and security they offer.

III. NATIONALISM AND TOTALITARIANISM—IMMORTALITY THROUGH A CAUSE

> The majority of men have not yet acquired the maturity to be independent, to be rational, to be objective. They need myths and idols to endure the fact that man is all by himself, that there is no authority which gives meaning to life except man himself.
>
> Erich Fromm (1941)
> *Escape From Freedom*, (p. xiv)

Totalitarian regimes are usually the outcome of the vacillations of socioeconomic forces, but their roots lie in the human psychological make-up. The destructiveness of Nazism and the Third Reich have been attributed to the "German" character; however, the seeds of this destructiveness lie in every person. In Erich Fromm's (1941) comprehensive explanation of the psychology of Nazism, he discusses the dynamics of *authoritarianism* as the basis for totalitarianism. His analysis, in some respects, parallels the author's thinking on this issue.

It has been my experience that the average person's desperate dependence on the group, idolization of the leader, and unswerving allegiance to a cause are all defenses against death. The bond with the group, with a leader, with a cause, allays anxiety about dying, and this association with a powerful idol or rescuer unconsciously relieves one's fears and symbolically cheats death.

Similarly, Fromm (1941) has written about the "tendency to give up the independence of one's own individual self and to fuse one's self with somebody or something outside of oneself in order to acquire the strength which the individual self is lacking." He describes people's search for "new, secondary bonds" as a substitute for the "primary bonds" which have been lost. In describing the "authoritarian character," Fromm writes of the parallels between religion and nationalism in relation to their restrictions on freedom:

> The authoritarian character loves those conditions that limit human freedom, he loves being submitted to fate.... Fate may be rationalized philosophically as "natural law" or as "destiny of man," religiously as the "will of the Lord," ethically as "duty"—for the authoritarian character it is always a higher power outside of the individual, toward which the individual can do nothing but submit. (p. 192-193)

The submission of one's will to a higher power or cause is not exclusively a characteristic of the "authoritarian personality." Indeed the author has found that most people reject a truly democratic process or government. To have a forum where they speak out or voice their own opinions reminds them of their individual existence and identity. This feeling of being alive and separate arouses their fear of death. Therefore, most individuals seek connections with authority figures to whom they can submit their will.

Thus, because of separation anxiety and later, the fear of death, people turn to leaders and causes in their search for immortality and security. They transfer the primitive feelings that were once embodied in their bond with their parents onto new figures and ideologies. Rank's (1978) statement that the transference object represents "the great biological forces of nature, to which the ego binds itself emotionally" (p. 82) describes the dynamics of forming a bond with persons, groups, and causes for the purpose of preserving one's life.

This transference of the emotional reactions that formed the early relationship with the parents is responsible for the submissive behavior of members of a group. Freud (1921/1955), in his work *Group Psychology and the Analysis of the Ego,* explains how people dispose of their opinions and independence when they join groups. Freud quotes Le Bon's (1895/1920) *Psychologie des foules*: ". . . the individual forming part of a group . . . is no longer himself, but has become an automaton who has ceased to be guided by his will" (p. 76). Later, in his description of the characteristics of the group, Freud continues: "The leader of the group is still the dreaded primal father; the group still wishes to be governed by unrestricted force; it has an extreme passion for authority; in Le Bon's phrase, it has a thirst for obedience" (p. 127).

Nationalism, Communism, capitalism, as well as any other "ism," also serve the function of being a narcotic, a psychic painkiller, that fosters a deep dependency in people who are desperately searching for comfort and security. Karl Marx (1927/1964) was well aware of the hypnotic spell cast by religion when he described religion as "the opium of the people." He was cognizant of this same quality in the political system—its ability to narcotize the individual through illusion:

> The abolition of religion, as the illusory happiness of men, is a demand for their real happiness. The call to abandon their illusions about their condition is a call to abandon a condition which requires illusions. . . .
>
> The immediate task is to unmask human alienation in its secular form, now that it has been unmasked in its sacred form. Thus the criticism of heaven transforms itself into the criticism of earth, the criticism of religion into the criticism of law, and the criticism of theology into the criticism of politics. (Marx & Engels, 1927/1964, p. 27)

In drawing this analogy between religion and the state, Marx suggested that political dogma held the same compelling attraction as religion and that the illusions each offered needed to be exposed and overthrown in order for real social progress to occur. Ironically, Marxism itself came to serve the same function as religion and other systems of political thought.

In any system other than a functioning democratic society, the individual subordinates the self in relation to an idea or a principle and experiences a false sense of power. The illusion of fusion and connection that comes from being a part of a patriotic or nationalistic movement is exhilarating and addictive. In capitalism too, man has subordinated himself as a "means to an economic end" (Fromm, 1941). Indeed, any cause or "ism," whether potentially good or evil, is capable of fostering a corresponding addiction in the individual.

In substituting an idealized cause for individual acts of mastery and personal power, people use the philosophy of their adopted cause to fantasize that they are being taken care of. They imagine the group to be "the ultimate rescuer" and try to merge their personality with that of the group, and become conformists. They attempt to obtain gratification for their dependency needs, unsatisfied in childhood, by forming a union with the Fascist Party, Communist Party, the John Birch Society, or any other aggressive, "patriotic" group. Very little distinction exists between the primitive bond with the mother and an imaginary connection with an heroic leader or a cause in terms of the kind of satisfactions sought. Strong leaders and political systems stimulate intense feelings of patriotism in their followers which lock them into their chosen cause. In this way, strong feelings of patriotism and nationalism indirectly act as a defense against death anxiety.

IV. COUPLE BONDS—ADDICTION TO THE OTHER AS AN ULTIMATE RESCUER

> As a rule, we find . . . in modern relationships . . . one person is made the god-like judge over good and bad in the other person. In the long run, such symbiotic relationship becomes demoralizing to both parties, for it is just as unbearable to be God as it is to remain an utter slave.
>
> Otto Rank (1958)
> (quoted in E. Becker, 1973, p. 159)

Many people expect far more security from couple relationships and marriage than it is possible to extract. There is an expectation that all of one's needs will be met in the relationship. In that sense, one's husband or wife becomes the source of all happiness. The burden these anticipations put on the relationship is enormous; obviously, no one person can fulfill such unrealistic expectations or live up to this idealized image. However, people's actions show that they believe, on some level, that by submitting their individuality to a more "powerful" person as in a bond, by giving up their independence and points of view, they are somehow achieving safety and immortality.

Equality, genuine companionship, and spontaneous, affectionate sex destroy the inherent inequality of this type of relating, where the partners alternate between submission and dominance, first being the parent and then becoming the child. Indeed, when a person perceives a mate as he or she really is, a mortal human being with flaws, weaknesses, and blemishes, generally the response is one of anger and disillusionment.

A further cause of hostility between members of a couple is their alarm and anger at the self-destructiveness of their mates. Though most people are quite successful at covering up their self-denial, they cannot deceive the person who knows them on an intimate level. Wives who nag their husbands about their drinking, smoking, or overwork and husbands who criticize their wives' careless driving or their lack of pride in their looks are genuinely disturbed and frightened by the deterioration they see in their loved ones. There is a deep, primitive fear of losing one's partner because of illness or death. There is both a fear of breaking the bond and a fear of losing the actual person.

To allay the fear of loss, people avoid dealing directly with each other's self-destructive defenses. Instead, they complain endlessly and ineffectively *about* their mates or they ignore each other's deterioration by fantasizing that their love is still alive. This pretense of love and the mutual protection of each other's defensive styles are significant aspects of the couple bond. The underlying purpose is to avoid a confrontation that would arouse anxiety about life and death.

V.   GENE SURVIVAL—IMMORTALITY THROUGH ONE'S CHILDREN

The wish to leave some part of oneself behind after death motivates many people to have children. To be able to leave a legacy in the world after our death, evidence that our life has made a difference, that we have left our mark on the world, eases our anxiety about dying. Our children give us a sense of surviving our own death. After all, they are products of our bodies, extensions of ourselves; they look like us and they "belong" to us. This need to feel that we have achieved immortality through our offspring leads to our forming a bond with them.

Traditionally, parents have exerted proprietary rights over their children due to this bond. Their feelings of being connected to their children foster a sense of ownership and "belonging" that has destructive consequences. Feelings of exclusivity and possessiveness stem from parents' hunger to have their own unsatisfied needs met by their children.

The disrespectful proprietary interest that many parents take in their children is very different from the genuine companionship and closeness that occurs in families that do *not* have dishonest or neurotic dependency ties. When family bonds develop, real togetherness is replaced by special attention, intrusiveness, and possessiveness on the part of parents. Children come to expect this counterfeit "love;" indeed, after a time, they demand it, using annoying behaviors like whining, excessive crying, and temper tantrums whenever they feel the absence of special treatment. For instance, if Mother returns from a shopping trip without a gift, the child dissolves into heartbreaking sobs. Children believe they are the most important thing in their mother's life, that she belongs to them, that they are special above anyone else. When the mother fails to produce tangible evidence of this, it threatens the bond and the child's sense of omnipotence.

Interfering with the family bond is taboo in our culture because tampering with these neurotic ties between family members causes considerable fear and anxiety leading to anger and defensiveness. To avoid facing this existential dilemma, our society preserves the sanctity of the family except in extreme cases. Even in families where there are pathological interrelationships and patterns of communication and where separation from a severely disturbed person is advisable, many therapists exert every effort to keep the family together.

When one family therapist was asked why this choice was made in the case of a sixteen-year-old schizophrenic patient where there was every indication of environmental causation the reply was "The tie with his parents, however destructive it is, is the only thing the schizophrenic has in his life. Remove that and there is only emptiness, the void, no identity." The author believes that this extreme reluctance to disturb the family bond is due to the fear of breaking into one of the strongest and most effective defenses against death anxiety.

VI.   CREATIVITY—"THE BURDEN OF GENIUS"

The true genius has an immense problem that other men do not. He has to earn his value as a person from his work, which means that his work has to carry the burden of justifying him. What does "justifying" mean for man? It means transcending death by qualifying for immortality.

Ernest Becker (1973)
The Denial of Death, (p. 109)

In attempting to satisfy his deepest, most urgent need—the need to survive his own personal ending—man strives for perfection and uniqueness in his life's work. Of course, the defense of being creative and producing original work that will be preserved by future generations is positive and constructive. It takes nothing away from the importance of these works to examine the part played by the artist's undeniable desire somehow to transcend death through his or her creations.

It has been said that the neurotic is an artist without talent. This cliché acknowledges the difference between the person who, sensing the inevitability of death, restricts the experiencing of life and the one who, having the same awareness, attempts to work out this problem symbolically through creative pursuits. The neurotic and the artist tend to perceive the world similarly; their personal views of the world do not generally correspond to the cultural solutions that allay the anxieties of most people. Nevertheless, artists, poets, architects, or composers are neurotic when they believe on some level that their special flair for creativity will allow them to cheat death, or when they lose sight of the personal conflict manifested in their work. If remnants of infantile feelings of omnipotence, in the form of vanity, overshadow their real endeavors, their work may take on a compulsive quality. In this case, their productiveness will be limited and feelings of self-defeat and despair will plague them, just as they do men of lesser talent. In that sense, a person's efforts to achieve immortality through creative endeavors can become restrictive like other, more conventional defenses regarding death.

CONCLUSION

The fear of death is inherent in being alive. Anxiety about death per se is *not* neurotic; however, attempts to *deny* the fact that one must die lead to psychological disturbance.

In one sense, humankind is cursed with an "incurable" neurosis. We fear death and naturally strive to remove the source of this fear from consciousness. To accomplish this, we withhold our feeling for the things and people in our lives that remind us of our mortality. We tread a thin line because we cannot afford to go too far in our avoidance or it becomes obvious that we are self-denying. If our self-destructive tendencies prevail over our strivings toward self-fulfillment, we feel progressively more guilty and demoralized about life.

We are trapped in bodies that will die and are always conscious of this fact on some level. Since it is not possible to overcome completely the anxiety and pain concerning our awareness of death, we are destined to suffer emotionally and experience a basic sadness. To some degree we must mourn our anticipated loss of life in order to retain feeling for our real existence. Without fully experiencing this sadness, our capacity to feel spontaneous and joyful is limited and genuine happiness is unattainable.

In this context, how can the therapist symbolically persuade the patient to face pain and therefore fully embrace life? A multidimensional therapeutic approach that frees the patient from neurotic defensive solutions is indicated. Within this context, the patient could learn to face separation, aloneness, and death without regression and alienation. In coping with basic existential issues, he or she would become acutely aware of the alternatives: whether to restrict and numb one's feelings in an attempt to escape death anxiety or to live fully, with humility, meaningful activity, and compassion for oneself and others.

PART III

IMPLICATIONS FOR THERAPY

Chapter 17

PSYCHOTHERAPY OVERVIEW

An individual's resistance to change is the most powerful limitation to the enjoyment of the closest personal relationships and deepest levels of self-expression. The author's life work as a psychotherapist has been devoted to the study of resistance. My investigations have been directed toward learning why most people, in spite of emotional catharsis, understanding, and intellectual insight, still cling to the familiar, yet destructive patterns of the past and refuse to change on a deep character level. I have concluded that resistance is centered in the pattern of thoughts and behaviors that act to preserve the core defense—the illusion of self-sufficiency and immortality achieved through a fantasized connection to another. The fantasy bond of connectedness extends from the mother to one's family, to symbolic parental figures, and even to institutions or causes.

THEORY OF RESISTANCE

Theoretical Issues and Implications for Psychotherapy

A comprehensive theory of psychotherapy is generally based on a specific view of human nature. In this respect, the author's theoretical orientation has some basic roots in psychoanalytic thought. "Psycho-analysis views the functioning of the mind as the expression of conflict-ing forces" and emphasizes conflict as "an inexorable dimension of the human condition" (Arlow, 1979, p. 1). This conceptualization parallels my own understanding of the role of conflict in the formation of psy-chological defenses. In Calvin Hall's (Hall & Lindzey, 1970) words, Freud's view of man "tries to envisage a full-bodied individual living partly in a world of reality and partly in a world of make-believe, beset by conflicts and inner contradictions, yet capable of rational thought and action" (p. 72). Freud perceived people as torn between unconscious impulses that seek expression and opposing forces that seek to deny these impulses. His assumption was that this conflict is created by sexual or aggressive urges striving for release against incorporated societal con-straints that are imparted to the child during the socialization process.

The author's view of the specific impulses or urges that give rise to this basic conflict diverges from Freud's psychoanalytic formulation. Throughout the present work, I have described this conflict as being the struggle between the drive for independence and separateness and the desire to remain dependent and connected to others in fantasy. This basic conflict expresses itself in an entire style of living. For example, a man who is in the process of changing in therapy may vacillate between these polar opposites in his everyday life, sometimes boldly pursuing his personal goals in spite of anxiety and other times becoming passive in his relationships and more involved in inward self-nourishing fantasy and behavior.

More commonly, though, "average" people have reached a state of psychological equilibrium where the balance between these two drives has achieved a certain level of stability. In a sense, they have found a solution to this basic conflict, one that allows them to proceed through life with a minimum of anxiety. Although their solution may be stable, it is generally established on a defensive level and can be very restrictive, self-limiting, or damaging. The neurotic resolution lies more in the direction of dependency, passivity, and fantasy gratification than toward independence and separateness. Therefore, their "adjustment" tends to interfere with their freedom of choice and movement rather than en-hance it. Ultimately, resistance serves the purpose of protecting the indi-vidual from experiencing anxiety states that would arise from threats to their particular solution to the basic conflict.

At the time of seeking therapy, people are generally in a state of anxiety because their fantasy solution has broken down to some extent. In many cases, their symptoms are a sign that a bond has been disrupted and a destructive defense process has been threatened; therefore, symptoms can be conceptualized to be manifestations of change, a possible movement toward emotional health rather than deterioration. Conventional therapies that attempt to restore patients to their premorbid anxiety-free state by strengthening their defenses inadvertently do these patients a disservice. In trying to relieve their pain and bring their inner life back into an equilibrium, they condemn the patients to a life of bondage. The patients' defenses will continue to limit them and interfere with their lives even though they may feel more comfortable. Both therapist and patient may misinterpret this process as a positive movement toward cure.

Levels of Resistance

Resistance in therapy is indicative of a deeper, more general fear and aversion to change. Theorists tend to categorize resistance along a number of dimensions. Fenichel (1945) discusses several types of resistance in his book, *The Psychoanalytic Theory of Neurosis*. He writes:

> An acute resistance, one that is directed against the discussion of some particular topic, is far easier to handle than "character resistances." These are attitudes which the patient had previously developed in order to maintain his repressions, and which he now exhibits toward the analyst. (p. 29)

Three types of resistance have been described by Blatt and Erlich (1982): episodic resistance, transference resistance, and fundamental resistance to change. In the therapeutic relationship, an attempt is made to transform the patient's more fundamental resistance to change into a transference resistance. Working with the distortions inherent in the transference, the therapist simultaneously challenges the new *bond* that the patient attempts to form with him or her and analyzes the resistance with a view toward eventually overcoming it.

In my private practice, I have had the opportunity to observe each form of resistance and study the many manifestations of this phenomenon. When I began my professional career as a private practitioner of psychotherapy, I was involved in a traditional form of psychoanalytic psychotherapy. I found that many patients were resistant to the use of free association as a technique. They censored their thoughts and feelings to a considerable extent and wouldn't adhere to the traditional rule to "say everything that comes to your mind, no matter how trivial or embarrassing." Other patients would come late for appointments, act out, or become delinquent in paying for their sessions. These behaviors, though quite specific and "episodic," were symptomatic of the patient's general underlying resistance to personal growth and change.

The major consideration in any therapy is the patient's fundamental resistance to growth or progress, that is, unwillingness, because of fear and guilt, to alter the defense system. When it manifests itself during the course of therapy, this resistance has been defined as "defense expressed in the transference" (Gill, 1981). This is generally understood to mean that following the initial, "honeymoon" phase of the therapy, patients project their "will to health" onto the therapist and take the opposing role, that of resisting the therapist's efforts to "cure" them. What has occurred is that in this initial phase of therapy, the patients' anxiety tends to be reduced or considerably relieved by the therapeutic process; they begin to experience alleviation of the symptoms that caused them to seek help. However, as they feel better, they typically become more resistant to challenging the basic structure of their defense system. They may be less motivated to change because they are in less pain psychologically than when they entered therapy. At this point, they may decide to terminate therapy, mistakenly feeling "cured." However, their basic style of being defended will still be intact and they will still be susceptible to the limitations imposed by their defended life style.

Many patients choose to leave therapy when they sense that by giving up a specific defense, they would have to change their style of defensive living. Some may become resistant at a point far removed from actually tampering with a deep character defense. Merely the hint that a basic defense may be challenged sometime in the future can trigger strong resistance or lead to avoidance or even premature termination.

> One of my patients, a building contractor, had an important insight in a session several months after he entered therapy. He saw that he had a lack of integrity and a basic disrespect for people in his business transactions and that he was corrupt in his practices. He realized that his desperation to achieve financial success sprang from a deep unsatisfied longing for love or approval. Being successful in business, no matter what the cost, was a sign to him that he was acceptable. However, he suffered feelings of guilt and remorse for the trickery and deceit he used to fool his customers. He left therapy immediately following a session in which he experienced considerable pain about his unethical practices. In this rather simplified example, it was obvious that the patient resisted changing because he felt threatened at the prospect of a possible loss of income and status. He chose to preserve his dishonest life style at the expense of his own well-being. Ironically, in this case, *his resistance had been mobilized by his*

own desire for a more decent, respectable life, expressed in his final session. After taking his own side, he resisted his impulse to change and held on to a life style of self-hatred.

In another case, a college professor had been married for several years to a psychotic, tyrannical woman who attempted to control her husband's life to an extreme degree. As he progressed in therapy, he began to be aware of how destructive this relationship was for him. He became more sensitive to the nightly interrogations, the jealousy, the angry threats and distrust, and the outright paranoia directed toward his friends. He felt acute humiliation at his wife's episodes of acting out and repeatedly embarrassing him at university functions. Discouraged by his wife's lack of progress after years of being in therapy and several hospitalizations, the patient began to contemplate divorce. However, he soon became resistant to talking about this prospect and within a few weeks had terminated therapy altogether.

Fear of separation and the anticipation of breaking a longstanding bond brought this man's conflict to an early resolution when he decided to leave therapy rather than leave his wife. His need for the security of the bond overshadowed his desire to be free. Despite the fact that his situation was untenable and that it was unreasonable for him to remain in the marriage, the patient could not tolerate the anxiety of being separate from this intensely damaging relationship. In both of these cases, the patients' resistance had become significantly stronger after they had expressed an urge toward health and personal growth.

Resistance as Manifest in the Compulsion to Relive the Past

Defended individuals involve themselves in a destructive process of reliving their past rather than completely experiencing their present-day life. Their tendency to recreate the conditions of early life is expressed in the bonds they form with significant persons in their interpersonal environment. The process of reliving is evident in these attempts to reproduce or recreate a parent in other persons or in institutions. The compelling need to repeat the past represents the basic resistance to a better, more enriched way of life that would necessarily contradict their earliest experience of reality.

The author's concept of reliving is analogous to Freud's (1920/1955) concept of *repetition compulsion* in one respect: we both believe that the patient goes through a repetitive process that is misguided and that cannot have a favorable outcome. However, my understanding of the *purpose* or goal of this compulsion differs from that of Freud's, according to which:

> They [repetitive activities] are of course the activities of in-
> stincts intended to lead to satisfaction; but no lesson has been
> learnt from the old experience of these activities having led in-
> stead only to unpleasure. In spite of that, they are repeated,
> under pressure of a compulsion. (p. 21)

Psychoanalytic thought suggests that patients repeat the patterns of
the past in a futile attempt to *obtain gratification,* that is, they try to
recreate a parent in other people in order to get the love they missed.
Fenichel (1945), in describing the psychoanalytic formulation of the
"compulsion to repeat," states that:

> *Repetitions due to the tendency of the repressed to find an outlet* . . .
> [are] the core of the characteristic psychoneurotic repetitions. . . .
> They are most pronounced in the so-called neuroses of destiny, in
> which the patient periodically evokes or endures the same experi-
> ence. . . . What has not been gratified strives for gratification.
> (p. 542)

In my conceptualization of reliving, patients recreate or provoke
those situations that protect the fantasy of self-sufficiency; in other
words, they relive the past in order to justify their defenses. In contrast
to the psychoanalytic formulation, the attempt here is to *avoid gratification.* Individuals are compelled to recreate the emotional setting of
childhood, the conditions to which their particular defenses are appropriate. *They relive patterns of hurtful behavior for the purpose of avoiding real
gratification, which would cause emotional pain and create anxiety by disrupting
the fantasy that they can feed and sustain themselves.*
Once people become defended in their earliest experiences in their
family, their total life style is constructed around protecting the self-
nourishing fantasy. They tend to develop unusually strong resistance to
positive intrusions into their defended posture. Unfortunately, maintaining their defenses becomes the principle focus of life, *not* a search for
the satisfactions they may have missed in childhood.
In addition to this distinction, the author differs from certain other
theorists in his concepts of the meaning and role of defenses. Many
psychoanalysts and conventional psychotherapists feel that psychological
defenses are necessary for the individual to function successfully in the
biosocial environment. This philosophy tends to support the view that
defenses are essentially adaptive. In contrast, it is my belief that the same
psychological defenses that warded off pain and protected us when we
were young later play destructive, limiting roles in our adult life. Because self-parenting fantasies of self-sufficiency act partially to gratify
drives and reduce anxiety and pain, individuals become compulsively

dependent on this defensive process. Indeed, they suffer from the delusion that they cannot live without their defenses. However, in remaining defended, they maintain a level of intolerance toward and rejection of the kind of life they really desire on a deeper level.

People's fear of stepping out of this mode is not in proportion to the reality of their current situation as they are no longer the weak and vulnerable children they once were. While they are in a defended state, patients imagine that their anxiety will be intolerable if they change. They feel, albeit irrationally, that their present-day situation is similar to the one in which they found themselves in the past. They are afraid that by separating themselves from the bond with their parents, or from present-day parental symbols, they will again be plunged into primitive feelings of helplessness, abandonment, and rejection. The patient's seemingly stubborn resistance becomes more understandable when viewed from this vantage point.

It is difficult to convince patients of what they themselves know intellectually: that as adults they have more control over their lives and that their fears could never be of the same magnitude as those which overwhelmed them as children and originally caused them to become defended. The skill of the therapists lies in the ability to encourage a new vulnerability which often leads patients to succeed in relation to personal goals. Later, the successful therapist must help the individuals to cope with the positive anxiety that they experience as they overcome their resistance and expand their life boundaries.

Theoretical Basis for a Multidimensional Approach to Resistance

To summarize, resistance is the core of the neurosis itself; as such, every aspect of the patient's life style can be conceptualized as being an expression of this process. The fundamental resistance is to a better life and it manifests itself whenever positive as well as negative circumstances threaten to disrupt the patient's solution. Individuals tend to protect their bonds and inner fantasy life, to avoid separation anxiety, to repress primal feelings of pain, and to prevent any change in identity that would arouse anxiety. Resistance also functions to prevent people from becoming attached to those who cause them to value their life and thus increase their vulnerability, and as such it is also a vital part of an individual's denial of death on an unconscious level. Indeed, the entire process of neurotic living is directed toward resisting a richer, more fulfilled way of life due to the fear of ultimate loss or separation. Throughout life there is a constant struggle between the drive toward actualizing one's potential and the tendency to be self-denying and self-destructive. A "successful" psychotherapy would be a catalyst for a lifetime process of growing.

The author realizes the problems and limitations confronting most psychotherapies in attempting to effect change in the face of this basic resistance. A truly effective therapy must challenge all aspects of the patient's neurotic life style: idealization of the family, negative self-concept, distortions of people outside the family, lack of compassion and feeling for oneself, withholding and self-denying responses, self-nourishing habits, and the bonds with the significant people in one's life. Defensive patterns are interrelated and efforts directed toward changing any one aspect interfere with other defenses and cause anxiety. Furthermore, the disruption of any specific defense is an indirect threat to the core defense, the process of sustaining oneself through fantasy gratification.

Living defensively necessitates duplicity in one's behavior and communication. In a defended state, individuals have learned partially to satisfy their own needs, to fulfill their own goals in fantasy. In imagining that they don't need anyone, that they are capable of taking care of themselves through self-parenting behaviors, they must react negatively to events and to people who offer *real* gratification. They become dishonest when they attempt to deceive themselves and others that they still want real satisfaction, real friendship or relationships.

The neurotic ploy is to maintain the fantasy, while at the same time keeping minimal contact with the other person and preserving enough symbols of the relationship to support the fantasy. For example, in a couple bond, both partners need symbols that they still love each other—the traditional Saturday night date, the anniversary and birthday gifts, the flowers—they require these outward signs and reassurances that their bond is still intact. When these symbols of love are not forthcoming, they react melodramatically, yet at the same time, they are often oblivious to real neglect or abuse in their daily interactions.

In protecting the original process of imagining fulfillment instead of obtaining it in the real world, a person has to distort other people, misperceive their motives, hate the self, and in some sense, preserve an idealized image of the family. An inward style of life and dishonest communications hurt the people closest. By contrast, living an undefended life means risking hurt and frustration in an honest pursuit of goals. However, a person can learn to develop an open, nondefensive life style, free from the deception and double messages so damaging to others.

The ultimate goal of therapy is to persuade the patient to challenge his or her inner world of fantasy and risk seeking satisfaction through goal-directed behavior. To this end, the author has developed a psychotherapeutic methodology that utilizes procedures that are very different in process and in technique, but that are consistent with respect to the underlying theory.

This multidimensional methodology, which has proved most beneficial in overcoming resistance and promoting change, makes use of the following therapeutic techniques:

A.   Feeling Release Therapy (with accompanying insight).

B.   Voice Therapy

C.   Corrective Suggestions and Experiences

(Voice Therapy and Corrective Suggestions will be discussed in subsequent chapters.)

We utilize all of these procedures in our work, but not as a rigid system applied to all persons seeking help or therapeutic intervention. The techniques may or may not be used in the order described, and there is no regimented treatment plan implied for all patients. Our therapy is adapted to the specific requirements of the individual.

We attempt to challenge the defense system in a manner that will be the most productive for each person's struggle according to the level of maturity and ego-strength. We prefer patients who are not locked tightly into a particular life style or relationship constellation because they have a greater potential for growth. This is an important prognostic factor. Even patients who are seriously disturbed can respond if they are relatively free of interpersonal bonds. Indeed, some individuals who are less distressed yet more restricted by family and personal ties fail to progress as well.

All of our therapeutic interventions challenge the patient's basic character defenses and inner process of fantasy gratification. The therapist who uses these techniques needs to have an understanding of each patient's particular areas of resistance. He or she should also be able to predict, with some accuracy, the critical points in the therapy that will create significant anxiety for patients and offer them sensitive help during difficult phases.

FEELING RELEASE THERAPY

Comparison with Free Association

Techniques of psychotherapy can be roughly divided, with obvious overlap, into those which emphasize the rational nature of human beings, those which emphasize the behavior, and those which emphasize the emotions. Historically, the psychoanalysts were concerned with developing a method whereby they could obtain a free release of thoughts as well as an emotional catharsis. They turned from early hypnotic techniques to free association as the "royal road to the unconscious." They felt that if the unconscious material—the impulses, repressed feelings and memories—were recovered, they could be integrated into the ego and the patient would be cured in the process. The analysts thought that through interpreting, analyzing, and integrating the material and through the analysis of the transference and the patient's resistance, the neurosis could be overcome and the patient could develop into a healthy, functioning human being.

Feeling Release Therapy utilizes techniques that elicit deeply repressed feelings and reawaken emotional pain from the past. After re-experiencing this pain, the patient usually has a flood of powerful intellectual insights and is able to integrate this awareness and understand the meaning of his or her present-day neurotic symptoms and behaviors. Feeling Release Therapy utilizes techniques similar in many respects to those of Arthur Janov's (1970) Primal Therapy, as described in *The Primal Scream*.

Feeling Release Therapy appears to be a significant advance over free association as a technique for recovering memories and experiences from one's childhood. It is more direct and in no way more radical or dangerous than traditional methods aimed at bringing unconscious material into the patient's awareness. The material that is unearthed verifies, in a straightforward manner and in a way that the patient can clearly understand, many basic hypotheses about the unconscious and the organization of human behavior. When I began working with patients using techniques of Feeling Release Therapy, I found that many of my concepts about the neurotic process were validated by the productions of patients who interpreted their own material and integrated it without assistance or intervention from the therapist. Because of the lack of therapeutic interference in the process, feeling release therapy has an excellent research potential, which has largely been neglected by practitioners and theorists in the field.

Techniques of Feeling Release Therapy

> When the neurotic becomes disengaged from his Pain, I believe he stops feeling in a complete way. The neurotic, until he really feels again, doesn't know that he isn't feeling. Thus, it is not

possible to convince a neurotic that he is unfeeling. Feeling again seems to be the sole convincing factor.

Arthur Janov (1970)
The Primal Scream, (p. 71)

Goal of Feeling Release Therapy.   A primary goal of Feeling Release Therapy is to put patients in touch with painful feelings from the past: the anger, rage, anxiety, sadness or grief that they found too threatening to allow themselves fully to experience originally. In shutting off this pain at an early age, people disengage from their real selves as a center of feeling, perception, cognition, and behavior. They disown their genuine reactions by projecting them onto others, or they feel guilty and hate themselves for having "unacceptable" feelings and try to cover them up. They numb themselves against their pain or suppress it altogether after they repress or depersonalize their memories of the traumatic events that caused them distress. They build a false self that is almost completely cut off from the pain they are suppressing. These repressed feelings are locked into the muscles of the body and experienced as tension. Patients are generally unaware that they still have these unresolved, disconnected feelings or that they are actively engaged in suppressing them.

Most professionals agree that it is destructive to repress one's emotional responses and free flow of feelings, but they tend to underestimate the degree of primal pain and its widespread damage to a constructive life. It is our belief that if people are cut off or removed from their innermost feelings, they cannot experience compassion toward themselves or have genuine empathy for other people. They tend to spend their time in an inward state, indifferent to the basic issues of their lives. The individual's loss of feeling is reflected in a society characterized by depersonalization and schizoid trends. The cut-off individual avoids feelings at the expense of joy and happiness. One who is fully in touch with one's feelings would be acutely aware of a limitation in time and would, at times, feel a poignant sadness about one's inevitable fate. This sadness, though painful, would cause us to feel a kinship with our fellow man. Without this appreciation of ourselves as mortal creatures, essentially alone in the world except for this sense of sharing, we remain alienated from ourselves and isolated from others.

Initial Sessions.   Most people have become so habitually defended against their primal pain that it generally requires special techniques to break through their tension to allow these long repressed emotions to surface. However, some individuals require very little encouragement and are able to get in touch with these feelings in their earliest sessions.

Those who elected to take part in the intensive phase[1] of Feeling Release Therapy were asked to comply with specific procedures prior to their first session. They were instructed to isolate themselves for 24 hours and to refrain as much as possible from smoking, drinking alcoholic beverages, taking medication, reading, watching television, and sleeping. They were also asked to eat very lightly during this time. They were told that it would be valuable to write down or record their thoughts and describe their inner emotional state.

The prohibition against these commonly-used self-nourishing habits had the obvious effect of artificially creating a state of deprivation, which gave rise to anxiety. In addition, interfering with these addictive habits induced a state of disorientation and stress in most individuals. In general, when the patients came for their first session, their underlying pain was close to the surface.

The method for helping people get in touch with their deeper, primitive feelings has been outlined in Arthur Janov's (1970) book, *The Primal Scream*. Lying on a mat on the floor, they learn to breathe deeply and to allow sounds to escape as they exhale. They are also encouraged to say or blurt out spontaneously any thoughts that come to mind while they are breathing deeply.

The large majority of the people who went through this therapy were able to learn this technique within a few sessions. Some began sobbing almost immediately. Others moaned loudly or shouted angrily, while a few uttered high-pitched screams, loud cries for help, angry expletives, such as "Leave me alone," "Get away," "I don't need you," and other emotionally-charged verbalizations.

People's physical movements, often tight and inhibited at the beginning of the initial session, generally became much freer as therapy progressed. People's verbal expressions, their screams and moans, seemed to become more coordinated and integrated with their body movements as time went on. The sounds were not forced; they seemed to emanate involuntarily from deep within the person. It was evident to the therapist that something remarkable was taking place—almost every patient seemed to be genuinely reliving, with intense emotional reactions, events and feelings from early childhood. It appeared that at a critical point in the distant past, these individuals had chosen *not* to feel the intense

---

[1] Intensive Feeling Release Therapy consists of daily, 5 times-a-week, one and one-half hour sessions that take place over a period of 5 weeks, followed by several months of once or twice-a-week sessions.

psychic pain that they were now allowing themselves to experience in the permissive atmosphere of the session.

Group Psychotherapy.   Just prior to the time when many people— patients, friends, colleagues, and associates—were involved directly in Feeling Release Therapy, they had participated in group sessions. In weekend marathons in the mountains and in intensive group sessions, these people gradually came to express their feelings with more freedom and abandonment. Eventually, they began to have reactions that I would call "primal," that is, deep expressions of intense childhood trauma. The atmosphere was unusually accepting of feelingful expression, and open expression of feelings was implicitly and explicitly encouraged. In these groups, when one person began to express a deeper level of feeling, the effect on the group was contagious. Participants would become aware of their own feelings of sadness while listening to someone else reliving a particularly traumatic event from his or her past. Group members generally tended to wait patiently and compassionately until the person had finished working and had clarified the meaning of his or her feelings; then another group member would become deeply involved in expressing his or her own primal feelings. The most noticeable change in the people going through this group process was a significant decrease in hostility and the emergence of a nondefensive posture. They were no longer as directly confronting of each other. Instead they were inclined to trace their feelings back to the original sources. They became much more open and expressive as their hidden feelings became more accessible to consciousness.

Case History.   In working with the people who participated in this phase of Feeling Release Therapy, my associates and I became acquainted with important facets of each person's inner life. Much was revealed in a direct and meaningful way. The patients expressed themselves and described their memories in a way that was unusually clear and lucid. It is difficult to do full justice to these subjective experiences in words. However, a few people were able to capture some of the flavor of the primitive reactions that they felt in the sessions in written records that were kept during the course of therapy. One talented and highly intelligent participant wrote her impressions in a journal immediately following each session. Her record provides insight into the powerful emotions and memories she experienced in the sessions.

Betty, thirty-five, and the mother of three, had lived a complacent and safe existence for the better part of her life, subordinating herself to her husband and living her life through his accomplishments, to the detriment of her own capabilities and intellect. She had hoped to gain a greater sense of self through the therapy and to become more independent in her relationship with her husband. Although she had a noticeably childlike voice and manner and tended to be somewhat unspontaneous in her emotional responses, her basic personality was intact with no symptoms of serious disturbances. In her first sessions, she recalled vivid scenes from her early years spent in a large lonely house on a ranch in the Southwest.

> *Session 1*:   I remember going back to my parents' house. I wandered through the rooms calling for my parents and no one answered. When I found my father, he was sitting in a chair reading a paper or listening to the radio. I could feel the cold leather leggings on his legs. When he talked to me I could not understand him—the words were too big or he spoke in Spanish. He did not look at me.
>
> I remember having difficulty breathing, my throat seemed to close and I could not talk. Then I realized that my mother's hands were covering my mouth. I felt that she was telling me that nice girls don't act that way, that I should be quiet and not say anything, not bother her.
>
> I felt that I wanted to tear something apart like splitting a peach, tearing, ripping, until the blood came out; it seemed to be my sister I wanted to split open. But I began to feel that it was my husband I meant to kill. I called angrily to him that I didn't want him to leave me. Then I asked my father why he never loved me—he was supposed to. I asked him to try, to pretend he loved me, just to act that way. I was appalled that I would be willing to settle for so little—it was pathetic.
>
> I remembered something that made me feel very ashamed. I remembered holding my baby and feeling anxious. I was ashamed at feeling anxious, afraid that the baby might have felt my anxiety. I felt like a bad mother. I wondered if that feeling of anxiety had been passed to me by my mother.
>
> I saw myself as a little girl, standing looking down at the ground, looking defeated and pathetic, wearing a dress too long, with long stringy hair. I attacked her for being a coward, for not looking at them, for not standing up to them—I hated her for being a coward, for condemning me to being a coward. I felt that if I could become her I could look around the corner and face what made her afraid.
>
> *Session 4*:   I was very angry. I made angry sounds, almost screeches. I could hear my father whispering to me: "I don't love you"—over and over. I cried and cried. I felt desolate. It was a

very bad feeling. I was on the floor playing next to my father's desk; he was at the desk sitting in a rocking chair. The rocker rocked over my fingers on the floor. My father reached down and kissed them to make them well. He didn't pick me up. He thought that only my fingers hurt. He didn't even know. He didn't know that I hurt inside. It wasn't just that he didn't care—he didn't even know. I was very sad.

Session 9:   I cried and whimpered a lot. I had a strong desire to suck, even put my fingers in my mouth, but I took them out again to feel the desire to suck. My stomach hurt, I gagged a lot. As I screamed I felt really uncontrolled.

Then I saw a white breast (only one). It was repulsive. It looked sticky like raw bread. When I was near it I felt uncomfortable, and my stomach hurt. I kicked and pushed away. I would rather not eat than be near it. Then I saw two brown breasts and I felt warm and safe, relaxed, completely happy and comfortable next to them. Then I became increasingly anxious. And I was snatched back to the white breast. I went back and forth from white breast to brown breasts over and over, with exactly the same feelings. (When I was a baby I had a wet nurse and my mother didn't want me to get too attached to her.)

When things are really going well for me I get anxious. "How long can this last?" And then I mess up and it doesn't last. I say to myself, "Now I have something to lose," and I get more uncomfortable. (I am more jealous when my husband, John, is really close to me.)

The patient's memories and experiences during her first sessions were notable in the quality of unconscious material and insight she experienced. Despite her regression within the sessions themselves, she functioned in an adult and rational manner during her everyday life outside the sessions. Her first session produced scattered fragments of remembered events which clearly revealed her parents' attitudes toward her. She felt very sad and described herself as a pathetic coward, desperate to sell out. She learned how she had projected the rejection by her father onto her husband, and recalled memories of intense jealousy and hatred toward her sister.

In later sessions, the patient had an even more powerful realization that not only did her father not care for her, but that he was inadequate, unknowing, and ignorant of her hurt and her need. This insight was basic. She found it difficult to accept her father's inadequacy when she was a small child, because it threatened her survival. She found this deeper insight about his rejection painful. Later she realized that by denying her parents' limitations, she blamed herself for their rejection of her and came to see herself as bad. She tried desperately to be good in their terms, to "win their love."

Others of her sessions touched on themes from a very primitive stage of development, where the patient relived memories pertaining to the frustration of her needs on an oral level. She became aware that this was the source of her current underlying dependency on her husband. Direct oral material of this nature, such as memories of frustration at the breast, are usually not accessible in traditional insight therapy to a person with the ego strength of this particular patient.

In general, a wealth of unconscious material was unearthed and integrated by the participants in our feeling release sessions. The material produced provided the patients with a more realistic view of their families and re-awakened a sense of compassion for themselves over the way they had been damaged in their early lives. In spite of the powerful emotional catharsis they went through in the actual sessions, most patients were able to conduct their practical affairs and continue their adult existence outside the session during the intensive part of this therapy.

Description of Patient Population and Results

For a period of 3 to 4 years, the author had the opportunity to work with approximately 200 patients, friends, and colleagues utilizing the innovative procedures of Feeling Release Therapy. Much time was spent evaluating the results, recording and transcribing the vast amounts of material from individual and group sessions, and assessing the advantages and disadvantages of this powerful form of therapeutic intervention. My associates and I came to the conclusion that everybody has a considerable amount of deep-seated pain and sadness that they are continually suppressing, and indeed, may be completely unaware of in their everyday lives. It seemed that no one was immune to this deep primal pain, that no one had escaped childhood without being scarred to some extent.

We found no fundamental difference in this regard between the patients seeking therapy and the professionals and friends who volunteered to go through this process. In other words, there were not two categories of people, those with pain and those without it—everyone in our sample population had repressed pain and everybody's life centered around the avoidance of it. We became increasingly aware of the fact that not only had people stored up painful experiences from the past, but that they maintained their defensive postures and arranged their lives in order to protect against ever having to feel their pain or even be aware of it.

Selection of Patients and Control of Acting Out

The technique of Feeling Release Therapy was not the treatment of choice in every case, even as an adjunct to insight therapy. To progress in this therapy, patients must have sufficient ego strength to exercise a great deal of self-discipline and apply rational thought to any intense reaction they may feel *before* acting on their feelings outside of the sessions. We feel that people with poor impulse control, delinquents, psychotics, borderline paranoid or schizophrenic personalities, or people with certain character disorders, would tend to do poorly in a therapy that strictly adhered to the techniques described above.

Similarly, Gestalt therapists have noted that therapy techniques which affect patients on a deep level and arouse intense feeling reactions are not necessarily recommended for all individuals. For instance, Shepherd (1970) has cautioned: "Individuals whose problems center in lack of impulse control—acting out, delinquency, sociopathy, etc.— require a different approach" (p. 235).

In examining the contraindications for psychoanalysis, Fenichel (1945) also lists personality characteristics of poor risk patients, including a "lack of a reasonable and cooperative ego," patients who achieve certain secondary gains by being ill, and people with schizoid and psychopathic personalities.

Despite the inclusion in our patient population of some seriously disturbed individuals, there were no psychotic breakdowns or attempted suicides or other dramatic forms of regression. There is no question that an explicit or even implicit selection process was operating in our sampling, but our treatment program was applied to a wide range of emotional disturbances. Among the percentage of applicants who were not accepted for intensive Feeling Release Therapy, there were a few who probably would have been rejected as candidates for other more traditional therapies due to their poor prognosis. For example, one young man displayed an immediate paranoid reaction in his pre-interview and was turned away because of a well-developed delusional system, which might have become more intense and volatile through the release of feelings.

Comparison with Primal Therapy of Arthur Janov

Arthur Janov's contribution to the field of psychotherapy was his discovery of a more direct road to the unconscious than the method of free association. Janov's view of the psychological defense system is similar to our own, in that he feels that defenses are limiting and destructive.

As in the analogy to pneumonia where the body's defense is more dangerous to life than the original germ, we feel that in neurosis, the defense becomes the disease on a functional level. The repression of deep feelings of pain causes neurotic patients to feel chronically tense and alienated from themselves, thereby preventing a natural healing process. Janov feels that defenses are a protection against feeling primal pain and that only through repeated expression and release could this reservoir of underlying pain be emptied and the patient cured of neurosis.

It has been our experience with the patients and colleagues who took part in Feeling Release Therapy that the primal "pool of pain," as Janov termed the repressed emotional pains from childhood, cannot be emptied as such, and that repeated primal sessions will not necessarily alter an individual's basic style of defense. Furthermore, we found that the reliving of primal feelings without good impulse control and personal self-discipline may increase a person's tendencies to recapitulate early situations in present-day life and may contribute to reacting overdramatically. Patients who successfully controlled their acting out progressed rapidly whereas patients who acted immaturely or childishly in their personal relationships did not improve as much.

On the positive side, utilizing this therapy procedure enabled our patients to relive traumatic events of childhood and directly experience repressed pain and sadness. The majority experienced unusual awareness and clever intellectual insights that explained their current behavior and illuminated their problems. We have noted, as did Janov, that the personal knowledge gained through Feeling Release Therapy was unusually direct and pure. It is as if the patients were able to envision their childhood situations and see through their present-day problems rather than intellectually "figuring them out" or analyzing them.

In spite of all these positive effects, this type of therapy does not in itself sufficiently challenge the patient's basic addiction to an inward style of existence. As important as it is to understand the connection between one's present-day behavior and past trauma and to have access to one's deepest feelings, this therapeutic process does not necessarily alter the basic conflict, which involves a holding on to fantasy gratification and an avoidance of real satisfactions in the outside world. The patients' fundamental resistance to changing themselves on a deep character level is embedded in their choice of life style, in their tendency to act out immature elements based on the past, and in their unwillingness to be the agent of their own change. It requires more direct therapeutic intervention, personal control over acting-out behavior, and corrective experiences, in addition to the release of feelings, in order to change significantly the basic neurosis.

Thus, patients who have undergone the feeling release part of our therapy and become less defended and more vulnerable still must challenge their basic character defenses. They must learn to accommodate to a more positive image of themselves and to the more realistic picture of their families that they gained from the sessions. More significantly, they must learn to tolerate the inevitable pain and aloneness that come from severing primary bonds and fantasies of connection. Living a richer, more fulfilling, outward life causes a new kind of pain and stress. Without conscious awareness of these reactions and their source, a person will generally return to the inward state so familiar to him or her. The dynamics of compulsively reliving destructive patterns, listening to the "voice," preferring fantasy gratification to the real, are not permanently shattered simply by emotional reliving.

In concluding our evaluation of Feeling Release Therapy and comparing it with Janov's work, it is our opinion that despite disagreeing with his statement that primal therapy is a "cure," properly understood and administered it is a valuable therapy and an excellent and legitimate research tool in understanding personal dynamics and unconscious material. The author feels that the true value of Janov's contribution has been marred by his own movement toward physiological explanations that were of questionable scientific value and by fear and prejudice in the psychological community relating both to primal material and the method of eliciting it. The unique methodology and its powerful effects, together with Janov's (1970) dramatic description in *The Primal Scream*, went against orthodox practices. Defining and describing the phenomena of a primal and developing primal therapy and theory were matters of great importance. Heralding it as a "cure" and the cultlike application of these ideas by would-be followers, together with a basic fear of the primal material unearthed, all acted to disenchant serious practitioners.

Chapter 18

VOICE THERAPY

In a sense, each of us lives in two different worlds, experiencing strong ambivalent feelings toward ourselves and others, and entertaining contradictory viewpoints of the events in our lives. At times we see our loved ones and other people in warm, friendly, compassionate terms. At other times, we are detached, cynical, and critical. While one part of us strives to be open and vulnerable, the other, negative view prompts us to see life as meaningless and insignificant. From our theoretical vantage point, the "voice" keeps us locked into our defense system, while our healthier side strives for freedom from the constraints of these defenses.

The "voice," as we conceptualize it, is the language of the defensive process. As such, it opposes the expression of feeling, undermines rational thought, and sabotages the pursuit of real satisfaction and goals. The voice represents an unconscious, ongoing pattern of thoughts that acts to depress one's emotional state and direct one's behavior toward negative, limiting, or self-destructive consequences. Self-hatred is a direct result of this negative thought process. The voice includes all the statements that one says to oneself in the process of preserving one's negative self-image.

Voice Therapy employs methods that bring these hostile thoughts and attitudes into the patient's awareness. The process of formulating

298

and verbalizing negative thoughts acts to lessen the destructive effect of the voice on the patient's behavior. In Voice Therapy patients learn to verbalize their ongoing internal dialogue with their voice, to expose their self-attacks, and eventually to separate their negative attitudes toward themselves and others from a more objective, nonjudgmental view. They learn to distinguish the negative defensive attitudes, incorporated from the family, from their real point of view. In learning to answer these internal criticisms and accusations with realistic appraisals of themselves, they improve their reality testing and attain mastery over the voice and its influence.

Voice Therapy, like Feeling Release Therapy, can elicit intense feelings that result in a powerful emotional catharsis with accompanying insight. The techniques of Voice Therapy are different, though, from those of Feeling Release Therapy in two ways: first, there are no special rules or restrictions placed on patients, such as isolating them or depriving them of customary emotional painkillers and routines prior to the sessions. Second, the level of emotional catharsis can be controlled in Voice Therapy. The therapist can choose whether to utilize a more cognitive approach or to elicit more emotionally-laden material.

The purpose of Voice Therapy is to bring the destructive aspects of the voice, which are primarily unconscious, under the conscious control of the patients so that they have more freedom of choice in directing their life. It elucidates the basic split in their thinking and feeling about themselves and their ambivalence about people and events. Voice Therapy acts to separate the individual from the incorporated parental values and attitudes that affect him or her adversely and that support the compulsion to repeat destructive patterns of the past.

BRIEF REVIEW OF THE CONCEPT OF THE VOICE

As we have explained earlier, the voice originates in childhood as the child incorporates the rejecting, negative viewpoint of the parents toward the self and other people. These incorporated parental attitudes are a basic part of the bond with the parents, and they come to have their own functional autonomy within the adult personality, effectively limiting one's independence and growth potential.

The process of incorporating the image of the rejecting parent and the negative, even hostile, thought patterns is analogous to the phenomenon of "identification with the aggressor," described by Bettelheim (1943/1980):

> The old prisoners' identification with the SS did not stop with the copying of their outer appearance and behavior. Old prisoners accepted Nazi goals and values, too, even when these seemed opposed to their own best interests. (p. 79)

When children are hurt and in pain psychologically, they don't want to be in distress, so when the situation becomes intolerable, they cease to identify with themselves. When they feel the most threatened, they will choose to identify with the person who is the source of their suffering in an attempt to possess that person's strength. Children assume the qualities of the parents through identification with them and assimilate their hostile, critical attitudes toward their offspring. In forming the bond with one's parents, one becomes at once the weak, bad child and the strong parent; the transgressor and one's own severest critic.

Most children learn gradually to withhold their feelings of affection for their parents in response to parental rejection and intolerance; the children, nevertheless, persist in their efforts to win love and approval. When they repeatedly fail and experience new rejections, they blame themselves and use the voice to castigate themselves. The voice or negative thought process eventually comes to subvert the child's point of view about everything in his or her world. It protects the core defense of self-sufficiency by interpreting reality in a way to preserve both a superior and inferior view of self.

Everyday manifestations of this critical thought process can sometimes be detected in the form of a voice or a style of speaking to oneself. In many instances, people are aware of this process and can actually detect the voice in operation. When they are participating in a new activity, they hear a critical voice saying, "You look so awkward—people are looking at you." When people make mistakes, they severely berate themselves. For instance, a ball player thinks to himself, "You idiot. You must be blind to miss that ball. You're getting too old to make it any more." A surgeon tortures himself, "What if you make a mistake?" A salesman broods, "Your selling streak is over; you were just lucky until now." A lover thinks, "You're going to lose your erection. You're not really a man. Why should she be attracted to you?"

The voice is directed externally as an attack on others as well as internally toward the self. More commonly, however, the voice tells the person that he or she is unlovable and undeserving, is not like other people, and is mean or "bad." This self-punishing content of the voice is more basic and substantive than the part that distorts others. For instance, when the therapist encourages a patient to give free rein to verbalizing and dramatizing the voice, more of the negative statements are directed against the self than against other people.

The concept of the voice must be distinguished from the rational consideration of alternatives and a realistic evaluation of self and others. It is not concerned with reality testing or validating perceptions. It is not a positive or even neutral force but a self-destructive process, with varying degrees of anger toward the self and others.

The voice is essentially an ongoing internal dialogue that attacks the self and perceives others as unfeeling and untrustworthy. Under normal conditions, only fragments of these self-attacks become conscious. The procedures of Voice Therapy increase the patient's awareness of this self-destructive dialogue and help him or her to counteract the voice's influence. Once exposed, it can come under control, and a person is able to make behavioral choices in a direction contrary to the dictates of the voice.

DEVELOPMENT OF METHODOLOGY

Early History

In developing the concept of the voice and a therapeutic methodology to counter its pervasive influence, the author has had many occasions to observe this process in both "normal" and neurotic individuals. Early in my professional career, I became aware that most people became angry and defensive when they were told things about themselves that they could construe as being critical or negative. Their defensiveness was not usually related to the accuracy or inaccuracy of the feedback they were receiving, but appeared to coincide with their own negative self-evaluations. Any quality that they particularly disliked in themselves constituted a sensitive area that they felt they must protect from outside criticism. If that were not the case, they would not have reacted so defensively whenever their personal qualities or behavior came under scrutiny. I came to the conclusion that appraisals and evaluations from others, when they validate a person's distorted view of him or herself, tend to arouse an obsessive thought process.

From these observations, I hypothesized that most people think and evaluate themselves in ways that are extremely self-punishing and negative. Since they already suffer from their own critical thoughts and attacks, they feel very threatened whenever other people disapprove of them. People's reactions to external criticism are usually out of proportion to content or severity. Any criticism or judgment, ranging from the mildest to the most harsh, can trigger a train of associations that are self-hating. Because of this, I thought it would be valuable for people to become aware of the issues to which they were especially sensitive. I wanted them to be alert to the events that stimulated their self-attacks. This type of research and investigation became an important part of my initial explorations of the techniques of Voice Therapy.

In order to study this phenomenon, several psychotherapists decided to form a discussion group where they would focus on revealing the negative feelings and thoughts they had toward themselves. They took as their frame of reference the ideas about the voice that the author was developing at the time. Within this same context, they discussed the traits and behavior patterns in one another which were offensive or undesirable. In their discussions, they found that they tended to react much more defensively to certain types of feedback than to others. Their findings corroborated my preliminary concept of the voice.

The practitioners then experimented with the technique of verbalizing their negative thoughts in terms of the voice. They discovered that the voice was easily recognizable and could be expressed in words that had a great deal of emotional impact. Indeed, negative thought patterns often occur in the form of a "voice." When self-accusations were spoken aloud, they were represented in the second person, and they sounded like: "You're no good;" "You're a phony;" "You so-and-so, you did this or that;" etc. Verbalization of the voice in this manner provokes strong supportive feelings for oneself. Once formulated, these self-attacks could be effectively evaluated and countered.

On the other hand, people who think negative things about themselves or make disparaging comments in the first person, such as, "I'm a failure," or "I'm too old to change," or "I'm incompetent at work," to varying degrees believe these self-perceptions and cannot easily separate them out from realistic self-appraisals and therefore cannot really defend themselves against them. In the neurotic individual, a great deal of energy is expended in an internal dialogue regarding self-worth, which does not basically alter the damaging effect of these self-attacks.

It became clear to the psychotherapists in the discussion group that this thought process not only affected them at times of stress or when learning new activities but could affect any area of their lives: concern with sexual performance, predictions of personal rejection, worries about competency, negative comparisons of themselves with rivals, and cynical, harsh judgments of others.

These more obvious examples were only the tip of an iceberg. The real clues to the depth and pervasiveness of the process were the reactions of fear and defensiveness that occurred when certain attacks were exposed. We could determine the content of our most severe self-attacks by noting the experiences that made us feel bad. We could sense the occurrence of an inner attack whenever we felt especially hurt or pained.

Later, when the concept of the voice was presented in lecture material to a class of university students, it was interesting to note how quickly the students grasped the concept. They easily understood and talked about the ways that they habitually attacked and criticized themselves and could provide numerous examples of the self-critical thoughts they had about themselves, especially when they were under pressure of exams or suffered from other stress. One student, for instance, told of the difficulty he had studying, because he was continually distracted by thoughts about upcoming exams. As he crammed, he told himself, "What's the use? You're going to fail anyway. Why study? Go out and have a beer instead;" or "If you don't get a B on this one, then you won't be able to get into graduate school." Other students analyzed their reactions to peer pressures, sexual problems, and career decisions with these techniques.

The voice is an abnormal or misguided form of self-protection that acts to preserve an individual's isolation and negative self-concept. To a great extent people make their behavior conform to these distortions of themselves. They talk themselves out of pursuing goals that are important to them with statements such as: "Why try, you'll probably fail," or "Don't show that it matters to you," or "Don't be a fool, you'll just be humiliated if she says 'no.'"

Expectations of failure and rejection logically follow from a pessimistic point of view, and acting on these thoughts leads to self-fulfilling prophesies and negative consequences. Important everyday decisions are constantly being made under the direction of the voice. Unchallenged, this thought process can lead to more serious pathology.

METHODS FOR ELICITING THE VOICE

There are three principal techniques utilized to assist patients in identifying the voice and differentiating it from their own point of view: (1) Dramatizing the voice: The patient is encouraged to blurt out emotionally whatever critical thoughts come to mind during a session. This method usually arouses deep feeling responses and spontaneous insights. (2) A more conventional psychotherapeutic approach: Patient and therapist explore the various aspects of the voice and systematically break down the patient's defenses into their particular components—the punishing aspect, the self-indulgence, the build-up, the anger toward others, and the basic misconceptions about the self. In this technique, the voice is verbalized and discussed objectively and analytically. (3) Answering the voice: This technique involves talking back from one's own point of view and challenging both the content and the dictates of the voice. The patient may choose to answer in dramatic, emotional terms or logically and matter-of-factly. On an action level one may choose to alter one's behavior by not complying with the mandates of the voice or by directly going against them.

A. Dramatic Verbalizations of the Voice

The technique of dramatizing the voice is straightforward and relatively easy to explain and demonstrate to the patient. First, patients are introduced to the concept of the voice and its relationship to their distressful symptoms. Then they are taught how to verbalize the self-critical statements they tell themselves in their everyday lives. Over a period of several sessions, they become familiar with the process of saying these thoughts out loud in the second person; then they are encouraged to express these sentiments *emotionally*: "say it louder," or "really let go," or "say it again with more feeling," and "blurt out spontaneously anything that comes to mind."

Direct expressions of hostility, meanness, and viciousness generally flow from these suggestions; many patients come by this method naturally, on their own, without needing much encouragement from the therapist. They sense anger behind specific thoughts and spontaneously express it along with the content. Others who are more inhibited in expressing themselves need support and permission to be more dynamic in their manner of expressing the voice.

Results.[1]   In individual and group sessions, most patients expressed intense feelings of self-hatred in powerful language and with strong affect. In one therapy group, for example, a young man was in the midst of verbalizing his thoughts and feelings about his physical appearance, when he suddenly yelled at himself:

> Get out of my sight, you simple shit! You pathetic, repulsive piece of shit! I can't stand the sight of you! You make me sick!

His face was contorted with the rage he was expressing toward himself; tears welled up in his eyes and streamed down his cheeks. He finally

---

[1]Excerpts from transcriptions of tape-recorded therapy sessions.

broke into sobs as he said, "You make me sick!" His outburst stirred deep feelings of sadness and rage in other group members who empathized with this man's struggle to accept himself. Soon they, too, responded with similar material. One woman who continually failed in her attempts to control her weight loudly condemned herself in strong language. She began by saying:

> I'm so discouraged by my diet. Every morning I look in the mirror and call myself names. It's like a voice saying, "You cow! You're disgusting. Look at yourself! People can't stand to look at you! You fat cow! You'll never lose weight! You're a failure. Hear that, a failure, a total failure!"

A man who had recently gone through a divorce tore into himself savagely in an individual session, telling himself that he had failed as a husband and father:

> Look at you! You can't love a woman! You couldn't even hold on to your wife and kids. You bastard! Nobody wants you! Nobody! You're an unfeeling bastard. You'll *never* get another woman. You've had your chance, you stupid bastard!

This man, who had been married for 15 years before his wife left him, was attacking himself in the same manner that his wife had criticized and nagged him throughout their marriage. In the absence of *her* criticisms, the patient's attacks on himself had increased considerably. He realized that he had used his wife as an external critic and now that she was gone, he could see that her criticisms had closely matched those of his own voice.

In our therapy groups, dramatic and powerful primal feelings are aroused in others when one person blurts out self-attacks in this manner. People tend to experience deep feelings for the person going through this process as well as compassion for themselves.

In still another case, a receptionist became flustered while talking to one of her company's clients. She felt humiliated when she heard herself stammering as she attempted to answer his inquiries about her company. She told her therapist that her voice had seized on this evidence of her shyness and reserve and had attacked with words such as:

> You idiot! You idiot, you can't even talk right! You're so stupid! You can't even say the simplest thing! You can't even say hello! You little creep. You are such a little nothing! You can't even talk plain! You'd let anybody humiliate you!

Another patient, Sara, a young legal secretary who doubted her ability to attract a man and typically appeared depressed and sullen, had an extremely punishing voice. The young woman had grown up in a remote area on a lonely farm with her parents and sister, who were cold and unresponsive. It was obvious that she had been an unwanted child and that her younger sister, in contrast to the patient, had been prized for her good looks.

In her sessions, Sara had focused on her angry, competitive feelings toward other women and her hostility toward men, whom she saw as rejecting her and preferring the company of more attractive women. She came to identify many of her self-attacks regarding her looks, her body, her weight, and an overall feeling of disgust she felt about herself. In this particular session, her therapist asked her to stay with the feelings of hatred and revulsion toward herself, and very soon she was in the midst of a tirade against herself, berating herself for not being the child her mother wanted.

In a controlled, tight voice, quite unlike her own slow, low-pitched voice, she launched into a vicious attack on herself:

> Sara (voice): Why can't you be like your sister? Look at her and look at you. Why can't you be like her? Look at her! She was beautiful when we brought her home from the hospital and look at your face, just look at your face . . .
>
> (Louder) You have the ugliest face I ever saw . . . of any child I ever saw in my life . . . I feel like I could kill you . . . I hate you so much . . . you won't die . . . You just keep getting sick . . . Why didn't you just die?
>
> (Louder, almost screaming) I just want you to be dead! You should have been one of the ones who died . . . and you didn't die . . . Why didn't you die . . . Why didn't you die (repeated many times). I just want you to die. I can't stand to look at you. You're the ugliest . . . filthiest . . . filthiest . . . person in the world. I want to kill you. I want to wipe that face off this earth . . . You look so terrible. Look at you! You're ugly, ugly . . . You're ugly (repeated many times). I'm so angry at you. I could just strangle you with my bare hands. Why won't you be more like Sandy? Why won't you be sweet like her? Look at her! She is so sweet to me . . . She knows all I've done for her . . . You won't be grateful. Why won't you be grateful? You should be grateful.
>
> (Sad) Why don't you just get out of here? I wish you would just get out of here. Why don't you just leave? . . . leave . . . (voice trails off, cries softly).

In the midst of her highly emotional state, when Sara was allowing her thoughts to emerge spontaneously, she recalled that her mother had once confided in her that she had had several miscarriages. She had told Sara of her disappointment and how she had always wondered how those children would have turned out if they had lived. This recollection explained Sara's feelings of guilt for just being alive. She had insight into her deep feeling of being undeserving in relation to having a better life than her family.

Following this cathartic experience, the patient had a clearer understanding regarding her mother's underlying hostile feelings toward her and the origins of her own self-hatred and lack of self-esteem. In subsequent sessions, she recognized the barriers she had put up to protect herself from becoming involved in a relationship with a man. In maintaining the image of "the ugly one" given her by her parents, she never had to feel the outrage and hurt from her past. Breaking with this definition or identity continued to cause her varying degrees of anxiety as she progressed in her therapy over the next weeks and months.

When the voice is expressed dramatically and forcefully, patients invariably become aware of the suppressed rage that they have always felt toward themselves. These feelings were repressed and exist on a deep level. Our patients are usually able to trace this anger back to its origins in their parents' spoken and unspoken feelings and attitudes.

Greg, a twenty-five-year-old carpenter, was pained by his increasing aversion to working with power tools and his tendency to "space out" when working long hours. In one session, he verbalized the thoughts that preoccupied him as he worked with the power saw in the shop. The following is an example of Greg's voice in operation:

> You'd better be careful tonight. You're tired. Just watch yourself. You're going to run your hand right into that blade. Careful now, see how close you came that time? C'mon, just see how close you can put your fingers to the blade. C'mon, just a little closer, it won't hurt. Just shove your finger right into that blade.

Greg was shocked at the seductive and tricky tone of his own voice as he gave vent to these thoughts. The injunction to injure himself was delivered in a soft, gentle voice until the final command to "shove your finger right into that blade." The gentle quality of the voice belied its viciousness, which was expressed in the tone of ridicule and sarcasm. This voice had a familiar ring for Greg. He recalled that his father had spoken to him in a similar tone of voice. Gradually, he had to face the fact that his father hated and resented him especially during the early years when the boy's mother had seemed to focus all of her attention on him to the neglect of her husband. He also remembered that his father, who had never attained success financially, had ridiculed his early interest in woodworking, insisting that he should aim for a professional career.

Recently Greg had had a number of minor mishaps in his shop and had become obsessively concerned about the possibility of more incidents. It appeared that this young man was living out his father's ill will toward him despite his own strong desire for success. Indeed, the fact that he had surpassed his father financially had awakened symbolic castration fears that were graphically expressed by his voice. Getting in touch with this self-destructive voice enabled him to gain some perspective on his work and allowed him to relax his extreme vigilance and overly-cautious style of working.

In another case, Robert had been living with his girlfriend for almost a year when he began to question her love for him. Robert was an extremely possessive young man who became enraged and self-destructive whenever he sensed there was a rival for his girlfriend. At these times, he would sulk and drink heavily. When she told him that she was having lunch with a business associate, Robert flew off the handle and began to tear himself apart:

> Robert: When my girl friend told me that she was going to lunch with a man who worked in her office, my heart sank. My whole body felt in pain. Strangely enough, I thought immediately of attacking myself. Mostly I was afraid that she would make love to this man and find out that I wasn't very good. If I put this line of thinking in terms of the "voice," I'd say:
> "She's going to find out you're nobody. She's going to find out what sex is *really* like. She's going to be with a man and she is going to find out what it is really like and not want to be with you again. You better just stop her. It's really the end for you and you're going to die, you're really weak. You've been protected up to now, you shit, but now you've had it. Now she's going to be ruined. Now she'll really be different. It will never be the same, you weak piece of shit, why don't you be a man and stop her?"

Jealousy and possessiveness were recurring themes in this young man's life. His insecurity and strong dependence on his girlfriend for endless reassurances of her love and his extreme possessiveness were ruining the couple's relationship. The current situation had triggered Robert's underlying fear of being abandoned that had begun in childhood when his mother was hospitalized for long periods of time due to a chronic illness. Following this session, Robert had a better understanding of his jealous feelings and fear of being alone.

Sometimes patients will have difficulty at the beginning when using this technique. We suggest that they express this blocking in terms of the second person. In other words, instead of saying: "I can't think of anything to talk about," or "I'm blank right now," the person is encouraged to try to say critical thoughts about expressing him or herself. One woman, in trying to overcome her resistance to talking, used this voice technique to initiate the conversation:

> Voice: You don't even know how to get started. I never saw anybody so stupid in my entire life. You don't even know what you are going to say. You think you have things to say here? You have nothing to say! People don't want to hear what you have to say. This man doesn't want to hear what you have to say. You're going to say something like a blubbering idiot. You're an idiot. You better keep your mouth shut before I kill you. You're nothing and you're an idiot. You'd better keep that big trap of yours shut because you're an idiot and you don't know what you're talking about. And you're a liar. What the hell do you think you're trying to do? Do you think you're going to change? Yeah, you just keep right on trying. I'm right behind you and you're *not* going to change.
>
> You think that you have some good feelings? Well, wait until morning. I'll make you wake up feeling shitty. You'll feel so shitty that you won't know what to do. You can't talk in here and then expect to feel good. I'll see to that. You're going to feel terrible if you talk about things.

It was clear to this woman that talking openly about herself was a threat to her voice because it disrupted the bond she still had with her family. She often felt like a traitor who was giving away the secrets of her family when she spoke of her childhood in therapy sessions.

Theoretical Implications.   As we refined this technique and more people began to loosen their controls while vocalizing the voice, we learned that these expressions of intense anger against themselves were not isolated occurrences. It seemed that many people hated themselves with a passion and intensity that surpassed by far anything they consciously *thought* they felt toward themselves. It was apparent there was a great deal of energy being expended by people in repressing these volatile emotions of murderous rage and self-hatred. Where did the intensity and viciousness of these attacks come from?

From interviews and talks with parents who had learned to be forthright and honest about their relationships with their offspring, we became aware that many parents have hidden desires and impulses to get rid of their children. The more defended the parent, the more hostility he or she feels toward the child, because of the child's innocent intrusion on the parent's defenses. Of course, parents feel extreme guilt about these unacceptable feelings and cover them up by finding fault with the child (usually they project their own self-hatred onto the child) or by being overprotective. The child's reactive anger at the parents for their rejection is also suppressed. The child turns this anger against the self and becomes self-hating and depressed. Thus, what we were experiencing and observing was an expression of this suppressed rage, both the parent's toward the child and the child's toward the parent. We hypothesized that this primitive rage is the basis of much of people's self-destructive and self-denying behavior.

When people enact the voice in a dramatic way and as they get to the emotionally charged content of their statements against themselves, there is often a remarkable change in their physical expression. The person's body takes on the posture and mannerisms of a strict parent delivering a lecture or issuing an ultimatum. The actual voice sometimes takes on the accent of one of the patient's parents. This phenomenon is especially obvious if the parent is of foreign birth. Occasionally people will stop in the midst of severely condemning themselves and report that the way they sound is exactly the way they remember their parent sounding. Often entire phrases and colloquial expressions are blurted out that are replications of the parent's speech. Patterns of intonation and pitch become quite similar to those of the parent when an individual is deep into the process of dramatically expressing his or her voice.

In conclusion, the technique of dramatizing the voice is an effective tool in unearthing the sources of people's feelings of self-hatred. It increases their understanding of the origins of their self-destructive urges and helps them separate from the incorporated parental view of themselves that is only an overlay on their real image of self. The emotional catharsis that accompanies this exposure of the voice relieves tension and promotes positive feelings similar to the results we have observed following sessions of Feeling Release Therapy. Further research is in progress with a view toward determining the overall effectiveness of this technique when it is utilized alone or in conjunction with other procedures.

B. Systematic Analysis of the Voice

In contrast to the technique of dramatically verbalizing the voice, the method of analyzing the content of the internal thought process utilizes a more cognitive approach. The level of interaction between therapist and patient is similar to that of psychoanalytic psychotherapy or other traditional forms of insight therapy. With this technique, people first identify the connection their negative thoughts have to important events in their everyday life. For example, if they notice that some time during the previous week they had engaged in a conversation with a close friend that left them feeling bad, the therapist would ask what they thought they might have been telling themselves at the time that made them depressed. The therapist would encourage them to try to give words to the thoughts they had. The patients would then attempt to recapture the self-critical thoughts they had in relation to the earlier conversation. They might say:

> Why are you so insensitive? He doesn't want to talk to you right now. Can't you see that he's bored? He's busy and you're taking up his time talking about trivia. You have no consideration for other people.

In contrast to the previous technique, this is done unemotionally and undramatically.

From this exposure to the content of their own self-accusatory remarks, people learn that their "bad moods" begin with their voice attacks. They gain insight into the specific ways the voice operates to depress their overall good feeling about themselves.

Results.   An analysis of the statements that people use against themselves reveals that misconceptions of the self are among the most common forms of self-attacks. These distortions act to separate people from each other by emphasizing the differences between them. For example, one general theme reported by people using the analytic technique was their tendency to compare themselves unfavorably with other people, particularly with rivals or potential competitors. Men described themselves as "unattractive to women," "weak," being "less than a man." These comparisons were especially prominent in the area of their sexuality. Men often told themselves:

> "You're not like the other men she dates."
> "You're too short."
> "You're not good-looking."
> "You don't know how to treat a woman."
> "You aren't going to be able to satisfy her."

Almost every man reported "hearing" an attack that his penis was too small. Similarly, almost every woman felt that either her breasts were too small or her hips were too large. Many were afraid that their vaginas were too big or that men would be "turned off" to them. Many women attacked themselves about their ability to attract a man or to excite him sexually. They tended to attack their appearance with such statements as:

> "You look awful."
> "Look at your complexion."
> "You're not the feminine type."
> "How can you expect to compete with those pretty young girls in your husband's office?"

Many women reported being distracted from feeling sexual when they were making love by thoughts such as:

> "You don't know how to touch him."
> "He's not going to have an erection."
> "You're not going to be able to have an orgasm."
> "Don't let him touch you or kiss your vagina."

Sometimes these thoughts were directed against the man. These distortions stood in the way of a satisfactory sexual relationship:

> "He doesn't know how to touch you."
> "He's too gentle/too hard."
> "He's so insensitive."
> "He's too quick to enter you."
> "All he wants is intercourse; he's not interested in how *you* feel."

We found that many men also distorted women and misperceived their behavior. Sometimes, however, their cynicism was a reaction to a woman's becoming more withholding sexually:

> "She's cold and indifferent. Forget *her!*"
> "She's so childish and melodramatic."
> "You can never trust a woman."

Or a man sometimes built up the woman in his mind:

> "She's much more personal and feelingful than you are."
> "She wants love and affection and all *you* want is sex."

Giving words to the thoughts and worries that are triggered during lovemaking had the effect of making the patients aware of how they were sabotaging their sexual experiences and interfering with their own satisfaction. Often there was a tendency to blame the partner for one's sexual problems. After verbalizing these dissatisfactions with their partners, most people came to recognize the part their own obsessive thinking played in diminishing their enjoyment of sex. Simply by verbalizing these self-attacks and the criticisms of their partners, they were able to relax more and allow their feelings to flow uninterruptedly. People generally reported progress after these voice sessions. Sexual partners said that they were closer to each other as a result of exposing their inhibitions as well as their hostility toward one another.

During each stage in analyzing the voice, the therapist consistently points out to the patient that whether one's self-evaluations or criticisms are accurate or false, the process of attacking and hating oneself is not appropriate or functional. In other words, the therapist impresses upon the patients that it would be legitimate for them to change their behavior if they don't like or admire it in themselves, but the process of belligerence and anger toward themselves is never constructive, even if there is confirmation of the criticism. If patients voice these self-attacks as if they are attacks from the outside, almost as if there were a parental figure chiding them, there is usually therapeutic movement. There is also evidence of a positive mood swing, as the process of sharing and analyzing the voice brings about a basic change in attitude toward self and others.

Voice Therapy in Psychotherapy Groups.   Both the analytic approach to Voice Therapy and the dramatic approach may be successfully utilized in group psychotherapy. In one group composed of married couples, partners were encouraged to expose what their voices are "saying" about each other and about their relationships in general. For example, one couple had been married only a few months and the partners were already at odds with each other. Both were stubborn, willful individuals who wanted their own way. They were childish in their style of angrily accusing each other of not living up to their expectations. In this particular session, they focused on clarifying the angry feelings that they had been harboring for some time. The therapist first instructed the husband to use the voice technique in talking about his anger.

> Husband (voice): My thoughts go something like this: "If she really cares for you, then why doesn't she work on it? You're just getting lost in the shuffle, she's involved with so many other things. What does she really care about you? Nothing, that's what, and her actions prove it."

At this point, the therapist asked the husband to say any angry, irrational feelings he had to his wife from *his own point of view,* in an attempt to separate them from the more cynical, hostile attitudes of his voice.

> Husband (to wife): I can't feel much of my anger towards you. I feel it more towards myself. I feel like there's something wrong with *me*. But when you're gone all day, it makes me feel angry and then I don't want to have anything to do with you. Then when I see you again, I do feel like I want something with you. . . . I feel lost. . . . I go back and forth in my feelings.

Next, the wife was encouraged to express her negative thoughts to her husband in terms of what her voice was telling her about him.

> Wife (voice): "Why should you give him anything? Who is he to think you should always go where *he* wants to go? He doesn't have anything to give you! He never wants what *you* want. Why should you always try to please him? You're a real sucker to give in like that."
>
> Wife (to husband): My voice says it the way I actually feel toward you sometimes. I feel like saying—"just leave me alone, I don't have anything to give you" (sad). I have really felt like being nice to you at times, being very giving, especially sexually. I feel like I've opened up, but then you pull away. So I really *do* feel rejected at those times. I think to myself "What's the matter with me, I try to be nice to you, but what's wrong?—don't you like me?" Then I get furious at being hurt.
>
> Wife (voice): Don't do that any more—don't try to be nice to him or please him. Stay away from him, show him what it's like to be rejected. He can't make a fool out of you.
>
> Husband (to wife): That's exactly the way I feel. I would have said the same thing. My voice is almost identical to yours. I feel scared getting into my feelings. I've wanted to protect myself from them. But what I really want to say is that I just want you to love me.

The next couple to work on their relationship during this particular session had been married for several years and had settled into a routine style of communicating in which each tended to blame the other for their unhappiness. An angry exchange the previous evening had left both partners feeling discouraged about the relationship. The source of their disagreement was a long-standing conflict over money and the wife's tendency to splurge on clothes and cosmetics.

First the husband spoke of being disillusioned by his wife's seeming disregard of their financial situation. He was also troubled by her habit of overspending:

> Husband (voice): "Man, she's going to take you for all you've got. Why won't you be a man and just *stop her*? You're such a fool. She's got you wrapped around her little finger. Look at her sitting here playing it cool, acting as if she's so innocent. You should tell everybody here about her. Let *them* see what a bitch she is."
>
> Husband (to wife): All I know is that I'm totally confused by you. I want to buy you nice things, but you always manage to beat me to it. You buy yourself a dress and then you're afraid to tell me what it costs. But I have to pay the bills, dammit, how can I keep us solvent if you keep on?

The therapist recognized that the patient's fury at his wife was not only connected with a fear of being drained financially but also covered up his deep hurt at not being allowed to give to her. After discussing this point with the couple, he asked the wife to say her voice about that.

> Wife (voice): "He'll never give you anything. Don't believe him when he says he'd like to buy you a new dress. He's lying, he'll forget. If you waited for him to buy you something, you'd wait all your life!"

Later, after analyzing her concern and distrust:

> Wife (to husband): I really don't want anything from you because then I'd owe you something. I know that sounds unreasonable but that's my gut-level feeling. (sad) I get so nervous and jumpy if you say you want to buy something for me. I guess I just don't want you to give things to me. I'd rather get things for myself. I don't know why. (cries)

As these two examples illustrate, the nature of a couple bond is that both people are usually "listening" to the dictates of their respective voices. Both ward off love from the other and use the voice to justify their anger and distancing behavior.

C. Answering the Voice

One of the most important therapeutic effects of Voice Therapy is the positive impact it has on an individual's self-image. Often the procedure of simply recognizing the voice and vocalizing it has a powerful curative effect. What has occurred dynamically is that a separation has been made between the incorporated parental attitudes that constitute the voice and the person's own opinions and desires. Prior to "saying the voice," patients have generally accepted these negative thoughts as true evaluations of themselves and have believed them. These have been part of their self-concept since childhood. The malice and ridicule expressed during Voice Therapy sessions reveal the malevolent subjective character of the feelings that accompany negative self-statements. Answering the voice with realistic appraisals of oneself diminishes the voice's influence on a person's behavior and feeling state.

When patients have fully articulated specific self-attacks, the therapist asks them to formulate an "answer to the voice." Some patients find this step more difficult and have trouble thinking of statements to make on their own behalf. They have little or no defense against the voice. The inward state in which many people live tends to support their voice attacks. If they are not externalized and viewed objectively, an individual's attempts to argue with his or her voice, that is, to carry on an inner dialogue between the self and the voice, are all too often exercises in futility.

When the therapist teaches patients to answer back to their own self-attacks, he or she may suggest one of two different techniques: one, the patients can "talk or attack back" dramatically, or, two, they may objectively enumerate their own traits and distinguish the characteristics in themselves that differ from the qualities they disliked in their parents. The therapist may suggest to the patients that they fight back by imagining that they are talking to the actual parent, a technique that is similar in some respects to psychodrama. Deep feelings of anger are usually aroused when the patient accepts this suggestion.

Dramatic Answering of the Voice.   One woman, whose mother dominated the family, had never been allowed to express hostility. When she attempted to answer her voice attacks with angry rebuttals, she drew a complete blank. Finally she said that she didn't want to be like her mother in *any* way. The therapist suggested that she tell this to her mother as if she were present.

> Patient: (angry and loud) I don't want to be anything like you. I don't want you as part of my life. I'm not going to make the same choices that you did. Even if I get mixed up sometimes and start to act like you, I don't like myself like that and I *hate* you like that. I'm not going to be disrespectful and mean. I don't hate and despise men. I don't see them as bastards. I don't want to join your battle against men! I saw the way you treated my father! I'm not going to be like that! like *you*!

Answering her voice, that is, the incorporated attitudes of her mother in relation to men, disrupted this woman's emotional tie with her mother. She began to separate her personal feelings of caring for men from her mother's characteristic hostility and condescending attitudes toward them.

A man whose father had the reputation of being a "loner" found himself becoming more and more alienated from his friends as he approached middle age. It seemed that he was repeating his father's habit of living in isolation. In answering his voice that continually warned him not to trust or depend on his friends, he said:

> I'm not a loner like you! I have friends who I care about a lot. I won't give them up like *you* did. I'm a loyal friend, but you were never loyal to anyone, not ever! You pushed everyone away, even me (sad). You couldn't even—(long pause)—you couldn't even be a pal to your own son. I feel sorry for you, but I won't live *my* life like that, alone with no friends. I don't want that kind of independence!

In another case, a young mother who was struggling against her tendency to feel burdened by housework and the care of her children answered her voice with the following words:

> Look, mother, I don't want you in my life. I can't *stand* you. I can't *stand* the way you are. You are just a lazy slob. That's all you are! That's all you are (loud). I hate you! You're a mean bitch! You're lazy! You're disgusting! You're disgusting to look at. You don't want to lift one finger for anybody!

A young man angrily attacked his family in a session while attempting to counteract his voice:

> You're all liars! We didn't have a family! We all sat in separate rooms staring at our own private TV sets. You didn't talk! You didn't listen! Why did you have us if you didn't want to talk to us or see us?

Some patients become deeply sad as they articulate their responses to the voice. For example, the young receptionist mentioned earlier, who stammered and then attacked herself for being shy and backward, broke down in tears as she said:

> I *am* a person, nothing special, nothing weird. I'm not strange—the way you used to see me. I'm just a regular kind of

person. All I wanted was somebody to take care of me. There's nothing wrong about wanting a mother when you're a child. That doesn't make me a shy creep, groveling around being humiliated by other people. That doesn't make me a creep (sad). That makes *you* a creep—not me—you're the creep, not me. You're the bad person! (Angry)

This young woman had been deserted by her mother when she was five years old and still suffered the effects of feeling humiliated whenever she showed a desire for a normal home life of her own. In this session, she recovered feelings for herself and was able to see her mother in a more realistic light.

One of the most powerful challenges to the voice I have heard was screamed out in a group by a man who had believed all his life that he was inferior to other people because he was strange or "weird." This man rarely talked about his parents, but on one occasion, as he was exploring the reasons behind his inferiority feelings, he mentioned how bad he had felt at home. His sister, who was also in the therapy group, concurred with his perceptions. Evidently her validation of his own point of view was enough to alter his basic misconception of himself for the moment, and he screamed out painfully yet triumphantly: "I'm *not* crazy! I'm *not* crazy!" As his sobs subsided, the patient explained that he had always believed that he was crazy and different from other people. There was a strong bond in this family and considerable pathology. Both children had to deny their real perceptions of their parents. When the son did speak up, his parents told him he was crazy. As a result he had to "swallow" much of what he perceived. He internalized the feeling that he was peculiar, because he disagreed with his parent's image of themselves as loving, caring people.

Realistic Appraisals that Challenge the Voice.   In challenging the power of the voice over their lives, behavior and emotional state, people can make objective statements about traits and actions they like in themselves and those they wish to change. In answering the voice, a person might say:

> 'I know that I have been stingy and tight with my money, but I intend to be more generous from now on," or "I realize that I haven't put forth my best efforts in working at this new job, but I feel that I have more motivation now," or "I know that I've always been afraid of sex, but I feel that I'm making progress in overcoming these fears."

These statements are part of the process of answering back to the voice in a realistic, nonjudgmental manner. Self-evaluations that are realistically negative but objective are far different from those of the voice that are loaded with meanness and hostility. For example, even if people have a low I.Q., their voice would not be right in saying to them: "You moron! You stupid ass! You're so dumb. You good-for-nothing!" Their limitation is real, but an angry attack on themselves is unjustifiable.

The voice also plays into the naive and stultifying assumption that people have a fixed and stable identity. It implies that people are the way they are and that is all there is to it. The voice sees identity as immutable and supports the neurotic solution. There is a desperate need to maintain psychological equilibrium at the expense of personal growth. However, individuals cannot be permanently labeled and pigeonholed. They exist in a dynamic state of flux and can change all but their most basic endowments.

Matter-of-fact answers to the voice accompanied by appropriate changes in behavior can be powerful tools in the hands of a person who is motivated to change. Patients are free to challenge their voice in any area once a self-attack has been articulated. The therapist will ask them to put forward an honest evaluation of themselves. Often, patients spontaneously compare themselves with the parent of the same sex. For example, one woman, who was a business executive, said to her voice:

> I'm not playing the big shot the way you see it. I'm not out to control anyone's life, but I feel that I have a good effect on people. I influence them in a positive direction. I like having that effect on people. I like making them happy.
>
> An interesting thought just went through my mind. I'd say to my mother:
>
> "When I die, I want to have had an effect on people. I don't want to die and not leave anything behind me, like you. *You're* not going to leave a mark on anybody that's constructive."

The young man, Robert, described earlier, who was jealous and possessive of his girlfriend, attempted to answer his voice by saying:

> You're wrong. I'm not going to fall apart even if she falls in love with someone else. Sure, I would be very sad and disappointed if she found someone, if she really rejected me. But if I'm feeling strong and self-confident, I could even handle that.
>
> I learned to be possessive from you, Dad. You wouldn't let mom out of your sight without worrying about whether she was faithful or not. You hounded her all the time—so she finally

rejected you. You drove her away with your suspicions. Well, I'm not going to repeat *your* mistake. I know that I can't imprison someone without eventually losing them. That's something *you* never learned.

Another woman revealed what her voice was telling her about her husband.

Think of yourself! What about you? You need your time, you need some time to yourself. Are you going to give all your spare time to *him*? Don't you ever get tired of being with him?

Later in the same session she answered back by saying:

Listen, this is what I *want* to do. I love doing things with Jim. I really like being with him. I love it. It makes me feel happy. I love doing all the things that we do together. I love sharing a project we're both working on. I enjoy being affectionate, and I especially like being sexual with him. I feel happy *any* time I can be with him. *That's* what I want to do.

Answering the voice is not to be construed as being a diatribe against parents. It serves no purpose to blame parents for the patients' current unhappiness, symptoms, or acting out. Talking back to one's voice is a challenge to the *internalized parental image,* not one's real parent. Indeed, it is rarely therapeutic to attempt to answer back to the original family members or to attempt to work on one's neurotic problems directly with them. Rather, it is better to recognize that one's conflict is an internal one, once the defenses are well-established.

The technique of answering the voice is similar to dialogues in Gestalt Therapy where people change roles as they articulate different parts of their personalities or dramatize and act out symbols from dream material. However, the traditional "Top Dog/Underdog" Gestalt dialogue (Perls, 1969) differs from our method of separating the verbalization of the voice from the process of answering it.

In Voice Therapy, patients first formulate all of the attacks on themselves. Only after they have fully expressed these attacks do they answer back with a counterattack from their own point of view. The purpose here is to separate out the patients' self-destructive thoughts from a legitimate point of view that reflects feeling for themselves. By contrast, Gestalt dialogues mix the two with sequential statements from the opposing sides in a give-and-take dialogue. In our experience with

Gestalt dialogues, we have found that a person often becomes confused by continually switching roles. One feels on both sides of the fence and can lose perspective. We believe it is important to separate clearly and decisively one's hostility toward oneself from speaking up for oneself. At this stage of our research, we found this method to have superior results.

SUMMARY OF FINDINGS FROM VOICE THERAPY

Voice Therapy is an active agent in breaking down the fantasy bond—the symbolic connection with the family. For this reason, there may be considerable resistance to Voice Therapy. Stubborn feelings are aroused because challenging the voice is so closely tied to behavioral change. In order for Voice Therapy to remain effective there must be changes in habitual behavior that go against the injunctions of the voice. Therefore, our therapeutic methodology includes the process of formulating corrective suggestions that modify behavior.

In conclusion, Voice Therapy is in a rudimentary stage of development, and there is a need for systematic research to further elucidate the defensive and self-destructive process. We are striving to improve our methodology and expand our techniques for both exposing and overcoming the effects of the voice.

In our present state of knowledge there is no question that there is an insidious process of sabotage and self-attack in every individual. Each person is plagued to varying degrees by an internal dialogue that is self-limiting and harmful. Techniques are available to give words to this process and help an individual to isolate and become conscious of the source of the majority of his misery. Combined with corrective suggestions, a person can begin to counteract the dictates of the voice and achieve greater personal fulfillment. Without this challenge, a person gradually submits to the destructive process of the voice and shuts down his or her real self and unique point of view. It is our opinion that Voice Therapy is a powerful therapeutic procedure and valuable research tool in understanding the anatomy of psychological defenses.

Chapter 19

CORRECTIVE SUGGESTIONS

The ultimate goal of therapy is to help patients to change the pattern of their lives and behavior so that they are able to tolerate more gratification in reality. In order to achieve this, the patient's psychological defenses have to be confronted at every level. Therefore our corrective suggestions are aimed at challenging the core of defenses, opening up the possibility of greater exposure and vulnerability and an honest life style.

Honest communication is impossible if one is leading an inward, defended life and gratifying one's needs in fantasy. People living on this level cannot be truthful about their lives. If they claim to be seeking success and love in the real world, they are basically untruthful because their behavior fails to live up to their words. On the other hand, when they attempt to be more honest by admitting that they don't want much from life, a fact that is borne out by self-denying behavior, they are only telling a *defensive truth*, because on a deeper level, they want to fulfill their personal destiny.

Therapeutic progress is characterized by an increase in patients' ability to tolerate the pain and anxiety of expanding their lives and changing their identity. Improvement is reflected in positive changes in the patient's self-image and in the ability to be open. In living a more honest, nondefended life, an individual has more vitality because energy previously expended in repression and defensiveness is freed for more constructive purposes. There is an absence of duplicity in communication and interaction with others; a breakdown of withholding and protective defenses; and a free flow of emotion, i.e., a real capacity both to give and receive love. There is also a gradual increase in tolerance for a better life and a broadening of personal choice and freedom.

An honest, more vulnerable existence is not always a happy one. Happiness depends in part on favorable conditions in a person's environment and in the real world. A nondefensive life simply implies being adaptive to the real circumstances of life and feeling appropriately about them. One's situation will largely determine the degree of happiness or unhappiness that one feels. An emotionally healthy person adopts an adventurous, direct approach to goals and is able to experience feelings for both the good and the less fortunate outcomes.

Corrective suggestions initiate changes in the patient's behavior; as such, they lead into a more goal-directed approach to living. Interventions that affect the patient's everyday practical life are a vital part of a successful therapy. Therapeutic progress is more than a function of freeing repressed material and interpreting it; it must also involve a process of creating and adjusting to a new environment.

The term "corrective experience" was suggested by Franz Alexander when he attempted to apply psychoanalytic therapy to cases that had been generally refractory to treatment. "Alexander (1932) felt that . . . most patients had been traumatized by parental mismanagement during childhood," and that "it was necessary for the analyst to arrange 'a corrective emotional experience' that would counteract the effects of the original trauma." (Arlow, 1979, p. 17) More recently, other types of supportive therapy have emerged. *Milieu therapy* or *situational therapy* makes use of guidance techniques and environmental manipulation to help the patient develop better inner controls. Other *supportive therapies* attempt to assist and strengthen the patient's ego through practical guidance and suggestions. These techniques are especially applicable to patients with poor ego strength and impulse control who are experiencing situational difficulties. In these cases, the therapist attempts to build up the defenses of the patient.

The author's use of the term "corrective suggestion" is meant to describe techniques that are usually *focused on challenging rather than supporting specific defenses of the patient.* Our corrective suggestions often lead directly to a corrective emotional experience. For instance, when patients stop provoking or negatively manipulating their environment, they generate a new set of circumstances, which creates a different type of emotional climate.

Our interventions or corrective suggestions fall into five general categories. While these categories may actually overlap to some extent, they can be separated as follows:

1. Suggestions that help control self-feeding habits and dependency behavior.
2. Suggestions that break into the patient's inwardness and involvement in fantasy.
3. Suggestions that control noxious or provoking behavior and interfere with withholding patterns.
4. Suggestions that disrupt destructive bonds.
5. Suggestions for exploring a new identity and overcoming fears.

In developing an overall treatment strategy for their patients, therapists must be aware of the particular pattern of defense that is being challenged. For example, if patients follow the therapeutic suggestion to refrain from acting out behavior that provokes anger in others, their relief from guilt will affect their negative self-concept. In other words, these patients disrupt their internalized "bad-child" image by controlling habitual behavior that they dislike in themselves.

Our corrective suggestions bear a direct relationship to specific dimensions of the defensive process. Because psychological defenses are interrelated, behavior change in one area necessarily challenges other defenses. For example, the patients described who began to like themselves better also started to perceive their families more realistically. This, in turn, led to real communication and a break in the destructive bond with the family. In this sense, there is a close relationship between corrective suggestions and underlying theoretical concepts.

Corrective suggestions act as catalysts to move patients toward new situations where they will be unprotected by their customary defenses. When they discover that they can live without the things they believed were absolutely necessary for their survival, they feel freer and more independent. In a sense, they must relinquish their crutches *before* they learn that they will not fall without them. They must give up their armor before they really learn that there is no threat. In addition, corrective suggestions act to eliminate dependency on fantasy and other painkillers that have served a lifelong purpose of alleviating pain.

In describing the technique and use of corrective suggestions, we are not claiming that our approach is unique. Every psychotherapist offers corrective hints or suggestions at one point or another. We stress the broadening of this process with systematic therapeutic interventions that directly challenge the character defenses at the core of the patient's neurotic life style.

It is important to distinguish our techniques from authoritative guidance or advice-giving, which is the treatment procedure of choice in "directive psychotherapy." In general, we are not parental in attitude or style; we encourage patients to explore alternatives and possibilities with us as equals and in an open manner. In frank discussions about the aspects of their lives that lock them into misery and conflict, both patient and therapist contribute corrective ideas that apply to the unique circumstances of each case. Our patients have demonstrated remarkable sensitivity to their own resistance and awareness of the importance of changing habitual behaviors that limit their lives.

When the therapist offers a suggestion to the patient, he or she has no stake in the patient's acting on the suggestion. The overall procedure has an experimental flavor and is generally undertaken in a cooperative spirit. This is not to say that resistance is not encountered when a particular suggestion "hits home" or that patients don't distort the therapist who is helping them formulate these practical changes.

But though collaborating on the suggestion as equal partners and free agents, patients can distort the entire situation and deal with it in a paranoid manner. They may believe that the therapist is telling them how to run their lives or accuse the therapist of making value judgments. They may even develop paranoid feelings similar to those expressed by one patient who indignantly asked her therapist: "What's wrong with reading?" and "Don't I have a right to my privacy?" The therapist, in this case, had merely commented that it would be better for her to spend less time alone reading. He had interpreted that this isolated activity probably contributed to her withdrawn state and depressed feelings. Angry paranoid reactions to the therapist's intervention in cases like this are a sign that the patient has projected his or her desire for change onto the therapist and has twisted the meaning and purpose of the relationship.

In working with our patients, our suggestions are usually made in accord with their personal goals and the areas they want to change. The way people live their lives and express their individuality is largely a matter of choice. Therapeutic suggestions are valuable primarily because they set into motion a process that increases the freedom and range of personal choice for each person.

1.   BREAKING SELF-FEEDING HABITS AND DEPENDENCY BEHAVIORS

Implementing a suggestion that breaks a self-nourishing habit pattern is often a first step toward change on a deep character level. The patient has typically used these types of behaviors to allay anxiety; however, they have interfered with personal growth and placed limitations on the scope of experience. Most self-nourishing behavior is directly related to the neurotic process of symbolically satisfying oral needs. The patient may use smoking, alcohol, drugs, or overeating as a substitute for real gratification. Dependency on these substances may reach the proportions of an addiction.

We agree with the position of many psychotherapists that the patient with a drinking or other drug-related problem must constrain drinking or drug use as a prerequisite for entering therapy. This creates the seemingly perverse situation of asking the patient to be cured in order to start therapy. Although it is extremely difficult for the alcoholic or heavy drug user to maintain the resolution to abstain throughout the course of treatment, it is necessary for a successful prognosis.

Use of addictive substances numbs the patient's feelings of pain and sadness. Unfortunately, other emotional responses are also blunted by these habits. Suggestions, or in serious cases, mandates, to stop addictive behavior leave patients vulnerable to the painful feelings they have been suppressing, often for years. Such feelings then break into an emotionally deadened state that has consistently kept the patient insulated from positive as well as negative experiences.

There are other self-nourishing habits that are *not* as closely associated with oral gratification which also serve to cut individuals off from a feelingful state and tend to isolate them from other people. Behaviors such as excessive reading, television-viewing, and addiction to computer games, for example, are painkillers in that they dull people's sensitivity to experiences in the real world. Compulsive masturbation and routine, mechanical sex without emotional contact keep one insulated and removed from others. Attempts to change this compulsive behavior arouse anxiety in a manner similar to challenging self-feeding habits, such as smoking or drinking.

It is obvious that watching too much television is psychologically damaging to children; yet many parents use it to put their children "to sleep" emotionally and to avoid any real contact with them.

> One young teen-age girl was asked to limit her television-viewing to one hour a day because it appeared to her therapist that she was living more in fantasy than in reality. She had become progressively more withdrawn and noncommunicative upon entering adolescence. In ostensibly following this suggestion, the girl attempted to substitute another habit—that of compulsive reading. She told her therapist that her life was too boring and too empty without these distractions from the pain of living in an emotionally barren home.

Most patients find it difficult to give up symbolic substitutes for the love they were deprived of as children. They dread the prospect of facing withdrawal with its psychologically unpleasant and often physically painful symptoms. They are reluctant to break a bond with themselves where they have been symbolically feeding and caring for themselves in order to preserve a secret sense of security and self-sufficiency.

The rationale and purpose behind the use of therapeutic measures that trigger anxiety states is to assist patients in gradually accommodating themselves to the tension involved in constructive change. As patients learn to tolerate unpleasant sensations of anxiety without regression or reversion to old behavior patterns, they are free to progress.

When self-nourishing behavior is abandoned during the therapy process, the habit may diminish or disappear entirely. This demonstrates the functional autonomy of some habit patterns; they are no longer related to the original need that caused them. For example, one patient was troubled about chronic masturbation and guilt when he entered treatment. At a certain point during the course of therapy, his therapist suggested that he give up masturbation, and instead call a friend and talk to him at those times that he felt lonely and anxious. There were no withdrawal symptoms and the patient gradually became accustomed to this methodology. In addition, he began to develop an important personal relationship. In following the therapist's suggestion, he progressed beyond his destructive habit of compulsive self-gratification and there was movement toward a better overall adjustment.

Breaking self-nourishing habits may be conceptualized as a re-education in living. In giving up a particular habit that has been used as a crutch or painkiller, patients expand their life space and go beyond self-imposed limitations.

Proper timing and the development of trust in the therapist is essential in getting people to cooperate with these suggestions. The proper follow-up requires a great deal of support and involvement on the therapist's part. It is important not to make these suggestions lightly. They can lead to serious anxiety states and possible regression.

2. BREAKING INTO THE PATIENT'S INWARDNESS AND INVOLVEMENT IN FANTASY

Suggestions designed to intrude on an individual's inward state reawaken repressed feelings and disrupt the inner world of fantasy. When people have been alienated from their feelings for long periods of time, they generally become impersonal in their interaction and communication with others, especially with the people closest—their family and children. To counteract this superficial level of communication, our therapists often recommend that their patients make it a point to talk daily to one trusted friend or to the person in their family with whom they feel the most open. The purpose of these dialogues is to learn how to talk more personally and honestly about one's practical life and goals. When these suggestions are followed, a person develops a stronger sense of self in relation to the environment and comes to feel more active and in control of his or her life.

Experiences designed to break through the barriers people erect in order to remain emotionally isolated are also valuable adjuncts to therapy.

> One couple who had been married for several years had become increasingly alienated, and each partner secretly blamed the other for his or her unhappiness. Their therapist recommended that they spend 15 minutes together each evening objectively verbalizing their criticisms of each other in an adult and rational manner. They were asked to reveal or "give away" their cynical thoughts or their "voices" about the behavior and traits of the other that they disliked the most. Following this exercise they were asked to tell each other any positive feelings they might have. Clearing the air of complaints and grudges from the past had an immediate effect on their feelings toward each other. In addition to opening up avenues of communication that had broken down, this experience appeared to have a positive effect on the couple's sexual relationship.

Breaking routines that give a false sense of permanence can be an effective intrusion into an individual's inward state. Almost any routine that a person consistently depends on is capable of becoming addictive in the sense that it can function to cut off pain and anxiety. We have sometimes suggested to patients that they change simple and mundane repetitive actions such as taking the same route to work every day, having dinner at the same time every evening, or the ritual of having a cup of coffee immediately upon rising in the morning. Seemingly innocuous changes in routines and schedules can be a first step in effecting change in an overall defensive posture. Even minor alterations can break into a patient's inwardness and increase energy level and vitality. An obvious example of this process can be seen in people on vacation. They often feel happier and more extroverted than at other times in their lives. These people have energy available to them that comes directly from breaking emotionally deadening routines. In this instance, they usually don't experience overwhelming anxiety because of the temporary nature of the change. They give themselves permission but only for a limited time.

To combat a patient's passivity and isolation, the therapist may suggest any number of activities: sharing a project or hobby with another person where active cooperation is required, saying one's negative feelings directly to another person rather than gossiping about him, going out to dinner with friends once a week rather than always eating alone, or interrupting patterns of sleep by waking up in the middle of the night and engaging in an activity or talking with someone. This latter exercise has important positive implications. We have found that many people regress to a less adult level or sink deeper into a self-hating mood during their sleep in such a way that they are somewhat worse off upon awakening. Some find it difficult to get out of the inward, cut-off state in the morning. Many people report that they feel quite well when retiring at night yet wake up the next morning feeling depressed and irritable. Interfering with the regressive process that occurs during sleep through sleep interruption has had a positive effect on many of these patients.

Corrective suggestions are often made in our psychotherapy groups. At one intensive session where the participants had reached a deep level of trust in each other, the therapist suggested that each person reveal his or her most shameful secret or humiliating experience. The effect on the people who chose to follow the suggestion was immediate. At first, there was a great deal of sadness and pain accompanying these revelations. Afterward, the people who had exposed their deepest secret felt a tremendous sense of relief and a significant decrease in their feelings of self-hatred. Many discovered that they had entertained fantasies that they were different from other people because of this hidden side of themselves. In revealing their secrets, their fantasies of rejection that stemmed from these feelings of unacceptability were dispelled. Most of the participants reported feeling more gregarious and outgoing than they had prior to the experience.

The experience of revealing hidden fantasies renders them less effective or compelling to the patient and is an intrusion into the process of gratifying the self inwardly. Breaking into the patient's fantasy life can sometimes be accomplished by involving another person in the isolated material. This technique has been used by Dr. John N. Rosen (1953) in working with psychotic patients and intruding into the autism by entering into the fantasy process. By joining the patients in their psychotic world, the therapist helps them leave their dream state. In a particularly vivid and exciting story, *The Jet-Propelled Couch*, Robert Lindner (1976) described a case in which, as the therapist became increasingly involved in a psychotic patient's fantasy, the patient began to move out of his fantasy and the protection it had offered him.

We have utilized this technique in our work. Many times the revelations and verbalizations of sexual fantasies in therapy can break the addiction to the fantasy process.

> It was suggested to one young man who secretly and compulsively attended pornographic films that he take a friend with him any time he had the impulse to see this type of movie. The combination of the therapist's nonprohibitive attitudes about these films and the suggestion to take someone with him effectively lessened the attraction these movies held for him. The suggestion implied permission to perform an activity that had made the patient feel guilty, yet it interfered with the sexual fantasies he entertained while watching these films. The patient could not actively maintain his isolation and fantasy life when he shared this experience with even one other person.

A significant characteristic of a neurotic or inward life style is evident in a person's progressive imitation of the parent of the same sex. Most individuals unconsciously imitate this parent's negative traits in spite of disliking them, and as they grow older they become more and more like this model from childhood. To counteract this compelling, primarily unconscious process, patients are counseled not to be ashamed of associating with and using as role models new people whom they admire. It is very valuable to imitate the positive and likeable traits of someone who is different from one's parent, yet there is generally guilt involved in the process of choosing an "outsider" over one's family. In supporting this process, the therapist might encourage patients to spend time in close proximity to a person they particularly respect and like. In close association with a role model, individuals tend to identify and unconsciously imitate and internalize new traits that they admire and respect.

This modeling effect occurs in the therapy process itself. Indeed, positive transference implies an identification with the therapist and an imitation of his or her good qualities. On some level this imitative process is going on during the entire course of therapy; thus, it is important that the therapist have personal qualities that are admirable and positive. Without strong identification, it is difficult for a person to develop a new sense of identity that is stable.

Some patients are fearful of losing their identity, or are embarrassed at using another person as a role model. Nonetheless, conscious and unconscious imitation of the positive traits of respected individuals can be a source of valuable incidental learning. Of course, this suggestion should not be confused with encouraging the person to become a follower or sycophant; rather, the intention is that each person will adopt those new traits that are in harmony with his or her own identity.

Some people have a stubborn, fundamental resistance to changing their negative self-image. Others who have a great deal of vanity or who are egotistical are generally not open to the process of forming a new identity or accepting therapeutic suggestions. It is important to overcome this resistance, as therapeutic suggestions and an experimental attitude toward behavioral change are an important part of any successful therapeutic process.

3. CONTROLLING PROVOKING BEHAVIOR AND INTERFERING WITH WITHHOLDING PATTERNS

A person can ward off closeness by isolation or by provocation. By creating antagonistic circumstances and a hostile emotional climate, one can manipulate one's world and effectively put distance between oneself and other people.

Provocation

Many patients become candidates for therapy because they have never grown up emotionally and are still reacting childishly and dramatically to present-day conditions. Others can't seem to cope with their practical affairs and provoke people with their helplessness.

> One young woman, a graduate student at the state university, "collected" large numbers of parking tickets and carelessly neglected to pay them. She seemed determined to provoke her husband with her forgetfulness. This habit, together with the substantial bills she ran up by not returning overdue library books, created tension in the relationship with her spouse and kept this young woman in the role of a child. The therapeutic suggestions for her were fairly straightforward—first, immediately to pay off her delinquent fines and library fees by securing a loan from the bank; second, to avoid getting any tickets in the future; and third, to return all books to the library on the due date. She had difficulty following the simple suggestion to return the books on time because she had a stake in keeping her husband in a parental mode with her. It gave her security to play the role of "child" with him but put a heavy burden on the relationship. Until she was successful some months later, their relationship remained unpleasant, and their bond, which recapitulated the parent/child relationship, remained intact.

In another marriage, the husband habitually refused to pick up after himself, leaving his wife to clean up. Finally, she decided to stop nagging him about this habit, which had provoked her for years. Stopping her part of the game where she had played the "mother" to his childish manipulation permitted important underlying problems to come to the surface. Once the bond was interrupted and these basic issues brought to light, there was progress in their relationship.

Some habits develop along sexist lines. Many women refuse to drive competently or carefully, and alarm and provoke their mates with their carelessness. Others rarely carry heavy packages or suitcases, leaving the man to look after them. These behaviors tend to encourage childishness in women and patronizing or parental reactions in men. Therapeutic suggestions to alter these patterns generally initiate important changes in both members of the couple.

Many people need help in correcting the angry, negativistic and passive-aggressive behavior that they were allowed to act out when they were young. Adult forms of temper tantrums or explosive angry reactions, pushiness, defensiveness, and other noxious responses are symptomatic of continuing to live on a childish primal level. One young woman was told that her dramatic outbursts toward her fellow workers as well as toward the members of her therapy group kept people at arm's length. She explored a variety of self-disciplinary techniques with her therapist, looking for an effective method of control.

Another patient, a lawyer, was asked to refrain from making "courtroom rebuttals" and condescending statements to other group members or friends who had things to say to him. He stopped this style of defensiveness and found that others were far less put off by him. He began to be likeable, and people actually had fewer negative comments about him.

Some people earn the reputation of being troublemakers because of their remarkable ability to provoke other people with an abrasive, irritating style of talking and behaving. One young woman talked in her therapy group of nothing but her weight problem and the psychological "reasons" she was unable to control her intake of calories. Once, in the midst of an analytic monologue about her weight, another group member interrupted her and told her that it would probably help her if she would resolve *not* to talk about her diet during the group. When she complied and talked about other subjects, she immediately became less irritating. Later, she went further in allowing people really to like her.

In general, the majority of our suggestions concerning noxious behaviors are designed to alter the milieu that the provoking person habitually establishes to protect him or herself. As such, acting on the suggestions permits a corrective emotional experience in a more positive environment.

Withholding

Patients who tend to be withholding act out their passive-aggression in ways that lead to unproductiveness at work and deterioration in their personal relationships. In the work area, they often find it difficult to finish assignments and tend to be disorganized, often to an extreme degree. For example, one executive was well known for his messy desk which was continually piled high with papers and unopened mail. Despite the efforts of his secretary to reduce his paper work, this man still managed to irritate clients by his apparent disregard for the documents they sent him. The therapeutic suggestion was simply to clear his desk each morning and at noon before going to lunch; he was not to start working until he had performed this chore. This simple suggestion had profound effects on this man and his business associations.

There is considerable stubbornness about changing withholding behavior because it is tied to the primary fantasy of being self-sustaining. By restricting their emotional transactions with others, people refuse to receive love from the environment or to give love in return. Withholding intelligence, looks, or loving and sexual responses from other people is a way of indirectly expressing hostility. It is a style of holding on to oneself and one's products to avoid feeling "drained." For many, the tendency to withhold positive responses involves broad areas of psychological functioning and, as such, becomes a basic part of their identity.

Patients who have learned to be withholding in their families continue to be tight and ungenerous as adults. Some withhold from themselves. One case in point is a patient who was self-sacrificing and spent large amounts of money on her children, but not herself. One of her therapeutic suggestions was to spend some money routinely on herself each week.

People who are tight with their money are generally withholding in other areas as well. They appear to be blocked or thwarted in their ability to give or express love. It was suggested to one man, who was self-centered and ungenerous, that he buy dinner for his friends. Another patient began doing small favors for others, an activity that was completely out of character with his reputation for stinginess and self-importance.

In general, we encourage our patients to be generous with themselves and their feelings and to get over the feeling of "being a victim or sucker." Breaking patterns of withholding leads almost immediately to a freer, more energetic feeling and a happier state. Changing withholding habits that alienate others significantly changes the patient's emotional life and social experience. The gratification and positive reinforcement that result act to support the learning of new responses.

4.   Suggestions for Disrupting Bonds

Essentially, fantasies of connection between individuals can be as addictive as painkillers such as alcohol or drugs. Suggestions that are directed toward changing behaviors that maintain these bonds lead to a break with the hungry and dependent life style that the patient developed in the family. For instance, when a patient is advised to stop asking advice or seeking reassurances of love from a mate or others, ties of dependency are threatened.

In order to achieve genuine close relationships in reality, people must break their bonds with the people in their past and present life. *They must understand the distinction between genuine caring and concern for another person and the symptoms of being connected to that person in fantasy.* They must be able to distinguish emotional hunger from real expressions of love. This is a vital step in the direction of learning to tolerate the satisfaction and fulfillment of a close personal and sexual relationship and is a prerequisite for developing a nondestructive interaction with one's spouse and one's children. The intense reactions that are inevitable in separating from these powerful connections make most people reluctant to break their dependencies on important figures in their lives. Some patients become intensely angry when their bonds are being tampered with and in various ways will punish their therapist for supporting them in their efforts to be independent.

The quality of the communication in a relationship is an indication of the presence or absence of a bond. Because most couples conceptualize their relationship as a union or merger of two personalities, which reinforces an imagined connection between them, we often suggest to married couples that they stop using the terms "we" and "us," and other phrases that imply a oneness, when talking about themselves.

> One man who appeared to be the spokesman for a couple talked in a therapy group of "wanting to work on *us*," saying "I'd like to talk about *us*." When he stopped talking in this style, he noticed that he felt very uneasy. His discomfort continued for several group sessions, and seemed to intensify each time his wife spoke about *her* perceptions or voiced her opinion. This man was unaccustomed to thinking of his wife as a person with views of her

own. As a result of the therapist's suggestion he had begun to see her in a different light and even this hint of separateness had frightened him.

The way that people in a couple talk *to* each other can either strengthen their bond or disrupt it. Suggestions that couples stop being protective of each other's defenses by underplaying their mate's destructive habits, by building up the other's vanity, or by complaining in ineffectual ways about the other's weaknesses, are valuable aids which break down the mutual protection and defensiveness.

Most couples need extensive help in simply learning how to talk together in ways that are constructive and nonhurtful. In analyzing their styles of communication in therapy sessions, patients become more aware of their tendencies to make fantasy connections with each other, as well as of their propensities for giving up their individuality. For example, communications between partners who play out the role of the child or the parent in relation to each other are commonplace. In one group, a woman persisted in talking in a shaky, tearful voice each time she tried to confront her husband with her complaints. Another group member finally interrupted her and insisted that she talk "straight." All were surprised when she complied with this suggestion and answered for the first time in a firm, adult manner. By dropping her childlike pose and dependent role-playing, this woman had taken an important step toward freeing herself from the restrictive bond she had with her husband.

Some couples have redefined the traditional roles of husband and wife that are the parameters of a stereotyped, sexist view of marriage, which incidentally support dependency and fantasies of connection. Women have taken over functions customarily referred to as "man's work," such as home maintenance, yard work, plumbing, and other mechanical skills, while men have learned to cook and care for the children. Stepping out of these roles promotes genuine companionship between men and women and disrupts the bond that is largely supported by role-determined behavior. Sharing equally in raising children promotes a genuine sense of working together for a common goal and breaks into the myth of maternal love (Badinter, 1982) which so often excludes the father. Innovations that disturb sexist role-playing can be instrumental in changing the couple's fantasy of love into real friendship and equality.

In most couples, there is an assigned leader, spokesman, or decision-maker, a process that personifies the dependency tie. In one couple of our acquaintance, decisions were always referred to the wife, ranging from choosing a restaurant or theater to buying a new home or managing financial affairs. When it was suggested that this woman temporarily refrain from directing the couple's plans, her husband felt a sharp sense of loss and disorientation. The gradual accommodation to this new situation allowed for potential growth in both partners.

Most people are afraid to be vulnerable and outspoken in sexual situations. Suggestions directed toward overcoming these fears include: being honest about one's desire or lack of desire to make love, openly admitting shyness or hesitancy about being looked at, voicing fears about being touched or about being experimental sexually and acknowledging when one or the other partner feels cut off or unfeeling during the sex act. Direct conversation about specific sexual matters has the effect of breaking into routine lovemaking, where the partners are often emotionally cut off from the experience and need fantasy to increase their excitement. Couples utilizing these suggestions become closer friends and feel a sense of companionship with their mates because these communications help break into their defenses.

Separating from a bond can usually be accomplished without the people actually separating. Once the symptoms of the bond between them have been recognized and corrected, a new relationship is possible, based on real feelings. However, temporary separations, such as taking separate vacations, can be beneficial for couples who have lost the excitement and romance that characterized the early phases of their relationship. People who have taken brief vacations away from the other person have usually returned to the relationship with a renewed sense of their own individuality.

Many people falsely equate breaking bonds with breaking up or leaving a relationship. For many, all that remains of the original caring friendship and respect for one another is a fantasy of love. There are no longer signs or operations in the warring or indifferent couple that could be interpreted as indications of genuine affection. Challenging this fantasy of love opens up the possibility of a renewed love relationship, even though there is a risk of further rejection or even the possibility of a real loss. For the majority of patients, rejection or divorce is another step toward an inward, unfeeling or self-denying life. In spite of the many rationalizations for leaving, in most instances the person is salvaging defenses rather than moving toward a positive life choice. For this reason, therapeutic suggestions often seem paradoxical in nature. They challenge the falseness of the bond which emphasizes form over substance but strongly suggest "hanging in" and developing greater tolerance for real friendship, love, and closeness.

5.   SUGGESTIONS FOR EXPLORING A NEW IDENTITY AND OVERCOMING FEARS

Neurotic individuals generally come to therapy with a false or con-fused sense of their own identity, having lived most of their lives within the restrictive definitions bestowed on them by their families. They are frightened of challenging these labels and definitions even though they reflect an unrealistic and often unfavorable self-image. When they no longer manipulate their environment in order to maintain a stable image based on past interactions, people feel as if they are living in an unfamil-iar world very different from the one they knew as children. Adapting to a more positive situation becomes the focus of their struggles, and they must learn to cope with the fear aroused by their changing circum-stances and the disorientation that comes with the exploration of a new identity. This process of accepting a changing identity rather than a fixed identity disrupts the neurotic solution or defensive posture. For this reason, corrective suggestions that challenge a person's rigid self-concept and open up new experiences play an important part in per-sonal growth.

People are resistant to changing the image of themselves in the family because it breaks the bond and there is a sense of loss. For exam-ple, one woman who was known as the plain one, while her sister was labelled the pretty one, attempted to live up to this definition by becom-ing overweight and looking unattractive. She followed her therapist's suggestion to lose weight and then buy a new wardrobe. However, when she had reached her ideal weight and others commented on her attrac-tiveness, she became anxious and found it difficult to continue her diet-ing regimen. She felt compelled to regain the weight she had lost when she became aware that men were attracted to her. She could no longer maintain the old image of herself, and this scared her. In her words, she felt that she was out on a limb.

In another example, a man in one of our therapy groups irritated people with his habit of name-dropping and his reliance on various status symbols, including expensive clothes and a sports car. His vanity was a compensation for underlying feelings of worthlessness. The therapeutic suggestion consistently to move away from these symbols was based on the strategy that his compensatory behavior really con-firmed his inner conviction that he was bad or inadequate. Changing this process involved coping directly with his feelings of worthlessness and inadequacy. This could only be accomplished by breaking down his de-fensive image of superiority. In general, offering suggestions to people that they stop catering to others or trying to impress them, together with the implementation of an honest, forthright manner, serve the same underlying purpose: that of establishing relations with others in an open, nondefensive style without a self-protective facade.

Parents often pick one child to be their "dumping ground" for their feelings of self-loathing. They project their negative self-image onto the child in order to avoid feelings of self-hatred.

> In one case, a mother suppressed her own feelings of being dirty and contemptible and treated her daughter as if she were a despicable child. As an adult, the daughter had great difficulty believing that she deserved much out of life and pushed away people who felt warmly toward her. In addition, she let her looks go and kept her apartment in disarray. She was encouraged to keep up her appearance and helped to see that by keeping her apartment and possessions in a mess she was supporting the "freaky" image she had of herself in her family. By reliving her past, she was perpetuating her misery.
>
> Our therapeutic suggestions were difficult for this woman to follow. As is often the case, anyone can comply with the actions involved in corrective suggestions—that part is easy. The difficulty comes from the anxiety engendered by the change in behavior. When this woman's friends began to respond favorably, she tended to regress and give up the constructive changes. Their concern for her well-being began to make her feel hostile. To cope with her discomfort, she increased her defensive maneuvers and maintained her image of being different and unacceptable, instead of feeling her anxiety and increased vulnerability. In a sense, she chose her rejecting family of the past over her new associations.

Not all suggestions for growth experiences originate with the therapist. Psychologically sophisticated patients who are participants in therapy groups often have keen insight into the idiosyncratic defenses of their fellow members. For example, one older man was told by another group member, a young woman, to pause for a moment when he hugged her at the end of the group meeting and let himself experience her affection rather than pulling back from her. Very soon the man, who had always put women off with his tough exterior, felt a warmth and sadness that surprised him and touched him deeply. He began to talk more freely about his life in the group sessions. Other people felt attracted to this man whom they had previously perceived as being distant and unapproachable. His long-standing evaluation of himself as a "cold fish" was challenged by this experience.

Overcoming Fears

Psychoanalysis as well as behavior therapy has traditionally been concerned with the patient's fears and phobias. Our therapeutic suggestions are applied to a wide range of fears, from a fear of public speaking to fears of being close to another person. In most cases, fearful people are listening to their inner voice's response to the activity or situation that they are afraid of. Prior to therapy, they have been acting in accordance with their "voice," that is, they have been giving in to their fears and have generally become demoralized in relation to the goals they want to pursue. Techniques of verbalizing the inner thoughts that operate to paralyze the patients' actions can facilitate changes in attitudes that allow the patients to meet challenges. By understanding the roots of their fear, they develop the courage to accept corrective suggestions to move toward situations that were previously too threatening.

Overcoming fears of physical activities, sports, heights, flying, and other dimensions of adventurous living can be an important focal point for constructive change. One man who was afraid of the ocean, but wanted to learn to sail, progressively desensitized himself to his fear of the sea and to boating by taking sailing lessons at a nearby marina. From sailing a small sailboat in the relatively safe channels of the marina, he gradually increased the scope of his voyages. Later he bought a larger boat and began to enjoy cruises to nearby ports. The process of overcoming his fears in this area filled him with exhilaration and confidence to challenge other areas of his life.

A colleague of mine who wanted to break out of his protected, regimented life decided to spend one summer in Europe traveling by motorcycle through several countries. This adventure, undertaken in a spirit of experimentation and with a great deal of enthusiasm, was more rewarding than he had anticipated. Through driving rainstorms, winding mountain passages, and many hardships, this man, who was middle-aged and trapped in a stultifying marriage, traveled through the Continent in an adventurous, hard-driving manner that belied his customary passivity. Needless to say he returned home in September more confident and far less willing to accept his submissiveness and passivity in relation to his wife.

Fears of intimacy and closeness in a sexual relationship are recurring themes with many patients. A specific technique that is often useful to couples who are having difficulty being sexually close involves learning how to be touched sensually and how to caress and touch one's partner. The specific directions of this exercise vary according to each partner's degree of inhibition or anxiety. In general, one person begins by stroking and caressing the partner while the other simply allows him or herself to experience sensations and feelings. The exercise is then reversed, with the partner who was giving pleasure now in a receiving mode. Each partner gives the other feedback about what feels particularly good or pleasant. Couples are instructed to carry out this exercise slowly, with tenderness and sensitivity. Patients report that they have been able to relax and let go of their restraints. They feel a sense of permission from this exercise that allows them to go further in their sexual expressiveness and freedom, and they develop a sense of compassion for each other in the process.

A few patients who have had long-standing relationships but were afraid to make serious commitments have been encouraged to try living with the person of their choice in order to acclimate themselves to having close contact on a daily basis. One woman who had been involved in a series of unsuccessful relationships revealed that she felt a stability in her life that she had never before experienced. Living in close quarters with another human being was completely alien to this woman before she took a chance. She had grown up as an only child with cold, unresponsive parents.

Corrective suggestions such as the ones described above, applied in a timely, carefully controlled and skillful manner, progressively desensitize patients to the pain involved in changing identity and expanding their lives. The process acquaints them with experiences that would have remained unfamiliar had they not entered the therapeutic situation. It teaches them on a deep emotional level that they can apply rational thought and insight to the control of their avoidance and distancing behaviors. By using self-discipline to increase freedom of choice, the individual is moving away from compulsively repeating past experiences. However, in order to move in that direction, people invariably have to take risks at certain crucial points, risks that frighten them and threaten to overwhelm them. If they manage to sweat out the anxiety, it gradually diminishes and there is movement. If they retreat, they must face this same situation in the future or they will remain fixated at a lower level of development.

CONCLUSION

The therapeutic interventions described in this chapter constitute direct attacks on neurotic activity in everyday life. They are directed at the behavioral manifestations of a defensive process. Corrective suggestions act to challenge the "voice" and attempt to alter the patient's behavior and life style outside of the office setting. They stimulate changes in the patient's actions that are consistent with changes in self-concept. At first glance, some of these suggestions may appear innocuous, but in truth, they interrupt a process of unusual importance. When complied with, they interfere with an inward posture characterized by fantasy gratification. They shatter defenses that have been deeply entrenched since earliest childhood.

The question arises as to what constitutes therapeutic progress. Does the absence of certain neurotic symptoms alone indicate that a "cure" has been accomplished? What are the criteria for evaluating effective psychotherapy?

The author strongly believes that the ultimate goal of psychotherapy is to help people to achieve an ongoing state of vulnerability in which they are fully in touch with their feelings and respond appropriately to both positive and negative events in their lives. They would approach life in a realistic manner, one which is neither idealistic as in fantasy nor cynical and denigrating. The healthy individual would still have to contend with painful issues in life. In the vulnerable state, he or she would be better adapted to pursue real goals and more likely therefore to effect positive outcomes.

Psychotherapeutic progress does not imply the absence of conflict or suffering; however, it results in less *unnecessary* suffering. A therapeutic process that successfully challenges defenses offers human beings the alternative to live life with sensitivity, dignity, and self-respect while coping with the pressures of the interpersonal environment and the limitation of mortality. Without this movement toward growth and a willingness to be exposed to a lifelong process of struggle and change, there is only a gradual deterioration and submission to the "voice" and the defensive process.

Chapter 20

THE PSYCHOTHERAPEUTIC COMMUNITY

> Until philosophers are kings, or the kings and princes of this
> world have the spirit and power of philosophy, . . . cities will never
> have rest from their evils, no, nor the human race, as I believe—
> and then only will this our State have a possibility of life and
> behold the light of day.
>
> Plato
> *The Republic*

Therapeutic progress involves continual exposure to a process of change and requires a willingness to relinquish outmoded ways of perceiving and responding to the world. However, most patients who have improved in therapy unfortunately return to a world or situation that is abrasive and destructive to the undefended person. The conventions and mores of our society are, for the most part, hostile to the state of vulnerability brought about by the process of dismantling major defenses. The negative circumstances and stresses of daily living tend to stifle a desire for further change. Therefore, many of the gains the patient has made during therapy are eventually lost.

In our Introduction, we described a situation similar to the one faced by many patients terminating therapy. We found that the majority of people from the weekend groups in the mountains were unable to sustain their undefended, feelingful state after returning to the "normal" world. Their daily interactions with well-meaning but defended family members along with other associates encouraged them to return to a self-limiting, defensive posture. However, there were certain individuals who, motivated by a powerful inner desire to continue to live a sensitive life and drawn to the environment of the weekends, developed strong friendships and ties that persisted into their everyday lives. As a result of ongoing socializing and an interest in psychology, they incidentally created a new social order or community, a society that was conducive to a continuous process of personal growth.

These people devoted themselves to minimizing or eliminating psychologically toxic influences from their lives. Because they valued the openness and vulnerability they felt with their new-found friends, in their ongoing talks they attempted to preserve the compassionate atmosphere of the mountains and made every effort to avoid returning to a defended, dishonest way of living. Over many years, an implicit code of ethics or morality gradually evolved that was nonrestrictive, nondemanding of conformity, and respectful of a person's feelings and individuality.

What is most remarkable about this community is that no person or group of persons set out with the purpose of establishing it; it emerged naturally as an extension of the original families and the surrounding friendship circle. There was no other method or means available for joining the group.

In their search for friendship and understanding, these people unintentionally created a new form of psychosocial milieu where the destructive elements present in the larger society have been considerably reduced. They unwittingly demonstrated that a society that enhances the well-being of its members *can* exist if those members are devoted and committed to this type of value system.

For the past 10 years, the unintentional community has not only served to implement a multidimensional approach to therapy, but has also functioned as a dynamic living psychological laboratory. The people in this mini-culture have succeeded for the most part in their efforts to lead an honest emotional existence, one that counters basic defenses. Over the years, they have developed a very deep level of communication built upon mutual trust, a style very different from routine or conventional life. Together they formulated and put into practice therapeutic procedures and corrective suggestions that challenged each individual's defenses and limitations. Close rapport combined with compassion and support of individuality characterize the interactions in this environment. Members exchange personal information freely and contribute to an ever growing pool of knowledge. In summary, a way of life has sprung up that is so different from life in the larger society that the emergent community appears worthy of anthropological study. For ourselves, this group of people has been one of the major reference populations from which our ideas and concepts have emerged.

In this chapter, we will give a brief narrative description of the dimensions of this community and an overview of its historical development, the style of communication evolved by the members, and the breadth and scope of the new environment. In the next, we will discuss a point of view based on hypotheses and conclusions derived from our ongoing experience and observations of this unique laboratory.

This chapter is interspersed with quotes from a written commentary by Stuart Boyd, Ph.D. (1982), psychologist and tutor at St. John's College in Santa Fe, New Mexico, who visited the community and observed the interactions and activities of its population for a 3-month period from February through April 1982. He summarized his findings in an essay about this society.

HISTORICAL DEVELOPMENT OF THE PSYCHOTHERAPEUTIC COMMUNITY

> This is a community of some 90 persons—women, men, children—who seem to have achieved the better life together with a minimum of dogma, political authority, withdrawal, mysticism, insulation, isolation, dispossession of the goods and comforts of modern technology. There is no golden lie, no coercion, no constitution, no turning out at the expense of in, no turning in at the expense of out. It is not, nor claims to be, Utopia.
>
> Stuart Boyd (1982)
> *Analysis of the Psychotherapeutic Community*

A Brief Overview

From a small group of friends, which 12 years ago consisted of seven families, an extended friendship circle of approximately 95 individuals has evolved. Although its growth in numbers was determined by many factors, it centered around two widely disparate areas of endeavor. The first was the project of rebuilding and refurbishing a large sailing vessel, which went on more and more challenging voyages and eventually circumnavigated the world. The second area, the one most relevant to the future of these people as a society, was their search for a richer, more fulfilling emotional and psychological life. This search grew out of the passionate concern of these friends with their own personal growth and development and that of their families. This was their central purpose and it enriched them and sustained them in all of their activities.

The author, an original member of the friendship circle, was persuaded in time to leave a large psychotherapy practice to involve himself in this project on a full-time basis. Because of my innate interest and ongoing study of resistance in psychotherapy, and the desire to pursue this subject in a social context, I was pleased to avail myself of the opportunity.

The story of this extended friendship circle has many diverse roots. Its beginnings may be traced to a fantasy that is probably common to all people, that is, a dream to share a better world with close friends. This fantasy was particularly strong in the people from this environment, though they never fancied themselves as pioneers of a new order. They saw themselves as ordinary people with a natural desire to find an atmosphere where they could be themselves, and where they could be generous and caring toward others. In their pursuit of friendship, however, they created an extraordinary life and unique set of circumstances.

We will briefly consider the succession of events that led to the creation of this new environment: (1) the original friendship circle; (2) the young people's discussion group; (3) the "Vltava" and the expansion of the friendship circle; (4) the specialized therapy group; (5) the discussion group of personal friends; (6) research into Feeling Release Therapy; (7) the cooperative apartment; and (8) involvement in Voice Therapy.

In addition to discussing the community's historical development, we will describe the important functions of the emerging psychotherapeutic community. A more complete discussion of the environment and the people, together with an enlarged analysis of the data it has provided, has been detailed in a book, *The Friendship Circle—A Unique Psychological Laboratory* (Firestone & Catlett, in progress).

1. The Original Friendship Circle

The people in the original families had, for a long time, shared in travel and vacations and helped each other out in crises. They were unusually good friends who had a strong desire for social and personal contact. The friendships were long-standing, averaging 10 to 15 years, and one relationship had been in existence for over 35 years. The individuals came from varying backgrounds and had different vocations, including engineering, teaching, business, and psychology. Yet, they had certain common characteristics. Most were highly individualistic, independent, and had a lively interest in people. In general, they were sensitive, intelligent people with a good sense of humor, who enjoyed discussing philosophical and psychological issues. They were questioning of life and concerned with childrearing and humanistic pursuits. They were not "joiners" in the conventional sense; in fact, they tended to stay away from structured social organizations and groups. Paradoxically, it was this group of individuals who formed the core of what was to later become a much larger aggregation of people.

2. The Young People's Discussion Group

In 1971, it was discovered that some of the children from the original families, who were then entering junior high school, had begun experimenting with dangerous drugs. All of the parents were deeply concerned that these children were becoming involved in this destructive pattern, which was typical of what was happening to many young people in the neighborhood. As a result, one of the fathers, a businessman, who had a natural rapport with the kids, was asked to lead a discussion group for the teenagers.

The youngsters met once a week to talk about their thoughts and feelings, their alienation from their parents, and their emerging sexual feelings. After several months of talking among themselves, they asked their parents to join their talks. Initially the meetings between the children and their parents were very painful for all concerned. Many parents were defensive when confronted with the feelings their children were expressing. It was difficult for them really to listen to their children, to see them as people in their own right, and to face their own imperfections and weaknesses as parents.

The talks had a powerful effect on both parents and children. Because these parents were concerned and because the content of these talks was reminiscent of their own childhood trauma, they experienced considerable pain and sadness. One father, a psychologist, still remembers the profound impact that the first meeting between the adolescents and their parents had on him personally:

> During the first part of the meeting, I kept trying to avoid glancing across the room at my kids. Then I heard my daughter, Jean, say my name, and I looked into her face and saw that she was crying. Between sobs, she screamed out words that really hit me hard. The scene is still etched in my memory. She said she wished that I had loved her the way I loved Mark, her brother.

She told me how bad she felt whenever I hugged Mark and walked right past her, time after time. Her voice shook as she spoke of her constant longing for some sign of love from me.

I was completely choked up and couldn't say anything for a long time. I knew that what she said was true. I've since forgotten how I finally responded or what I actually said to Jean, but everyone in the room was deeply moved and many people were crying openly. I thought back to my own childhood and how I had always wanted affection from *my* father, and now my own daughter was telling me the same thing. I never had the guts to talk to my father the way the children were talking to us that day. It was one of the most painful moments of my life to sit in that room and listen to them struggling to say what they really felt.

The democratic exchange of perceptions and the sincere expression of feelings that occurred during these meetings between parents and children gradually dissolved the generational boundaries. Parental roles began to be discarded and the adolescents related to their parents on a more equal basis. Incidentally, the discussion group did succeed in its original goal: the young people gave up their use of drugs and the dishonest, rebellious attitudes that went along with it. In becoming friends with each other and openly relating to their parents, the children exposed the hurtful ways their parents had treated them. They challenged the hypercritical, judgmental attitudes that they had grown up with and spoke out against condescending and disrespectful treatment. They began to ask for real acknowledgment and respect from their parents.

When parents first began to relate to their children as equals, with mutual respect, many of them felt threatened. When their children called them by their first names rather than mom or dad, they felt as if they were losing something vital and basic to the relationship. As the group discussions progressed, however, the parents realized that they were losing only their parental roles, losing the form while gaining the substance of a relationship with their children. Through honest relating, they were breaking down a fantasy of connection, a bond that had actually kept them apart. They became aware that, because of this change, their children no longer were tied to them or *belonged* to them in that sense, but were becoming their friends. These parents began to value their children's honesty and they recaptured loving and close feelings that had been dormant or lost altogether. Interestingly enough, it was this group, numbering eleven young people, that later became the basic crew of the schooner that eventually sailed around the world.

3.   The "Vltava" and the Expansion of the Friendship Circle

The people in the original circle had been friends for a number of years when the idea of buying a boat captured their imagination. At the time the schooner, *Vltava,* was purchased, early in 1973, no one thought ahead to voyages across oceans or around the world. In fact, only two or three of the men had sailing experience.

The novice sailors gradually increased the distances they sailed from their home port and built up their confidence in themselves and the ship. In the next 3 years, they completely rebuilt the schooner— lowering the engine, cutting hatches, re-engineering the rigging, and subdividing and redecorating the interior—until she was seaworthy and functional.

The boat became a vehicle not only for journeys and adventure but also for people's personal growth. For example, one man who had never held a hammer in his life learned to build cabinets and bulkheads for the ship's interior. Others who had habitually procrastinated at work learned to complete projects according to set schedules, because their fellow workers were dependent on their cooperation.

The boat also became the focal point for new friendships and acquaintances. Many people who heard about her voyages asked to come along, and the interest in sailing paralleled the interest in people and psychology.

In the course of working on the boat, people began to meet on a weekly basis to discuss plans for sailing and construction. This meeting, at the home of one of the families, gradually enlarged its format to include the expression of personal feelings as well as offering feedback about work or sailing issues. These talks became as meaningful and as therapeutic as any psychotherapy group; indeed, they were even more relevant to everyday life. For example, in a talk, a person might gain insight into his unproductive ways of working and subsequently use the boat-building project as a means to change his behavior. Another might learn to cope with her fears of the ocean or her reactions to her or someone else's being in authority. Still others might share intimate personal memories and reactions while exploring new relationships.

Many of the new friends became interested in their self-development and felt a sense of kinship with the people in the original families. Through the process of talking together and facing hard truths about themselves and their relationships, those who finally made the voyage around the world were a hardy crew, unified through their personal interaction. Their habit of working toward a common goal while combining it with personal exposure persisted throughout their travels and activities.

In November 1976 the schooner, *Vltava*, set sail on a 17-month voyage around the world. More than 80 people participated at various times in the trip, which covered over 26,000 miles. Because of the adults' work schedules and commitments at home, parts of the journey had to be made by the 11 teenagers without adult supervision. During the years of preparation and sailing, they had learned the basics of boat-handling, engine mechanics, electronics, navigation, and medical procedures, skills that would be necessary at those times when they assumed total responsibility for the ship. Their expert handling of the ship and their increasing maturity and sense of responsibility had earned the young people the adults' respect, and from among their members, they elected their own captain, who was sixteen years old at the time of departure.

During storms that the young people encountered both in the Indian Ocean and in mid-Pacific, the tradition of talking openly proved to be very valuable. The early talks about drugs and personal feelings made it easier for them to talk about their basic fears and other feelings, especially under frightening sea conditions.

The circumnavigation was a great achievement for the teenagers as well as the adults and represented the culmination of years of hard work and planning.

> The voyage pointed out that people working together in close communication can overcome differences and expand their boundaries, both in sailing expertise and in individual personality growth. The journey taught the young people to cope with separation, and they developed a sense of independence and self-sufficiency. It gave them a true sense of perspective and taught them the value and personal meaning of life and experience in the face of a finite existence.[1]

The completion of the circumnavigation in 1978 was reported by the Los Angeles *Times* and the San Francisco *Chronicle* (1978): "The real meaning of the voyage was 'people struggling to expand their boundaries—in friendship and closeness'." Almost everyone fulfilled their deepest desires for adventure. For many, the days they sailed on the *Vltava* were the happiest times they had ever known.

The *Vltava* served as a laboratory of life, a microcosm of society, for

---

[1] Quote from film *Voyage to Understanding* (Parr, 1983) (author's concluding statement).

years before the journey, and it served this function especially well during the voyage. The data gathered from what people experienced as a result of living in close quarters on board the ship contributed much to the author's understanding of psychological defenses and these issues were a central theme of the ongoing discussion group.

4. The Specialized Therapy Group

An important developmental influence on the new community was the formation of a unique and specialized psychotherapy group. During the same period of time that the young people's discussion group was formed, I became interested in applying to group psychotherapy therapeutic concepts that I had been utilizing in individual sessions.

I carefully selected, from a number of patients who were in the process of terminating therapy, 10 individuals who were interested in exploring psychotherapy as a life style. These people were unusually honest and open in talking about themselves and were compassionate and empathetic toward others. My choice of participants had been made with the goal in mind of its being a long-term project. I believed that neurosis had originated in a social setting and that the manifestations of neurosis could be effectively dealt with in the new social atmosphere that the ongoing group could potentially provide.

Group psychotherapy was to be an important point of departure for me, though this weekly group had been formed with some apprehension on my part. I had a certain amount of discomfort with groups and formal organizations because I was aware of the possibility that any group might detract from the individuality of its members, and I was searching for methods that would be helpful and productive for the growth of individuals, not subordinate them to a preconceived system. My choice of people for this group was made with this consideration. The initial group members were sturdy, independent individuals who were highly motivated to pursue both personal and professional goals.

The first meeting of this group aroused some anxiety in everyone. From the start, however, the participants displayed an openness and a courage that was unusual, and this group came to be a most meaningful experience for these people and significantly affected my own life as well. As the members of this group progressed, other people joined, and eventually more groups were formed. Still, there was something unique and more advanced about this particular group of people compared to the other groups I worked with during this time. These men and women were unusually sincere and knowledgeable about human behavior. They were always seeking creative methods to ameliorate the deadening aspects of their everyday lives.

In the original therapy group one of the men suggested that they meet outside the sessions in order to socialize and get to know each other in real-life situations. He and, as it turned out, other participants had a strong desire to extend the honesty of that hour and a half each week to include their everyday lives. This idea challenged both the traditional role of the therapist and the function of the group as strictly a laboratory setting. It appeared that something important might be lost if that laboratory were to be translated into a real-life setting. On the other hand, it seemed to me contradictory and even harmful to impose constraints on these people in an authoritarian manner. I also had an intuitive feeling that this development was part of a natural process and that I should not interfere with the flow. I could not prohibit their movement toward deepening their friendships. By not placing limits on the members of this group, I was removing the traditional restriction that generally applied to groups of this sort. The process was not taken lightly, and filled me with trepidation.

As these men and women met outside the group setting, they became interested in pursuing a variety of activities. An unstated ethical code emerged from their free exchange of ideas and their openness and trust in one another. The unusually high regard for freedom and mutual respect that was manifest in this group proved to have considerable therapeutic value for its members.

These individuals made a concerted effort in their talks to communicate their perceptions about the characteristics in each other that were offensive and hurtful. At the same time, they attempted to control the traits and behaviors in themselves that they thought would be damaging to others—snobbishness, sarcasm, phoniness, status-seeking, vanity, or hostility. In communicating within the group they didn't intrude upon or disregard each other nor were they overbearing or hypercritical. They continued to pursue their investigation of the relationships that had damaged them as they grew up and the experiences that still hurt them in their present-day lives.

This specialized therapy group and its enlarging membership contributed significantly to the development of the new environment evolving at the time. The next stage of this growth process involved the families who had been part of the original friendship circle.

5. The Discussion Group of Personal Friends

The next phase in the growth of this community or environment was stimulated by the formation of a discussion group made up of close personal friends and colleagues. Though these people had talked together often on an informal basis, the idea of meeting together on a weekly basis was new.

When I had told my professional associates and some of my friends about the results achieved in the specialized therapy group, they were eager to start meeting together themselves to talk at a deeper level. They were very interested in the ideas and concepts that were evolving at the time and looked forward to these groups fulfilling an educational function as well as a therapeutic one.

The people in this latter group were from somewhat different backgrounds from those in the specialized group. They were older by 10 or 15 years and were of a different generation. They appeared to have more empathy or patience with others. They were more mature and responsible in many respects and their concern for people and sense of loyalty and compassion appeared to be more developed.

By contrast, the participants in the original therapy group were in some respects typical of the so-called youth movement of the time. These younger people were often more direct and honest in expressing their feelings and in confronting each other about issues important to them. They were less conventional and more experimental than the men and women in the original friendship circle.

Both groups began meeting for extended periods of time in a setting away from the city. During these gatherings, described in our Introduction, the participants were able to break through many barriers and reach their deepest feelings. These weekend talks gave them an inkling of the kind of life they wanted to live.

Later, several people in the specialized therapy group expressed a desire to get together with the circle of personal friends. I felt strongly that because of their complementary characteristics, the two groups had a great deal to offer one another. (I decided to select out of the therapy group those individuals who were the most motivated and who I felt would contribute a great deal to my friends and colleagues.) Subsequently, these individuals from the specialized therapy group joined the friends' discussion group and began to mingle socially. Both populations enjoyed their new acquaintances, whom they liked and admired, and immediate friendships sprang up. It was this mix of people that began to explore innovative techniques and therapeutic procedures and that eventually formed the core of the expanding community.

6.   Research into Feeling Release Therapy

Within the enlarged group, people continued to progress and to develop their relationships, and we became interested in experimenting with new approaches that might assist individuals who had reached points of resistance to progress. The group was eager to participate in this research project. During the weekend talks, where constant exposure to each other had stressed people's defenses, there had been powerful expressions of emotion accompanied by important insights, and I began to search for other methods that would facilitate this type of primal expression.

Later, through a technique of deep breathing and letting out sounds, these people were able to re-experience many repressed feelings. They interpreted the verbalizations of these feelings and their content and gained a great deal of insight into the dynamics underlying the pain, rage, and sadness they were expressing.

For a period of 2 to 3 years, they were very much involved in this new therapeutic procedure, and they underwent some basic changes in their overall approach to life and in their attitudes and feelings toward one another. These people appeared to be altering deep-seated character defenses that had been basic parts of their personality make-up.

The effect on these people as a community was profound. In their groups, their style became less confronting than before. They stopped projecting much of what they disliked in themselves and their families onto their friends and instead looked more to themselves for the sources of their discontent. They were remarkably less defensive when hearing or receiving negative feedback.

The depth of feeling tapped during the sessions resulted in an increase in people's capacity to feel on a deep level generally. Most people were closer to their feelings than ever before, especially feelings of sadness. In everyday situations, they were very responsive to stimuli that were sad and were easily moved to tears. The community as a whole went through a period of sadness, which, interestingly enough, did not make people feel bad or depressed. Quite the contrary, depressive moods and melodramatic suffering over trivial incidents appeared to decrease considerably as people felt more real sadness.

In an atmosphere that was less confrontational, the men and women developed a depth of compassion and mutual trust that surpassed the understanding that already existed between them. They lost the remnants of the superficial hardness or facade that most people depend on to face the everyday world, becoming softer and more vulnerable. Although they were even more active and energetic in pursuing their goals and appeared to have more vitality than before, they were quieter and more self-contained about their lives. Physical tenseness or agitation was relatively absent, which contributed to their relaxed state, and the pace of their lives slowed down, allowing them time for reflection.

During these years, people also developed more perspective on their lives. Some realized that they had never had a true picture of what had happened to them in their personal history. They were able to see more clearly the traumatic events that had made them repress early memories and feelings. Rather than remaining embedded in the past, they were able to put distance between that time and the present and to separate the deep, reliving experiences in their sessions from their responses to present-day events outside the sessions. The techniques of this therapy gave most of the participants a realistic picture of their childhoods and helped them to become more independent of their families and their styles of interacting.

The people in the group became very conversant with how they used current relationships to perpetuate the unhappiness of their childhoods and were able to develop insights into their pasts beyond any they had achieved in traditional psychotherapy. In addition, their involvement in Feeling Release Therapy affected their overall style of talking to one another. Their participation in this therapy significantly changed the nature of the groups and deepened their existing relationships. This change was quite evident at the beginning of group discussions or talks, during the transition from small talk to meaningful communication. In this relaxed, quiet period of time, as people shifted from a superficial level of experience to a deeper one, they were able quickly to get in touch with their underlying feelings of sadness or pain.

7. The Cooperative Apartment

As the group of friends grew in numbers, practical necessities dictated another important step in the evolution of the community. There were two primary motivating factors behind this next step: first, the increased expense of financing the voyage around the world; and second, the need for a place that would be large enough to accommodate various meetings, discussion groups, and social events. To solve the first problem, steps were taken toward more formal cooperation on a financial and practical basis. In preparing for the anticipated circumnavigation, several individuals had already contributed large sums of money, and others had said they wanted to share in the financial backing. They decided to contribute a set amount monthly to cover the extensive improvements and new equipment being purchased and installed on the boat. A "cooperative" to support the expenses of the upcoming voyage was formed in 1975. Following this arrangement, many more people indicated an interest in sharing in this project and contributed according to their financial ability.

The problems that had come about because many of the meetings were taking place within a quiet neighborhood had to be solved. Increasing numbers of people were using one particular home for a meeting place, and an impossible parking situation had developed that created a problem for the rest of the neighborhood. Therefore, we decided to look for a more central location with larger accommodations and more adequate parking. Eventually, a large, recently-completed apartment complex was located and purchased. Within a few months, many of the people from the extended friendship circle had moved into this new building. With this step, the community of friends that had lived separately up to that time became a residential community.

The arrangement was originally meant to serve a temporary function and to provide a central location for the duration of the voyage. However, sharing the adventures and dangers of the voyage around the world drew everyone closer. People came to value the experience of living together for extended periods of time, and when the voyage was over, they decided to continue living together and sharing expenses cooperatively.

Prior to the voyage, the friends had formed a general partnership where they contributed a certain percentage (33 percent) of their gross income to pay for rent, food, utilities, and boat expenses, and they decided to continue this financial arrangement on a permanent basis after the voyage was over. Later, an investment fund was started; with this new financial arrangement, each member of the "cooperative" became an equal partner in a general partnership. As each new baby is born into this community, the capital is re-divided so that the new "member" receives an amount equal to any other share.

Though the cost of living is shared by everyone on a graduated basis, the community is not socialistic in philosophy or practice. There is no equal disbursement or division of funds or redistribution of wealth.

At their first general meeting, members of the new community elected a committee of 15 people to be responsible for overseeing the practical problems of group living. The committee handles finances and the maintenance and improvement of the physical surroundings. Members of the committee also arbitrate any internal disputes that arise, though over the years the committee has rarely had to convene for this purpose. Despite the fact that there is no formal therapy available, the committee offers corrective or therapeutic suggestions to anyone who requests help. This committee, together with several consultants, offers all types of assistance ranging from practical counseling to ideas for further personal development.

The most meaningful aspect of our living cooperatively continues to be our involvement in the talks that take place twice a week. The community as it exists today would probably be unworkable without these talks. Over the years people have come to value highly the perceptions and insights of their friends. They feel very protective of this forum; in it, they continue their struggle to overcome the anxiety and guilt inherent in pursuing a better life. The survival of this small culture is inextricably tied to the survival of this form of interaction.

8. Involvement in Voice Therapy

For many years, my professional associates and myself had been exploring techniques designed to elicit and challenge the destructive thought process we have referred to here as the "voice." Later, we applied this understanding to the people in the new environment as an aid in their struggle to accommodate themselves to a better life. Many of them had reached plateaus in their development, having become frightened of their progress. They tended, at this point, to revert to old habit patterns and regressive behavior that interfered with their happiness. The destructive way of thinking that these individuals were engaged in was essentially a "voice," which could be expressed, or verbalized. When people were able to identify this thought process, they were better able to control the negative behaviors that accompanied these setbacks.

Because of their interest in Voice Therapy, some people decided to meet several mornings a week to talk about their negative thoughts and in this setting, the techniques of Voice Therapy were further refined and elaborated. Interestingly, participants noticed that whenever one of them talked openly about an area where he or she had progressed or overcome a serious limitation, this person became more vulnerable to self-attacks from the "voice." As a part of their exploration, the participants also investigated activities and actions that helped them to oppose the dictates of the "voice."

This early morning "voice" group served three purposes: it furthered systematic research in relation to the "voice;" it contributed to the development of several innovative procedures of Voice Therapy (described in Chapter 18); and it helped the participants accommodate to the positive changes they were making in their lives.

DIMENSIONS OF THE COMMUNITY

A ship, an apartment building, and a triad of businesses . . . comprise the environment of the Friendship Circle. Within this triangle the group has its life and meaning. Plato described a tripartite division of the soul into reason (located in the head), courage, virtue, honor (the heart), passions (loins). For the group, the business corporation may be seen as the expression predominantly of reason, the ship, of courage, the building, of passion. Of course, there can be none but an artificial splitting of functions in any human, but some differences of emphasis in description may help in illuminating the meaning of this venture.

. . . They share a set of beliefs and consequent behaviors that have embraced all of these ventures in a web of feeling and motivation that has led to adventurous courage on the high seas, to spectacular business success, and to a remarkable complex of living and loving relationships where it would seem that energy and laughter and good feeling significantly outweigh their opposites.

Stuart Boyd (1982)

The Business Enterprises

In order to pick up the thread of the history of the business endeavors, it is necessary to retrace our steps to the time prior to the developments just described. The evolution of the businesses closely paralleled the cooperation evidenced in the round-the-world sail. Again, it is a story of people working together to fulfill a dream—in this instance, of working together and sharing in the success of their own business ventures.

In 1966, several members of the community formed a partnership to invest in a jade-importing business, owned by a close friend. As this company grew and flourished under its new management, the partners began also to pursue investment in real estate and other ventures. However, the importing business was felt to be the most exciting because it offered the opportunity for travel and adventure in the Orient.

By 1975, this company had become one of the largest importers of fine jade jewelry in the United States, with gross sales over $1.7 million a year, demonstrating relatively early that this group could successfully combine friendship and business.

Concomitant with the voyage, the group started a computer distribution firm and a commercial interior design company, and these enterprises began to employ an increasing number of friends. Inspired by their easy sharing and cooperation while traveling together on the world cruise, the principals of these two companies, together with the original partners in the importing business, decided to relocate the three entities in one place and form a conglomerate.

These companies eventually went on to employ more than 50 people from the extended circle of friends. The computer company generated enough business over the next four years to become one of the principal suppliers of computer terminals for major business firms across the country. Several of the young people, upon their return from the voyage, entered sales and management trainee positions and, because of their competence and leadership potential, quickly rose to positions of responsibility. The youthful captain of the *Vltava*, for example, became the company's vice-president in charge of operations within 2 years. The commercial interior design company grew from a small operation employing two designers to one of the fastest-growing privately-owned corporations in the country. As of this writing, it employs some 54 people and has annual sales approaching $10 million.

The Work Environment and the Application of Psychological Concepts to Business

The conglomerate that was formed by merging the three diverse companies was characterized by open exchanges between management and employees. There were frank discussions of business problems and management-personnel relations. There was open evaluation of personnel on all levels and analysis of personal conflicts. Poor work habits were not tolerated but were talked about honestly. Employees with poor performance records were given many opportunities to improve. People were given the chance to discover and explore their interests and aptitudes. Every employee was encouraged to seek his or her own level and could move up through the ranks quickly when appropriate. Management often used personnel across companies. For instance, a salesperson in the computer company might also help with sales in the design firm, or a manager from one company would offer particular expertise to another.

The talks between employees and management contributed to a powerful sense of energy and vitality as the company grew. Psychological defenses underlying nonproductive working styles were identified and worked through as people talked together in the direct, compassionate style that they had developed in other areas of their lives.

The work environment reflected the pride that the employees had in owning a part of their own company. The aesthetics of the office setting, designed by their own firm and located high above the city with a beautiful view, had a positive effect on their mood and morale. People enjoyed the informal, relaxed atmosphere where they could energetically pursue their professional goals. At the same time, they were able to maintain their friendships and share in the project. The overall combination stimulated sales and led to high productivity, which assured the profitability of the enterprise.

The business environment provided the author another valuable opportunity, this time for clarifying his ideas about power and leadership. For example, we found that many individuals who were capable of rising through the ranks to positions in middle management or executive positions found it difficult to sustain the quality of work or level of performance that had brought these promotions. We concluded that a number of factors contributed to this phenomenon. As we have noted earlier, many people prefer to gratify their wants in fantasy rather than achieve real goals in the real world. Their accomplishments become threatening as they begin to approach long-dreamed-of goals. These real successes interrupt a fantasy process that these individuals have relied on since childhood and represent a change of identity that they find difficult to tolerate.

It was also observed that some people avoided assuming real power and authority because they preferred the leverage that negative power gave them. For example, some individuals use passive-aggressive techniques and withholding in order to manipulate their world. These techniques and other forms of acting out date from childhood and become important in the business world because many people have never progressed beyond this stage of development in their relationships with authority figures. Still others avoid power because they fear retaliation and assume that they will be hated or seen as "mean" when *they* become the boss. These fears cause them to retreat from positions of leadership and authority. Many individuals are frightened and guilty about surpassing the parent of the same sex professionally or financially so they limit themselves with defensive behavior and withholding patterns that interfere with their succeeding in life. All of these issues were continually dealt with in management meetings and seminars and everyone experienced significant progress in challenging their defenses.

The involvement with business ventures is still a vital dimension of people's lives. Their basic business philosophy can be summarized as follows: "Business success is for people; to enrich their lives personally and professionally, not merely to acquire power or to build an empire. Financial gain, in proper perspective, can contribute to the independence and freedom of people." (Firestone & Catlett, in progress) The story of the business ventures has been in every sense the ideal American success story, brought into reality by a group of friends who valued both achievement and personal fulfillment.

The Talks

> The talk is disciplined in the sense that it is not the chatter you hear when a large group of people come into a room to-

gether, which swiftly escalates to a roar as everyone talks at once and no one hears. These meetings are a blend of the informal, some announcements, some joking of a personal nature, relevant and good-natured. Then often the emergence, spontaneously, of a problem of pain someone is having with the self or others, in the most intimate of relationships, or in work or some aspect of the community.

The communication of circumstance and the open expression of feeling, negative and positive, the deep impression of community relationship, the respectful listening and participation by others than those directly involved is a moving experience.

Stuart Boyd (1982)

Underlying the personal development of the people in this community and the ease with which they interact is a style of communication that evolved from the original therapy groups. In spite of the active and varied pursuits that occupy the friends—sailing, business, travel—they appear to value participation in these talks more than any other activity. People's involvement in these intellectual discussions and compassionate encounters is a vital part of their lives, and these talks have been the principal agent of change for many of them. They have come to value the opportunity to reveal their innermost thoughts and feelings in an atmosphere of understanding and acceptance and have struggled over the years to maintain this atmosphere against their own resistance and the pull to resume a more inward, defended life style.

Participation in the talks has also enabled them to live and work together in a remarkably harmonious way. The normal, routine bickering of everyday life has been diminished to a considerable degree. The right of each person to speak his or her mind freely and to talk about very personal feelings is cherished and protected. The process of maintaining a forum for the exchange of perceptions and feelings (without fear of retaliation for what one has said) has made it possible for these people to get along with a minimum of friction.

In addition to a large discussion group, there are many auxiliary talks. These can take place in many different ways, either organized or arising spontaneously. People often meet to discuss a specific practical matter, i.e., travel plans, or investments, or child-rearing, or maintenance of the apartment building. Sometimes the talk is about philosophical issues, at other times about personal feelings. There are small groups such as couples' groups and parents' talks that meet weekly, as well as a children's group. During vacations while at sea, people often gather in the cockpit and talk, sometimes shutting the motor off in order to sail along quietly. While traveling, time is taken to continue this ongoing dialogue, and many people meet in parks or in hotel rooms wherever they go.

The subjects discussed are varied. Individuals might choose to talk about their dreams, their fantasies, their anger, their fears. They may have positive or negative perceptions about another person that they feel would be relevant to the other's development. In the talks, people actively seek realistic perceptions about themselves from others. They have confidence in the process of change and feel that they can effectively alter their lives and become the kind of people they want to be. Therefore, if they hear negative information, it can even be more favorable to their development than being told something positive, because they can use the constructive criticism to develop themselves.

After years of talking together in this style, most people have become remarkably open; for instance, they tend not to be embarrassed about revealing their innermost secrets. Because they have deep, personal feelings toward each other, even the large talks take on the feeling of a close, intimate group.

This style of talking stands in sharp contrast to the communication that occurs in most traditional families. Most perceptions are generally not shared within the family; freedom of speech is usually not the rule. In most families, members cannot say what they really think and feel; honest feedback is often resented and retaliated against.

Talks with the new generation of children, ranging in age from ten to fourteen, take place every morning at breakfast and then as a special talk once a week. In this group setting, the youngsters share their personal feelings in a manner similar to that of the original adolescent group. The degree of psychological knowledge and self-understanding naturally manifested by these children is unusual. Because they have been included in their parents' lives, they are able to communicate in a forthright way with each other and with their parents, and they feel at home with other adults as well.

Couples' talks also occur on a weekly basis and are a vital part of the partners' attempt to sustain the quality of their relationships. In our experience, the most compelling problems for this community of people are found in their most intimate relationships. The people in this environment, as in society as a whole, are the most defended with their mates and their children. They all feel that the process of learning how to remain friends with their spouses on a deep emotional level is not only a worthwhile endeavor, but essential to their well-being.

Because they have experienced so much change as a result of these various talks, these people feel optimistic about overcoming long-standing behavior patterns and deep-seated emotional problems. Indeed, the people in the extended friendship circle have improved dramatically, many of them without any traditional psychotherapy.

Goals

> The attempt to cut loose from the demoralizing influence of the larger culture by small communities of like-minded individuals has usually ended in material wretchedness or internal dissension and dissolution. It is therefore arresting to me, as a social-scientist and liberal artist, to find myself among a community of harmony and happiness, personal growth and fulfillment, economic independence and power, that hasn't withdrawn from the larger destructive society, nor become involved in the political power game; and that has done so without resort to force or loss of liberty, or submission to cultism or pseudo mystic or religious principle, without dogma or inviolable code; and with commitment to experiment and change. . . .
>
> There is undoubtedly a principle—the commitment to honesty of feeling, and the appropriate expression of this.
>
> Stuart Boyd (1982)

The major focus for these friends is still their pursuit of freedom, independence, personal maturity, and self-fulfillment. They are as devoted as ever to the process of contending with their fears and limitations. There is a deep commitment to the continuation of this life style. People have already observed the positive effects of this way of living on their children. As a general rule, the children are well-behaved and well-adjusted. They stand out in their appearance and demeanor, according to teachers and other observers. They appear to be developing into decent, sensitive individuals and are particularly knowledgeable about their feelings.

There is still a desire for travel and adventure, and a strong possibility of another circumnavigation in the future. Members want greater financial freedom and more time for personal pursuits. Because they feel best when they are involved in sharing an adventure or a project, they are working toward the goal of having the time to spend together in group activities and travel. They enjoy each other's company very much yet are always excited to meet new people, who bring with them the hope of making new friends and acquaintances. In order to have the freedom that comes with financial independence, people are attempting to raise their overall minimum standard of living, which is already fairly high. To this end, they encourage new ventures and support each other's initiative in business, particularly those people who are just starting out in their careers.

It is interesting to note that the community has become more like an extended family in the sense that several children of the original friends have intermarried; consequently, many people are now related by actual family ties. In the past 5 years, ten babies have been born into the friendship circle. The birth of these babies has been very meaningful, not only to their parents, but to everyone in the small community. Each woman who has had her baby in this environment has expressed a strong desire to have her husband, family, and friends present at the delivery. These women were fortunate enough to have as friends a doctor and two nurses who provided the necessary medical expertise to enable them to have their babies at home.

Many of the young children, who are an integral part of everyone's life, have been present at the deliveries. One birth was recorded on film by a professional camera and sound crew. The filming was arranged by an independent film-maker who was recording various aspects of the community, and it resulted in a moving documentary film entitled *Of Birth and Friendship.* The completed film has received several film awards including best in the category of Family Process in the National Council on Family Relations film competition.

Other films, articles, and books have been produced or written that describe the community and its unique life style. One documentary has been broadcast on national public television channels across the country. The film, *Friendship under Sail,* describes the voyage around the world and its significance to the people who participated in it. Another recently completed documentary, *Voyage to Understanding,* is an adventure film depicting the story of the eleven young people who sailed the *Vltava* on her circumnavigation. A book entitled, *The Truth, A Psychological Cure,* published in 1981 by Macmillan Publishing Company, presented the author's concepts and ideas in a style directed toward the general population.

The people living in this miniature society welcome other social scientists to study and observe their community and to analyze the information that has been documented and recorded thus far. There is a vast accumulation of knowledge about human behavior as a result of the ongoing open discussion of personal issues. The author feels committed to further dissemination of these findings to other professionals in the field.

In conclusion, despite the fact that no one deliberately set out to establish a community, now that it exists, its members are actively seeking to continue the dynamic process. The people in this friendship circle have a strong desire to perpetuate their value system of personal regard for all individuals and further to integrate these principles into their everyday lives. They want to preserve the new environment because they want their children to grow up and flourish here. It appears that they have succeeded, to a large extent, in ameliorating the effects of their own upbringing and have interrupted, to a considerable degree, the negative defensive process that is generally passed on to succeeding generations.

If the community, for whatever reason, were to be dissolved tomorrow, it *did* exist as a viable, successful alternative to conventional living for a number of years and has left its mark. Nothing can erase this experience from the memory of some ninety people who have lived differently than they had ever lived before, nor can the positive impact on the lives of their children be negated. In their shared endeavor, these people have attempted to change generation upon generation of thought within the short span of their own lives. They are involved in a complex process of acculturation. Having inadvertently evolved into a new culture, they are now attempting to live in it and accommodate to the vast differences between their new world and the world they knew as children.

Chapter 21

POINT OF VIEW

> By understanding how pain and neurosis are passed down from generation to generation, [people] might decide to break that chain. They could choose to live by an implicit code of morality that . . . doesn't fracture their feelings and experiences or those of others, a morality that enhances their well-being and personal development . . . creating a society that is sensitive to the emotional and psychological fulfillment of all its members.
>
> Firestone & Catlett (1981)
> *The truth—A Psychological Cure* (p. xiv)

The author has observed and participated in the life of this psychotherapeutic community for a period of approximately 10 years. My associates and I have developed a number of hypotheses and preliminary conclusions from our study of this population that we believe are generally valid for human behavior in the larger society. We have assembled and documented much information about the emotional damage that people sustained as children and how their specific defenses and reactions to stress perpetuate their suffering throughout their lives. Our investigations have led to conclusions about both the type and quality of experience that is conducive to the well-being of individuals and therefore growth-enhancing, as well as those experiences that are destructive and limiting.

Certain of our hypotheses and interpretations are innovative and a few are controversial. Some may be contrary to current psychological thought, but all are closely related to clinical material in the sample population. We are aware that our findings are not final or incontrovertible truths about human nature, yet we feel strongly that they should stimulate thought and scientific inquiry.

The uniqueness of this population as a living psychological laboratory lies in the style of open discussion and sustained observation. In talks over the years, people have revealed the dynamics of their inner lives and their innermost secrets and feelings. At the same time, their outward behavior has been visible, providing systematic objective data. Thus, it has been possible in this context for my associates and me to study the full extent of a neurotic or maladaptive psychological function. For example, if a man were passive, we could see all the dimensions of his passivity—in his work, in his personal interactions, in his sexual life, in sports, and other activities. His personality dynamics and problematic style of interacting with others could be elucidated in the context of a total life experience.

Though the therapist may learn a great deal about a patient in the office setting, many areas of the patient's functioning remain hidden or open to speculation. By contrast, in the community of friends, over a long period of time and under varying conditions, we observed an individual's pattern of defensive behavior and its consequences on self and others. Because people's friendships are of such long duration, the depth of feeling and the breadth of subject matter discussed in the talks far exceed the level of interaction and range of topics in typical psychotherapy or encounter groups.

The open style of communication has impinged upon the psychological defenses of each person. By contrast, routine communication in conventional society serves to maintain defenses, to conceal rather than to reveal. Of course, all of the people here have had to struggle against their stubborn resistance to information about their life style and intimate relationships. However, because of their overall willingness to remain open in spite of strong resistance, they have contributed extensively to our knowledge of the defensive process.

In the following pages, we will discuss preliminary conclusions derived from the information revealed. These hypotheses have reached a certain level of predictability and have been validated by the continuing process of self-disclosure. Paradoxically, the generally favorable living circumstances enjoyed by this population have provided a unique opportunity to study resistance to "the better life." For example, my associates and I have been able to anticipate the critical points in people's lives when resistance and regressive behavior are most likely to occur. It has been more difficult, however, to pinpoint precisely or to determine in advance to what degree an individual will react to these circumstances. Nevertheless, the set of constructs set forth in this work is well understood by the reference population and has generally proven reliable and valid in the context of the group. Indeed, the lives and everyday experiences of the people here have repeatedly borne out the concepts and theoretical orientation offered in this volume.

The conclusions and supporting clinical material that we will summarize in this chapter include the following topics: (1) Motivational Dishonesty: People Don't Want What They Say They Want; (2) The Duplicity of Communication in Bonds; (3) Withholding; (4) The Success and Failure of Manipulations Through Guilt; (5) The Inevitable Destructiveness of Defenses; (6) Conclusions that Contradict Popular Myths about Men, Women, and Sex; (7) The Essential Damage of a Conventional Life Style; (8) Application of Our Concepts to Child-Rearing Practices; (9) The Therapeutic Value of Friendship; and (10) Existential Issues.

1. MOTIVATIONAL DISHONESTY: PEOPLE DON'T WANT WHAT THEY SAY THEY WANT

For those who cannot turn away from the world and who are still committed to the search for happiness within it, there remains the problem of why there is still the pervasive unease over success or over the appearance of the wished-for.

If the problem lies in the mother-infant symbiosis, and in the development of the primary fantasy bond as a defense against the devastation, even annihilation, of the self, in the face of an inadequate, defective, even malign relationship, then the solution is two-fold. One aspect involves working socially and therapeutically with the individual who has been damaged in this way; the other involves the provision of a milieu in which such initial damaging bonds will not be formed. The Friendship Circle and The Environment attempt to deal with both of these aspects.

Stuart Boyd (1982)
Analysis of the Psychotherapeutic Community

The unusual advantages available to people living in the community—the excitement and adventure of sailing throughout the world, the opportunities for financial success, the warmth of close friendships, the acknowledgement of individual accomplishments, the support for developing each person's unique abilities, talents, and careers—all of these advantages combine to expose a fallacy under which most people operate. The fact is that *people are generally dishonest about their motivations and aspirations.* In fact, people don't really want what they say they want.

Members of this community have found in this environment much of what they sought after all of their lives. However, they discovered that they had great difficulty tolerating or accepting the actual satisfaction of their wants. They found that, to a significant degree, they were not desirous of actualizing or fulfilling their fantasies when they had the opportunity. Real success, genuine love, and friendship interrupted an inward, self-gratifying fantasy process that they had depended on since they were young, and this disruption caused them anxiety and pain. Furthermore, the anxiety and sadness that were generated were sometimes of a magnitude that threatened an individual's defensive equilibrium, and therefore achievements, friendships, and relationships were many times pushed away or discarded.

It became clear from people's negative reactions to positive circumstances that *there is an enormous discrepancy between what people say they want and what they can actually tolerate having.* When one's dreams come true in reality, they are no longer under one's control. One can no longer conjure up the satisfaction of these wants in fantasy and obtain partial gratification and escape or relief from psychic pain. It appears that most people are well-adapted to being *unsuccessful,* to *not* getting what they want. Anything that disrupts their fantasies of always waiting for and hoping for success, while at the same time blaming their failures on external circumstances, is usually strenuously avoided.

As an illustration, people in the community have generally been resistant to formulating personal goals and consciously mobilizing activity toward their achievement. For example, when they first began to benefit from the growth of the business ventures, many found it difficult to adjust to the financial rewards and higher standard of living. Often we observed that an individual would not sustain performance if it entailed a basic change in identity which brought him or her to a level of professional competence above that achieved by the parent of the same sex, or if it fulfilled the person's fondest hopes. Gradually, over the years, there has been an adaptation to success but not without considerable suffering.

Many people have advanced considerably in their personal development and have gone beyond the limits and boundaries imposed by their upbringing. However, certain individuals reached crucial high points in their growth where their fear of further progress caused them to regress and return to their former defensive postures. At these times, even the talks became double-edged as people projected their own desires for personal fulfillment and change onto their friends and took the other side. When this occurred, they became paranoid about hearing feedback, very resistant to change, and negative toward the life-style.

Even in these instances much was learned as people attempted to keep the ongoing dialogue of the talks alive during the setbacks. In fact, these regressions provided us with information that might never have been made available had people not reached these personal heights in their development and then faltered. From these experiences, we concluded that, in general, *a person who is actively defensive cannot tolerate an open forum for honest communication.* He or she tends to have an aversion to a democratic process and to an equal sharing of views.

We also observed that the probability of regression was highest for people whenever they achieved personal goals that were especially meaningful to them, whenever they approached the life "they always dreamed of." Some reactions were dramatic, and symptoms of regression developed suddenly; in other cases, the deterioration was more gradual but could still be serious over a period of time. Regression usually took the form of a retreat into an inward, emotionally-deadened state characterized by childish behavior and primal reactions. Other symptoms of regression were split loyalties—people appeared to act against their own interests and there was confusion about important issues in their lives. Indeed, even their appearance changed, and they didn't look like themselves in the open state. They became self-doubting and self-hating where previously they had been confident and insightful. They tended to imagine rejection and anticipate disapproval from people who, in reality, liked and supported them in their personal endeavors. On occasion, serious depressive states were triggered, characterized by a wide range of pathological symptoms, including suicidal ideation, strong desires for isolation and escape, and other self-punishing tendencies.

More often than not, happy moments and unusual success preceded the onset of the symptoms. The precipitating events themselves varied from one individual to another: for one man, it was finding friendship and companionship after years of being isolated and alone; for another, a woman, it was the acknowledgement of her personal effectiveness in the talks that interrupted her long-standing awkwardness and reserve in social situations. One man became aloof and distant after receiving a gift from his friends, one that held a great deal of personal meaning for him. Another man resumed his pattern of self-destructive drinking after achieving his long-standing goal of earning $100,000 a year at his job. A woman regressed after being admired by her friends for being a good wife, another for being a good lover, still another for being powerful in her job.

For many people, basic changes in identity leave them feeling anxious, and they experience sensations of being disoriented. Their reactions tended to validate our ideas about the pervasiveness of the negative self-concept and its resistance to change. Most people have difficulty assimilating a new, more positive image of themselves and usually quickly give it up to return to the familiar. They refuse to accept their new identities and disregard or even reverse behaviors that were significantly valued. For one man, this identity change meant accepting himself as an intelligent, clear-thinking adult instead of an inarticulate, defiant "kid," a role he had felt stubbornly proud of. For another man, it was becoming aware that he had tender feelings toward children when all his life he had thought he was harsh and unfeeling toward them.

Significant changes aroused anxiety because they represented a marked separation from parents and other family members. For example, one woman learned to accept herself as a loving woman and mother instead of running away (literally) from her family as her own mother had done. After feeling at ease with her new identity of being a good mother for several months following the birth of her baby, she felt compelled to destroy this image by repeating her mother's behavior and deserting her husband and child for a period of time.

The attainment of sexual maturity was also linked to regression in a number of women. The ability to have an orgasm for the first time symbolized an adult level of sexuality and often caused adverse reactions that extended into other areas of living. We also noted in group discussions that almost every woman who verbally reported improvement in the area of her sexuality suffered a relapse and became unresponsive sexually for a time. Many men who talked about overcoming their sexual fears and feelings of inadequacy had similar reactions. It has been of great concern to all who studied this phenomenon that virtually any man or woman who *publicly* acknowledged improvement or a major change in an important area of his or her life manifested symptoms of regression following the disclosure.

By far the greatest resistance has been to the process of combining a close personal friendship with a satisfying sexual relationship. *People are the most refractive in their most intimate relations, where there is both an opportunity for an affectionate and feelingful exchange and an animal or physical response.* They tend to pull back first in one area and then the other, yet always avoiding the very special combination of love, sexuality, and tenderness that is the most rewarding or ideal.

2. The Duplicity of Couples in a Bond

> It seems that what is now stimulating, reenergizing, and mov-
> ing the community is the insight into the nature of relationships
> as they constitute connections and dependencies and manipula-
> tions, versus equalities, freedoms, and responsibilities.
>
> Stuart Boyd (1982)

The fact that most people *don't* want what they claim to want sets up a style of dishonesty and duplicity within the couple that is damaging to both partners and extends to their children and even their friends. From our study of couples in the community, we are able to predict that there will be negative trends in behavior following significant events in the lives of the members, such as getting married, buying a home, or talking about or actually having a child. When people reach these milestones in their lives, they are expected to be more mature and responsible. Paradoxically, it is at these times that regression usually occurs, and people actually become *less* mature in their outlook and their behavior. Because this disparity is socially unacceptable, it encourages more inwardness and less communication, which further damages their relationships.

People appear to be terrified of those steps in life that signify full maturity and adulthood because they symbolize separation from parental figures and a movement toward old age and death. Events that were expected to bring happiness and expansiveness often result in the opposite. For example, one couple in our community was very compatible until they bought new furniture for their apartment. The purchase signaled the beginning of a real living arrangement and a deeper commitment to one another. For months afterward, this couple's relationship was one of constant bickering and mutual hostility.

Frequently the women who emotionally acknowledged in group discussions their strong desire to have children tended to regress, and sometimes there were serious consequences as a result. Often they lost their spontaneous interest in sex at the very time they were trying to become pregnant. Neurotic symptoms reappeared, and some women re-experienced sexual problems that they believed they had permanently overcome. They also tended to become more self-hating and self-denying, and these feelings prevailed for the duration of the pregnancy.

Negative reactions to movement and progress in people's lives shed light on the subject of bonds and bond formation. All the symptoms of bonds that we have described have been demonstrated by the couples in the environment: the substitution of dependency, obligation, and a pretense of love for genuine friendship and spontaneous sexuality; a progressive giving up of individuality; an increase in self-hatred and self-attacks by the "voice;" and hostile thoughts and negative feelings toward one another. The partners appeared to be recreating the same type of circumstances that had existed in their original families and tended to blame each other for the unhappy situation.

Almost every individual in the community who married in the last several years has undergone some period of regression where he or she has returned to a more defended posture and in so doing has inadvertently punished the mate. During these phases, both men and women were less open about their relationships and became dishonest and vague when speaking about their problems. Despite this resistance, the talks have revolved around this crucial problem as people attempted to continue their dialogue about bonds. A great deal of time and energy has been expended in trying to save couple relationships and reawaken the original good feelings. Couples' groups were started to explore techniques that would break into these bonds and to encourage the independence of each individual. In dealing with these basic issues between men and women, we have arrived at a number of tentative conclusions about the nature of withholding and the part it plays in the deterioration of people's most intimate relationships.

3.   WITHHOLDING

Withholding is a defensive pattern that develops early in life as a response to a rejecting home environment. If a child's love and direct emotional response to the parent are threatening to the parent's defense system, the child comes to believe that his or her feelings are unacceptable. Consequently, the child begins to hold back expressions of love and affection.

Many complicated factors shape withholding patterns, such as hostility, passive-aggression, and a fear of being drained or depleted. Children raised by emotionally hungry or intrusive parents are afraid of being consumed or "swallowed up" in the parental interaction. They become tight and are reluctant to enter into a psychonutritional exchange of products with other individuals. These patterns persist into adult life and into personal relationships, affecting the formation of new families. Though withholding represents a basic self-denial or self-deprivation, it nevertheless has an incidental destructive effect on others and on relationships.

Sexual withholding refers to a holding back of natural sexual desire and all its expressions, including physical attractiveness, affection, touching, and other aspects of one's natural, healthy sexuality. *This form of withholding appears to be at the core of a couple's emotional life—its effects are devastating to both men and women.*

We have studied this process of withholding for many years. The subject has been pursued despite considerable resistance; men and women alike were often reluctant to reveal the pain in their relationships and to expose their style of holding back from their mates. Invariably the atmosphere in the talks was heavy whenever the subject came up. It was clear that something deeply entrenched was being exposed. As the talks progressed, the logic of this resistance became more explicable: men's and women's most basic illusions of security were being threatened by their explorations of these dynamics. Withholding was a core defense. In exposing withholding, people were disrupting bonds with their families and fantasized connections, and this aroused deep anxiety.

We found that, in general, *both men and women hold back sexually and emotionally from their mates when they revert to a defended stance; however, the tendency to withhold appears to be greater in a woman.* A woman's bond with her mother often takes precedence over her relationship with a man. When she becomes anxious or fearful, a woman will often revert to childish responses and become emotionally distant.

Whether or not she is conscious of withholding from a man, the process of holding back feelings that were once natural to her causes a woman considerable guilt and significantly increases her self-hatred. Women refuse, for the most part, to enter into an equal partnership with a man sexually. They generally do not honestly express their desire for sex and closeness. When they hold back their natural responsiveness or enthusiasm for sex, a shadow is cast on the relationship, and the effects are profoundly detrimental to *both* partners. Most women refuse to be equal partners in other aspects of married life as well. Many hold back their abilities and talents in order to be taken care of by a man. This is particularly true in practical areas and financial matters.

Many men also have been seriously damaged early in their relationships with their mothers and have become accustomed to holding back their affectional responses to women. They become passive and stubborn and hold back from a feelingful investment in their mates. In some instances, a man may be so emotionally hungry toward women that he is unable to sustain a mature sexual relationship or may be unconsciously seeking revenge for the damage he sustained as a child.

A woman who is withholding loses her sense of identity as a mature person and is seriously affected in other areas of her functioning. The man who is married to a woman who has begun to withdraw her sexual responses is deeply affected and tends to blame himself rather than identifying his wife's withholding. He generally blames himself for his failure to be attracted to his mate or for any reluctance or failure in his sexual performance, i.e. impotence, premature ejaculation, etc., though these symptoms are often the *result* of the woman's holding back her genuine sexual responses. Self-hatred and feelings of inadequacy are inevitable for the man involved in this type of relationship.

We have observed that when a woman is withholding, and thus not operating from her own point of view, she displays a curious lack of compassion or concern for her mate. True, she may experience painful feelings of guilt, but she appears unresponsive to the emotional pain she is causing her loved one. She tends to perceive herself as being "bad" in a childish sense. Sometimes she attempts to be sexual out of guilt and feelings of obligation, which further confuses the situation.

We have concluded that *women who have become withholding are incapable of having empathetic feelings toward the men in their lives. When a woman regresses and connects to her mother, she tends to become immature in relation to her sexuality.* She strives for an unfeeling, automatic connection similar to the bond with her mother. As described in our discussion of *The Oral Basis of Sexuality*, sex is often perceived as a feeding experience. When a woman is withholding, she is in a regressed state and desires to be fed (symbolically) and taken care of by a man. In her retreat from mature sexuality, she seeks a fantasized connection to relieve her primitive feelings of emotional hunger.

Both men and women tend to be withholding toward people whom they perceive as powerful or who assume leadership positions. In a sense, they surrender their own initiative and autonomy and manipulate through weakness and incompetency in order to maintain a fantasized connection with parental figures. In fact, if there is anyone in the surrounding environment that people can identify as a "rescuer" or "savior," they are quick to give up their own independent points of view for an imaginary connection with such a figure. They preserve the connection through the same withholding patterns and bids for negative attention they acted out as children in relation to their real parents, only in a more refined, sophisticated form. By attempting to fuse their personalities with that of a leader, they avoid the anxiety of being separate individuals with opinions of their own.

Our experience with people in this reference population lends support to our theories about separation, regression, and fusion. As stated earlier, any step away from the Primary Fantasy Bond with the mother and toward individuation and separateness and power has resulted in dramatic reversals in personality development and in an increase in withholding behavior because of the fear inherent in having a *separate* life.

The terror of separation is also evident in the strong resistance to Voice Therapy. An increased awareness of the "voice" and attempts to formulate one's self-attacks in terms of the voice tend to break down this form of internal security. For many people, there is an illusion of being parented in listening to this inner voice or dialogue. The harangue, however unpleasant or negative, gives them a feeling of security. The relative absence of this internal thought process is often experienced as an emptiness or lonely feeling. The voice functions as an internalized parent. Separation from the voice occurs when the voice is expressed publicly or scrutinized or analyzed in Voice Therapy. This process is analogous to separation from the actual parent. It disturbs the Fantasy Bond with the parent and creates anxiety states.

Once withholding is well-established, a sense of obligation takes the place of real desire or initiative. Acting out of obligation, form or tradition is deadly, because giving up one's ability to act out of free choice is equivalent to giving up life itself.

One of the most damaging moves a person can make in living is to conform to what is acceptable and place form and obligation above own's own desires. Even if one's value system is positive, one cannot force feelings to fit values; one can only control or limit behavior. Once the process of withholding sets in and an individual is acting out of obligation, even a conscious resolve to change behavior is rarely effective. It is much more productive to investigate the sources of the withholding and self-denial. Often, in trying to make one's behavior conform to one's sense of obligation, slips occur that reveal the true nature of the withholding and leave the individual filled with guilt and self-recrimination.

If individuals consistently subjugate their own feelings and defer to conventions and popular opinions, they will become progressively removed from their own point of view and feelings. To substitute obligation for free choice is to give up a function that is peculiarly human, and it symbolizes living more on a herd or an imitative level. It is, in fact, a desperate attempt on the part of an individual to regress to a level where there is no awareness of separation or death. The more one gives up of life by denying priorities and choices, the *less* one feels alone and separate.

4.   Manipulations Through Guilt and Anger

A powerful theme for me in the discussion was the nature of an initial commitment to another person. What was stressed here

> was that it is damaging to make promises contrary to your nature
> to another person, or extract or expect such in return.
>
> Stuart Boyd (1982)

In our study of withholding, we have concluded that a person generally attempts to control those closest to him or her. This is possible because people have been taught early in life that they belong to their families in a proprietary sense. Thus, people don't have a sense of belonging to themselves or feel that they have a right to their own lives. For these reasons, they are subject to manipulations which play on their guilt. Both members of a couple learn that they can successfully restrict the lives of their mates and get them to conform. However, these maneuvers often backfire because they provoke angry responses and tension in the relationship and create more problems than they are worth. *People can successfully imprison one another, but they damage the relationship in the process.* In fact, the *manipulation of another person through guilt subverts any genuine feelings that may exist.* These maneuvers preserve the form of a relationship while the richness, the substance, and love are being destroyed.

Manipulations through guilt are particularly characteristic of people in a strong bond who are losing the real love in their relationship. Though restrictions and conventions are often effective in controlling the behavior of each partner, the people involved lose a sense of dignity and self-respect. People can be nagged or badgered into the desired behavior but the rewards are short-lived. These maneuvers perpetuate a vicious cycle of damage. We have found, in relationships characterized by this style of manipulation, that it is often beneficial for the individuals to separate temporarily and then come together again on a voluntary basis out of a renewed sense of choice and not out of loyalty or obligation. Indeed the only hope for any couple is that they sustain their freedom of choice and not limit or place demands on each other through rules and restrictions.

5.   THE INEVITABLE DESTRUCTIVENESS OF DEFENSES

From the subject matter that we have discussed throughout this work, it becomes apparent that *people cannot be innocently defended.* When individuals protect themselves from anxiety, pain, and sadness—emotions that are inherent in close relationships—they push away or punish people who care for them the most. Although this damage is minimized with acquaintances, in casual relationships, or in more distant social contacts, it still takes a toll there as well. There is no way to be self-denying or self-destructive without damaging other people. This presents a serious problem for the community, just as in the family. We have consistently found that parents who are defended in an area cannot be sensitive to their children in that area; a woman who cannot tolerate an image of herself as a lovable person will punish the man who offers her love; a man who sees himself as cold or unattractive will be suspicious of a woman who shows an interest in him and will be rejecting toward her. If a person cannot tolerate generosity, he will hurt the gift-giver. If he needs to think of himself as bad or inadequate, he will act accordingly, thereby damaging a joint effort to live happily. If he needs to provoke aggression, he will stir up anger and resentment in others, which damages their good feelings.

Through their talks with each other, people in this friendship circle have learned at first hand how they have hurt their friends and families when they suffered setbacks that made them become more defended. The exchange of information about the pain they experience from present-day rejection, withholding, or acting out has made people in this community acutely aware of the inevitable repercussions of their own defensiveness.

6. CONCLUSIONS ABOUT MEN, WOMEN, AND SEX THAT CONTRADICT POPULAR MYTHS AND SEXUAL STEREOTYPES

> These people I speak of look different, certainly, but it is a difference in the positive direction of the cultural norm—health, posture, attractiveness of presence and clothing, happiness, adventure, striking generosity and friendliness, success in most of the ways of life. And the living through of critical sexual problems to a different, clearly comfortable, and happy level is one striking instance.
>
> Stuart Boyd (1982)

Within the community, there is a strong emphasis on a healthy, active sexual life. In conventional society, there is a great deal of manipulation and dishonesty in sexual relationships. People in the society at large rarely receive real or accurate feedback or information about their sexuality. They don't know much about their performance and they probably have had very little honest feedback from their partners. By contrast, the individuals in the friendship circle have had the benefit of this kind of dialogue for years and have explored this subject matter in depth.

In their talks, men and women have admitted feelings of possessiveness, jealousy, and competitiveness. From years of dealing with
these feelings in an open forum, people came to the conclusion that a
person's sexuality belongs to himself or herself and cannot be assigned to
or possessed by another person. Just as they feel that a child does not
"belong" to the parents, they realized the wives don't "belong" to husbands or vice versa. In other words, they hold strong convictions that no
person has proprietary rights over another person's body.

One significant finding that emerged from the exploration of competitiveness and rivalry was the observation that *feelings of jealousy are
often intensified when a person holds back feelings and physical expressions of
affection and sex from a mate or loved one.* In other words, once a person is
withholding in a relationship, he or she is more inclined to feel hostility
toward potential rivals, and this passivity leads to a morbid and jealous
brooding over imagined losses. In overcoming many of their more primal feelings of jealousy and in learning how to express a healthy competitiveness, these people became closer and rivals found that they could
also be friends. *In fact, honest rivalry is necessary for genuine friendship,
particularly between members of the same sex.*

Men and women here have discovered that if sex is uncomplicated
and easy, it is a relatively minor issue in their lives, although it contributes much to their general sense of well-being. However, when sex is
withheld, or avoided or feared, it has a powerful negative effect on an
individual's overall functioning. We have learned that, unless a man is
depending on fantasies to increase his excitement, *his successful completion
of the sex act is almost entirely dependent on the woman's genuine sexual desire.* It
has been repeatedly demonstrated, by women in the community who
have been honest enough to admit their lack of interest or desire, that
the woman's withholding was the principal factor that interfered with
the man's performance and pleasure.

In our explorations of the subject of sexuality in the new environment, we have come to several other conclusions about men and women
that contradict popular thought. *We have found that women tend to be more
selective in their choices of sex objects, yet at the same time they are often less
personal and less compassionate in relation to their mates, especially in their
sexual relationships.* This became more obvious as we observed that
women tend to crowd around and attach themselves to strong men,
leaders, or popular figures. When this person is no longer present, they
attach their interest to the next in line. This predisposition may in part
be determined biologically but we have found that the tendency appears
to be based on a woman's bond with her mother, which she projects onto

the man in her life. Because of this process, her relationship with a man often reveals a fantasy of connection and security rather than a desire for real affection or caring.

It appears that men tend to be more random in their sexuality, yet are more personal and concerned in their overall contact with women. Most of the women held a distorted view of men and perceived them as harsh, "mean," and unfeeling, and many men have even shared this negative view of themselves. Upon honest investigation and reflection we have found the opposite. Men in the community have typically been more personally concerned about their women and their well-being than vice versa. In most cases, the men here are so concerned about the overall well-being of their mate that they rarely feel good unless she is happy and content. Indeed, her happiness and companionship is so sought after that it is the central issue in their lives and in the talks.

In conventional society, men control the so-called important activities of life—affairs of state, economics, scientific research, etc. Women, however, control the family and the social world and are seen as masters of interpersonal relations, child care and the couple's social life. In all of the important personal areas women dominate and manipulate the interpersonal scene and the emotional life of the family. However, we have observed that men have an equal capacity to offer sensitive, tender care to infants and children.

Women are able to control men through building up their vanity and by sexual withholding. They generally manipulate them through their childish maneuvers and weakness. If all else fails, a woman's tears generally bring about the desired effect of maintaining control. This form of manipulation can be quite subtle and generally is successfully concealed in the traditional nuclear family.

We have found that both men and women are physically and even sexually attracted to women and that this basic attraction is not an abnormality. It is based on the early physical attraction to the mother and is part of the child's earliest feelings. Although men also are physically attracted to other men, their attraction doesn't appear to be as powerful or compelling. This comparison is due only partly to the cultural taboo regarding affectionate contact between men. We discovered that most women were afraid of their feelings of loving sexuality toward other women and were embarrassed to reveal that they found other women attractive. They were especially uncomfortable with their attraction to breasts, hips, and sexual parts. We observed that the inhibition of these positive feelings leads to controversy, exaggerated competitiveness, and regressive behavior in many women.

We have observed that *women take their cues from other women in terms of their emotional states or their propensities to be self-denying*. For instance, rather than compete with another woman who is depressed or self-denying, a woman is more likely to withdraw and become self-denying herself. She tends to imitate another woman who has suffered a setback rather than separating herself from her and maintaining her own pursuit of personal goals. This reaction is symptomatic of a more serious process of intimidation that affects both men and women in relation to a woman who becomes self-destructive or who shows signs of a possible emotional breakdown. We have traced people's susceptibility to this form of intimidation to their early interactions with weak, emotionally unstable, dependent or self-denying mothers. Members of both sexes are afraid to confront or to be direct with a woman who is self-hating because they sense that she will use the information against herself and become even more self-hating. Basically they fear the loss of the mother or her symbolic substitute in the present-day situation and tend to hold themselves responsible for her vacillations in mood.

The fear aroused by this intimidation cannot be overestimated. It has had powerful negative consequences in this community, especially in the talks. At different times, women have responded adversely to honest feedback in discussions. Their reactions have reminded everyone of the restrictive atmosphere in their original families, where no one dared to criticize or express disapproval of the mother, particularly when she was upset, depressed, or unhappy. The effects of this intimidation are experienced in the community as a breakdown in communication in talks, a holding back of feelings and perceptions, the suppression of rage and turning it against oneself, and the succumbing to a passive or defended posture. The results of this intimidation are a subtle form of control. The tyranny of weakness, passivity, and helplessness has been exerted by members of both sexes but seems considerably stronger, more effective, and more widespread among the women of the community. Reactions of intense anxiety and fear are manifest in the group while confronting or exposing perceptions of a woman who refuses to give up her self-hatred. Her misery has a powerful influence on the mood of the man in her life as well as on other women who are closely associated with her.

In conclusion, *both men and women are emotionally hungry and dependent on the primary woman in their lives and seek safety and reassurance in a bond with her*. In this bond, they hold back their opinions and perceptions because they fear the possibility of driving her into a self-hating state. The free flow of communication is seriously limited by the threat of breaking this bond and challenging this form of intimidation and control.

7. THE DESTRUCTIVENESS OF CONVENTIONALITY

> How the community lives raises some very interesting issues
> for moral and ethical philosophy but as far as "conventional"
> morality is concerned it's no contest—truth versus hypocrisy;
> manifest improvement in happiness and stability versus anxiety
> and broken, hating relationships.
>
> Stuart Boyd (1982)

In our estimation, the institutions and conventions of society are a pooling of individual defense systems, which in turn support and help maintain each person's defenses. The duplicity within couples and in the traditional family is replicated in many of society's institutions. This duplicity is also expressed through society's double messages; that is, the ideals professed by members of the larger society are contradicted by their actions. As a result of this large-scale defensiveness and protection, people who live in fantasy in relation to their goals are rarely challenged about their dishonesty or lack of integrity. If they fail to achieve their goals or find themselves involved in one disastrous relationship after another, society supports their explanations and rationalizations of their failures. Thus, there is a general tendency to blame others for one's misfortunes, and people continue to deceive themselves and others about their real wants.

The conventions of society are replete with rules and roles that support people's tendencies to categorize others, to be exclusive, to feel superior, to force feelings into molds, to act out of obligation and guilt, and to coerce other people through weakness, illness and withholding. The illusion of being connected to other people is strongly supported in conventional society. The traditional family myth of closeness and security is perpetuated by the mistaken belief that people are connected or belong to one another.

People living in our small society have found that contact with the institutions of society, including the traditional family complex, continues to exert a damaging effect on their development. It is difficult for these people to have meaningful contact with family members and relatives who only want the imagined security and dependency of a bond or who are involved in role-playing instead of honestly expressing their feelings or thoughts. Contact with the traditional family is often destructive because it exerts conscious or unconscious social pressure on the individual to become self-denying and withholding in a style similar to that of the role model. For example, many men date the onset of the serious decline in their love relationship with their wives with the advent of her mother's visit during the period immediately following the birth of their first child. In many ways, there was an obvious transformation from what was to be a happy and joyful period to one that was filled with tension and conflict.

The philosophy of self-denial and selflessness instilled in children by most traditional families is propagated by society's institutions, notably traditional religion. Most religious teachings are representative of the incorporated negative parental view of the child. This view is composed of critical self-evaluations and hostile attitudes toward the body and physical person which support a posture of self-denial. Often religious prohibitions and teachings lead to the very immorality that they are trying to avert. By denying natural outlets for physical affection and sexuality and a positive regard for the self, they increase hostility and therefore contribute to destructive antisocial behavior.

In general, we have concluded that *religious dogma acts as a neurotic defense.* The believer gives up real life for an afterlife, the body for a hypothetical soul, sexuality for a union with God or for ethereal brotherly love, natural power for martyrdom, honest strivings for selflessness, desire for self-fulfillment for self-abuse, honest wants and needs for unnecessary sublimation, and a decent and fair view of human nature for the concept of original sin. Plagued by a false sense of unworthiness and badness, people cling to a connection with an all-powerful parent in the sky. When parents feel unworthy and lack self-love because as children *they* were taught these values and beliefs, they cannot accept the love of their own children and in turn damage *their* self-esteem. Through the process just described, religion inadvertently perpetuates the cycle of destructiveness that abounds in society, offering false security and causing unnecessary suffering, while stifling efforts toward progress and change.

8. Application of Theory to Child Rearing

It was good to see young ones present during the discussion. There seem to be no inhibitions or taboos of content or language among them, and they are learning the tales and anecdotes. The process of transmission through generations is preserved. The young ones are respected as children but are not encouraged to be falsely childish—and of course there is a considerable difference in the two conditions, a difference that the community is sensitively aware of. They are never given token recognition of

their presence, and then ignored. They have their rights for recognition and audience and serious attention respected too, and
they are never brushed aside or cut off in what they are saying, or
trying to say. The youngsters are such fun to be with and are the
bright hope of the community.

Stuart Boyd (1982)

In observing and interacting with the children in the community, we
have been impressed with the early age at which the defensive process is
formed and solidified. By the time a child is one or two years old, one
can see negative traits of the parents in the child's personality, qualities
that he or she will hold on to into adulthood, as though holding on to the
actual parent.

Once they have established defensive patterns of behavior, *children
are no longer innocent or pure, as usually conceptualized.* Very often they
choose to maintain their misery, and both provoke and exploit their
parents. In an attempt to avoid potentially painful feelings, particularly
sadness, they learn early in life to fantasize and select activities that will
cut them off emotionally. The avoidance of sad or tender feelings regu-
lates the behavior of children and, later, adults and renders them insensitive to others.

We have observed that *all* of the children in the community idealized their parents to a considerable extent and consequently blamed
themselves for family problems and for their parents' unhappiness.
They are hostile and defensive toward anyone, including their own parent, who attempts to present them with a more realistic picture of their
family.

Children generally represent themselves as more helpless and inept
than they actually are. They function at a level far below their real
capabilities and continue to do so as adults. In fact, children rarely outgrow their childish manipulations; in general, they are *not* going
through a phase characterized by seemingly age-appropriate patterns of
bad behavior as many experts and parents believe. Unless their self-
destructive habits are firmly interrupted, they will act out the same infantile patterns and display the same neurotic proclivities when they
reach adulthood.

We have learned that the *elements involved in correct or preventative
child rearing are very similar to the methods of effective psychotherapy.* There
are definite steps that parents can take to prevent the formation of
destructive defenses in their children and to minimize the types of experiences that are known to contribute to neurosis. Each dimension of the
defensive process described earlier in this book represents an area where
parents can identify and interrupt negative tendencies in their offspring

before they become habitual patterns of behavior. We have encouraged parents to represent themselves as they really are and not feel obliged to build themselves up in the child's eyes. Parental honesty to some extent prevents the child's idealizing the parents and family to the child's own detriment. Similarly, we have suggested to parents that they perceive their children realistically and not build *them* up falsely. It is important that parents do not shield or protect children from reality nor, on the other hand, teach them to be cynical about the world as a form of self-protection.

If parents allow their child to act babyish or cater to the child's manipulations, they give him or her a false sense of omnipotence that will lead to maladaptive social responses later on. In order to be effective in maintaining discipline and effectively socializing a child, a parent needs to accept his or her own anger and ambivalence. Parents would strive to control acting out in themselves in order to control this process in their children and not become evaluative, judgmental, nor parental in the negative sense. We have discouraged people from teaching children critical or suspicious attitudes toward people outside the family circle, including prejudicial views or stereotyped thinking. We encourage a healthy attitude toward the body, sex, and sexual functions, and discourage a sneaky or dirty view of sex and bodily functions.

A fundamental part of successful child rearing involves discouraging self-nourishing habit patterns—overeating, compulsive, repetitive behavior, excessive television-viewing, or dazed daydreaming. Children can be encouraged both to feel and appropriately express their feelings, but should be discouraged from utilizing dramatic emotional outbursts as a manipulation. This distinction is very important. Children can be taught very early about ambivalent or irrational feelings and can learn to verbalize their anger and not act it out by sulking or tantrums.

It is important to teach children to be generous and not withholding. It is important also for parents to be respectful of children's productions, without fussing over them, "swallowing up" their traits, or taking over their achievements. It is vital that parents not mislead their children about their positive or negative feelings. Many books on child rearing do an untold amount of damage because they promote duplicity; they teach parents to act the "proper" responses rather than express their genuine feeling. Ideally, parents would not distort their child's perception of reality with double messages and reassurances of love at times when the parents are in fact feeling hostile or angry toward him. Similarly, they would not shelter their offspring from the reality of death or illness with false beliefs and the denial of basic existential issues. Instead they would share the happiness and pain of life with their children on a level appropriate to each child's age.

9. THE THERAPEUTIC VALUE OF FRIENDSHIP

The central theme of the life style in the community is the core of close and long-lasting friendships. Some of the unique characteristics of the friendship circle that are of special therapeutic value include the freedom to pursue one's priorities, honest communication, and the opportunity to share equally in a democratic process, project or activity. Close friendships stand in opposition to bonds. They provide companionship that is nonintrusive and nonobligatory, qualities that lead to self-awareness and encourage a person to emerge from an inward or isolated posture. We have found that meaningful interaction with close friends on a daily basis diminishes "voice" attacks and significantly interferes with neurotic tendencies to be self-denying and self-hating.

In society at large, it is rare for a person to maintain close friendships. It is unusual to achieve an adult level of communication between people on any personal subject. A respectful dialogue pertaining to real issues without coercion, manipulation or parent-child role-playing is difficult to come by. When people are defended, adult communication, uncomplicated by phoniness, dishonesty, and efforts to make points, becomes almost impossible.

Occasionally, during wars or disasters or extraordinary projects such as the space program, people are able to transcend themselves and work together efficiently, with a spirit of real cooperation. These rare times are treasured in spite of adversity and have special therapeutic effects. In fact, if one had to choose whether to create a community based on psychological principles or one based on a work project, shaped by friendship, equality, and an honest division of labor, there would be more chance of success with the latter. An aggregate with goals that supersede one's petty preoccupations and that is based on sound practical principles that challenge a person's defended posture has real therapeutic potential. A community based on psychological principles alone would tend by its very focus on defenses to increase resentment and stubbornness. It is unlikely that such a community could survive for very long in a vacuum without meaningful work and strong personal ties.

Effective psychotherapy is a mutual project with many of the important characteristics of close personal friendship. In addition to his or her specialized knowledge, the ideal therapist would be open and nondefensive, avoid a judgmental attitude, and be compassionate and forthright in communications.

The patient in this type of therapeutic atmosphere would be provided with the opportunity to correct distortions and defenses in a new form of social interaction. In order for successful psychotherapy to take place, the therapist must remain in close association with the patient, despite the patient's efforts to distort and provoke distance in the relationship. The therapist must interrupt rather than facilitate the patient's attempt to establish illusions of connection or dependency ties in significant relationships.

The patient's neurosis, formed originally within the family bond, can be successfully counteracted only in a relationship that is *not* a bond. The author believes that *role-playing in a therapy situation, that is, substituting an unequal doctor-patient relationship for the original parent-child bond, cannot effect deep long-lasting change.* Paradoxically, as we have indicated, patients consistently struggle *against* having an equal exchange with the therapist because their overriding urge is to form a Fantasy Bond or connection with him or her. We have concluded that in successful therapy, we must address the patient's resistance to living his or her life as a separate person.

10. EXISTENTIAL ISSUES

> The theory suggests that at an unconscious level, the combination of the defensive distortions based on the primary fantasy bond and the consequent distorted threat of death is of such power as even to defeat our chances of success in life, in work, in love, in play; or to turn the taste of victory to wormwood and gall, and later to lead to decreased energy, vision, motivation, defeat in the areas of our greatest competence or longing.
>
> Stuart Boyd (1982)

Our ongoing, in-depth study of individuals in this community has exposed the basic split that exists in all people, the split between their desire for self-actualization and fulfillment and their tendency to retreat from life and move toward the controlled destruction of self. This dualism is apparent in the agony and ecstasy of the ongoing life style. Before they succeeded in establishing successful cooperation in business, adventurous living, and personal friendship, they had very little awareness of how much fear, even terror, is generated by achievement, personal power, and loving, tender relationships. They underestimated the pain involved in establishing a new identity, long and intimate relationships, and a life without destructive bonds. In no way could they anticipate the amount of energy and effort required to counteract the seemingly perverse behavior with which people push away warm or rewarding experiences.

In our studies, we found that *the negative reactions of guilt, anxiety, and self-hatred, which generally followed positive events, relate dynamically to a fear of separation, aloneness, and, ultimately, to death anxiety.* The powerful and frightening aspect of the specter of death, the inevitable submission to nothingness, represents a total loss of control. The prospect fills us with dread, a helpless, terrified feeling that is beyond our capacity to tolerate. It is akin to the despair and torment the infant experienced when painful needs were unfulfilled in the face of total helplessness. Because of this intrinsic fear and basic existential threat, an individual strives desperately to maintain some sense of control over his destiny. Once we know, on a deep level, that we must die, we choose, in various ways, purposely to give up our life in order to dispel the unbearable feelings of helplessness and dread.

In the attempt to elude death, people effectively give up their lives; they ration their aliveness and spontaneity, carefully doling out and restricting pleasant or enriching experiences. They become indifferent to important or relevant events and numb themselves by attending to life's trivialities. Later they use the same defenses they built as children to defend against separation anxiety in futile attempts to avoid the fact of their mortality.

The process just described is visible in this community and limits the active functioning of its members. Despite the fact that an observer would note the enthusiasm, vitality, energy, efficiency, and achievement, there exists on another level an undermining, self-destructive process that is an integral part of each individual. Without constant attention to this process, there is inevitable regression; without exposure, there is consistent deterioration both internally in attitudes toward self and externally in relationships with others. When this process is neglected and crucial issues are overlooked, there is at first a slow overall decline, then a rapid acceleration in the destructive process, as people return to bonds, conventional habit patterns, and routines. People first experience guilt and fear about their full lives and rich experiences, and then start systematically to give up their most satisfying endeavors.

Living a full life, with humility, meaningful activity, compassion for ourselves, and a poignant awareness that all people share the same fate, appears to be too agonizing for most of us to endure. Most are not strong enough to live fully in the face of dying, and so we slowly commit suicide, causing inevitable hurt to the people who care about us and love us. The central conflict between first investing ourselves emotionally in life and in other people and then renouncing or taking back our investment because of fear is the nature of resistance in therapy.

SUMMARY OF THEORY OF RESISTANCE

This book represents a summation of the author's current thinking about resistance to change in psychotherapy and everyday life. Many of the statements and hypotheses set forth in this section describing our point of view have been elaborated in our other works, *The Truth—A Psychological Cure* (Firestone & Catlett, 1981), *The Friendship Circle—A Unique Psychological Laboratory* (Firestone & Catlett, in progress), and *Closeness Without Bonds—A Study of Separation Therapy* (Firestone, 1976). In these works, I presented my view of the essential problem in psychotherapy and related it to our observation of the people in the experimental community.

In summary, it is ironic that people want the destructive, conventional forms of safety, security and "closeness," and tend to reject real closeness with people and a better life. They want to relive and maintain the illusion of connectedness more than they want happiness and loving responses.

As we look around at people, what they're doing with their children, with each other, with their wives, with their husbands, we see that most of their behavior is directed toward maintaining illusions and bonds. To some extent, all people cling to these security mechanisms and are frightened of their real aloneness. However, aloneness is not a sad or pathetic or terrible thing. It *is* when it's related to primal feelings of helplessness, dependency, and infantilism, but it's a glorious feeling, too, in the sense of really feeling happy, free, and strong. All of us have known that kind of feeling at one time or another, and all of us have rejected it when it became too frightening.

One of the functions of the community is to share perceptions of one another, pointing out bonds and immaturity. It is sometimes difficult to live in this environment because a person becomes very conscious of being separate.

The question arises as to whether people can live in an environment where defenses are so exposed. Can people live without their defenses? Indeed, there are some people who feel very uncomfortable, who can't seem to find themselves in this type of situation. They cling to mechanisms that are childlike and hold on to one another in couples. When this is revealed, they feel terrible. They want to maintain an illusion of being taken care of. They cling to sentimentality and conventional behavior more than others because this type of thinking appears to offer safety and comfort, and that's what they're after.

It is true that all people here have some discomfort in a changing, more positive environment. However, most people have felt more excited and alive than usual, and seem to thrive in an atmosphere of sharing and exposure. Life is exciting and revealing, and there is a good feeling among them. These individuals are alive in the sense that they see themselves as always changing, as compared with other more static living conditions. The group process is almost always pure, that is, there is almost always support for personal freedom and valuing of self. The environment as a process is warm and responsive to people who are struggling for life and fighting for themselves.

People here are deeply committed to self-enlightenment, each in a style that reflects one's own history, but the essential process is the same. They break through their wall of defensiveness, their self-imposed internal death, to reach the sadness and the vitality of their abandoned child-self.

To the extent that a person has recovered this lost child, he or she is able to live in a world that is perpetually new. It is a world in which experience is open-ended, rather than a continual reliving of the past. It's as if a person who is well-defended and whose feelings are cut off lives life in a single room. Then he or she is finally able to fling the doors open, and a whole new landscape is revealed.

It is my belief that only by giving up the fantasy of love in the traditional family when it is not present in reality, and by abandoning attempts at security that deny separateness in new relationships, can positive change take place. Only by relinquishing the hope of eternal life and defenses that sustain the illusion of living eternally through our children can a person grow and develop. Progress invariably upsets the psychological equilibrium established when bonds were first formed and defenses erected. Therefore, contending with polarity and conflicting drives is an essential part of any real therapeutic process. Understanding the sources of resistance, attending to them, creating a social process to cope with them and keep them in the foreground of awareness, can have a powerful and broadening effect on people's lives.

Paradoxically, the more people give up their crutches, the soothing mechanisms of their lives, their self-nourishing habits and deadening routines, the more they are able to embrace life. The more they give up false security, the greater the opportunity they have for real security in genuine relationships built on honest choices and priorities. Only through breaking loose from bondage and fantasies of connection can we really be free to fulfill our human potentiality.

REFERENCES

Chapter 1

Becker, E. *The revolution in psychiatry*. New York: The Free Press, 1964.

Bettelheim, B. Individual and mass behavior in extreme situations. *Surviving and other essays*. New York: Vintage Books, 1980. (Originally published, 1943.)

Erikson, E. H. *Childhood and society* (2nd ed.). New York: W. W. Norton, 1963.

Firestone, R. W. *A concept of the schizophrenic process*. Unpublished doctoral dissertation, University of Denver, 1957.

Firestone, R. W. A concept of the primary fantasy bond: A developmental perspective. *Psychotherapy*, 1984, *21*(2), 218–225.

Grotjahn, M. *Psychoanalysis and the family neurosis*. New York: W. W. Norton, 1960.

Kaiser, H. The problem of responsibility in psychotherapy. *Psychiatry*, 1955, *18*, 205-211.

Rosen, J. N. *Direct analysis*. New York: Grune & Stratton, 1953.

Winnicott, D. W. *Collected papers*. London: Tavistock Publications, 1958.

Chapter 3

Firestone, R. W., & Catlett, J. *The truth—A psychological cure*. New York: Macmillan Publishing Co., 1981.

Greer, G. *The female eunuch*. New York: McGraw-Hill, 1971. (Originally published, 1970.)

Lawrence, D. H. *Women in love.* New York: Viking Press, 1960. (Originally published, 1920.)

Satir, V. *Conjoint family therapy* (Rev. ed.). Palo Alto: Science and Behavior Books, Inc., 1967.

Chapter 4

Firestone, R. W. *A concept of the schizophrenic process.* Unpublished doctoral dissertation, University of Denver, 1957.

Sullivan, H. S. *Conceptions of modern psychiatry.* New York: W. W. Norton, 1953.

Chapter 5

Arieti, S. *Interpretation of schizophrenia.* New York: Robert Brunner, 1955.

Chapter 6

Bowlby, J. *Separation, anxiety and anger.* New York: Basic Books, Inc., 1973.

Fenichel, O. *The psychoanalytic theory of neurosis.* New York: W. W. Norton, 1945.

Firestone, R. W., & Catlett, J. *The truth—A psychological cure.* New York: Macmillan Publishing Co., 1981.

Gallwey, W. T. *The inner game of tennis.* New York: Random House, 1974.

Laing, R. D. *The divided self.* New York: Pantheon Books, 1969. (Originally published, 1960.)

Rubin, T. *Compassion and self-hate.* New York: David McKay Company, 1975.

Chapter 7

Arieti, S. *Interpretation of schizophrenia.* New York: Robert Brunner, 1955.

Raimy, V. *Misunderstandings of the self.* San Francisco: Jossey-Bass Publishers, 1975.

Chapter 8

Becker, E. *Revolution in psychiatry.* New York: The Free Press, 1964.

Firestone, R. W. A concept of the primary fantasy bond: A developmental perspective. *Psychotherapy,* 1984, *21*(2), 218–225.

Frankl, V. E. *Psychotherapy and existentialism.* New York: Simon and Schuster, 1967.

Janov, A. *The primal scream.* New York: G. P. Putnam, 1970.

Chapter 9

Firestone, R. W. *A concept of the schizophrenic process.* Unpublished doctoral dissertation, University of Denver, 1957.

Friday, N. *My mother, my self.* New York: Delacorte Press, 1977.

Friday, N. *Men in love.* New York: Delacorte Press, 1980.

Hainline, L. D. Developmental changes in the scanning of face and non-face patterns by infants. *Journal of Experimental Child Psychology,* 1978, *25,* 90-115.

Horney, K. *Our inner conflicts.* New York: W. W. Norton, 1945.

Laing, R. D. *The divided self.* New York: Pantheon Books, 1969. (Originally published, 1960.)

Chapter 10

Bruch, H. *Eating disorders.* New York: Basic Books, Inc. 1973.

Firestone, R. W., & Catlett, J. *The truth—A psychological cure.* New York: Macmillan Publishing Co., 1981.

Freud, S. Introductory lectures on psycho-analysis. (J. Strachey, ed. and trans.), *The standard edition of the complete psychological works of Sigmund Freud* (Vol. 16). London: Hogarth Press, 1961. (Originally published 1916-17.)

Jansen, J., & Catlett, J. *The love diet strategy.* Los Angeles: Glendon House Publications, 1978.

Chapter 11

Bowlby, J. *Separation, anxiety and anger.* New York: Basic Books, Inc., 1973.

Fierman, L. B. (Ed.) *Effective psychotherapy—the contribution of Hellmuth Kaiser.* New York: The Free Press, 1965.

Freud, S. Three essays on the theory of sexuality. (J. Strachey, ed. and trans.), *The standard edition of the complete psychological works of Sigmund Freud* (Vol. 7). London: Hogarth Press, 1953. (Originally published, 1905.)

Freud, S. Thoughts for the times on war and death. (J. Strachey, ed. and trans.), *The standard edition of the complete psychological works of Sigmund Freud* (Vol. 14). London: Hogarth Press, 1957. (Originally published, 1915.)

James, W. *Principles of psychology.* New York: Holt, 1890.

Katz, B. Separation-individuation and marital therapy. *Psychotherapy: Theory, Research & Practice,* 1981, *18*(2).

Klein, M. *Contributions to psychoanalysis 1921-1945.* New York: McGraw-Hill Book Company, 1964. (Originally published, 1948.)

Rank, O. *Will therapy and truth and reality* (J. Taft, trans.). New York: Alfred A. Knopf, 1972. (Originally published, 1936.)

Chapter 12

Arieti, S. *Interpretation of schizophrenia.* New York: Robert Brunner, 1955.

Firestone, R. W. *A concept of the schizophrenic process.* Unpublished doctoral dissertation, University of Denver, 1957.

Fromm-Reichmann, F. Transference problems in schizophrenia. *Psychoanalytic Quarterly,* 1939, *8,* 412-426.

Rosen, J. N. *Direct analysis.* New York: Grune & Stratton, 1953.

Rosen, J. N. *Transference in schizophrenia.* Paper presented at the International Convention of Psychoanalysts, Switzerland, July 1954.

Sechehaye, M. *Symbolic realization: a new method of psychotherapy applied to a case of schizophrenia.* New York: International Universities Press, 1951.

Sullivan, H. S. *The interpersonal theory of psychiatry.* New York: W. W. Norton, 1953.

Chapter 13

Bowlby, J. *Attachment.* New York: Basic Books, Inc., 1969.

Caplan, P. J. *Between women.* Toronto: Personal Library Publishers, 1981.

Deutsch, H. *The psychology of women* (Vol. 1). New York: Grune and Stratton, 1944.

Firestone, R. W. *A concept of the schizophrenic process.* Unpublished doctoral dissertation, University of Denver, 1957.

Freud, S. Three essays on the theory of sexuality. (J. Strachey, ed. and trans.), *The standard edition of the complete psychological works of Sigmund Freud* (Vol. 7). London: Hogarth Press, 1953. (Originally published, 1905.)

Freud, S. An outline of psycho-analysis. (J. Strachey, ed. and trans.), *The standard edition of the complete psychological works of Sigmund Freud* (Vol. 23). London: Hogarth Press, 1964. (Originally published, 1940.)

Friday, N. *My mother, my self.* New York: Delacorte Press, 1977.

Harlow, H. F., & Harlow M. K. *Behavior of nonhuman primates* (Vol. 2). (A. M. Schrier, H. F. Harlow, & F. Stollnitz, Eds.). New York and London: Academic Press, 1965.

Klein, M., Heimann, P., Isaacs, S., & Riviere, J. *Developments in psycho-analysis.* London: Hogarth Press; Toronto: Clarke-Irwin, 1952.

Lawrence, D. H. *Women in love.* New York: Viking Press, 1960. (Originally published, 1920.)

Chapter 14

Bateson, G. *Steps to an ecology of mind.* New York: Ballantine Books, 1972.

Bateson, G., Jackson, D. D., Haley, R., & Weakland, J. Toward a theory of schizophrenia. *Behavioral Science,* 1956, *1*(4), 251–64.

Laing, R. D. *The politics of experience.* New York: Ballantine Books, 1967.

Lubenow, G. C. When kids kill their parents. *Newsweek,* June 27, 1983, *101,* 35-36.

Miller, A. *For your own good* (H. & H. Hannum, trans.) New York: Farrar, Straus & Giroux, 1983. (Originally published, 1980.)

Chapter 15

Anthony, S. *The discovery of death in childhood and after.* New York: Basic Books, 1972. (Originally published, 1971.)

Beck, A., Sethi, B., & Tuthill, R. Childhood bereavement and adult depression. *Archives of General Psychiatry,* 1963, *9,* 295–302.

Becker, E. *The denial of death.* New York: The Free Press, 1973.

Brown, N. O. *Life against death—the psychoanalytical meaning of history.* Middletown, Connecticut: Wesleyan University Press, 1959.

Feldman, M. J., & Herzen, M. Attitudes toward death in nightmare subjects. *Journal of Abnormal Psychology,* 1967, *77*(5).

Freud, A. *Normality and pathology in childhood: Assessment of development.* New York: International Universities Press, 1965.

Freud, S. Thoughts for the times on war and death. (J. Strachey, ed. and trans.), *The standard edition of the complete psychological works of Sigmund Freud* (Vol. 14). London: Hogarth Press, 1957. (Originally published, 1915.)

Freud, S. An autobiographical study. (J. Strachey, ed. and trans.), *The standard edition of the complete psychological works of Sigmund Freud* (Vol. 20). London: Hogarth Press, 1959. (Originally published, 1925.)

Hilgard, J., Newman, M., & Fisk, F. Strength of adult ego following childhood bereavement. *American Journal of Orthopsychiatry,* 1960, *30,* 788-98.

Mahler, M. D. *On human symbiosis and the vicissitudes of individuation* (Vol. 1). New York: International Universities Press, 1968.

Mahler, M. D. Symbiosis and individuation. In R. S. Eissler, A. Freud, M. Kris, & A. J. Solnit (Eds.), *The psychoanalytic study of the child* (Vol. 29). New Haven: Yale University Press, 1974.

Nagy, M. The child's theories concerning death. *Journal of Genetics and Psychology,* 1948, *73,* 3, 4, 26, 27.

Rank, O. *Modern education: A critique of its fundamental ideas.* New York: Agathon Press, 1968.

Rochlin, G. How younger children view death and themselves. In L. A. Grollman (Ed.), *Explaining death to children.* Boston: Beacon Press, 1967.

Zilboorg, G. Fear of death. *Psychoanalytic Quarterly,* 1943, *12,* 465-475.

Chapter 16

Becker, E. *The denial of death*. New York: The Free Press, 1973.

Brown, N. O. *Life against death—the psychoanalytical meaning of history*. Middletown, Connecticut: Wesleyan University Press, 1959.

Butler, R., & Lewis, M. *Aging and mental health*. New York: New American Library, 1983.

Freud, S. Group psychology and the analysis of the ego. (J. Strachey, ed. and trans.), *The standard edition of the complete psychological works of Sigmund Freud* (Vol. 18). London: Hogarth Press, 1955. (Originally published, 1921.)

Fromm, E. *Escape from freedom*. New York: Avon, 1941.

Kierkegaard, S. (1849/1954). *The sickness unto death*. Cited in E. Becker, *The denial of death*. New York: The Free Press, 1973.

Le Bon, G. [*The crowd: a study of the popular mind*. London: 1920.] *Psychologie des foules*. Paris: 1895. Cited in S. Freud, Group psychology and the analysis of the ego. (J. Strachey, ed. and trans.), *The standard edition of the complete psychological works of Sigmund Freud* (Vol. 18). London: Hogarth Press, 1955. (Originally published, 1921.)

Marx, K. *Selected writings in sociology and social philosophy* (T. B. Bottomore, Trans.). New York: McGraw-Hill, 1964. (Originally published as Marx-Engels *Gesamtausgabe*, 1927.)

Rank, O. *Beyond psychology*. New York: Dover Books, 1958.

Rank, O. *Will therapy and truth and reality*. (J. Taft, Trans.). New York: Alfred A. Knopf, 1972. (Originally published, 1936)

Rank, O. *Will therapy*. New York: W. W. Norton, 1978.

Sheehy, G. *Passages*. New York: E. P. Dutton, 1974.

Styron, W. *Sophie's choice*. New York: Random House, 1979.

Yalom, I. D. *Existential psychotherapy*. New York: Basic Books, Inc., 1980.

Chapter 17

Arlow, J. A. Psychoanalysis. In R. J. Corsini (Ed.), *Current psychotherapies*. Itasca, Illinois: F. E. Peacock Publishers, 1979.

Blatt, S. J., & Erlich, H. S. Levels of resistance in the psychotherapeutic process. In P. L. Wachtel (Ed.), *Resistance*. New York and London: Plenum Press, 1982.

Fenichel, O. *The psychoanalytic theory of neurosis*. New York: W. W. Norton, 1945.

Freud, S. Beyond the pleasure principle. (J. Strachey, ed. and trans.), *The standard edition of the complete psychological works of Sigmund Freud* (Vol. 18). London: Hogarth Press, 1955. (Originally published, 1920.)

Gill, M. Analysis of the transference. In H. J. Schlesinger (Ed.), *Psychological issues monograph series* (No. 53). New York: International Universities Press, 1981.

Hall, C. S., & Lindzey, G. *Theories of personality* (2nd ed.). New York: Wiley, 1970.
Janov, A. *The primal scream.* New York: G. P. Putnam, 1970.
Shepherd, I. L. Limitations and cautions in the Gestalt approach. In J. Fagan & I. L. Shepherd (Eds.), *Gestalt therapy now.* New York: Harper & Row, 1970.

Chapter 18

Bettelheim, B. Individual and mass behavior in extreme situations. *Surviving and other essays.* New York: Vintage Books, 1980. (Originally published, 1943.)
Perls, F. S. *Gestalt therapy verbatim.* Lafayette, California: Real People Press, 1969.

Chapter 19

Alexander, F. *The medical value of psychoanalysis.* New York: W. W. Norton, 1932.
Arlow, J. A. Psychoanalysis. In R. J. Corsini (Ed.), *Current psychotherapies.* Itasca, Illinois: F. E. Peacock Publishers, 1979.
Badinter, E. *Mother love, myth and reality.* New York: Macmillan Publishing Company, 1982. (Originally published, 1980.)
Lindner, R. *The fifty-minute hour.* New York: Bantam Books, 1976.
Rosen, J. N. *Direct analysis.* New York: Grune & Stratton, 1953.

Chapter 20

Boyd, S. *Analysis of the psychotherapeutic community.* Unpublished manuscript, 1982.
Firestone, R. W., & Catlett, J. *The friendship circle—A unique psychological laboratory.* (in progress)
Parr, G. (Producer and Director) *Voyage to understanding* [Film]. Los Angeles: Environmental Films, 1983.
Viets, J. Epic voyage by a teenage crew. *San Francisco Chronicle,* April 6, 1978, p. 4.

Chapter 21

Boyd, S. *Analysis of the psychotherapeutic Community.* Unpublished manuscript, 1982.
Firestone, R. W. *Closeness without bonds—A study of separation therapy.* Unpublished manuscript, 1976.
Firestone, R. W., & Catlett, J. *The truth—A psychological cure.* New York: Macmillan Publishing Co., 1981.
Firestone, R. W., & Catlett, J. *The friendship circle—A unique psychological laboratory.* (in progress)

INDEX

Acting-out behaviors, 39, 97, 127, 140, 169, 185, 295–296
Addictions, 156, 157–169, 326
  alcohol, 161–162, 167, 326
  dependency, 168–169
  drugs, 167, 169, 326
  food, 158–161, 167, 326
  routines, 162–164, 165
Aging, 262–268
  self-denial in, 262, 266
  self-indulgence in, 266–267
Alcohol abuse, 156, 158, 161, 167, 185, 326
Alexander, Franz, 323
Anger
  case studies, 68, 112–113
  constructive, 118
  conversion of, 117
  expressed, 88–89, 306, 316
  parental, 107–109
  at separation, 42, 174, 179
  sexual, 223

suppressed, 96, 137, 310
  at withholding, 65, 66
Anorexia nervosa, 160–161
Anthony, Sylvia, 245, 247
Anxiety, 36, 42, 71, 78
  avoidance of, 82, 85, 232, 280
  and change in negative self-image, 100
  emotional, 35, 80
  parental, 43
  primal, 23, 37, 244
  in schizophrenia, 206
  separation, 46–47, 71, 72, 178–179, 182, 189, 387
  sources of, 81–82
  see also Death anxiety
Arieti, Silvano, 95, 118, 193, 195, 207–208, 209
Arlow, J.A., 280, 323

Bateson, Gregory, 238

399